THE KANSAS BEEF INDUSTRY

THE KANSAS BEEF INDUSTRY

Charles L. Wood

THE REGENTS PRESS OF KANSAS

Lawrence

Library of Congress Cataloging in Publication Data

Wood, Charles L   1937-
The Kansas beef industry.

Bibliography: p.
Includes index.
1. Cattle trade—Kansas—History. 2. Beef cattle—
Kansas—History. I. Title.
HD9433.U5K3   338.1'7'621309781   79-22730
ISBN 0-7006-0197-X

To

ALMA AND THE FIVE YOUNGER WOODS
Mark, Greg, John, Marice, and Lisa

Contents

List of Illustrations

List of Illustrations

Preface

From the late nineteenth century to the present, beef cattle raised on the lush prairie grasses and plump grains of Kansas supplied the steaks and roasts that graced the dinner tables of millions of American homes. The Kansas beef industry, like that of surrounding states, played an important role in the evolution of western beef production, from the expansive open-range methods of the nineteenth century into the well-organized ranching industry of today.

The first cattle appeared in Kansas before the Civil War as a result of missionary activities with the Indians and of the traffic on the Santa Fe and Oregon trails. These were, for the most part, scrub cattle from the East, and carried with them the Anglo techniques for producing beef that had been evolving and moving westward since the Colonial period of American history. Later, the Longhorns that were driven north from Texas mixed with these eastern cattle, blending in the Hispanic bloodlines and techniques that had come into Texas from Mexico. After the Civil War a boom occurred in the Plains beef business when it was discovered that a $5 steer was worth $30 to $40 in a northern market. Soon, with the population centers of the Northeast providing the demand, with the railroads that had pushed their tracks into the grassland supplying the means, and with Missouri, Kansas, Nebraska, and other states providing the terminal-point cowtowns, almost all the grass of the Plains was being used. Hundreds of prospective cattlemen joined those already engaged in raising cattle, all hoping to find the El Dorado they expected from the free or cheap grass and the natural reproductive tendencies of bovines. Besides cattle, millions of dollars from eastern banks and money from Scotland, England, and Western Europe also found its way to the West.

Few, however, harvested the easy fortune that they craved. As the optimistic early 1880s gave way to the latter part of the decade and the early 1890s, nature helped deal the jerry-built, overstocked industry a fatal blow. Blizzards, droughts, and, eventually, a world depression propelled the beef industry out of the realm of adventure and into the domain of sounder business operations. Moreover, nature and economic conditions were not the only stimuli for change. The railroads that had first made western cattle profitable, for instance, helped destroy the initial stage by bringing pioneer farmers to the new land. When thousands of farmers began to turn up the wrong side of the grass, as some put it, the transient cattlemen were forced to abandon the area or adapt their methods to new circumstances. While most of the reckless, adventurous sort left the business, many of the more serious-minded stayed and developed permanent ranches.

While much has been written about the colorful early period of raising beef on the open range and many studies have been done on individual cattle-raising empires, comparatively little has been produced on the beef industry of the twentieth century. And the latter period, in my view, is more important than the earlier one in explaining the importance of beef in American history. This study, then, traces the production and marketing of cattle into the twentieth century; analyzes the forces of change confronting cattlemen and their capacity to adapt to new conditions; and investigates the shifting relationships among beef producers, industry, and government. Though the work is focused on the Kansas experience, the broader implications of its findings transcend the borders of the state. As a whole, the beef industry after 1890 became more rationally organized and efficient in production; more representative of improved stock; and more concerned with industries associated with marketing and with the actions of government. In the end, raising beef became more a business than an adventure, and in the process it carved out the significant sector of the nation's economy that it holds today.

I naturally accumulated large debts in producing this work. As is customary, I wish to thank all who contributed their time and expertise. George L. Anderson, who taught me how to undertake scholarly research, and Paul Wallace Gates, Lloyd Sponholtz, Robert Richmond, Donald R. Ornduff, and Walter M. Kollmorgen—all of whom suggested improvements in the manuscript—were helpful. John G. Clark, who read these pages several times, and Jacquelin Collins, a colleague at Texas Tech who patiently directed my attention to split infinitives, dangling participles, and other errors, were especially important in getting the work into its present form. The writings of John T. Schlebecker and those of James C. Malin have greatly influenced my thinking on the development of the Great Plains. Staff members of the Kansas Live-stock Association, the Animal Health Department, and the Kansas State Historical Society were also generous with their assistance.

During final preparations, I had the generous support of Texas Tech University. Lawrence L. Graves, Dean of Arts and Sciences, and J. Knox Jones, Vice-president for Research and Graduate Studies, provided money for travel and typing. Dorothy Schmanke patiently proofread the initial drafts, and Joan Weldon typed the final copy. David Jones produced the illustrations. Finally, my wife, Alma Moravek Wood, and our five children deserve much credit; they too made many sacrifices. Alma proofread and typed preliminary drafts, and performed many of the chores of raising a family in order that I could devote more time to this work.

To these people, then, and to others who remain unnamed, I express my sincere appreciation.

I am tempted to share with all those mentioned above the responsibility for any errors that may have crept into the work. That, however, would be unfair and not completely accurate. I reserve for myself, then, the right to be mistaken.

1

Raising Beef during the 1890s

The first real blizzard of the season struck Kansas on January 23, 1894, forcing temperatures down to fifteen degrees below zero in some parts of the state. One can imagine an old cowboy the morning after the big snow, urging his reluctant team into the small corral where the hay had been stacked the previous summer. It was still cold, and the breath of the horses mixed with his own before disappearing over his shoulder and settling along the fresh track that his hayrack had just made as he went about feeding the cow herd for another day. Winter feeding was an increasingly popular practice now that there were more ranchers, fewer cattle, fenced pastures, and white-faced bulls. The old cowboy knew that there was no longer any profit in raising cattle unless they were fed during the winter months when snow covered the grass.

Many cowboys could remember when, only a few years before, they had not spent winters feeding cattle, but rather huddling next to a pot-bellied stove in a drafty bunkhouse, endlessly playing cards, or thumbing through a dog-eared Sears, Roebuck catalogue, or drinking in a saloon when they could get to town. They waited for spring work to begin, when they would drive cattle north from Texas, work on a roundup crew, or simply herd a large bunch of cattle from one stand of grass to another, always making sure that a creek or river was close by. Now, windmills provided water almost any place on the range, and the quiet summers were disrupted, more often than not, by clanging mowing machines.

Although some of the older cowmen may have longed for the "good old days," beef production in Kansas by the 1890s was well along in its transition from the open range to the ranch of the twentieth century. The original cattle-

1

men had spread across the West during the last half of the nineteenth century, their number multiplying as the railroads extended lines into the new territory. During the early 1880s, they enjoyed a degree of prosperity. Their scrub cattle grazed the free or cheap grass, often with little attention except for branding and the selection of aged steers destined for slaughter. Hundreds of unattended cattle died each year from extremes in the weather, and some overgrazing occurred in the rush to beat the other fellow to the grass. Little fencing was done, nor were the cattle upbred. The relatively few owners of cattle in this open-range situation employed mostly a transient labor force, often men who were unmarried and, some said, unchurched. Although many have found the early cattle industry colorful and romantic, it was in fact wasteful of grass, livestock, and manpower.

The open range disappeared and serious ranching began as larger numbers of cattlemen and farmers took over the land. They paid taxes and developed communities. Having built fences, they cared for their cattle the year around, and arranged for aggressive Hereford bulls to march in from the Midwest to take over the cow herds. Fences and better herd management reduced cattle thefts. Mowing machines and hay stackers came into common use to provide winter feed. Consequently, most cattle survived the winter and cows produced a much larger calf crop. Specialization into calf production, the maturing of stockers, and the fattening of feeder cattle became more pronounced. Ranch work was well organized, purposeful, and more profitable for a larger number of people, although it did become routine and rather prosaic. Cowhands more often now were married and even attended church, acquiring domestic and social concerns along with their greater attention to the cattle. These ranchers of the late nineteenth century and after, who transformed beef raising into the important national industry that it is today, are the real heroes of the cattle business. The greater credit is due to them rather than to their forefathers, who in fact helped themselves to the public's grass, paid few if any taxes, and wasted the lives of cows and men, all in the process of producing rather poor beef.

While much changed when the expansive method of producing beef gave way to modern ranching, some things stayed the same. Grass and cows were still basic. John J. Ingalls, a senator from Kansas from 1873 to 1891, once said, "Grass is the forgiveness of nature—her constant benediction. Fields trampled with battle, saturated with blood, torn with the ruts of cannon, grow green again with grass, and carnage is forgotten. . . . Forests decay, harvests perish, flowers vanish, but grass is immortal." Cattlemen agree with Ingalls' high opinion of grass, realizing that good grazing is the foundation of the range cattle industry and the basic reason it has remained permanent in the West rather than transient, as it had been in much of the East. The cow, not particularly intelligent or prolific as animals go, is a hardy specimen, whose unique, four-compartmented stomach can convert relatively low-grade natural vegetation into highly desirable protein food. "She is," one observer noted, "a mobile, selfpowered processing plant that needs no other raw material except water" to produce one of our most popular foods. As in ages past, then, there can be no beef industry without grass and cows.[1]

Kansas is in the transitional zone between East and West as far as environmental factors such as flatness, timber, aridity, and native vegetation are concerned. Even a casual observer is struck with the contrasts that appear within the state. The eastern third has trees, rolling hills, and long grasses, while many of the trees disappear and the flatter land produces short grasses in the western third except, of course, where the native vegetation has been replaced with wheat and other grains. The central third, roughly the area between the 95th and 100th meridians, has environmental features characteristic of both the eastern and western sections.

Environmental traits, along with human adaptation to them, accounted in large part for the variations that were found in the Kansas beef industry during the late nineteenth century. A more detailed examination of different sections of the state, first the Flint Hills, then the areas to the east and west of these famous hills, demonstrates the importance of environment as well as the variety of techniques that were used to produce beef in Kansas.

The Flint Hills, central to the Kansas beef industry during the late nineteenth century and for many years thereafter, encompassed some of the most extensive ranches in the state engaged in beef production. James C. Malin, a highly regarded Kansas historian, outlines the region "as a somewhat elongated oval-shaped area about 200 miles from tip to tip, with Pottawatomie County, Kansas, at the northern end and Osage County, Oklahoma, at the southern end, the intervening country being some fifty miles, or somewhat more than two counties, in width." There have been other attempts to define an exterior boundary, but essentially the Flint Halls are the "Central third of the eastern half of the State." They include the whole or some part of about fifteen Kansas counties.[2]

The beautiful bluestem pastures of the Flint Hills, covered with both long and short grasses, supported thousands of transient cattle each summer, shipped in from Texas, the Southwest, or western Kansas for a few months of growth and fattening before moving on to a slaughtering plant or to a specialized feedlot in the Midwest. The Flint Hills also helped stabilize the beef industry, not only of Kansas but of the Southwest as well, by grazing breeding herds during summers of extreme drought. And a few permanent cow herds existed, especially those dedicated to producing breeding stock for use in upgrading herds in Kansas and westward, while a few cattle were fed grain. Nevertheless, the most distinctive operation in the area remained the pasturing of transient cattle.

Many of the first settlers to reach the Flint Hills after the Civil War passed through the region's tall grass, preferring the rich, deep-soiled plow lands farther west. Only a few stopped to take up land in the fertile valleys along the several streams that permeate the region. This is surprising, as the thirty to thirty-five inches of annual rainfall is adequate for farming, and most of the upland area has adequate soil fertility and depth for extensive cropping. Nor are all of the bluestem pastures in hills. Many are on terrain that is remarkably flat, free of chert or flint outcroppings, and quite suitable for the plow. But for a number of reasons farming was never extended to all the areas it might have been. During the 1870s the slow experimental process of specializing in the grazing of transient cattle began and helped differentiate the Flint Hills from the wheat country to the west and the mixed farming area to the east. In the end, this disproved early boom literature promising immigrants that livestock interests would dominate only until the demands for a more intensive land-use necessitated crop farming—a sequence that had happened repeatedly in areas to the east.[3]

The cattle boom of the early 1880s and the drought at the end of the decade also discouraged plowing. The former made the practice of producing breeding stock for areas farther west more profitable, while the dry years, combined with the increased numbers of cattle in the Southwest, placed a premium on Kansas grazing lands. More ties with out-of-state ranching interests were thus encouraged, and many large pasture areas were created by purchasing railroad lands or by taking land already assembled into large acreages by some organization.

In 1882, for instance, a Scottish syndicate purchased 75,000 acres of Flint Hills land from the Santa Fe Railroad and an additional 20,000 acres from the Missouri, Kansas, and Texas Railroad. This large tract of land became famous first as the Diamond Ranch and then as the 101 Ranch, when it "was used in

Loading cattle for the Swenson Land and Cattle Company, Stanford, Texas. Thousands of cattle such as these were shipped into the Flint Hills each year for summer grazing. *Courtesy of the Southwest Collection, Texas Tech University, Lubbock, Texas.*

part for pasture-fattening steers from its 160,000-acre sister operation in Hartley County, Texas."[4] Other links with out-of-state interests were developed, and cattlemen like the Roglers, Crockers, Saubles, and Tods soon spread throughout the West the virtues of Flint Hills' grazing.

Many Kansans also brought cattle into the region from other parts of the state to graze on either rented land or ranch land that they owned. Frank Arnold, Lyon County banker and cattleman, for instance, synchronized stocker production in western Kansas with maturing cattle on Flint Hills grass. Arnold had purchased a ranch of 20,000 acres near Ashland, which he and his son, Francis, operated for many years. He had been attracted to the small town by a real-estate boom during the early 1880s, when a stream of settlers poured into the Southwest to take up government land. When drought appeared ten years later and many of these farmers and small cattlemen were forced from the land, Arnold began to purchase their property, much of it for only the taxes due. Despite the rustlers, who operated out of what is today the Oklahoma Panhandle, the Arnolds and many others across the state shipped thousands of cattle into the Flint Hills each year.[5]

The movement of western Kansas cattle to eastern parts of the state, notably the Flint Hills, continued throughout the eighties and nineties and then increased during the early years of the twentieth century. Some indication of the movement can be gained from the reports of a single shipping point on the Santa Fe branch line to Ashland. A 1906 issue of the local newspaper, for example, noted that over 160 cars of cattle had been shipped to the eastern part of the state for summer grazing in 1905 and nearly 200 cars in 1906. A year later, the paper reported over 500 cars of aged steers headed east.[6]

The railroads helped to establish the Flint Halls as a distinct area during the eighties and nineties by facilitating the inshipment of cattle. The Santa Fe, with its main line running through the Flint Hills, western Kansas, Colorado, and the Southwest, and many of its branch lines linking southern points, provided cattlemen with the means of transporting cattle into the Flint Hills without disturbing any of the intervening farmers or ranchers. The Missouri, Kansas, and Texas Railroad as well as a few other lines participated in the same business. Cheaper feed-in-transit rates also contributed to the quantity of inshipped cattle. These special tariffs allowed owners of cattle to pay the rates for a single long haul from the point of origin to the final destination at a slaughtering plant rather than the higher charges that would have resulted from the short hauls that actually occurred.

State legislation in the area of disease control encouraged the grazing of transient cattle by ensuring the health of inshipped cattle. By the nineties the Kansas Legislature had been passing and amending the state's quarantine laws for over three decades. To keep the ravages of Texas fever out of Kansas, for instance, the legislature generally restricted cattle that had not spent a winter north of the tick-infested area of Texas from moving into some parts of the state except during the winter months from December to March. By 1867 all of Kansas except that part south and west of present McPherson was protected. The unprotected section was gradually reduced until the whole state was placed under quarantine in 1884 and 1885. The laws, however, were more often violated than honored, and it was not until the 1890s when more knowledge was gained of Texas fever and how it was transmitted that the federal and state sanitary agencies were able to provide a degree of security to those cattlemen engaged in the business of grazing transient cattle. Improvement came largely through closer inspection of cattle and dipping procedures. Although attaining widespread protection from the fever was a gradual process not fully accomplished until the near demise of the tick well into the twentieth century, cattlemen felt there was less risk in importing cattle once inspections and quarantines were established.[7]

The unique grazing of transient cattle, then, was by the 1890s a major business in the Flint Hills and was to a large degree based on environmental factors. The Emporia *Gazette* reported in 1894 that over 200,000 cattle were already being shipped into Kansas each year, many arriving in the Flint Hills during April and May. Four to six months of grazing followed before the stock was shipped to slaughter or to cornbelt feedlots. Shipping out occurred principally during August and September. The length of the grazing period was determined by the protein levels of the native grasses, which "run from ten to fifteen percent from April to June . . . and then break rather sharply in July to seven to ten percent." The decline continues through August and September and may dip as low as four percent.[8] The levels of declining protein of the long grasses in the Flint Hills differ sharply from those of the buffalo and gramas of the short-grass region, which retain a higher level of protein well into the winter months. In a larger sense, the protein factor helped determine whether a producer specialized in calf production or in the maturing of stockers.

The managerial practices necessary for handling these transient cattle in the Flint Hills took several forms. Sometimes the owner of stock leased bluestem pasture, then cared for his cattle himself or hired others to do so. At other times the owner of the grass bought cattle for grazing, or had ranch land in other parts of the country that produced the stockers he needed. The operation of the 101 Ranch, with land in Texas and the Flint Hills, illustrated the latter method. Speculators sometimes got involved, buying both the cattle and the right to use the grass. The anticipated market levels at the end of the grazing season often determined which course the owner of the land or cattle took.[9] Most often in the 1890s, and for many years thereafter, the transient cattle belonged to one person, the grass to another, and in between the two was a unique individual known as the professional pastureman. Two or three of these professionals developed in each community, representing the landowner to those who owned the four-, five-, and even six-year-old steers that needed final grass fattening before slaughter. The Rogler family exemplifies professional pasturemen as well as any in the Flint Hills, using at different times several of the different techniques.

Charles Rogler migrated from Germany to Kansas before the Civil War, settling north of Matfield Green on land that is still in the family. His son,

Cattle pens at Eskridge, Kansas, used for holding cattle that were moving into or out of the Flint Hills. *Courtesy of the Kansas Department of Economic Development.*

Henry, and then later his grandson, Wayne, became pasturemen. The Roglers initiated their dealings with transient cattle soon after the Santa Fe Railroad pushed through the area during the 1880s. Working for a percent of the pasture rent, the Roglers and other pasturemen took care of the thousands of cattle that they had contracted for in the name of the landowner. The contracts were written rather than oral, specifying a certain acreage to graze, and guaranteeing water, salt, and protection against straying and theft.

Spring arrivals of cattle from the Southwest and early fall departures of the same stock after a gain of two hundred or three hundred pounds each were occasions for enjoyable social events for the people of nearby communities not unlike the gatherings that occurred at threshing time in farming areas. Pasturemen, cattle owners, cowboys, and a miscellaneous assortment of other folk clustered around the railroad stations waiting for the arrival of stock cars. Some pitched horseshoes or played cards, others told each other tall tales, and all talked intently about cattle prices or the condition of the grass. A small but usually good café was central to the pageant, providing roast beef and strong coffee to speed the hours spent waiting for the train.[10]

Besides grazing transient cattle, a few stockmen in the Flint Hills kept breeding herds the year around and supplemented their winter feed with grain and cottonseed products or roughage feeds such as alfalfa. Breeding herds were most adaptable to those parts of the Flint Hills where a higher percentage of short grass was mixed with the long bluestem. Several of these herds were purebred cattle used for the production of improved breeding stock for the range.

In addition, some local or inshipped cattle were partially or fully fed on grain before being marketed. The Emporia *Gazette* reported the extent of feeding in a single county of the Flint Hills, noting that more than 20,000 cattle would be on full- or half-feed in Lyon County during the winter of 1895. Sixteen feeders were listed as each having 300 or more cattle, with the partnership of Tom Price and William Martindale topping the list with 3,000 head.[11]

Finally, the Flint Hills helped stabilize the beef industry in Kansas and the Southwest during times of severe drought. According to J. J. Moxley, a long-time rancher in the Council Grove area, the "Flint Rock pastures absorb the rainfall in the spring and then give it back in the heat of the summer." This enabled quite a number of breeding herds to survive the dry years of the late eighties and early nineties as well as several droughts in the twentieth century.[12]

Kansans took great pride in the Flint Hills. In singing its praises they referred to it as the best cattle region in the state, if not the Untied States or even the world. It was most often compared to the Sand Hills of western Nebraska, with the Nebraska region always coming out second best. The Emporia *Gazette* reported in 1905 that a circle with a radius of fifty miles around the town would include eight of the greatest cattle counties in Kansas. It further noted that the area within the circle had the "best natural grass in the world," that it was the "garden spot" of the state, and that 40 percent of the "top cattle" sold on the Kansas City market came from the area. Emporia itself was labeled the "capital of steerdom."[13]

Some of the paper's claims needed modification, however, as other parts of Kansas were also raising good cattle and engaging in the transient stock business. Not all of the rural residents of the Flint Hills were cattlemen; nor was all the land used to graze stock. Crop farmers also lived in the region, many of whom were not at all or only slightly interested in grazing cattle.

Stockmen in the mixed farming area to the east of the Flint Hills, roughly a sixth of the state, engaged in several phases of beef production, but the geography and the methods of production were not as distinctive as those in the Flint Hills. A few transient cattle spilled over from the Flint Hills and were matured on grass. Herds of purebred breeding stock also dotted this section, complementing the feeder cattle and commercial cow herds that grazed the unplowed long grasses or ate much of the grain that was produced.

The eastern section was usually referred to as the cornbelt of Kansas. An overall emphasis on a corn-hog economy, much like that of the Midwest from whence most of the settlers had come, was evident there by the 1890s. The good corn, which grew in a section that received more than thirty inches of annual rainfall, was sometimes used to feed cattle. A few farmers had relatively large feeder operations, but most feeders full- or half-fed less than a hundred head of their own or inshipped cattle. After a winter of feeding, the stock was marketed for slaughter in the spring or, if still young, sent to summer grazing for more growth and maturity. Hog and cattle production was often complementary, with the hogs following the cattle in the same feedlot and fattening on the corn that passed through the bovine's digestive system.

The drought and depression of the 1890s hurt this section as well as the rest of Kansas and the whole grassland region. The low market price for corn encouraged some farmers to increase cattle feeding in an attempt to reap greater profits from their grain crop; but the drought and the drop in beef prices, especially up to 1895, brought about a decline in the number of the state's beef cattle. The middle nineties was the low point of Kansas beef production for the decade. One newspaper suggested that there was profit in cattle only through the by-product of hog fattening, while another said that many cattle were being shipped to Texas and the Southwest because the Kansas City market was glutted with cattle "too thin to butcher, and [too] light to feed corn."[14]

Beef production in the section immediately west of the Flint Hills, approximately the central third of the state, was determined largely by the sizable influx of farmers during the 1870s. Its agriculture was similar to that in the eastern section except for a greater emphasis on wheat, although the northern tier of counties specialized in the corn-hog economy. Cattle, usually small cow

Branding calves on the Salt Fork, Barber County, in the 1890s. *Courtesy of the Kansas State Historical Society.*

herds, and hogs were most often the livestock raised on the diversified farms. But there were also some large ranch operations along the western border of the Flint Hills and in the southern counties to the west. Feeder cattle were sometimes a part of the farm operation, as were herds of purebred cattle. In fact, some of the state's first purebred Herefords were raised in this central region.

Much of the full feeding of cattle in the 1890s occurring in this section as well as the other areas of Kansas took advantage of several new feeds and combinations of feeds that were developed at Kansas State Agricultural College. The results of experiments with stock diets were reported to feeders requesting help from the college. Corn, which was sometimes soaked in water or mixed with various types of roughage, was still the basic ration; but with an abundant supply and the drastic decline in prices in 1894, wheat was becoming increasingly popular.

The *Kansas Farmer* reported, "Never before in the history of Kansas was such vast quantities of wheat fed to growing and fattening stock as at the present time, and the practice is general throughout the West. . . ." Several writers for the *Farmer* felt compelled to advise feeders that it was not wicked to feed wheat to cattle when there were people in the country who were hungry for the bread the grain might produce. Evidently, in a folk-culture where wheat was thought of as a food for humans, people had to be persuaded to use it as livestock feed. The agricultural college joined the *Farmer* in advising the use of wheat, pointing out that it was especially good for bone and muscle development before the final layers of fat were put on with corn.

11

Because of a significant increase during the 1890s in the amount of cotton-seed that was crushed for livestock feed, it became a popular diet for cattle. The seed, sometimes crushed into a meal and mixed with roughages such as cob meal, ensilage, hay, or straw, was considered a high-powered diet. Some feeders believed that a judicious use of cottonseed in a balanced ration would "lay on flesh faster than any known food." In addition to its use with feeder cattle, cottonseed cake became important in the diet of range stock. Made from the pulp of the seed-meat after the oil had been extracted, cotton cake was especially important as a supplement to the roughage fed to cattle during the winter months. Besides cottonseed, the expanded use of alfalfa, several varieties of sorghum, and the Russian-developed crested wheat grass produced more forage for cattle. The sorghums were especially significant for their drought-resisting qualities.

The revolution in the methods of full-feeding stock that resulted from the use of new feeds and the scientific research into diet combinations decreased the amount of time required to finish cattle for market approximately by one-half, depending on their condition when entering the feedlot and on the degree of finish desired at the end. This, of course, represented a considerable saving for the cattleman. Despite several new feeds, however, corn remained a popular basic diet for fattening stock.[15]

Merritt M. Sherman's business operations typified some of the activities of other stockmen in this section in the beef industry during the 1890s and into the twentieth century. Sherman, a short, stocky man who usually sported a neatly trimmed beard, was a colorful and innovative cattleman. Born in New York and educated in philosophy and mathematics in an eastern university, he moved to Arizona for reasons of health and began a short teaching career. During the 1880s and the big cattle boom, Sherman was engaged by an uncle, Lewis H. Lapham, and his partners to purchase and manage ranching property for their New York firm. This he did by purchasing well over 100,000 acres south of Bisbee, Arizona, in Mexico, for ten cents an acre. This Mexican ranch, the San Rafael de La Nora, produced stocker and feeder cattle, many of which Sherman matured and fattened on whatever Kansas grass he could lease.

Importing cattle from Old Mexico, however, was not as simple as bringing stock from Texas and the Southwest because tariffs were involved. During the last decade of the nineteenth century, Congress pushed through three major tariff bills, all with varying effects on the Mexican trade. The McKinley Tariff of 1890 had relatively high rates, but these were lowered four years later by the Wilson-Gorman plan. Rates were raised again, however, when the Republicans were instrumental in passing the Dingley Act in 1897. Because they wanted to avoid the severe competition afforded by the Mexican producer, most cattlemen favored restrictive rates on imported cattle.[16]

Sherman, however, was out-of-step with the majority of his fellow cattlemen, arguing that low rates were needed to encourage Mexican cattle to utilize the Kansas grass crop. His position might have been expected, as his beef operations continued to grow. In 1896, 25,000 acres of grass were purchased by the New York firm near Crawford in Ellsworth County, while additional grassland was leased in the area. Thus began what came to be known throughout the West as the Sherman Ranch.

Soon after acquiring the Kansas ranch, Sherman turned it into a full-feeding station for Mexican cattle en route to market. As many as 7,000 cattle were fed some years, even after the Dingley Tariff raised rates to 20 percent *ad valorem*. The Sherman Ranch also produced Shorthorn bulls that were later shipped to the Mexican ranges, and served, too, as a hog-fattening center. During some years more than 10,000 hogs were fattened in conjunction with the large cattle-feeding operation. Sherman, who chain-smoked factory-made cigarettes, which he wrapped again in paper that he imported especially for that purpose, continued the feeder cattle and hog operation until just before World War I. Then an epidemic of cholera killed thousands of his hogs, and the interests of the firm turned to producing grain to fill the inflated demands of the war.

About half of the Kansas property was plowed and planted to wheat, corn, oats, and a few other crops. Sherman mechanized this large farm—which some claimed was the largest in the world under fence—by purchasing tractors, binders, and other machinery. Nearly two hundred hired hands were engaged during busy seasons, all of whom, according to Sherman, were not to drink, join a labor union, or believe in the principles of the Democratic party. The farming operation fell on hard times after the war, and was eventually broken up and rented to small farmers in the area.

Cattle continued to play a role in the Sherman operation, even though half the original ranch was farmed, and connections with the Mexican property were maintained. The large cow herd Sherman kept in the Flint Hills illustrated the fact that the area was not exclusively the domain of transient cattle. Sherman's operation successfully integrated cattle raising and highly mechanized farming, but nevertheless the mighty empire died during the Great Depression. In 1937 the Mexican government confiscated the San Rafael de La Nora, while grain and cattle prices in this country had recovered only slightly from their lows during the early 1930s. By this time Sherman was more than eighty years old. After disagreeing with Lapham heirs over the sale of land to the Kanopolis Dam project, he retired in disgust and moved to California. There he died the following year. Cattlemen in the area bought the famous headquarters of the ranch, but some of the land is today flooded by water impounded by the dam.[17]

The western third of the state, where the short grass grows, was more distinctly a beef-producing area during the 1890s than the central third, especially in the northwest and in the area along the Arkansas River. Irrigated farming was developing in the Arkansas valley, with sugar beets and alfalfa two of the principal crops. In most of the area where irrigation was impossible wheat was becoming an important crop.

The area around the Arkansas River was more exclusively devoted to cattle production during the 1890s than any other area of western Kansas, and it illustrated two problems frequently encountered in the West beyond the 100th meridian: first, the failure of the federal government to provide legislation that was adequate for the legal acquisition of the large land parcels necessary for ranching operations; and second, the reluctance of immigrants from more humid environments to adapt their agricultural pursuits to the scarcity of rainfall.

Before the 1880s most of the southwestern and south-central grasslands of Kansas were grazed by large herds on open range, a practice that was to a large extent a natural outgrowth from the times when herds were trailed to northern railroads from the south. The herds frequently ranged back and forth across the Kansas-Oklahoma border. Grazing associations and pools were established to facilitate the cooperative use of the grassland, and portions of the public domain were sometimes illegally fenced after barbed wire became readily available in the late 1880s.

The relatively unrestricted use of the land by cattlemen, however, did not continue without competition. During the early and middle eighties a wave of farmers poured into the area, took over parcels of government land, and attempted to diversify agricultural pursuits. This influx of thousands of settlers forced the cattlemen to adjust their operations, an adjustment that was lauded and encouraged by several local newspapers. One noted that during the early eighties the only occupation of the few inhabitants was raising cattle, with at

Branding in Scott County during the early 1900s. Like threshing in farming areas, branding was sometimes a festive occasion attended by women. *Courtesy of the Kansas State Historical Society.*

least one man having 25,000 head. But with the "advancement of civilization and cultivation and increased rainfall," which the editor believed the influx of settlers had caused, the large herds were being broken up. The writer concluded that the settlers "by taking up the land, force range cattle to more limited pasture, until at last every foot of the land will be taken by actual settlers. Then and not until then, will all the resources of this country be developed, and all utilities economized."[18]

Despite the distinct prejudices of some local editors, the farming boom was over by the late 1880s. Depression, drought, increased amounts of debt, and a general disillusionment with homesteading brought a common fate to small farmers and stockmen. Many of them left the area, returning to the East whence they had come. Less rainfall than they were accustomed to and their failure to adapt to the relatively dry conditions were responsible for many failures. Rather than adjust their endeavors to the environment, many fell victim to the theory that the coming of civilization, as it was embodied in the plow, and the extension of a timber culture would cure the heavens of their forgetfulness. "It has been rationally demonstrated," noted one local newspaper, "that this progress of timber culture and growth will work beneficent climatic changes, in which the annual rainfall will be more equally distributed. . . ." But several seasons during the late eighties and early nineties disproved the theories when neither the plow nor the newly planted trees produced moisture. In 1893, 1894, and 1897, for instance, Ashland received less than thirteen inches of rain annually, while over twenty inches was normal for the area. The theory that rain followed the plow was buried, along with the plow, in Kansas dust.[19]

Cattlemen repossessed much of southwestern Kansas as the settlers gradually thinned out, but the process of adjusting their unrestricted operations had begun and would continue well into the twentieth century. The size of individual holdings became smaller, more of the land was owned by the operator, upbreeding was more pronounced, and fencing was evident.

The days of cooperative grazing of large tracts were not completely past, however—only modified. Thousands of cattle sometimes grazed across "big pastures," with the cooperative roundup still in use on occasion. The large pastures, enclosed with barbed wire, confronted many cattlemen of the southwestern part of the state with a land ownership problem. The Wichita *Beacon* remarked in 1897 that many of the ranchers in the southwest were enclosing land "largely held by non-resident owners, many of whom no doubt think it a great hardship to pay taxes on land producing no income." The use of land without remunerating the owner and the continued use of the public domain were also alluded to by another writer, who promised that ranching in western Kansas required ownership of only a quarter section or at most a whole section. "The land you hold," he said, "will control grass on several sections adjoining, or [it] can be leased at very low figures."[20] Fencing and using these large pastures turned out to be an effective middle step in the evolution from open range to smaller, enclosed ranches.

Keeping cow herds to produce young cattle for eastern feeders was the dominate type of cattle operation in this area of the state during the 1890s and for many years thereafter. Stocker and feeder production allowed the western cattleman to pass on most of the risk to the eastern feeder, some said, and there was money in it toward the end of the decade. A few cattlemen claimed that the stockman had weathered the depression better than anyone else in agriculture, that in the 1890s "there never was a better outlook in western Kansas," and that by comparison "the stock breeder of the 'short grass' country is reaping far better returns for his capital and labor than the stock breeder dwelling within the cornbelt portion of the state." Some of the advantages enjoyed by the western cattleman were attributed to the better managed, smaller ranch.[21]

There was also some grazing of transient cattle in southwestern Kansas, much like that described earlier for the Flint Hills. There were numerous instances of Colorado cattle, unhampered by the quarantine laws, grazing Kansas pastures, as well as large numbers from Texas and other areas of the

Southwest, and even Old Mexico. It was estimated in 1897 that as many as 80,000 head from the Texas Panhandle alone would be in western Kansas "before snow flies."[22] Grazing inshipped cattle developed because many of the first cattlemen in western Kansas were Texans who retained cattle interests in their original state, many of the southern ranges produced more cattle than they could mature, and the building of cow herds sufficiently large to utilize the abundant grass was a slow process. Professional pasturemen, however, were not as common in the southwestern section as in the Flint Hills.

The return of much of western Kansas to the cattlemen after the unsuccessful farming boom was temporary. As the decade of the 1890s expired, other developments began to threaten the cattle empire. A few large spreads were poorly managed, and several local editors were again prompted to hurl insults at the large producers. There were "too many would-be cattle barons," one reported with Populist-like fervor, "who think they have capacity to run thousands . . . when in fact they can't handle 100 successfully." These barons, it was charged, tried to "fence in the bigger portion of the country" and spent their money in Kansas City, or at least outside the immediate area. Some of the cattlemen refused to pay for the use of other people's property, the editor scolded, but rather they had begun "a few years ago with nothing. They have grazed off much grass with many cattle; have paid all the profits out to thieving commission companies and are today not worth a dam." The bulwark of the country, the editor believed, was the man who owned a limited herd, paid his taxes, and bought his supplies from local dealers.[23]

The prevalence of a disease variously known as scabies, mange, or cattle itch and a severe winter in 1899 that had caused heavy stock losses contributed to the editor's dissatisfaction with the large cattlemen. He found it difficult to be completely objective when the stench from the rotting corpses of hundreds of dead cattle filled his office while he worked at publishing the weekly news sheet.

Earlier the same paper had castigated the barons for their fencing practices. While Kansas never had the controversy over fencing that other states experienced, there was a bit of fence cutting and some unhappiness over gates on public roads. Although the editor of the paper could overlook cutting wire on land that was not owned by the large operator, he threatened that "there will be a quietus put on unprovoked wire cutting sometime." Later he announced that "people building fences across public roads seems to have occasioned some inconvenience, some hard feelings and not a few 'cuss' words." The editor believed that a traveler compelled to open and close the rickety wire gates in the community "loses his patients [sic], slits his raiment, and knocks more or less skin off his hands." He advised abolishing the wire gate in favor of a wooden one "that can be opened without profanity, or loss of skin."[24]

The operations of C. D. Perry, rancher and farmer for over twenty years along the southern border of the state in Clark County, exemplified many of these developments in the southwest around the turn of the century. He was a large rancher but not really one of the irresponsible barons objected to by local newspapers. Perry had immigrated to Kansas in 1885 along with thousands of others interested in farming. He was fresh from real-estate developments in Chicago and differed from most of the other immigrants in two important considerations: he had no previous experience in agriculture, and he had considerable money in his pocket.

Perry purchased 10,000 acres of short-grass prairie and immediately began ranching and farming on what he called the Claremont Ranch. Imported Shorthorn cattle and later Herefords were used to upbreed the native stock that he purchased in the area. He was always experimenting—with crops, farming methods, and different breeds of livestock—or promoting something— a bank, a town, railroads, experimental farms, or sugar mills. By digging a shallow seven-mile canal from the Cimarron River in Oklahoma to his ranch in Kansas, Perry was able to irrigate several thousand acres of small grains, alfalfa, and tame grasses. All this was accomplished before 1900.

By the time Perry sold his holdings during the early years of the twentieth century, he had accumulated over 20,000 acres, 1,000 of which were irrigated, and over 2,000 head of well-bred cattle. He sold out in 1907 in order to retire to a California alfalfa farm, but, unfortunately, he died in an auto accident the following year.[25] Before his move, Perry had not only witnessed but encouraged several changes in western Kansas. He had engaged in both dry land and irrigated farming, encouraged more restricted ranching, fenced all or most of the land he used, and upbred his stock. Finally, he helped stimulate another threat to cattlemen that developed during the early years of the new century in the form of a wheat boom.

The Medicine Lodge *Cresset* was one of the first papers to note the second wave of immigrant farmers moving into the southwest in less than a generation. It reported in 1905, "Western Kansas is going to be the great wheat field of the world. Lands that have been thought only fit for short grass is proving that it can produce wheat, and the western counties are attracting immigrants from all over the country. . . . Fine farms can be seen where only a few years ago was a broad expanse of nothing but grass. . . . Land values are on the increase and there is a disposition of the owners to cut up the large ranches into farms."[26]

Two years later the Wichita *Eagle* observed that "one by one the big ranches of southwestern Kansas are disappearing and in their places are appearing farms. . . . Free range is almost unknown."[27] One factor that contributed to renewed interest in farming this area was the belief that the Campbell method of dry farming—essentially a method for summer-fallowing cropland—would solve the climatic deficiencies. C. D. Perry was one of the first in the area to experiment with and advertise the method. Parts of his Claremont Ranch that had farming potential were divided and sold to some of the new immigrants. But even with the influx of wheat growers the southwest remained largely cow country. Much of the short-grass prairie was already owned by cattlemen before the new immigrants arrived, some of the land was not adaptable to the plow, and the Campbell method was not a complete answer to the variance in annual rainfall. Wheat cultivation too was destined for many poor years.

Specialization, then, was evident in the different sections of the state engaged in raising beef, although a single area often practiced several phases of growing and maturing cattle for slaughter. During the nineteenth century, cattle were often born in one section of the country and matured over a period of several years in another, before being marketed as either grass-fat slaughter beef or feeder stock that needed additional fattening. If the latter was the case, a different owner often performed the task in a feedlot. Frequently it was undertaken by stockmen in another region, notably the Midwest.

Specialization into several stages occurred for a number of reasons, but basic to its development was the fact that the grassland production of cattle exceeded available grain supply, while the midwestern states chose to market much of their grain by feeding it to stock. This way more profit was expected from the grain. Also, midwestern land values were much too high by this time for profitable grazing of stock. Intensive production of corn for the fattening of cattle born and matured in the grasslands was more suitable, and, as a result, the regions complemented each other quite well.

Producers also expected to save money on transportation by putting as much weight on the animals as close to the large marketing centers as was possible. Not only were shipping rates on cattle usually cheaper than those on grain, but transporting midwestern feed to the source of stocker-feeder production would have necessitated shipping it back again a few years later in the form of beef. The necessity of a yearly income without a delay of several years while awaiting full maturation of the cattle, as well as the cost of separate pens and other equipment necessary for full-feeding operations, also contributed to specialization.

The practice of using several stages in the production of slaughter beef became increasingly popular during the twentieth century. Rarely did a single grassland operator retain ownership of cattle from birth to slaughter until the development of large commercial feedlots after World War II. Even then few producers retained ownership throughout the whole process of converting a little calf into a large critter ready for the packer.

By the 1890s Kansans had acquired relatively large numbers of cattle, and the production of beef was making a significant contribution to the state's agricultural economy. As a result of consistent growth since the 1860s, the state had over 2.2 million beef cattle and calves by 1890. After a decline during the middle nineties, the number had grown to almost 2.9 million by 1900, which represented the largest number for the nineteenth century (see Figure 1).

Figure 1 also reveals the relative balance that existed between the state's hog and cattle populations from 1890 to the early 1930s, even though fluctuations in numbers did not always coincide. After 1930 beef cattle became the dominant species of livestock in Kansas, largely as a result of the demands of World War II, the postwar consumer preference for beef, and the growth of large commercial feedlots. The state's hog industry, meanwhile, never regained its former stature after the depression, drought, and government controls of the 1930s combined to reduce swine numbers, although increases did occur as a result of World War II and the expanded demand for meat in the 1960s. Decreased amounts of corn harvested for grain paralleled the declining hog industry.

By the 1890s the pattern of distribution for Kansas beef cattle had already been set, with the heaviest concentrations in the Flint Hills (see Map 1, p. 70). This pattern did not vary greatly throughout the next fifty years, although prolonged droughts caused greater concentrations in the Flint Hills. The availability of grass and water, corn for feeding, and the total number of stock were important factors in determining the location of the state's cattle.

The contribution of livestock to the agricultural economy of Kansas increased along with the numbers of cattle. Livestock and its products consti-

Figure 1. Numbers of Livestock in Kansas, 1890-1970 (in million of head)

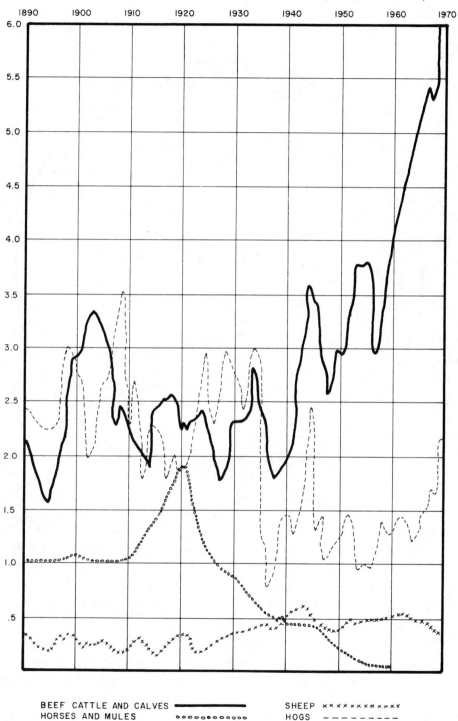

BEEF CATTLE AND CALVES ———————
HORSES AND MULES °°°°°°°°°°°°°
SHEEP ×××××××××××××
HOGS — — — — — — — —

Source: *Fifty-Fourth Rept., KSBA* (1970–1971).

Figure 2. Average Percentage of Farm Value of Selected Kansas Products, 1891–1895

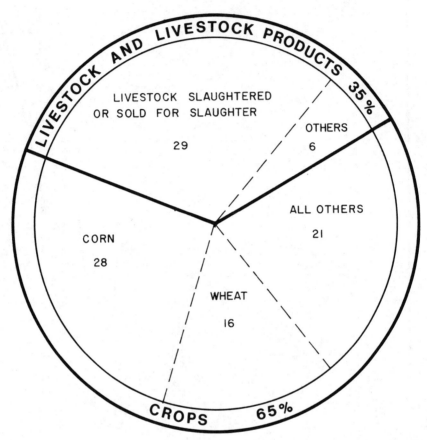

Source: "State Summaries," in *Repts., KSBA* (1891–1895).

tuted a higher percentage of the economy during the 1890s than at any other time during the next two decades (see Figures 2 and 3), accounting for over 35 percent of the total value of farm commodities. Actually, the contribution to farm income from livestock was probably larger than this figure indicates. The value of grain fed to stock, for instance, was apparently included in the crop sector, when in fact its cash value was attained only through livestock. Cash receipt figures from the marketing of farm and ranch products would have been a better indication of livestock's real value to the agricultural economy of Kansas, but these figures did not become available until 1925. Nor

Figure 3. Average Percentage of Farm Value of Selected Kansas Products, 1896–1900

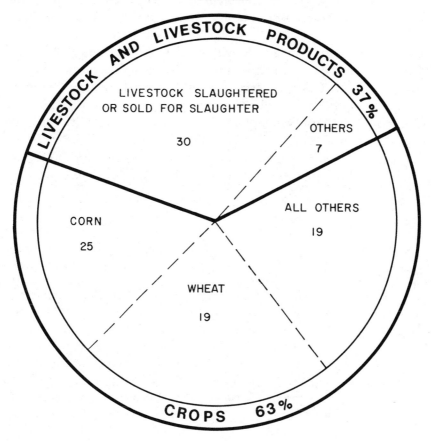

Source: "State Summaries," in *Repts., KSBA* (1896–1900).

was it possible to differentiate the contribution of beef cattle from that of livestock as a whole until after 1925, but that of cattle was the largest single contributor during most years.

The Kansas beef industry was an important local industry by the 1890s, but its significance went beyond the local area. In addition to the millions of beef cattle produced exclusively within the state thousands more were shipped in from Colorado, Oklahoma, Texas, and other states of the Southwest for maturing and fattening before going to market as grass-fattened or as partially fed animals. Some of these transient cattle were slaughtered immediately after leaving the grass, but large numbers were also shipped to feedlots in Iowa, Illinois, Indiana, and other cornbelt states. The intersectional link eventually proved far more important to Kansas and to the nation's beef industry than the earlier role of the state as the terminal point for the Texas drives.

As a whole, cattle raising in Kansas at the end of the nineteenth century had largely completed its transition from a frontier institution to a modern ranching industry. This necessitated a number of modifications. Ownership of land, for example, was requried as the public domain disappeared, and greater managerial skill was necessary as the spread between market prices and production costs narrowed. Finally, the upbreeding of stock, which was also begun during the nineteenth century, gained new importance in the modern industry's drive to improve management practices and increase profits.

2

Purebreds Move West: The 1890s

One of the most interesting and important single contributions that Kansas cattlemen of the late nineteenth century made to the western beef business was in the area of upbreeding. Before the century ended, thousands of well-bred cattle were sired and matured in the state and then shipped to the western range country. Prior to the 1890s most of the well-bred cattle had originated in England and Scotland or in the midwestern states of the Mississippi River valley. Kansas, initially a transfer point for these bovine aristocrats, gradually began to add its own improved stock to the growing flow westward.[1]

The westward path of improved stock was counter to the traditional movement of cattle. To the flood of stocker and feeder cattle that moved out of the West toward the midwestern markets was added a stream of upgraded stock moving in the opposite direction. This movement continued well into the twentieth century—until western producers had established their own purebred herds—and a shadow of it remains even today.

In a larger sense, upgrading of range cattle was an integral part of the transition from open range to ranch. It was both cause and effect. Because improved stock was dependent upon close herd management, cattlemen recorded few successes in improving their herds until after fences were built. A little barbed wire enabled stockmen to improve their herds and, most importantly, to harvest the products of good sires. Upbred stock, since they were more valuable, deserved more winter feeding and water close at hand, and required supervision during the calving period to minimize the risk of calf losses, all of which were possible only on a well-managed ranch.

Small and large farms that specialized in purebred production supplied much of the upgraded stock that moved West. The owners of these farms worked seriously at improving the breed and spent a good deal of money in the effort. Range producers then bought the bulls for use with commercial cattle or to start their own purebred herds for bull production. Frequently, these purebred establishments were owned by men who had considerable money, made not in agriculture but rather in some urban business. Some men made money and gained fame in the business, while others accomplished neither, but most contributed some impetus to transforming the long-legged scrubs into modern beef-producing machines.

Almost from the beginning there were attempts to upgrade the nondescript cattle that stocked the grasslands, but not until the 1870s and 1880s did the movement reach full force. Reasons abounded for upbreeding, but pride and profit were the prime movers. Most cattlemen had always desired to produce the best stock that their particular circumstances allowed. Improved cattle were more pleasing to the eye, a source of pride for the owner, and, most importantly, more profitable. During the last half of the nineteenth century, when the country was becoming increasingly urbanized and industrialized, there were demands for increased quantity and quality in the beef trade. A growing export trade, especially to England, also contributed to these demands. Many cornbelt feeders had stopped feeding Longhorns by the 1870s and were in the market for upbred feeder stock that fattened better and did not bring the dreaded Texas fever into the Midwest. Upgrading stock and the turn away from Longhorns, then, helped ensure profits for those who fed cattle.[2]

An Ohio correspondent to the *Kansas Farmer,* who was typical of those who fattened stock, wrote that cornbelt feeders wanted animals that gained weight rapidly and thus reduced feed costs. Further, he said, feeders desired "compact, medium-sized, thick-fleshed, easy keepers, that will mature at 3 years old and make a 1,500 to 1,700 pound steer." A quiet disposition, no horns, broad backs, deep loins, and massive quarters were highly desirable qualities too, because, he noted, "it costs no more to produce a pound of steak than a pound of neck or tripe."[3] Another correspondent suggested that an improved digestive and circulatory system that utilized feed to the best advantage was the most desirable quality in the upgraded stock. Only blooded animals could fill the requirement of increased quantity and quality. The upbred steer often weighed 500 to 600 pounds more at three years of age than his poorly bred counterpart. Reports of experiments at Kansas State Agricultural College that were published in the *Kansas Farmer* and other agricultural publications supported the gainability qualities of blooded stock when compared with scrubs.[4]

The premium paid by meat packers for quality stock obviously helped stimulate the feedlot demand for upgraded cattle. The packing industry played no small part in the upbreeding process. Not only did packers help create the demand, but several engaged directly in purebred production themselves. Kirk B. Armour of the famous packing family, for example, bought the herd of C. M. Culbertson, when in the 1890s depression forced the latter to liquidate his famous herd. Armour placed this herd on his farm near Excelsior Springs, Missouri, expanded it through additional purchases, and sent most of the increase to the range country. George A. Fowler, a Kansas City meat packer, was associated with William J. Tod, long-time rancher of Maple Hill, Kansas, in the production of purebred cattle, many of which were used in the Flint Hills or were sent to upgrade the commercial herd on their Crosselle Ranch in New Mexico.[5]

As a result of observing these improved animals, many range producers by the late nineteenth century agreed that not only did blooded stock adapt well to range conditions but they were also better money-makers. Only the specific breed—Shorthorn, Aberdeen-Angus, or Hereford—remained a matter of dispute.

As early as the eighties some improvement was noticed in the cattle being trailed from Texas. This improvement was largely the result of cattle moved south from Kansas shipping points to the Texas ranges. A. M. Lord of Dodge City, for example, assembled 1,300 yearling bulls from Missouri, Iowa, and Illinois and trailed them south from Dodge City in 1882. Lord's cattle must have passed several herds of Longhorns moving in the opposite direction on the first leg of their journey to urban markets. Also during the 1880s, the Burlingame, Kansas, firm of Finch, Lord, & Nelson estimated that they had sent around 10,000 Hereford bulls to Texas between 1881 and 1888, and Lucien Scott shipped breeding stock from his Ridgewood Farm near Leavenworth. Scott, a banker by trade, used his upbred Kansas cattle to improve the quality of the stock on his LS Ranch in the Texas Panhandle, a spread that became famous throughout the West. Other Kansans followed the example of the large exporters of fine cattle, much to the advantage of beef producers in Texas and throughout the Great Plains.[6]

Shorthorns were the first breed to be used extensively in upbreeding programs. The first were imported into the United States during the late eighteenth century, with hundreds more following during the next century. By the 1860s Shorthorns had migrated as far west as Kansas, where a few farms were being devoted to upgraded stock. Samuel S. Tipton, a cattleman in eastern Kansas, brought about fifty Shorthorns into Kansas Territory from Ohio after a brief stay in Iowa. As early as 1859 he recorded fifteen of these purebreds in the breed's herd book, the first purebred Shorthorns known to have existed in the state.

Additional Shorthorn cattle appeared soon after the Civil War. Albert Crane early in the 1870s kept a famous herd at his Durham Park farm north of Wichita. Crane had graduated from Harvard Law School before making a fortune in Chicago real estate and investing in Kansas land and cattle. He soon bought Shorthorn bulls to use on 3,000 Longhorn cows, while building a small purebred herd of his own with cattle brought from the Midwest or imported from England. For a while during the seventies, cows that Crane had purchased for more than $20,000 apiece, as well as a bull from England at $25,000, grazed the bluegrass that he had sown after plowing under the native grass. It is doubtful that Crane's heavy investment in fine cattle ever paid for itself, but he did sprinkle some fine Shorthorn blood throughout central Kansas.[7]

George Washington Glick, first Democrat to govern Kansas, also bred Shorthorns. A threshing machine accident that severely injured both feet had forced young Glick from his father's Ohio farm and into the law office of Rutherford B. Hayes. After some experience with Hayes, Glick practiced law in Ohio, then moved to Atchison, Kansas, where he prospered in both business and politics. But practicing law did not satisfy Glick's longing to improve the agriculture of his adopted state. Thus, during the 1870s he bought what was called the Shannon Hill stock farm west of Atchison, and there built a herd of more than a hundred purebred Shorthorns. Glick claimed that he chose the breed because of its large, well-marbled carcass, its early-maturing qualities, its mild disposition, and its superior milk production. Murdo Mackenzie, manager of the Matador Land and Cattle Company, bought many of Glick's bulls for use with range cows, paying $80 to $120 per head during the 1890s. The herd was finally dispersed in 1900, when Glick went to Florida to spend his twilight years on a citrus farm.[8]

The master Shorthorn breeder during this early period was W. A. Harris of Linwood. According to C. W. McCampbell, beef cattle specialist at Kansas State Agricultural College for many years, Harris had the "most famous herd in America during the '80s and '90s." Harris made his specific contribution by following the lead of the great Scottish Shorthorn breeder, Amos Cruickshank. Both men devised matings and made herd selections based on individual merit rather than on ancestry, as the Bates Shorthorn people had tended to do. Using many animals of Cruickshank breeding, which he obtained from Canada, as well as a few superior Bates cattle, Harris revolutionized the type of Shorthorns raised in the United States. His cattle, when compared to the older Bates Shorthorns, improved markedly the size and fleshing ability of the breed. His fame spread even to the British Isles, where some of his cattle were exported during the late eighties and early nineties.

The depression of the 1890s and a growing interest in politics forced Harris to sell his prized herd. He was first elected a United States congressman, then a United States senator in 1896. His famous herd was dispersed the same year, but his Shorthorns had already made their mark in American breeding circles, not least of which was the effect they had on the Tomson cattle, probably the most enduring herd of Shorthorns in Kansas.[9]

T. K. Tomson, who had migrated to Kansas during the Civil War, established a farm near Dover and another south of Topeka, around Wakarusa. It was 1886, however, before he got into the Shorthorn business with a small herd of common grade cows. To this he added a famous bull named Phyllis Duke, which he purchased at a sheriff's sale in Kentucky for the paltry sum of $25.50, as the bull was in poor flesh. Thistletop, a bull bred by Cruickshank, was also placed in the herd. Then during the 1890s John and James G. Tomson became their father's associates, and the purebred business was expanded. Young Jim Tomson displayed early the shrewdness and determination that was essential in making their herd famous. Jim, the genius who built the herd, became known as one of the best judges of cattle in the country. Kansans tell the story that W. A. Harris mistakenly listed for sale one of his coveted herd sires, Gallant Knight, in a letter to young James Tomson, who insisted that the letter constituted a bona fide offer, and Harris was persuaded to sell this excellent bull that he had intended to keep for his own herd.

Gallant Knight and several good cows purchased later at the Harris dispersion sale were added to the growing herd of Shorthorns, aiding in the development of what came to be known as the Tomson Type, cattle that were of "scale and substance, thickly and evenly fleshed, combined with quality and breediness." During the twentieth century the Tomson name became almost synonymous with Shorthorn, especially in Kansas. The contributions of the Tomson Shorthorns to their home state can be judged from the fact that over half of their production was sold to Kansas breeders. A few were sent west, and the remainder were sold in states to the east of Kansas.[10]

The black Galloway and Aberdeen-Angus, nature's dehorners, were not far behind the Shorthorns in arriving on the western scene. George Grant is usually given credit for importing the first Aberdeen-Angus into the United States. Grant had made a fortune as a London cloth merchant, part of which, it was said, came as a result of his cornering the supply of black crepe at the time of Prince Albert's death. Be that as it may, he did have money. After visiting Kansas he decided to plant a colony on the state's western grassland. Thus, in 1873 he brought a group of immigrants and four black bulls through the port of New Orleans and on to a site a few miles east of Hays, which he called Victoria. The colony soon failed, but the bulls sired hundreds of calves from Texas Longhorn cows.

At the time of Grant's death in 1878, over 800 crossbred calves had been dispersed from his herd. These mixed-blood calves "created a sensation" when their rapid gainability became evident to eastern feeders. McCampbell, who may have been a bit too laudatory, noted in his study of upbreeding that Grant's importation "more than any other single factor stimulated a desire for better sires." It was an odd turn of fate, McCampbell continued, "that Angus cattle which furnished the inspiration that really started the work of improving Kansas cattle, were not used extensively in this work." The greater availability of other breeds accounted for the smaller role of Angus cattle, but one might also question McCampbell's evaluation of the blacks as the inspiration. Shorthorns were already established to some degree by 1873, and the great Hereford boom was not far off. But Grant's work did help stimulate interest in the Aberdeen-Angus and contributed to the founding in Kansas of several herds of purebreds.

Probably none of the other purebred herds descended from Grant's importations, although no one knows for sure what became of the original four bulls. T. J. McCreary of Highland had one of the first purebred Angus herds in the state, and he was joined shortly by J. S. and W. R. Goodwin of Beloit. A representative of the Goodwin herd won a major prize at a Kansas City stock show as early as 1885. Many of the finest Angus herds in the state, however, were begun around the turn of the century, or several years after.[11]

Shorthorn and Angus cattle certainly helped upgrade stock, but it was the white-faced Herefords that played the most significant role both in Kansas and throughout the West. The Herefords' popularity was based on their availability, their attractive appearance, and, most heavily, upon the belief that they were the best winter and summer grazers, especially on scanty pastures. Ironically, the poor milking ability of Herefords when compared with Shorthorns enhanced their popularity, because udder and nursing problems were reduced and the cow's strength was not spent producing milk. Rather, Hereford cows had excellent records of breeding back quickly and producing calves the following year, even though drought might have ravaged their pastures. Hereford bulls were even more popular than the female stock. They were virile and aggressive breeders during the hot summer months, and even came through long winters in good physical condition when feed was short. It was the Hereford bull, more than any other single factor, that increased the size and quality of range cattle, enabling any producer to increase his beef production without necessarily enlarging his land holdings.

Herefords fattened well, too. Their quiet dispositions in feedlots and their ability to manufacture grain into a highly desirable meat were cited repeatedly by those who championed the breed. The fattening ability of the breed was indicated by the prices paid at marketing centers. During the first forty years of the twentieth century, for instance, the highest price paid each year for fat steers at Chicago went to Herefords more than half the time.[12]

The Hereford first came to America after being developed in England during the eighteenth century in response to the increased demands for meat in the growing urban centers. Breeders in western England were responsible for Hereford development, especially the elder and younger Benjamin Tomkins of Herefordshire, a county in England adjacent to Wales. Henry Clay, United States senator and frequent presidential hopeful, as well as an agriculturalist, from Lexington, Kentucky, imported the first Herefords into the United States in 1817. But to avoid continuous inbreeding, Clay soon mixed the breed with Shorthorns and their identity was lost. A few whitefaces were brought over after Clay's initial importation and were used sparingly from New England to Ohio. Although there is an authentic record of Clay's import, the first importation of Herefords to the United States that resulted in the founding of a breeding herd of a substantial basis, a shipment from England in 1840 consisting of twenty-two head, was made by William H. Sotham of New York.

Importations of purebred Herefords before the mid-1870s, however, were not great and probably did not exceed 250 head. This changed rapidly during the next decade. New imports, along with the cattle already here, helped establish several Hereford farms in midwestern states during the 1870s. Thomas Clark, for example, produced excellent Herefords, first in Ohio, then Illinois. About the same time, T. L. Miller, whose industrious promotional work was equally as important as the quality of his cattle, and C. M. Culbertson helped move the center for Hereford production from Ohio to Illinois. Culbertson, a wealthy Chicago packer, imported the first Anxiety blood, a line destined to have great influence on American Herefords. He also persuaded other men of wealth to enter the purebred business, among the most significant of whom were Moses Fowler and W. S. Van Natta. These men, along with many others, worked not only to improve the breed but also to spread it into the West.[13]

Hiram Woodward and Walter M. Morgan, both of Marshall County near Blue Rapids, share the honor of introducing Herefords into Kansas. Both had connections with Thomas Aston of Elyria, Ohio, who had brought some of the original Tomkins blood to the United States when he migrated from Herefordshire. Woodward brought the first Herefords into the state in 1872 and showed them at a Leavenworth fair a couple of years later. But Woodward died in 1877, before the cattle were fully developed, and the herd was sold to T. L. Miller.

Walter Morgan did more to popularize Herefords in the state than did Woodward, as his herd advertised the breed from the 1870s until a year before his death in 1916. Morgan had migrated from England to Ohio in 1852 and there became associated with Thomas Aston. Several years after beginning this position, he married Aston's daughter, and they moved to Kansas in 1876. With them the Morgans brought Aston cattle that had been crossed with blood from T. L. Miller's herd. They attempted to show their cattle almost as soon as they arrived, but getting the Hereford accepted by fair judges as a legitimate beef breed was no small task. Morgan's son reported many years later that it would have been as easy for "Governor Al E. Smith to get justice in a K.K.K. lodge in 1928 as for Herefords to win over Shorthorns at that time." Despite prejudice, however, Morgan's herd eventually won many prizes at top shows, and soon established Marshall County as the "Herefordshire of Kansas."[14]

Other Hereford herds were established in widely scattered areas of the state soon after the pioneering work of Morgan and Woodward. Shockey & Gibb near Lawrence, J. S. Hawes of Colony, T. J. Higgins around Council Grove, and W. E. Campbell, whose headquarters were near Kiowa, all had

Herefords during the early period. Campbell was especially significant in introducing the breed to range herds.

W. E. Campbell had been one of the first to trail Texas cattle into the state after the Civil War, and he eventually bought grazing land of his own southwest of Wichita. To his herd of native cattle he introduced blooded Shorthorn bulls and championed their value throughout the Southwest. Neighbors called him "Shorthorn" Campbell, but this sobriquet soon gave way to "Whiteface" Campbell when he began using that breed in 1879. His enthusiasm for Herefords grew to more than double that which he had expressed for the former breed. Campbell even established a purebred herd, which produced bulls for his range cattle and won top prizes at the best stock shows in the area.

Campbell's greatest contribution was in demonstrating the Hereford bull's ability to transmit his desirable qualities to scrub cattle. In 1881 six of his small south Texas cows strayed into the pasture of his purebred herd and were serviced by Hereford bulls. Three of the calves from this chance mating were carefully fed before becoming Campbell's demonstration exhibit at the Kansas City Fat Stock Show in 1883. His favorite, a heifer called Texas Jane, weighed 1,260 pounds as a yearling, some 500 pounds more than the Texas cow that had mothered her. Texas Jane was kept for three years in a special pen at the Kansas City market where she demonstrated before hundreds of range producers the results from good Hereford bulls.[15]

With men like Campbell showing that added weight on upbred cattle resulted in increased profits, and with many of the agricultural journals urging stockmen to eliminate the plug, scrub, and runt, it is not surprising that the upbreeding of range herds became an important concern towards the end of the century. The Hereford was in a prime position to facilitate the change, especially after breeders had eliminated some of the deficiencies in the breed.

The Herefords' thin, cat-hammed hindquarters were their principal fault and the source of much criticism during the early years of their development in the United States. This deficiency was especially significant because many of the more expensive beef cuts come from the hindquarters. When improvement of this trait occurred, not only was the Herefords' meat-producing abilities enhanced but also their popularity. The Hereford boom in the 1880s followed closely the first successful steps to solve this hind-end problem.

Charles and James Gudgell and Thomas A. Simpson were most responsible for taking the first step that led to enlarging the hindquarters. These transplanted Kentuckians did much of their early breeding work around Pleasant Hill, Missouri, where they founded in 1876 a purebred herd that was to become easily the most famous and influential of its time. Later, they moved their headquarters to Independence, Missouri. Donald R. Ornduff, in his history of the Hereford breed, judged that "in ultimate influence upon the Hereford breed in America, no contemporary herd came close to matching the contributions of Gudgell & Simpson and no bull that of Anxiety 4th 9904." Regarding this bloodline, Ornduff had written earlier that there was little doubt that Anxiety had "supplied the foundation upon which the improvement wrought in the United States in the old English-type Herefords was primarily based."[16] Even today most purebred Herefords trace their ancestry to Anxiety 4th.

Thomas A. "Governor" Simpson, a quiet man with an endearing dry wit, was a distant cousin of the father of the Gudgell brothers, and had been a partner from time to time in some of the elder Gudgell's farming activities. Perhaps as a mark of his willingness to make decisions, he was nicknamed "Governor" early in life, and the Gudgell sons, who were some twenty-five years younger, naturally picked up the term, as did his friends in the Hereford field. Upon their father's death before they attained their majority, the "Governor," who never held political office, became their legal guardian.

The Gudgell brothers became engaged in the range-cattle business at Las Animas, Colorado, more by circumstance than by deliberate design. When they first came to Missouri they entered the employ of a bank in Kansas City. When hard times struck in the early 1870s they acquired a financial interest in a cattle operation through a transaction which had to do with a loan the bank had made. Their partners in this venture, which eventually reached into Oklahoma and Kansas and gave them an insight into the need for high-grade range bulls, were Major W. A. Towers and John R. Towers, the firm operating as Towers & Gudgell. Simpson never had a financial interest in this venture.

Following the death of his wife, Simpson made his home for the remainder of his life in Charles Gudgell's large home in Independence. This house also served as the first office of what was to become the American Hereford Association, and became a renowned meeting place for important cattlemen from throughout the country. Simpson always kept on hand a barrel of excellent Scotch whisky, which was always available to guests, he himself professing to indulge a bit only when struck by "a cold." Gudgell & Simpson also made notable importations of Aberdeen-Angus cattle from Scotland, but sold them out within a few years. They were, however, charter members of both the Angus and Hereford breed associations, and Charles Gudgell served as the secretary of both organizations from the office in a large room in his home in Independence.

Charles Gudgell, whose brother James had died in 1897, continued the purebred business alone after Simpson's death in 1904 until the entire herd was dispersed in 1916. The Gudgell sons had no desire to continue the purebred business, although ranching interests, including land in northwest Kansas, were retained. The elder Gudgell retired to California soon after the dispersal of the purebred cattle and began construction of a beautiful new home. Death, unfortunately, claimed him barely three months after the herd was sold. Observers of the Gudgell & Simpson enterprise have given both men equal credit for its accomplishments. Gudgell received praise for his keen business sense and willingness to provide capital, while Simpson was lauded for his remarkable ability to judge cattle and plan breeding programs.[17]

An often-repeated story concerns Simpson's journey to England in 1881 to find a bull with a "hind-end on him," as he had been admonished by Charles Gudgell. This was the trip that produced the famous Anxiety 4th, a son of the original Anxiety that had died shortly after arriving in 1879 in Illinois. Through a judicious and skilled use of linebreeding—a practice of mating animals that have as close a relationship to the foundation as possible and the least amount of relationship to each other except through the foundation—Gudgell & Simpson were able to concentrate Anxiety 4th's blood in his numerous progeny. Much criticism and many predictions of failure were leveled at the firm by those who failed to understand that linebreeding was a useful form of closebreeding when accompanied by a rigid culling of the herd. The bull Don Carlos, which in turn produced Beau Brummel and Lamplighter, was the most famous son of Anxiety 4th; but another son, Beau Real, the sire of such famous sons as Kansas Lad and Wild Tom, should not be overlooked. These six bulls and many other bulls and heifers represented the high concentration of Anxiety 4th's blood that was destined to make major improvements throughout the nation.

It has been estimated that Anxiety 4th had more effect on Kansas upbreeding than any other animal, by improving such influential purebred herds as those of Shockey & Gibb, Scott & Whitman, C. S. Cross, and Robert H. Hazlett. But the effect that Gudgell & Simpson had on purebred herds was only part of their magnificent story, as they also directly influenced many commercial range herds. The Horace G. Adams family and the Tod-Fowler interests, all of Maple Hill, along the northern edge of the Flint Hills, were only two examples of the many who used Anxiety 4th breeding on large range herds. Likewise, the Gudgell brothers, as previously noted, had ranching interests where Anxiety 4th's blood was used on commercial herds. The firm of Gudgell & Simpson also eventually raised purebreds in Kansas, first on a ranch near Richmond, then on a ranch of nearly 10,000 acres in northwestern Kansas, near Edmond. In fact, the entire breeding herd was sent to the Edmond ranch after 1909, with only small holdings retained in the Independence area for show or sale. This latter location near Kansas City, where hundreds of prospective customers patronized the stockyards, was helpful in spreading Gudgell & Simpson's blooded cattle.

It is not surprising that the Gudgell & Simpson influence was so widely felt when one considers that their purebred herd sometimes approached 800 head and that it "shelled-out" bulls by the carload. Fully two-thirds of Anxiety 4th's own sons and literally thousands of bulls with Anxiety 4th's blood went into commercial range herds, most of which grazed the plains of Kansas and the Southwest. Gudgell & Simpson enlarged the hindquarters of the Herefords, improved their "mellowness of flesh" and easy feeding characteristics, and helped decrease the age at which they matured. Even more important, they had demonstrated to American breeders that the blood of a superior animal could be sucessfully concentrated through linebreeding.[18] It was this practice that the Kansan Robert H. Hazlett employed in becoming one of the greatest Hereford breeders of the twentieth century.

One of the largest purebred Hereford herds in Kansas during the 1890s, if not the largest, was that of Charles S. Cross, who had built a herd of 300 cows by the end of the decade. In addition to fine breeding on his model Sunny Slope farm, a few miles northwest of Emporia, Cross illustrated again that purebred breeders frequently had large financial resources, money that was often made in nonagricultural pursuits. The literature abounds with examples of men who had made fortunes in oil, real estate, banking, or other urban-centered businesses before going into the purebred trade. The Cross experience illustrated several other characteristics of purebred production during the 1890s as well, especially the widening influence of Anxiety 4th, the continued ties American breeders retained with England, the large amount of capital that was required, and the precarious nature of the investment. Finally, Cross exemplified a certain mystique that developed around this class of breeder and his livestock.

C. S. Cross had come to Emporia with his parents just after the Civil War. His father invested in the First National Bank in Emporia a couple of years before the financial panic in 1873, but neither the panic nor the depression permanently harmed the Cross banking interests. At his death in 1891 the elder Cross passed to his son his interest in the bank, which must have exceeded 50 percent. C. S. Cross first diversified his economic interests during the middle 1880s when he began to fatten stock for slaughter. Then, with the depression in the 1890s and the low prices for purebreds that resulted, Cross was encouraged to enter the purebred business. He bought foundation stock from Shockey & Gibb, who were forced to liquidate, Gudgell & Simpson, Fowler & Tod, and several other well-known breeders. Among the cattle purchased from Fowler was the bull Wild Tom, a grandson of Anxiety 4th, which became not only the most important sire for the young herd but also a nationally famous bull. All of the stock was kept at Sunny Slope farm, which consisted of a large residence, a bunkhouse, several large barns—all scrupulously kept in the finest condition—and over 2,000 acres of land. Some 760 acres of this land belonged to Cross, and the balance was leased. The day-to-day work was performed by a manager and a score of other hired hands, while Cross divided his time between the farm and the Emporia bank.

A practice not uncommon for fine cattle breeders was that of keeping purebred hogs. Cross kept quality Poland China hogs until he disposed of them in 1896 to make room for more cattle. The hog sale was reported as one of the biggest social events of the year for the community. It needed, according to the local newspaper, "only a red lamp shade and a head prize to get into the *Gazette's* society column."

Moreover, there were a number of other sales prominent in the Cross story. The yearly progeny of the large cow herd were sold at special auctions or by private contract to those who visited the farm. The *Gazette* proudly announced in 1898 that Sunny Slope was the one famous thing in Lyon County and that "buyers from all over the country come here to buy fine stock." The largest and most publicized sale at Sunny Slope was one that was held in March, 1898. Billed as the highlight Hereford auction of the decade, it included in the listing forty head of highly blooded animals that Cross had recently imported from England at a cost of over $150 a head. The *Breeder's Gazette, Harpers Weekly,* and dozens of newspapers covered the two-day sale, which was attended by over 3,000 people. Gross receipts totaled over $61,300 for an average of $407 per animal.[19]

Almost four decades later, one of the auctioneers remembered the sale in 1898 as one of the greatest he had ever attended. Advertised in many national stock journals and by an elaborate catalogue bound in red, velvet-like cloth, it attracted the leading breeders of the nation. Bidding was moderate to begin with, but when a gentleman from Virginia finally bid $3,000 for the bull Salisbury pandemonium broke loose at ringside. The enthusiasm carried through the remainder of the sale. Some have said that the national attention that surrounded the event, as well as the nationwide attendance, did more for the breed during the difficult 1890s than anything else. "It was without doubt," one observer said, "the greatest sale of Herefords ever made in America up to that time."[20]

With the assets of "unlimited capital, energy, and brains," according to the local newspaper, Cross built one of the largest herds of blooded cattle in America. The herd was the source of much pride in the community, as the Cross cattle not only attracted many distinguished visitors to the Emporia area but advertised the small town by winning top prizes at most of the shows on the western circuit.

All the transactions of the Cross enterprises were not apparent, however, and when the financial crash came the community was shocked. The crisis became visible several months after the large sale in March, 1898, which was a last desperate attempt by Cross to regain financial stability. The effort failed, however, and a bank examiner closed the First National Bank in November, 1898. The Cross bank had lent so much money that less than 16 percent of the deposits were on hand, while other local banks, by comparison, maintained close to 40 percent. Cross and his partner had been heavy borrowers, mostly without adequate collateral. Cross alone was estimated to have borrowed as much as $150,000, with Sunny Slope as collateral; but only a month after the bank was closed the model farm and remaining stock were sold for only $40,000. On the day that the bank's activities were officially suspended, Cross paid a final visit to his beloved Sunny Slope and there, in an upstairs bedroom of the large house, shot himself. He had lived just forty years.[21]

Cross had built what many breeders could only dream of, but he had done so at great expense. His own small fortune was lost, as well as the deposits of many members of the community, although the bank did eventually pay much of its debt after several years of litigation.

The Cross experience related directly to some of the larger problems of financing purebred as well as other cattle herds toward the end of the century. Long-term, low-interest loans to cattlemen were almost nonexistent, unless of course one owned a bank, as Cross did. Short-term loans that were rediscounted by commission firms or smaller banks and passed to the larger sources of capital in the East were more common and even quite adequate in the view of some, but the long-term needs of cattlemen were seldom satisfied. Interest rates were also high, sometimes approaching 10 percent, and the availability of capital did not correspond well with the need. During depressions, when there was an increased need for credit, as in the early 1890s, cattlemen had more difficulty in finding capital, while the reverse was true when there was a great deal of optimism about the beef industry. In fact, the greater availability of money towards the end of the decade and the lack of precaution exercised by some bankers led to several situations in Kansas similar to that of C. S. Cross.

An eager, swashbuckling young man named Grant G. Gillett, for instance, was able to parlay his self-imposed reputation as the largest cattle feeder in Kansas into a small fortune of borrowed money without ever having adequate collateral. Gillett had a small cattle-feeding operation near Abilene during the last part of the nineteenth century that was moderately successful, but he was impatient for fortune and began to expand rapidly. Soon, hundreds of cattle began arriving at the Gillett farm and departing with such rapidity that the bank examiners did not bother to keep adequate count of the cattle or the dollars that were involved. A score of banks in a half-dozen states were involved in loans to Gillett, some on the same cattle and some on stock that did not exist. Gillett, meanwhile, traveled around in a private railroad car with his own cowboy band and hosted lavish parties for his friends and creditors in Kansas City and other large cities. But someone became suspicious in 1898, counted the cattle and dollars, and found some $200,000 to $600,000 in loans—other estimates ranged up to a million dollars—while only a few cattle could be found.

Before the audit was completed, Gillett beat a hasty retreat with a relay of fast horses to Chihuahua, Mexico. "It was reported that he took with him $100,000 in gold," but not his young wife, one newspaper reported. She and their small son joined him later, followed, it was said, by a mysterious stranger, dressed in black, and wearing a heavy, sandy mustache. Legend has it that the stranger intended to steal the gold, or kidnap Gillett and bring him back to the United States. In fact, there probably was not much gold, although the cattle king did eventually make enough money in mining and real estate to repay part of his debt. Accusations of stock frauds, and even some arrests, dogged Gillett's footsteps for the rest of his life. He died in the 1920s, living as if he were wealthy even if he was not, after crashing a "fast car" into a telephone pole in California.[22]

After another disaster in western Kansas similar to the Gillett affair, a local editor lamented philosophically that the big busts experienced by some cattlemen have a "redeeming feature, for they hasten the time when any kind of a little 2 × 4 cow-boy with only a six-shooter and a stinking cigarette can't buy a thousand head of cattle for his individual note and mortgage."[23] And the editor was right. Procedures for loaning money on cattle needed revision. The dishonest hustler only increased the prejudice that some lending institutions already had against cattle paper. But most of all, those cattlemen who had collateral needed more long-term, reasonable credit. This situation, some feel, has not been entirely corrected even today, although there has been notable improvement during the twentieth century.

Financial shenanigans and subsequent disasters were not confined to these two men. Others besides Cross and Gillett also exploited the loosely organized system of financing the cattle industry. Yet in the case of Sunny Slope, the demise of Cross caused only a temporary setback in the farm's increasing importance to the purebred trade. In 1898 C. A. Stannard, who already had a large Hereford interest as well as extensive oil properties, purchased the farm and combined his purebred stock with what remained of the Cross herd, doubling the number to almost 600 head. Stannard also reinstituted the practice of raising hogs at Sunny Slope, with a herd of 300 registered Berkshires.

The farm grew in fame, and probably fortune, under the astute management of Stannard. He spent much time on the show circuit and dispersed purebred breeding stock to many sections of the United States at almost double the rate that Cross had. Sunny Slope stock was included in auctions held in widely scattered towns and cities, including Fort Worth, Denver, and Kansas City. Many sales also continued to be made at Sunny Slope itself. One, in 1903, included on its list of large purchasers the name of Frank Rockefeller, a younger brother of the famed industrialist John D. Rockefeller. This is another example of nonagricultural money being brought into the purebred business. Led by young Frank, the Rockefellers had become interested in Kansas ranching as early as 1876, buying several thousand acres in Kiowa County and engaging in general ranching and the production of purebred Shorthorns. A herd of 400 registered Shorthorns had been accumulated by the middle 1880s. When C. S. Cross staged his large sale in 1898, Rockefeller added Herefords to his line of stock and continued to increase the number until by the early twentieth century it equaled the size of his Shorthorn herd. The Rockefeller interest was important to upbreeding in Kansas and surrounding states for several decades, for it provided an outlet for stock bred at Sunny

Slope and also helped to distribute registered stock among many range herds.[24]

A disastrous fire in "barn #3" during the winter of 1904 was about the only setback in the growth of Sunny Slope under Stannard ownership. Almost a hundred head valued at over $20,000 perished in the flames. Judging by the local newspapers, the farm remained a source of much pride in the community even after the fire. "Best" and "largest" in Kansas, "larger than the Gudgell & Simpson's herd," and "largest thoroughbred Hereford herd in the World" were only a few of the superlatives aimed at Sunny Slope. A degree of the community's pride, as well as the mystique that often surrounded purebred cattle operations, might well be judged from an unusual obituary written by the editor of the *Gazette*. He wrote:

> Several days ago one of the most distinguished inhabitants of Lyon County died and no telegraphic reports were sent out of town, and the *Gazette* wouldn't have heard of it but for the fact that a friend of the *Gazette* went out to Sunny Slope farm Thursday and asked to see Wild Tom and was told by one of the men that Tom had been "laid away" . . . . He has won blue ribbons from cattle shows all over the United States and Canada, and his picture hangs in the rooms of all lovers of white face cattle in this country and England. At one time, while Wild Tom was the property of C. S. Cross, an offer of $25,000 was made for him and refused.[25]

Stannard continued to operate Sunny Slope until 1910, when political obligations and an increased preoccupation with his oil interests forced him to sell. The luster of purebred breeding had also declined for Stannard by this time because of personal misfortune. His only son had contracted typhoid fever while showing Sunny Slope cattle at a county fair and died in 1907, and his wife succumbed to the same disease the following year. In 1910 the entire herd, down from over 800 head to less than 250, was sold at public auction. Sunny Slope was sold privately to a local resident and then resold the following year. Both buyers were described as "successful businessmen" who were seeking rural investments. The sum of $60,000, or more than double what Stannard had paid for the land only twelve years earlier, was cited as the sale price in each transaction.[26]

Any picture of upbreeding in Kansas during the 1890s or in any other part of the country, for that matter, is apt to overemphasize the importance of the colorful producers of purebreds because they were the men who caught the fancy of the press. The owners of range herds who patronized the purebred breeders were often relegated to obscurity, even though these were the folk who used the purebred animal for the basic purpose for which it was bred. But the producers of purebreds were important because their herds were the fountainheads of improved blood. Several herds in Kansas had acquired national stature by the 1890s, and these were often owned by men of financial means who seemed to engage in the purebred business as something of an avocation. The depression in the early part of the decade eliminated a few herds, but the business had recovered well by the end of the decade.

By 1900 the Hereford was well on its way to becoming the most popular of the several breeds of beef cattle. Most important for the twentieth century, however, was the fact that this blooded stock had begun to work its magic on the range as more and better beef was being produced in a shorter period of time from fewer cattle and on fewer acres of land. The "blue jeans roasts and corduroy steaks" that had formerly stood for Kansas meat were fast becoming a thing of the past. Finally, there was much optimism toward the end of the nineteenth century about the present and future condition of the industry. One enthusiast went so far as to predict that the whole country would soon recognize Kansas as the "hub of the cattle industry of the United States, and consequently the world." The northwestern section of the United States, the article noted, had too much winter weather and not enough grain for major cattle production, while the South had less grain and more "greenhead" flies, and the East had land and grain that were too high-priced. Only in Kansas, he said, were the conditions and resources ideal for large-scale beef production.[27]

Production, however, was only the first step in putting steaks and roasts on the American table, and in many ways it may have been the least complicated. After growing and fattening the stock, cattlemen were forced to confront the several large businesses that were in charge of the marketing and processing phase of the industry. As a result, many disputes between producers and big businesses arose, and cattlemen were compelled to spend increasing amounts of time and energy in attempting to resolve these disagreements. The box score of the cattlemen–big-business confrontations revealed both their successes and failures.

3

Big Business and KLA: The 1890s

Between the range or feedlot and the consumer's dinner table was the marketing phase of the beef industry. Here the cattleman came into contact with big business in the form of railroads, stockyards, and packing plants. As independent-minded stockmen individually confronted the greater power and organization of big business, the first result was conflict; but before long the cattlemen saw the need to organize and thus to speak with a stronger, united voice. In due time this produced the Kansas Livestock Association (KLA), a weak and ineffective organization for several years, except in dealings with railways, but also the foundation upon which stockmen later built a strong association. Ultimately, KLA became an organizational response to industrialization, not unlike that taken by farmers, laborers, and big businesses.

After 1871 the stockyards and packing houses in Kansas City were the destination of most livestock produced in Kansas and much of the Southwest. These two industries were tremendously important in the development of the Kansas and Southwestern beef industry throughout the last quarter of the nineteenth century and much of the twentieth.

Kansas City, like other large central markets in the West, developed simultaneously with improvement in transportation, increased livestock production, and the migration of eastern packers toward the primary sources of supply. These central markets served to concentrate supply and demand and to provide the facilities and coordination necessary for the transfer of ownership. Skilled employees of the stockyards, as well as the commission men who operated under the rules of a livestock exchange, supplied the coordination. Feeders or graziers bought the younger stock for additional maturing, while

43

packers took the older cattle and transformed this beef on the hoof into products ready for consumption.

During the nineteenth century a typical group of cattle arrived at the Kansas City stockyards by railroad car. The unloading and recording of the stock's origin, number of head, and location within the yards were accomplished by stockyard employees. Then a commission company, selected by the shipper, assumed responsibility for the animals and saw to their feeding, watering, and eventual sale. After the sale was completed the animals were weighed under the supervision of the commission company and then delivered to the buyer by stockyards personnel. The commission company deducted various charges and paid the shipper the balance, usually on the same day.

Besides facilities and coordination, central markets provided auxiliary functions. During the nineteenth century prices paid for livestock sold in as well as outside the central markets were set by the markets themselves. Supply and demand supposedly determined prices, and few questioned the practice. During the first two decades of the twentieth century, however, producers increasingly accused the large packers of arbitrarily setting price levels. Central markets also developed banking and credit facilities for buyer and seller, provided market news services, and performed some sanitary control. From the buyer's point of view the large volume of transactions handled, the regularity of receipts, the facilities for handling and weighing cattle, and the guaranteeing of titles were the principal advantages. The seller appreciated the standardization of price and classification at the central markets and the market information that eventually became available. The seller often felt that higher prices were received when there were larger numbers of specialized buyers, that his poor stock sold better when there was more off-grade stuff available, and that the weighing and grading were more satisfactory in the central market.[1]

Railway companies were responsible for the origin and development of the Kansas City yards. As early as 1867 the Kansas Pacific Railroad established a small area in the town as a rest and feeding station for southwestern cattle that were en route to Chicago or midwestern feedlots. The yards were located just south of the confluence of the Kansas and Missouri rivers on the Kansas side of the state line. As the yards expanded eastward in subsequent years, many of the activities covered an area in both states. Some 35,000 head passed through the feeding station in 1867 and double that number the following year. Three years later L. V. Morse, a superintendent for the Hannibal & St. Joseph Railroad, and James F. Joy, president of the Chicago, Burlington,

& Quincy, had permanent pens built and scales installed. Though the presence of scales indicates that some animals were being sold locally either to butchers or feeders, the yards for several years remained primarily a rest and feeding station.

In 1871 the Kansas Stock Yards Company was organized with a capitalization of $100,000. J. M. Walker of Chicago became president of the company, although ownership was reported to be largely local until 1876. These were the first yards west of Chicago, predating those in St. Louis by a year and those in Omaha, Denver, and St. Paul by about fifteen years. Receipts in 1871 included over 120,000 cattle, 40,000 hogs, and 4,500 sheep, but these figures may have included some stock that passed through only for feed and rest. Growth was slow until the late eighties, but by 1900 the Kansas City yards were receiving over two million cattle a year in addition to other livestock. Cattle usually accounted for about 75 percent of all receipts. Stocker and feeder sales, by 1900 amounting to over half of the cattle trade, became the most significant part of cattle marketing, and Kansas City eventually became the largest stocker-feeder market in the world.

An eastern group of financiers, headed by Charles Francis Adams, Jr., of Boston, became in 1876 the principal owners of the yards, which they reorganized into the Kansas City Stock Yards Company with Adams as its president, a post he held until 1902. These financiers also had interests in the railroads that served Kansas City, and there were several instances of railroad personnel filling key managerial positions in the new organization. The new company initiated a policy of expansion and development that lasted well into the 1890s. It was responsible for adding land on both sides of the Kansas-Missouri border, and for building new pens and unloading facilities, bridges across the Kansas River, and a new and enlarged Livestock Exchange Building. Charles F. Morse, a Harvard-educated Bostonian with Burlington and Santa Fe railroad experience who became general manager of the yards in 1870, received much of the credit for developing the Kansas City market. After the period of expansion that temporarily ended the nineties, the stock-yards company had a capitalization of over four million dollars.[2]

There were few local markets for livestock in Kansas in the nineties, and a number of cattlemen no doubt shipped to the large central markets outside the state. Chicago, for example, was usually considered the best market for fat stock; St. Louis was active, as was St. Joseph, which for many Kansas producers was the closest central market outside the state. The development of the St. Joseph yards was similar to that which had already occurred in Kansas City. The yards, originally used for feed and rest stops by the Hannibal & St. Joseph Railway, developed into a central market during the late eighties. Compared to Kansas City, however, the packing industry played an earlier and larger role in their development.[3]

Within the state, Wichita also had a major market but nothing comparable to that of Kansas City. It had been one of the original shipping points for Texas cattle trailed north during the 1870s, but not until 1888 was the Wichita Union Stock Yards Company opened for business. Initial capitalization for the stockyards company was $200,000; twenty years later it had more than tripled. The interests of Jacob Dold, Francis Whittaker, and other small packers were important to the development of the Wichita yards, although Cudahy packing interests eventually became a large stockholder.[4] The proximity of the large beef-producing areas to the southwest contributed to the growth of the Wichita yards because of lower freight rates, while the many cow herds in these areas encouraged the stocker and feeder trade.

Railroad rates and connections were extremely important for the development of all stockyards, and a major consideration of cattle shippers in deciding which market to patronize. The additional expense of freight charges influenced many Kansas shippers to avoid the Chicago market even though it might have paid higher prices. Sometimes a railroad favored one stockyard over another. The Santa Fe, for example, attempted during the early 1870s to continue their carrying trade to Chicago by avoiding the Kansas City yards and routing trains through Atchison. But the practice gave way after a few years as the Kansas City yards grew and shippers insisted on using them.

The meat processing industry complemented production: the packers were the harvesters, so to speak, of the meat crop. More important than processing, though, the industry found a market for the surplus meat produced in the thinly populated West in the more heavily populated areas of the Midwest and the East.

As the eastern packers were migrating west, first to Milwaukee and Chicago, then to Kansas City and a number of other cities on the fringe of the large beef-producing area, they were also developing a system for the national distribution of their products. This highly efficient wholesale marketing system was of prime importance to the growth and centralization of the packing industry. Gustavus F. Swift and his brother, Edwin, are usually given credit for leading the development. Their nationwide system, which was built around a network of branch houses established during the 1870s and 1880s in most of the major towns and cities, forced other large packers to follow their example or remain relatively small local companies.

A number of problems had to be solved before western meat moved smoothly into eastern markets. Railroads first discouraged the shipment of dressed meat with freight charges that were much higher than rates for live shipments. Even the reduction in bulk between live and dressed shipments failed to equalize this rate disparity. Livestock shipments had been a lucrative business, except when rate wars absorbed the profits, and the lines reluctantly accepted dressed meat. But not until the advent of refrigerated cars, developed and owned for the most part by the large meat processors, were the Chicago and Kansas City packers able to force lower rates. As the number of refrigerated units owned by packers increased, it became customary for the railroads to pay for the use of these cars by a reduction in the established hauling charges. Eventually this refrigerated traffic became, as William Z. Ripley has pointed out, "large in volume, very regular and highly concentrated as to source." Volume increased even more as packers began to ship fruit and other produce that could be successfully refrigerated. These large tonnages were easily diverted to that railroad which best showed its appreciation through reduced rates or secret rebates, resulting in the western packers having significant power to influence the rail lines. The influence continued until the Hepburn Act in 1906, and resulted in fewer shipments of live cattle to the East and the growth of midwestern packing.

In addition to the discouragement from railroads, the opposition from retail meat shops, stockyards, and livestock dealers in the East, all of whom were in line to lose profits from predressed meat, had to be overcome. And finally, the public prejudice against cattle that were slaughtered thousands of miles from the place of consumption had to be eliminated before western beef became common fare on eastern tables.[5]

The development of a national distribution system and the increased centralization of the packing industry in a few locations were interrelated developments. Both were dependent upon a number of technological innovations. Of utmost importance was the refrigerated railroad car, pioneered successfully by Swift in the late 1870s. Built and owned largely by the packers, refrigerated cars solved many of the problems of the long-distance transportation of fresh meat and ended the packers' dependence on salting, curing, and canning for the perservation of their products. They also provided an important source of revenue and served as the packers entrée into many other lines of distribution, especially of foods that were highly perishable. Distribution of

California fruit, for example, was almost monopolized by Swift and Armour by 1900. Refrigeration also was important to the packing plants because it allowed year-round operation with little fear of spoilage.

Developments in the slaughtering process during the last quarter of the nineteenth century were also important to the spectacular growth of the packing industry. The moving conveyor belt, or the disassembly line, as packers called it, speeded the butchering process by allowing a more specialized utilization of space, machinery, and labor. Some plants were ingeniously arranged. Animals were herded up to the top floors, killed, and hung on a line. Gravity then assisted the movement toward the lower floors as different parts were separated from the hanging carcasses. At the end of the line waste products were converted into fertilizer.

Increased use of by-products from animal slaughter both stimulated and resulted from this growth and centralization. Desire for larger profits and the difficulties of disposing of waste also contributed to more frequent use of by-products. The Armour interests pioneered the large-scale practice of utilizing every part of the animals they butchered, and by the 1890s all the large packers were doing so. The by-products were manufactured into marketable commodities by the packing plant itself or in separate plants located close to the slaughter point. By the nineties most of the by-product manufacturing that had originally been started by small businessmen was owned by the major packers.[6]

The development of Kansas City as a national packing center, like its development as a central market, was dependent upon the railroads. There were a couple of antebellum packers supplying the local market with meat during the 1850s, but it was not until the late 1860s, after railroads had reached Kansas City, that today's packing industry originated. Most of the initial plants were owned by local citizens. The first outside money for the industry came in around 1870 with the Armour brothers and their partner, John Plankinton. These early plants provided Kansas City with what one historian has called a "thriving packing business" a year before the Kansas Stock Yards Company was chartered.[7]

Before the 1880s, when rapid transportation and refrigerated cars allowed the fresh beef trade to develop, Kansas City's packing was heavily dependent upon the pork and the specialty beef trade. Beef was packed in salt, then later in cans, some of which became an item in international trade. The importance of the pork trade can be judged from the fact that in 1880 the number of hogs slaughtered was about seventeen times greater than the number of cattle. In the late 1880s, however, after refrigeration had developed, cattle slaughter as well as the whole packing business grew rapidly.

The growth of the central market and the new possibility of using Kansas City as a slaughter point for the national fresh meat trade attracted a number of additional packing interests during the 1880s. Fowler & Sons, for example, moved in from Atchison a few years before moving to Wichita; Morris & Butt initiated a plant that became Wilson & Company in 1915; and Kingan & Company built a plant that was taken over by Cudahy in 1900. There were others besides these, but the most significant addition to Kansas City's packing industry during the eighties was the attraction in 1887 of Swift's large half-million-dollar plant. Then, with their combined strength, Swift and Armour were able to stop much of the railraods' discrimination against dressed beef. Success in adjusting railroad rates contributed much to the increase in cattle slaughter from 79,000 head in 1885 to a kill of over half a million in 1890.

The patronizing attitude of the stockyards company was also important in attracting packers. Swift received over $62,000 in land, while Armour was given $500,000 worth of stock in the Kansas City Stock Yards Company for locating its new million-dollar plant in the city. At least $200,000 in land or cash was paid to four other packers.

Given these land and cash incentives, the mechanical developments that were occurring, and the choice location of Kansas City, it was not surprising that the packing industry continued to expand late in the nineteenth century. By 1900 the lion's share of Kansas City's meat processing was in the hands of the large national packers, and it was the largest single industry in the city, supplying incomes to over 35,000 people. One historian has noted that "perhaps nothing was so important to Kansas City's industrial growth before 1900 as meat packing." This industry "more than any other aspect of the livestock business," he continued, "made Kansas City a metropolitan center." Much the same thing could be said for Kansas City's packing houses in their effect on the Kansas and southwestern beef producers.[8]

While packers, stockyards, and railroads were expanding westward during the latter part of the nineteenth century, their relations with agricultural producers were becoming more and more strained. Rural producers, after failing to correct through individual effort the abuse they felt, protested vehemently through the Grange, Alliance, and Populist movements and also advertised their grievances through a number of other regional and state groups. Cattlemen, for instance—who complained of high railroad rates, yardage fees, and low prices for their stock, all of which were the result, they claimed, of the monopolistic power of the large industries—often sought relief and security by cooperating with their neighbors in livestock associations. They used either the old associations, which were redirected to conform more with the increasingly complex economic conditions, or newly created organizations, which were also directed toward meeting the new circumstances. Preeminent among the latter was the Kansas Livestock Association. The rationale for its creation, contrary to earlier associations in the West, yet consistent with the new economic situation, was not related to any particular problem that cattlemen faced in range production. Rather, the railroads and their freight-rate policies were more responsible than any other factor in spawning this significant group. Begun as an organized lobby against rising freight rates, however, KLA was soon involved in many other developments that directly or indirectly affected livestock producers. This involvement has continued to the present time.

The exact origin of the association is shrouded in mystery and conflicting evidence. Though the earliest secondary accounts point to May, 1894, as its beginning, no primary material can be found to support this early date. The first accounts probably refer to a local or county association that preceded KLA. The first statewide organization, the Kansas Livestock Association, most likely had its origin in 1897.[9]

William Allen White's Emporia *Daily Gazette* proclaimed the new organization in its August 30, 1897, issue. Cramped between a story of "a boy tramp from Dodge City" who had stolen a pair of shoes and an advertisement for two-quart hot-water bottles that sold for seventy-five cents was an inconspicuous note that said "stockmen from all parts of the state met at the courthouse this afternoon and formed a state organization. The principal object of the organization is to get freight rates which will be just and equitable . . . ." In its issue for the following day the paper listed other objectives of the new group as reducing theft, preventing the shipment of diseased animals, and protecting "in every manner possible the interests of dealers and shippers of livestock." For over a decade, however, the freight-rate battle pushed other concerns out of the picture.

KLA began, then, with little fanfare. Perhaps its founders expected it to dissolve in a few years, as other organizations had done before. But it struggled along for a decade or so and then blossomed into one of the more prominent stock associations of the twentieth century.[10]

Although the exact origin of KLA may be debatable, the names of several prominent Kansas stockmen can definitely be associated with it in its early years. James W. Robison of Towanda, sometimes hailed as the proprietor of the "biggest farm in Kansas," located in Butler and Sedgwick counties, was the association's president from its inception until his death in 1909. This stockman was born in Scotland in 1831 and raised in Illinois. Before migrating to Kansas in 1882, Robison farmed in that state, beginning, as he said later, with a "stumpy forty acres" rented from his father. By the late 1890s Robison owned and leased over 10,000 acres in Kansas, including 4,000 acres of crop land. He planted corn for the most part, using the remainder for grazing his 1,800 head of cattle and horses. His cattle included many feeder steers that were marketed after grass and corn fattening. He also sold about 2,000 hogs each year. Even though, the Topeka *Daily Capital* noted, "everything on the Robison farm is as handy as a pocket in a shirt," a labor force of sixty to seventy-five men was required to run the extensive operation. By 1901 Robison's holdings were reported to have increased to over 16,000 acres. Robison was also active in several other promotional organizations in addition to KLA. At various times he served as president of the Kansas Improved Stock Breeders' Association and as vice-president of the State Horticultural Society. He was also president of the State Bank of El Dorado and served a two-year term on the Kansas Board of Railroad Commissioners.

Robison's fame reached beyond the borders of the state as well. His obituary noted that he had acquired international fame as the "breeder, importer and handler of the big black handsome Percheron horses." One of his sons continued the registered horse business on his famous Whitewater Falls Stock Farm long after the father's death, but the efficiency of the tractor, the depression of the 1930s, and the death of the son forced the sale of the famous Percherons.[11]

George Plumb, brother of United States Senator Preston Plumb, was the most important early member of the KLA, serving as its secretary during the first decade of its existence. He and his parents had migrated from Ohio during the spring of 1857 to a Kansas prairie site that was destined to become Emporia. The Plumb family built one of the first wooden shanties on the town site. Plumb had served with several Kansas cavalry units during the Civil War, spending much of his service time in the West, before he began extensive sheep and cattle raising in the Emporia area on his 3,000-acre ranch. Plumb was a member of the state legislature from 1905 to 1907, and the chairman of the 1911 Board of Railroad Commissioners that organized the Kansas Public Utilities Commission.

51

Plumb's principal contribution to KLA was his knowledge of freight rates, and he early became one of the state's most vehement critics of railroad policy. Sharing his ranching duties with a son, James R., during his later years, Plumb continued until his death in 1933 to advance the interests of Kansas livestock producers.[12]

Though Robison and Plumb were the most active members of KLA during this early period and often seemed to be the whole organization, they were by no means the only prominent stockmen in the ranks of the new group. H. B. Miller of Osage City was the first vice-president, and W. P. Martin of Cottonwood Falls the first treasurer. Thomas M. Potter, rancher and cattle feeder from the Peabody area, was also a charter member. Before his death in 1929 Potter had acquired a long list of accomplishments in addition to his participation in KLA, including membership in the state legislature, a gubernatorial candidacy, the presidency of the Board of Agriculture, and membership on the University of Kansas Board of Regents. A small reward for the last service was his becoming the eponym of Potter Lake on the campus of the University. Jacob Heath, Frank Arnold, George Donaldson, W. J. Tod, and Melville C. Campbell also helped guide the new association.

Campbell became especially well-known for his long service in KLA and more generally as a Kansas rancher and businessman. He had begun his cattle interests by trailing herds north from Texas during the 1880s before he settled more permanently on a ranch in southwestern Kansas in 1891. Early in his cattle business Campbell was associated with a younger brother, James P., who also made a distinguished reputation for himself as a Kansas rancher.

Campbell was also an active businesman in Wichita, first as a commission man at the stockyards, then as a banker. But the cattle business was always his first love, and he had a good deal of experience with livestock associations before KLA was ever conceived. During the 1880s he was a member of the Cherokee Strip Live Stock Association, the Western Kansas Cattle Growers' Association, and the group that eventually became the Texas and Southwestern Cattle Raisers Association. He served on the board of directors of the last organization for many years. The KLA executive board from its beginning until a few years before his death in 1932 also benefited from Campbell's wide experience.

During the 1890s Campbell was busy buying, or blocking up, as it was called, some of the public and private land in Clark County that he and other stockmen in the area had been using. Wisely, Campbell was making the transition from free grass to ranch. Most other cattlemen had already done so, although the change was delayed a few years in the southwestern part of the state.[13]

The Campbell ranch, some 20,000 acres of grazing and meadow land along the Cimarron River, eventually became one of the best-known spreads in the state. This was due not so much to the ranch itself, although an efficient steer and cow herd operation developed, but to the people associated with it. Campbell, of course, became widely known and respected for his business interests and his long-term participation in the public affairs of stockmen. In 1918 he formed a partnership with his son-in-law, Jesse C. Harper. This young man had only recently retired as coach and athletic director at the University of Notre Dame, after having persuaded the university to hire Knute Rockne as its football coach.

Though Harper's background was unusual, his common sense and willingness to work in the interest of stock producers soon won for him a respected place among ranching folk. Like his father-in-law, Jesse was honored with the presidency of KLA, although his term of office was interrupted by his returning to Notre Dame after the tragic death of Rockne for a stay of two years. Harper's son, Mellvin C., also became a KLA president. The ranch prospered under their astute management, and it continues today with the third generation of Harpers actively involved.[14]

KLA was not the first significant stock association in the state or the West as a whole. The number of associations was legion before KLA ever came to be. In Kansas, sectional and county associations predated KLA, as did organizations to promote a single breed of stock. State associations in Colorado, Wyoming, Texas, Utah, Nebraska, and South Dakota were among those established earlier than KLA.

There were also attempts in the 1880s to form a national association, initiated first by western stockmen who gathered in Chicago in 1883 to discuss the possibilities of federal legislation to retard the spread of Texas fever and pleuro-pneumonia. The National Cattle Growers' Association and the formation of the Bureau of Animal Industry followed the Chicago meeting. But the National Cattle Growers was not in fact a national organization, as it tended to represent only northwestern cattlemen. Southwestern stockmen, reluctant to accept the responsibility for Texas fever and determined to have a national cattle trail to northern ranges, established the following year in St. Louis a rival group known as the National Cattle Growers' and Horse Association. The two worked at cross purposes for a while, then merged into the Consolidated Cattle Growers' Association, and finally ceased to exist after the disastrous winter of 1886–87. Today's National Cattlemen's Association, a name adopted in 1977 after several name changes during the twentieth century, does not descend directly from any of these early attempts. It originated early in 1898 as a result of a meeting called the year before by the Denver Chamber of Commerce and the Colorado Cattle Growers' Association.[15]

KLA was thus part of the phenomenon of stock associations, local, regional, statewide, and national, that sprang up all through the West during the last quarter of the nineteenth century. Similar movements toward consolidated action were apparent in the industrial and financial sectors of the economy as well.

The associations in the livestock business can be divided roughly into two groups. The ones established before the 1890s were concerned primarily with internal problems that were related to the peculiar nature of open-range production. Regulation of round-ups, use of grass, and the control of theft were typical issues that demanded attention. After 1890, however, the older associations that continued and the new ones that were created became more concerned with problems that were external to range production and inherent in the industrialization process. KLA represented the latter group.

The tendency of stock associations to emphasize new directions after the early 1890s followed, though somewhat tardily, the larger developments that were occurring in the nation's economy. Not only had the open-range method of producing beef largely disappeared, but western farmers and ranchers were at the peak of their struggles to adapt their operations to the demands of the agricultural and industrial revolutions. Industrialization had provided agriculture with larger domestic and international markets and the transportation necessary to service them; it had supplied the machinery that was necessary for expansion; and it had generated hopes that the agricultural producers' share of profits from the nation's economy would be greatly increased. But industrialization had another face, too. The increased efficiency of agriculture and the expanded acreages that had come into production as a partial result of railroads, new machinery, government land policies, and increased immigration led to a surplus of agricultural products. As a result, farm prices were low, and a number of industries hoped to keep them that way. Cheap raw materials from agriculture were indispensable to low production costs in industry, as were tariff policies that actually raised the expenses of farmers and ranchers.

Besides the effects of industrialization that tended to restrict profits, farmers and ranchers had to contend with an unreliable climate, an antiquated tax structure that depended heavily upon real and personal property, labor costs that could rarely be reduced by layoffs, and the fact that returns on capital investment were often delayed for several years. In short, commercial agriculture had come to the West, and farm and ranch producers had been thrust into the money economy where their need to show a profit could not be matched by their ability to effect significant economic change.

Farmers and ranchers were small-unit producers and relatively small shippers and marketers, wholly unable to compete with the commercial giants that had developed by the 1890s. Agricultural producers could set neither the prices they received for their products nor those they paid for the manufactured goods they bought. It was a continuous struggle for them to raise an effective voice even in the relatively small area of marketing expenses. It was indeed a troubled time. Agriculturalists had been schooled to believe that they were the chosen people of God and the guardians of the nation's virtues, and that their endeavors were basic to a healthy economy. They had believed that industrialization would enhance the importance of their endeavors, but now found that the opposite was closer to reality.

Cattlemen in Kansas responded to industrialization with KLA. But this was only a partial response and one that followed a long line of attempts by agricultural producers throughout the nation. Early in the period farmers and ranchers tended to follow the lead of the Grange, which introduced cooperative marketing and purchasing associations and stimulated renewed interest in political activities. Then the belief that control over the political processes would enable the oppressed to curtail the evils of industrialization grew and blossomed into the Populist party of the 1890s. And while there are many different views of the Populist phenomenon, there is little dispute that it was in part a manifestation of agrarian discontent with problems that were related largely to industrialization.

Kansans participated in the early attempts of the Grange movement to maintain an honored place for agriculture in the developing economy, but not until the 1890s and the advent of the Populists were any large-scale efforts made to improve agriculture's economic position by gaining control of the state's political processes. Kansas populism, like that for the nation as a whole, developed from the Alliance movement, which had first come to the state in the interest of combating monopoly. Its strength increased rapidly until its fusion with the Democrats in 1896 and a rise in agricultural prosperity initiated its decline. Populist success in the state included the Kansas electoral vote for presidential candidates James B. Weaver in 1892 and William Jennings

Bryan in 1896, the selection of William A. Peffer to replace the seasoned United States Senator John J. Ingalls, and the election of several congressmen. Included in the latter group were at least two cattlemen, Jerry Simpson, who lost his accumulated wealth as a result of a Kansas blizzard, and William A. Harris, the Linwood Shorthorn breeder.

Populist success on the state level may have been even more striking. With about 40 percent of the state's vote in 1890, the Populists were able to cast the decisive votes in the legislature, and they gained control of both the executive and legislative branches of state government by 1896. But the latter victory was accomplished only by fusion with the Democrats, a union which eventually led to the death of populism as a separate entity. By 1896 intra-party strife also plagued the Populists and blunted their legislative efforts. Their direct success in mitigating the economic ills of the state's farmers and ranchers was negligible during the 1890s, but many of their proposals gained new life the following century. The overriding contribution of these late nineteenth-century movements was in awakening the populace to the importance of government regulation of monopoly.[16]

There is little evidence that producers in Kansas who were devoted more or less exclusively to cattle raising ever became Populists in large numbers. Simpson and Harris were, of course, both Populists and cattlemen, but Simpson was a cattleman and Harris a Populist for only brief periods. The leaders in the cattle industry appear to have remained, for the most part, in one of the old parties, primarily the Republican. O. Gene Clanton's study of Kansas Populists has shown that only 35 and 29 percent of the party's leaders were farmers or stockmen in 1890 and 1896, respectively; but whether farming or stock raising was the dominant interest remains unknown. Most were probably diversified in their interests, as many Kansas producers were, and raised both crops and stock. The political sympathies of the rank-and-file cattlemen are also a matter for some speculation. They were undoubtedly sympathetic to a number of Populist demands, but, as far as party affiliation is concerned, there is no reason to believe that they varied much from Clanton's conclusions regarding Populist leadership.[17]

Although the state's cattlemen were not in the vanguard of the Populist party, its failure left them without an effective lobby other than the Republican and Democratic parties. These parties were helpful at times, but cattlemen needed something bipartisan and dedicated exclusively to their interests. KLA picked up some of the slack and in so doing followed the trend already set by business and labor. Ineffective individual effort gave way to an organized response; cooperative action in the face of common problems overcame rugged individualism.[18]

The whole association movement spoke well for the western cattlemen's ingenuity and willingness to cooperate in the solution of problems common to the whole industry, to a particular region, or to a single state. The twentieth-century cooperative marketing and purchasing movement, for example, derived much benefit from the effects that the earlier agrarian organizations—including livestock associations—had on the thinking of producers.

On the other hand, some of the activities of these organizations were less laudable. Cattlemen's associations were sometimes employed to forbid the use of public lands to latecomers or sheepmen, and sometimes the associations implemented the cattlemen's concept of justice. Indians and other claimants to range land or cattle were often the recipients of this "justice," sometimes when it was unjust. The despicable activities perpetrated by stock associations were not unlike those of some manufacturing associations, who fought unionism, maintained artificially high prices, and took unfair advantage of businesses too small to protect their own interests. Association policies were essentially the extension of the ideas of a group of businessmen. Their activities led one historian of the cattle industry, C. L. Sonnichsen, to categorize their basic motivation as selfishness—a selfishness, one might add, that was often necessary in a competitive economy. Pointing his comments toward livestock associations in general—but they would apply to manufacturing organizations as well—Sonnichsen wrote: "[They are] out to 'protect the interests' of their constituents—that is, get as much for them as they can. They are dominated by rich and powerful men and they are frankly and proudly selfish, as all organizations must be which work for the welfare of a special group."[19] Sonnichsen's views are partly true of KLA.

Of all the complaints that agricultural producers voiced against big business during the 1890s, few if any exceeded in intensity those that were raised against the railroads. Cattlemen were among those who became increasingly concerned with rail lines. In Kansas, as was shown earlier, this concern led to KLA. At times, shippers complained of poor service or some other unpopular practice of the lines, but the most frequent and concentrated attack was upon freight rates. To complicate matters, railroad rate schedules and the process of arriving at them were exceedingly complex and difficult for the average shipper to comprehend. Most rural shippers understood only the cost of transporting their goods to market and not the complicated procedures of arriving at various schedules. To them, the rates were simply too high, in view of their own diminished purchasing power during the early 1890s. These shippers knew the railroads could not operate without earning a "fair" profit, but they believed that rates were higher than necessary, considering the increased efficiency and the expanded carrying trade of the lines and the high freight charges they themselves paid for the goods which they bought. They also believed there was corruption, mismanagement, and overcapitalization in railway circles.

It is difficult to determine, however, the level of combined long- and short-haul tariffs. Most authorities agree that rates in general had started to decline in the decades before the 1890s and continued to do so until about 1900. It was estimated, for example, that the average charge for transporting one ton of freight for one mile was around 2 cents in the late 1860s but only .73 of a cent by 1900.[20] This represented a reduction of over 63 percent. The Santa Fe system, one of the most patronized roads in Kansas and the Southwest, had reduced its ton-mile rates from about 2.3 to 1.1 cents between 1881 and 1895.[21]

These declines seemed to indicate that rate increases were justified by the 1890s in order to ensure the roads a reasonable profit, but such was not the case. The level of rates was not the only criterion of the roads' ability to show a profit. William Z. Ripley, in a detailed analysis of the subject, concluded that the level of rates did not always indicate profit or the lack of it. Other sorts of information, much of which the railway companies were reluctant to divulge, were necessary for an accurate evaluation of profits, and it was often impossible to reach a definite conclusion. Not even the fact that a number of railroads failed in the 1890s and went into receivership was convincing evidence that freight rates were too low; mismanagement or a number of other factors might have caused the failures. In the end, Ripley was unable to reach a definite conclusion on the justice of rates during the 1890s.

John F. Stover, another student of railroads, suggested a possible answer. He concluded that before 1900 rates did generally fall more rapidly than did the general price structure, and that they continued to lag behind for the first decade of the twentieth century.[22] But the relationship of tariffs to the general price structure was not of prime importance to shippers of farm products. Stover's study included all freight rates, some of which were relatively low, as well as all prices throughout the economy, some of which were relatively high. People in agriculture were interested only in the cost of transporting manufactured goods from east to west or the expense of getting livestock to a central market. In addition, rates probably did not decline as rapidly as did rural income. The justice of the railroads' position on interstate rates during the 1890s, then, remains somewhat clouded—except in the view of most rural shippers.

The evidence is a bit more conclusive on intrastate rates. As competition and the railroads' inability to establish effective pools pushed long-haul rates down, local or short-haul charges tended to become whatever the traffic would bear.[23] Some declined, others remained constant, and some actually increased during the last part of the nineteenth century, judging by reports made to the Kansas Board of Railroad Commissioners. A report in 1892 showed that the cost of shipping a carload of cattle or hogs 50 miles had declined from $22.00 per car in 1883 to $18.00 in 1892, a reduction of 18 percent. For the longer haul of 250 miles, rates had decreased from $72.00 to $43.50, or 39 percent. If the report was accurate, there had been a reduction in local rates; but even so, it did not occur with the same speed that interstate rates had declined. But the reports themselves were subject to question. The commissioners noted in 1891 that the statistical information included in their report was as full and accurate as was possible, but also that the complicated nature of the task made it possible for the railroads to make any showing they desired.[24] The inability to determine exactly the rates that were charged, as well as the method of establishing them, accounts in part for the contradictions that often permeated the rival claims of shippers and railway companies. Cattlemen, for example, were not cognizant of any decline in local rates during the 1890s, and in fact claimed repeatedly that rail tariffs were going up.

There was no effective federal agency that shippers could appeal to during the 1890s for redress of local rate grievances. The Interstate Commerce Commission was usually considered too cumbersome, time consuming, and expensive, and the practice of figuring on an extended basis whether the lines charged more for a short than a long haul made it difficult to establish that local rates were too high. This practice allowed railroads to charge relatively high rates for short hauls in areas without competition, as long as cheaper rates in areas with competition reduced the total charges for several short hauls to equal that of the long haul.[25]

On the state level, shippers could appeal to the Kansas Board of Railroad Commissioners—composed of three members appointed by the governor—which had been established in 1883. According to the legislation establishing the institution, the board had the power to supervise most activities of common carriers, require statistical reports, conduct official hearings, and, in the view of shippers, issue binding orders on rates to specific cities. As the century drew to a close, however, it became evident that the board did not have the power to determine freight tariffs; indeed, it had little power at all if a road stubbornly refused to abide by the board's decision or had them set aside through appeals to the courts.

The board's limited ability to determine rates was largely responsible for Populist moves to strengthen it. And efforts to increase the board's power soon provoked a heated debate. Most shippers were willing to strengthen the board, but other prominent Kansans insisted that it was too powerful as it was. William Allen White, an outspoken foe of the Populists, charged from Emporia that the men who formed the commission were "ignorant and mercenary, with the morals of bandits and the crude intelligence of arrant demagogues. These men too often regard the railroads as their prey and the people as their dupes." State railroad boards in general and the Kansas board in particular, White held, stood between the shipper and justice. In contrast, others claimed that the lines were affected little by the board, as they frequently refused to abide by its rulings, and used the courts to shield their excessive rates.[26] By 1896 the Kansas board had heard over a thousand cases, 354 of which had been decided in favor of the rail lines, and 483 in the shippers' favor. The railroads had disregarded twenty-two rulings of the board.[27] A tabulation such as this, however, meant little. The key was not how many but rather which cases the shippers won.

Several attempts were made in the Kansas legislature during the nineties to pass a stronger railroad bill, one that would establish maximum freight tariffs or give the board of commissioners the undisputed power to fix rates. Most attempts engendered partisan disputes between the Populists and the Republicans and eventually failed. Early in 1897 the legislature passed a new railroad bill, but Governor Leedy vetoed it on the basis that it was too weak. Then in December, 1898, this Populist governor called a special session of the legislature to consider railroad legislation. The lame duck session—voters had turned Leedy and several of his Populist supporters in the legislature out of office a few months before—created a Court of Visitation to replace the controversial railroad commission. The new bill gave a panel of three elected judges the right to decree freight rates, and also several other powers.

The new Republican governor, William E. Stanley, gave the new law a fair trial, but in 1900 the Kansas Supreme Court declared the Court of Visitation unconstitutional on the basis that the law had granted legislative, executive, and judicial powers to the same body.[28] These ill-fated attempts to regulate the state's railroads were to take several other forms during the twentieth century, but for most of the nineteenth century, the Kansas Board of Railroad Commissioners was the only body to which stockmen and other disgruntled shippers might appeal for help. If the railroads were inclined to follow the recommendations of the board, shippers received some relief.

The specific contest in Kansas between stockmen and railroads that led to KLA centered on the recurring question of increased freight rates. This was far from the first confrontation between Kansas cattlemen, or most western stockmen for that matter, and the railroads; but by the 1890s the effects of the depression, the growing power of railroads, and the other complexities of an increasingly industrialized economy put the dispute into a different perspective and added urgency to the search for a solution.

The question of rates also involved the contestants in issues related to the method of charging for freight and in the quality of railroad service. Almost a decade before the formation of KLA, shippers and railroads disagreed on the mode of charging for services. The railroads had traditionally billed stock shippers on a carload basis, with specific charges per carload, dependent upon the size of the car and the distance to market. Neither the number nor the weight of the livestock in the car mattered. Then in 1888 the lines initiated a new system based on weight shipped. The new plan stimulated numerous complaints to the Kansas Board of Railroad Commissioners, as the stockmen viewed it as only a ploy to raise rates. After a hearing the board directed that the new system be abandoned.[29] The railroads unsuccessfully attempted to change the mode of rate charges again in 1890, then they made no serious attempts to modify the established system until 1896. Most of the complaints to the board during the first half of the 1890s involved discrimination in the form of rebates, drawbacks, false classifications of freight, free personal transportation, or the practice of billing at underweight. The secretive nature of these arrangements between the railroads and their favorite shippers made regulation by the commissioners difficult.[30]

On January 11, 1896, the railroads again inaugurated the system of charging shippers by weight rather than by carload.[31] Stockmen immediately protested and pressured the railroad commissioners into summoning representatives of the lines to a formal hearing. Several hundred stockmen, according to the *Kansas Farmer,* journeyed to Topeka on the appointed day in order to register their complaints; but most of these were mere spectators. Forty-nine witnesses, including cattlemen, bankers, commission men, and freight agents, testified on behalf of the shippers.

The railroads, "represented by a splendid array of their best legal talent," according to the *Farmer,* argued that the new rates were not higher or, if higher, that the increase was minimal. They also argued, correctly, that the new system of charging was more equitable to the small shipper who was not always able to fill a car to the same capacity as large shippers, yet still had to pay the full carload rate. In addition, they claimed that the carload rate had encouraged overcrowding of cars, which resulted in the added expense to both shipper and carrier of injured or unmarketable stock.[32] Decreased brutality to animals and fairness for small shippers, then, appeared to be the cornerstones that supported the railroads' argument for a new system of rate charges. William F. Zornow, however, suggested another possible motive. The profits from Kansas railroads, he said, had been declining steadily since 1893, so that by 1896 only two out of the twenty-six companies in Kansas could pay dividends.[33]

The representatives of the shippers, among whom the cattlemen exerted a major influence, argued convincingly that the new mode of charging had resulted in a 15 to 50 percent increase. W. J. Tod of Maple Hill, for example, testified that the new rates increased the charges he paid for the sixty-eight mile haul to Kansas City by $6.00 to $7.50 per car, while James P. Campbell attested to an $8.22 increase per car for the several hundred mile trip from western Kansas.[34] James W. Robison, who later became the president of KLA, complained that his rates had risen by $8.00 a car, and that he had driven some of his stock to the Wichita market rather than pay the rate to Kansas City.

Then Robison emphasized other major complaints of stockmen. The necessity of weighing the stock cars in Kansas City and the practice of weighing the cars while they were still coupled and in motion left stockmen with no foreknowledge of shipping charges and in considerable doubt as to the accuracy of the railroads' scales. Robison argued that weighing moving cars, considering the uneven coupling devices commonly in use at the time, resulted in some cars recording an excessive weight. This meant that a shipper might pay for more freight than was actually carried because he might be charged for weight in the car either ahead or behind his. One of the three attorneys representing the Missouri Pacific countered Robison's argument by suggesting that "experts" had determined weighing cars while in motion actually resulted in short weights for the shipper. This conclusion, according to the testimony, was based on much the same principle as that which accounted for a moving skater being able to cross thin ice. Finally, stockmen maintained that the new system increased the suffering of stock by causing delays in weighing and by encouraging the practice of loading fewer cattle in the cars than was advisable for safe travel.[35]

In response to the skillful prompting of their Topeka attorney, cattlemen emphasized their desire to lower rates and to eliminate other abuses by returning to the old carload system of charging. The value of their testimony, however, was weakened somewhat by two inconsistencies. First, the stockmen found it difficult to justify adequately the inequities of the carload system to the small shipper, except to say that all shippers, sooner or later, ship "light" and "heavy cars," or that the small shipper could always cooperate with a neighbor in order to obtain a full carload. Many of them did this. But the railroads' contention that the large shippers favored the old carload system so that small shippers subsidized their freight charges, in part, also had merit. A second problem revolved around the question of why the stockmen demanded more cars to ship the same number of stock under the new system if, as they contended, they had not been overloading under the old system. This question was partially answered when some stockmen admitted that the increased demand for cars was a deliberate attempt to frustrate the new system.

The railroad commissioners recognized that the testimony had suggested at least two major issues: the mode of charging for freight, and the question of whether the new system had raised rates. They agreed with the railroads that the new mode of charging was more "just and equitable," but they were opposed to the apparent rate increase. They did, however, postpone a final decision on the questions until time permitted them to digest several hundred pages of conflicting testimony and numerous documents that had been introduced. In the meantime, the board ordered the railroads to return to the old system.[36]

The fact that the railroads again attempted to establish rates according to weight in 1897 indicates that the board eventually required the continuance of the old system. The change in 1897 prompted another hearing before the railroad commissioners, but the arguments, the witnesses, and the results were not much different from those of the earlier hearing. The railroads did, however, change their argument from the "no increase" position of 1896 to that of a reasonable and justifiable increase. Most important for the cattlemen of Kansas was the relationship of this hearing to the origin of KLA. The need for a united front against the tariff increase, as well as the lack of organization in previous disputes, was the major stimulus that led cattlemen to meet in Emporia and form the new association. James M. Robison and George Plumb both testified at the 1897 hearing, and both were referred to as officers of a stockmen's association.

While the cattlemen won the first few rounds with the railroads—Plumb, in fact, claimed that the success of stockmen in preventing rate increases saved livestock shippers $300,000 to $400,000 a year for many years—the fight was far from over.[37] A short notice in the May 16, 1898, Emporia *Gazette* relating to the second meeting of the young KLA implied that the organization was in dire need of money for the continuing struggle with the railroads. An order that KLA officers were "instructed to look after the injunction cases now pending" suggested that the railroads were not always following the dictates of the railroad commissioners and that the conflict had moved into the courts. The railroads' use of federal and state courts to protect their rate schedules was a major stimulus to the legislature that created the Court of Visitation. While few cattlemen recorded their view of the new court, the implication that the court was a stronger regulatory agency than the board should have put the stockmen squarely on the court's side.

The new Court of Visitation, however, proved to have no more success in regulating the railroads than had the old board of commissioners. The 1899 meeting of KLA, the first in more than a year, was devoted almost exclusively to plans for raising money to continue fighting rates. The railroads had again initiated new schedules, which were "in many localities . . . from 40 to 50 percent higher than the old rates." KLA officers appointed a committee to encourage the formation of a livestock association in every county of the state, with the expressed purpose of raising money for the renewed fight.[38]

Thus began a struggle between Kansas cattlemen and railroads that continued into the 1930s. Motor trucks were destined to figure prominently in, if not actually to eliminate, most of the strife between stockmen and rail companies. This earlier confrontation, however, taught many stockmen that only by cooperating with their neighbors could their voices be made audible.

In the few years of its existence during the nineteenth century, KLA had made a notable beginning on its journey toward becoming the most effective and cooperative stockmen's lobby in the state. Yet many of the early members of KLA were reluctant to give up their concept of themselves as rugged individualists who were able to care for their interests alone.

A popular story, told and retold over the years, typifies the view that many had of cattlemen, in general, and of the founders of KLA, in particular. In a small town in western Kansas during the height of the 1890s depression, the story went, folks were taking inventory to see what government aid they would need to get through the winter. One of the poorest members of the group refused to ask for help or to cooperate with the others. They were sure that he would starve and urged him to reconsider, but the old man replied that he would get along with his cow. "But you have no feed for your cow," the others protested. "Oh, she'll get along," said the old man, "she sucks herself." The author of the story went on to say that the old man was a stockman, that he was resourceful, and that all he wanted was to be left alone. "His reply typifies the spirit always present among stockmen," the author concluded.[39] The incident, however, hardly characterized KLA or any other livestock association. Rather, they were the antithesis of individualistic self-help. Although cattlemen continued to think of themselves as being individualistic and self-reliant, they sought help from others, and wisely so.

Kansas stockmen were quite willing to cooperate. They turned eventually to state and federal agencies for help in protecting and promoting the interests of their industry. Unfortunately, advancing the interests of some stockmen was sometimes harmful to the interests of others, at least in the case of KLA's attempt to preserve the carload system of freight rates. Small cattlemen suffered most from this position. The story of the early period of KLA's existence indicates that it was not representative of all the stockmen in the state, but rather was the organ of a few relatively large cattlemen. It was also apparent that the driving force behind early KLA activities came more specifically from the well-established stockmen in the Flint Hills who were heavily involved in grass-fattening transient cattle, which meant a greater dependence upon the railroads for in and out shipments.

Developments during the nineteenth century laid the foundation for the beef industry of the future. Production had stabilized to some extent, and the industry had become specialized, with some stockmen developing cow herds, some maturing stock, and others raising purebred breeding animals. The necessary links between grasslands in Kansas and dinner tables in the urban East had been provided by the movement westward of railroads, stockyards, and packers. To individual producers these big-business middlemen often seemed omnipotent, but through organizations such as KLA stockmen acquired the power to force acceptance of some of their demands. By the late nineties Kansas beef producers, as well as those throughout most of the West, were fairly well prepared for the future. Into the new century they carried few regrets, much optimism, and the beginning of a better understanding of the increasingly complex economic system in which they were forced to operate.

4

The Transition Completed:
Producing Beef, 1900-1920

Most historians view the first two decades of the twentieth century as a period of prosperity for ranchers and farmers—the "Golden Age" of agriculture, some have called it. While this was generally true of Kansas, there were a number of upturns and declines within the twenty years. Cattlemen swung from pessimism to optimism and back again. The stockman's mood often reflected the sharp fluctuations in cattle numbers, market prices, and purchasing power, or his continued dissatisfaction with big business. The prosperity usually associated with the early twentieth century was not always evident at the time, becoming obvious only when the cattleman stood squarely in the 1920s or 1930s and looked over his shoulder.

Despite the fact that cattlemen were dejected periodically, advances occurred in many areas. Upbreeding continued, and the quantity of forage crops and the amount of winter feeding reached new heights. Sorghums, for example, moved up to fourth in acreage among Kansas crops by 1910, behind corn, wheat, and alfalfa. New methods of utilizing forage crops were also significant. An Emporia paper, for instance, proudly announced that an Oklahoma man had developed an alfalfa meal that was a perfect feed. The meal consisted essentially of dehydrated green alfalfa and was, according to the report, "so attractive, and has such a pleasant taste, that men, as well as cows like to eat it."[1] Other crops, notably wheat, were also expanded, so much so that some stockmen felt the grassland was disappearing at an alarming rate. This feeling, coupled with the impact of several droughts, produced an increased awareness among cattlemen that the supply of grass was shrinking.

Stockmen met the second decade of the twentieth century with about the same misgivings and uncertainties as other sectors of the economy. The level

67

Haying scene, Scott County, 1906. *Courtesy of the Kansas State Historical Society.*

of domestic and foreign demand, the prices received and paid for goods, and the short labor supply were major concerns. But progress was made in adjusting to these difficulties. When the major developments in production are considered, it is evident that the grasslands beef industry during this period completed the transition that had begun during the closing decades of the previous century.

The number of cattle on the western grasslands actually declined during the first decade of the new century, by as much as a third in some parts of the Great Plains. Numbers in Kansas reflected this trend (see Figure 1, p. 21). But before the decline began, Kansans reported almost 3.4 million head in 1903, a figure not reached again until World War II. Following 1903, numbers declined steadily to 1.8 million in 1914, which was one of the lowest levels during the twentieth century. Then numbers increased to match the demands of the war. There were 2.7 million head by 1919. These were large fluctuations in relatively short periods of time, amounting to declines and increases of 50 to 67 percent.

The general distribution of the state's beef cattle had been pretty well established by 1890, and changed little during the next fifty years (see Maps

1, 2, and 3). By the final decade of the nineteenth century, eight of the top ten counties in number of cattle were located completely or partially in the Flint Hills, and throughout the next four decades little change occurred. Only the period around 1920 varied much from the norm. Increased production in other areas rather than a decline in the Flint Hills accounted for this change. During severe droughts cattle were always pushed back into the Flint Hills to graze on the lush bluestem.

The preeminence of the Flint Hills rested largely on the geographic advantages of abundant grass and water, and on the historic fact that pioneers, and the landowners who followed them, refused to turn the sod for crops. As a result, beef raising was firmly established in the area early in the state's history, even in those parts that could have been plowed.

The one or two tiers of counties on each side of the Flint Hills were secondary areas of concentration in 1890 and remain heavily populated with cattle up to the present, reflecting the availability of grass and corn for feeding livestock. Corn is heavily favored in the northern tier of counties as a crop, and much of it is fed to cattle and hogs. Relatively large numbers of cattle were also found along the southern border of the state, sometimes as far west as Meade County. Although beef raising in these areas was more mixed between the production of calves and the maturing of local or inshipped stockers than was that in the Flint Hills, concentration was largely for the same reasons: the availability of grass and water, and the reluctance of landowners to plow the grassland. In the western part of the state the relatively scant amounts of rainfall and the difficulties this presented to crop farmers also helped preserve much of the native grassland. Thus, while the major cattle-producing areas remained substantially the same between 1890 and 1940, there was a slight tendency for shifts toward the west and southwest. The movement toward the western part of the state before World War II became a flood with the coming of the fifties and the development of irrigation and large commercial feedlots (see Map 4).

The decline in cattle after 1903 revealed a facet of the beef industry that became generally recognized by cattlemen only after World War I. This was the fact that cattle numbers, prices, and purchasing power varied cyclically. For those associated with the industry, each cycle seemed unique and unpredictable; only in retrospect did a pattern become clear, and even then the many causes remained obscure (see Figure 4).

Between 1903 and 1911 the cycle was in its second major downturn since the origin of the grassland beef industry; the first had occurred between 1890

Map 1. Distribution of Beef Cattle in Kansas, 1890 (in thousands of head per county)

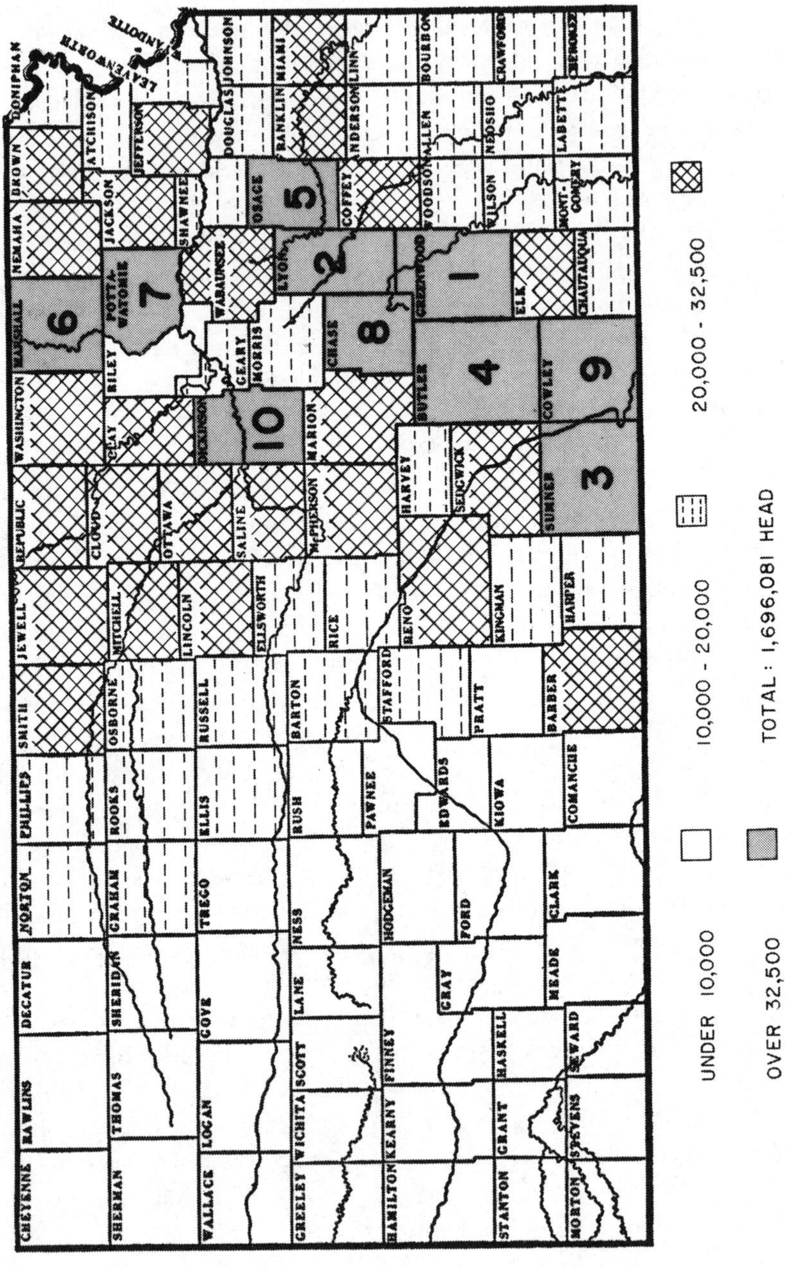

UNDER 10,000

10,000 - 20,000

20,000 - 32,500

OVER 32,500

TOTAL: 1,696,081 HEAD

Source: *Seventh Rept., KSBA* (1889–1890).

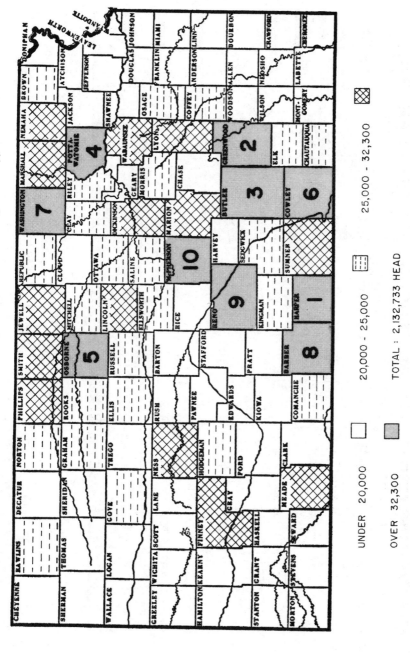

Map 2. Distribution of Beef Cattle in Kansas, 1920 (in thousands of head per county)

Source: *Twenty-Second Rept., KSBA* (1919–1920).

UNDER 20,000

20,000 – 25,000

25,000 – 32,300

OVER 32,300

TOTAL: 2,132,733 HEAD

Map 3. Distribution of Beef Cattle in Kansas, 1940 (in thousands of head per county)

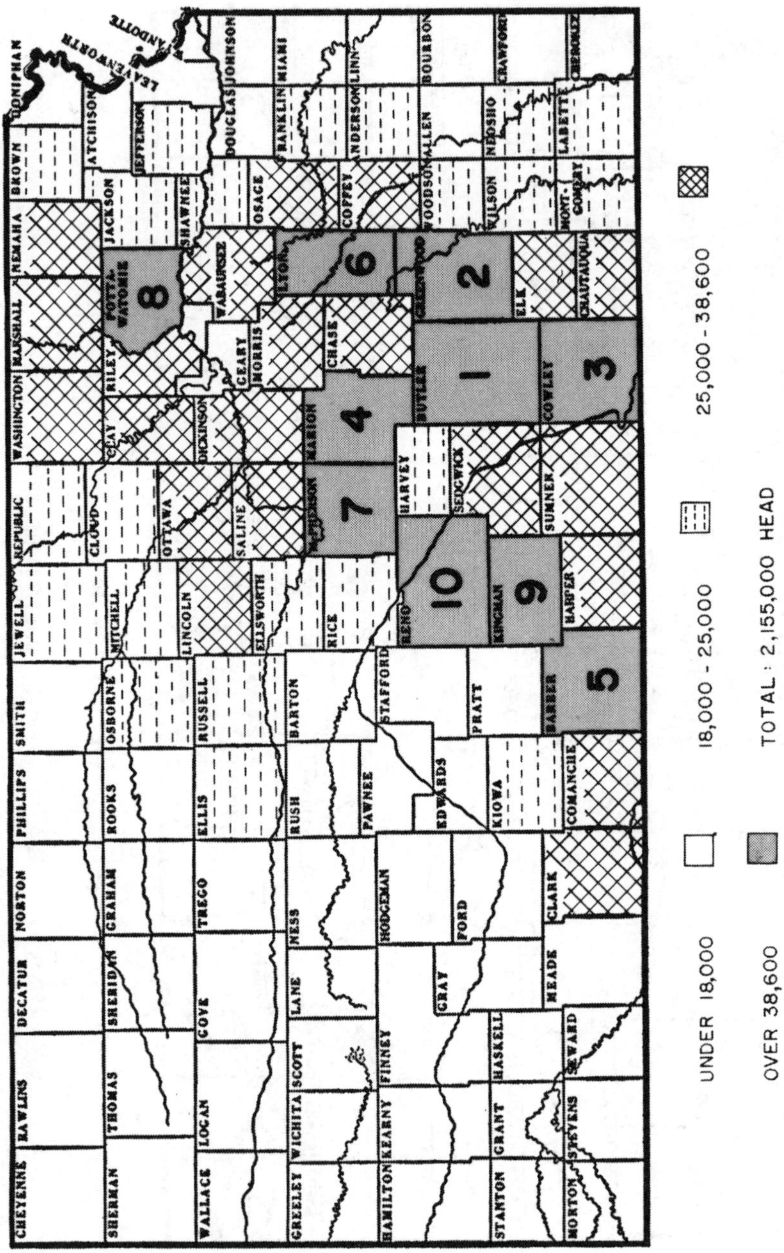

Source: *Thirty-Second Rept., KSBA* (1939–1940).

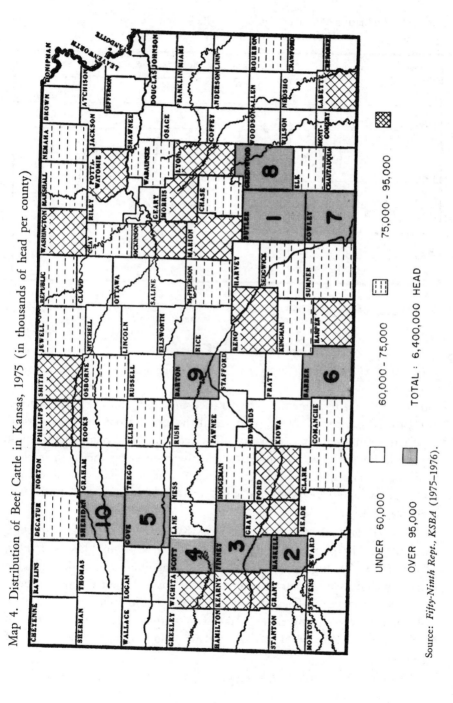

Map 4. Distribution of Beef Cattle in Kansas, 1975 (in thousands of head per county)

Source: *Fifty-Ninth Rept., KSBA* (1975–1976).

UNDER 60,000

60,000 - 75,000

75,000 - 95,000

OVER 95,000

TOTAL : 6,400,000 HEAD

Figure 4. Purchasing Power of Cattle (in dollars) and the Number of Beef Cattle in Kansas (in millions), 1865–1935

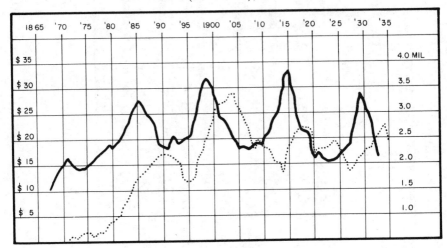

———— CATTLE PRICES EXPRESSED IN PURCHASING POWER PER HEAD, THE ACTUAL PRICES BEING CORRECTED BY THE BUREAU OF LABOR STATISTICS INDEX NUMBER OF WHOLESALE PRICES.

·············· NUMBER OF BEEF CATTLE IN KANSAS.

Source: *Fifty-Fourth Rept., KSBA* (1970–1971); *The Cattleman*, November, 1933.

and 1895. Thereafter, downturns that varied in length and intensity occurred in each decade between World War I and the 1960s. Complete cycles lasted anywhere from nine to sixteen years. This variation alone made them almost impossible for producers to anticipate, and therefore of no use in their planning. Stock prices, depression, war, drought, the availability of feed, and consumer demand were only a few of the interrelated conditions that increased or decreased numbers.

Between the 1880s and the middle 1950s Kansas beef cattle passed through six fairly distinct numerical cycles. Highs were reached in 1889, 1903, 1919, 1934, and 1955 (see Figure 1, p. 21). After 1957 the number of cattle increased, with only slight setbacks, at an unprecedented rate. Almost 6.4 million head were reported in 1970.[2] The last figure indicated that in 1970 there were more than three times as many cattle in the state as there had been just prior to World War I. Commercial feedlots and irrigation, again, explain much of the increase.

The number of cattle in the state at any one time, however, rarely excited cattlemen as much as did stock prices. Here again there were several fluctuations. The average price for western range cattle in 1900 was $4.35 per hundredweight. By 1905 the price had declined to $3.80, before a gradual upswing to $5.40 by 1910, and $7.40 just prior to World War I. Fat stock prices were a few dollars higher at times, but only if the cattle were choice.

After 1913, prices increased steadily until 1920. According to statistics from the Department of Agriculture, the average price for all beef cattle marketed in the United States rose from $6.52 to $9.88 per hundredweight during the war. The price of Kansas cattle went up even more. One historian claimed that the average price for western range cattle advanced from $7.65 in 1914 to $14.50 in 1918. An all-time high for the period, a price of $20.50, was paid for a native steer in December, 1918, a record not surpassed until the 1940s.[3]

Unfortunately for stockmen, rising production costs were often unrelated to the rise and fall of market prices. This disparity is most evident when the purchasing power of cattle—established by collating cattle prices to the costs of other commodities—is considered (see Figure 4). This was a comparison that cattlemen were forced to make every time they bought something, and it often led to much unrest. Statistics from the Bureau of Labor showed that the purchasing power per head for beef was about $28.00 in 1900, but had declined $10.00 a head by 1905. After this decline, it ranged upward again to about $28.00 by 1913, and continued to climb throughout the early years of the war. By 1915 it had moved to the highest point it was to reach before the 1940s, with an average of over $33.00 per head. After 1915 the increasing costs of other commodities caused purchasing power to decline rapidly to $16.00 by 1920. Purchasing power tended to follow a cyclic pattern similar to that of numbers of beef cattle, but highs and lows did not necessarily occur during the same years. There was a tendency, however, for highs in purchasing power to precede those in numbers by two to four years.[4]

As a result of this unpredictability, cattlemen were forced to operate with a large amount of uncertainty. Long-range production plans were often spoiled because they could be based only on guesses as to what purchasing power and numbers might be. In addition, the purchasing level of beef was probably less subject to modification by producers than was the number of cattle because they had little control over livestock prices and even less control over the prices of commodities they had to buy. A rapid rise in the general price index, as occurred during the latter part of World War I, caused a significant slump in the purchasing power of beef, even though prices for the latter were also rising.

Numbers and prices had a variety of reciprocal effects, but many other factors were also important in determining the prices stockmen received or the number of stock they produced. Domestic consumption, which was relatively high between 1900 and 1920 compared to the 1890s and to the decade that followed the war, affected prices and numbers. Annual per capita consumption of beef was almost eighty pounds between 1905 and 1910, and averaged around seventy-five pounds for the whole period. Increased consumption sometimes coincided with decreased numbers of cattle, suggesting that more beef was being produced from fewer animals.

Foreign demand was also a factor in domestic prices and numbers. England imported beef throughout this period, but France and Germany almost terminated their purchases a few years prior to the war. When the war came, exports to Europe increased; and this, in turn, was an important factor in the growth of production after 1914, as well as in price rises. The United States exported, primarily to England, an average of 6.2 percent of its total production each year during the war, compared to only about 2.2 percent for each of the previous seven years. Foreign exports declined soon after the war ended, but the effects were not felt to any large degree until the early 1920s.[5]

When prices were high, increased production was also stimulated by easy credit from lending institutions that were available to cattlemen (such as the commercial banks and cattle loan companies) and by the discounting practices of the Federal Reserve Banks, to a lesser degree. As is usually the case, much of the beef industry during this period was financed with borrowed money, especially during periods of rapid expansion. In fact, an official of the Federal Reserve Bank in Kansas City, M. L. McClure, said during the war that the cattle industry was always more dependent on borrowed capital than any other sector of the agricultural economy. Ranchers' excess capital, he believed, tended toward land investment, which necessitated credit arrangements for additional livestock. Kansas cattlemen were reminded of this fact during the 1915 KLA convention, when a Wichita minister opened the meeting with a prayer asserting that cattlemen held their stock only in trust. The next speaker immediately agreed with this thought, but, differing with the minister, pointed out that the cattle were owned by the banks rather than some higher power.

Capital was easy to obtain as long as prices remained at war levels, usually from local banks or those at the central markets that sometimes served as intermediaries for the larger banks and loan companies in the East. But, by the time of World War I, much of the eastern money that had been such an important part of cattle production during the nineteenth century had disappeared from the West. In its place arose local and regional banks, as well as cattle loan companies. Packer money often found its way into the production phase through the efforts of the latter institutions. The new Federal Reserve Banks were indirectly involved in livestock financing through their practice of rediscounting cattle notes, which were considered quite desirable when prices were high. McClure reported that by 1918 the reserve bank in Kansas City had discounted over $98 million worth of livestock paper throughout the Tenth District, which included five states. He also estimated that all lending institutions in the district combined had more than $300 million loaned on livestock most of the time, much of it to cattlemen.[6]

Although there was usually adequate money available while stock prices were high, cattlemen were troubled by the short-term nature of most loans. Cattle paper discounted by the Federal Reserve, for instance, had a six-month maturity—sometimes a six-month extension was granted—and this tended to be characteristic of most loans on cattle. Some even matured in three months. These short-term arrangements, while adequate for most feeding operations, were wholly inadequate for foundation herd expansion, which often required money for as long as three to five years. Long-term loans provided by the government would have been desirable, but not until the postwar depression was public money directly involved and then only on a relatively short-term basis.

Despite declining numbers and purchasing power of beef cattle, a disastrous flood in the state during the spring of 1903, and several dry seasons, Kansas agriculture as a whole was generally prosperous during the period 1900 to 1920, especially when compared to the years of depression that had gone before and those that followed. The years 1899 and 1900, as well as the period from 1908 to 1910, were outstanding crop years, and the state reached its all-time high in hog numbers in 1908, with three and a half million head. Cattlemen also enjoyed some of this prosperity. They were aware of declining numbers and prices but were not as cognizant of the significant decline in the purchasing power of beef until several years later.

Most of the time cattlemen had confidence in the future. Because of high prices and an abundance of feed, stockmen were expecting more prosperity when they journeyed to Wichita for the 1915 KLA convention. The Wichita *Eagle* remarked that "wrinkled-faced men, young men, middle-aged men and

Stacking second crop of alfalfa, Scott County, 1906. *Courtesy of the Kansas State Historical Society.*

fat-faced men swarmed into the Peerless Princess last night all talking cattle, horses, hogs or sheep—mostly cattle." The stockmen, according to the paper, said that the cow country was full of feed and that "the winter has poured gold into their pocket." When William J. Tod asked the members to help defray a $1,000 KLA debt, over $2,000 was raised in less than thirty minutes. "The eagerness, rapidity and spontaneity with which Kansas stockmen coughed up money yesterday, would make Billy Sunday envious," the *Eagle* stated.

Nor was Tod the only one eager to separate the cattlemen from some of their gold during this convention; many Wichita merchants were anxious to accomplish the same end. The 4,000 stockmen from Kansas and surrounding states who attended were expected to leave over $50,000 in town when they departed after the two-day meeting. "The cattlemen are liberal spenders" the paper noted, and if their spending caused them to "frisk around in the city a little" and they were "rounded up" by police, they could expect to be "dealt with gently by the law." The paper used the occasion to urge local promoters to establish a stock show similar to the American Royal in Kansas City so the city could stage a convention every year that would keep the cattlemen around for a full week. "Think what that would mean to the merchants of Wichita!" the *Eagle* cried. Two years later a stock show was actually established.[7]

With the attitudes of some Wichita businessmen in mind, a few of the state's cattlemen may have felt something like the Texans who had driven their cattle to market in Kansas, including Wichita, several decades before.

The cowtown merchants, some Texans claimed, were paper-collared Comanches who bought the trail herds, then waited in ambush with various entertainments to see that the weight of the gold did not burden the cattlemen on their trip back home.

Higher stock prices and a general feeling of prosperity during the early war years led to significantly higher prices for cattle feed. A drought in much of Texas and the Southwest also contributed to the high cost. By 1918 some supplemental cattle feeds had doubled in price since the beginning of the war. Cottonseed products rose from $30.00 to $60.00 a ton, tankage was up from $55.00 to $100.00 a ton and corn sold for $1.50 a bushel compared to 90 cents a few years before. Joseph H. Mercer, executive secretary of KLA, carried a strong protest to Herbert Hoover and the Food Administration. Though Mercer was able to get the amount of cottonseed meal shipped from droughtstriken Texas to Kansas increased, he accomplished nothing toward the reduction of prices.

The Food Administration was one of several efforts by President Wilson to gear the United States economy to the continuing war. Through this agency the government attempted to exercise authority over the production and distribution of vital food commodities. The production of wheat, for example, was encouraged by setting the minimum price at $2.00 a bushel. Sugar and pork received similar treatment, but no minimum price was ever set on cattle. Hoover apparently felt that the nation's beef producers were responding adequately to verbal encouragement to expand production, that prices were already high enough to provide incentive, and that the administration's meatless days were adequate to meet the crisis.

As a result of the war, the cost of renting pasture in the Flint Hills more than doubled, and much of the same rate of increase occurred for pastures throughout the state. In 1900 cattle owners paid as little as $1.00 per head for six months of grazing, and $5.00 to $6.00 in 1911. Three years later, $7.00 to $7.50 was the average; and, towards the end of the war, rates increased to as much as $20.00 per head for aged steers and cows. Average prices at this time were probably about $17.00 a head or less. Increased pasture rates reflected higher stock prices more than they did appreciated land values, although the price of Kansas land also shot upward. Flint Hills pasture could be purchased for $3.50 to $5.50 an acre in 1900; by 1911 it had advanced to $18.00 to $30.00; and by the end of the war the 1911 prices had nearly doubled.

Despite the increased prices, pasture was in great demand. Repeated notices in the *Kansas Cattleman* and the *Stockman* asked landowners to advise Mercer of available grass so that he could coordinate supply with demand. During the spring of 1918, the *Stockman* reported that more than 7,000 cars of cattle detrained in the Flint Hills. Over 38 percent of these cattle had originated in Texas, 28 percent in Kansas, and 19 percent in Oklahoma; and the remaining 15 percent came from states like New Mexico, Arizona, Colorado, Arkansas, and Missouri. Accurate figures on the number of transient cattle that grazed the Flint Hills during the war are not available, but James C. Malin estimated that between 213,000 and 319,000 head were accommodated annually during the early 1900s, and that 263,000 to 278,000 were definitely grazed there each year between 1925 and 1929. The level for the war years probably fell somewhere between the numbers for these two periods; and, of course, cattle in the Flint Hills represented only a portion of the in-shipped stock that were grazed throughout the state.[8]

Some of the state's cattlemen naturally took advantage of higher wartime prices for stock and grass to expand their operations, although few stockmen were as fortunate as Walter S. and Evan C. Jones, who nursed a few acres into an empire that lasted for more than half a century. And what an empire it was. At the time of their deaths, both in 1953, the brothers left a fortune estimated to be worth between six and eight million dollars in land, cattle, and oil to Walter's wife, Olive.

Few cattlemen made that kind of money, nor did many local banks encounter the predicament that dropped into the lap of an Emporia institution. Olive's will made several specific bequests to institutions and relatives, and after her death in 1957 the Emporia bank became responsible for dispensing the remaining large income from the estate. According to the will, money could be disbursed only for the medical needs of the poor in the several counties around Emporia. Soon, however, dollars were coming in faster than they could be dispersed. The court eventually broadened its interpretation of the will so that today the fund provides medical assistance and college educations for some of the local poor, as well as recreational facilities for people in the Emporia area.

The Jones brothers were a notable example of cattlemen moving up the ladder from leasing land to owning it. Raised in a poor family, Walter once claimed that not until he was an adult did he discover that a chicken had more than a neck. The brothers formed a partnership about the turn of the century with 200 acres of inherited land. In 1904 they moved a few miles east of Emporia to Lebo, the headquarters of their cattle operation. They became pasturemen, leasing land in the Flint Hills and grazing up to 10,000 transient cattle each year, including many steers from Isaac L. Elwood's famous Spade Ranch in Texas. Some of the cattle were fattened in feedyards at the south edge of Lebo after they were taken off grass.

The brothers made good money during World War I and invested much of it in land. Several thousand acres were acquired around Lebo; then, during the twenties, the brothers took advantage of the agricultural depression and bought more than 40,000 acres near Higgins, Texas. Although the presence of oil was unsuspected at the time, oil pumping machines began to dot their Texas grassland after World War II.

Big Walter, as he was called after he grew to weigh over 300 pounds, was known to be a shrewd cattle trader who spent much of his time traveling several states to find the cattle the brothers' pastures demanded. Evan, the more introverted of the two, tended the day-to-day requirements of their wide interests.

The family was rarely ostentatious with its wealth, but all of them enjoyed a few luxuries. Evan at one time left the ranch for the prestigious Julliard School of Music in New York, but returned when officials thought him a bit old for voice training. Big Walter loved to chauffeur people around his pastures in the largest Chrysler he could buy, while Olive never failed to serve visitors a huge platter of the finest steaks—a far cry from Walter's chicken-neck days. On the other hand, Olive made her own soap.

Friends liked to tell the story of Walter's encounter with several Texas ranchers in the lobby of the old Broadview Hotel in Emporia, a favorite watering hole for out-of-town cattlemen who were seeking grass or tending to other interests in the Flint Hills. Walter spent many happy hours there, enjoying the conversation as well as conducting much of his cattle business. One day, the story went, a number of Texans were sitting around bragging about how their wives were spending large amounts of money. One was wintering on the Riviera, another was in Rome, while a third was in New York attending the latest Broadway plays. Noting that Walter had not volunteered any information regarding his wife, someone asked him directly. "She's home making soap," he replied, totally unintimidated by his friends' braggadocio.

Although wealthy in land and cattle, the Joneses were plain folk to most of their neighbors, and they spent little money foolishly. When they did spend, however, a check for any amount signed "Jones & Jones" by one of the brothers or Olive was never refused.[9]

Few cattlemen were as prosperous as the Jones brothers, but many made a good living throughout most of the period before and during the European conflict. Toward the end of World War I, on the other hand, higher labor costs, government-encouraged meatless days, drought-induced feed shortages, and the rising prices of other commodities threatened not only the cattlemen's optimism but also their profits. Stockmen were unaccustomed to the high prices they received during the war; yet, only a few noted that price levels were abnormally high. This was understandable, for only when one failed to consider purchasing power were prices actually high. As the purchasing-power figures show, beef prices failed after 1915 to keep pace with the whole-sale prices of other commodities, and in the end the high levels made the sharp decline during the postwar depression in agriculture much harder to bear.

As a result, the feeling of prosperity early in the war gave way to doubt and skepticism during the closing years of the conflict, and the change in atttiude accurately reflected conditions. Increased labor costs and a shortage of farm and ranch workers, which was related to the international conflict, encouraged skepticism. Some workers were in the military service, but the primary cause of the shortage was the loss as many moved to towns and cities where higher wages were being paid. One stockman lamented to the *Cattleman* that the government was paying $45 to $50 a week for construction work at Ft. Riley to laborers who had not made half or a third that much on Kansas farms and ranches before the war. Organizations that represented the distressed stockmen and farmers were successful in getting draft deferments for some "real" agricultural workers, but cattlemen could do little to curtail the migration to the cities except increase their costs by raising wages. KLA at one time suggested strongly that military manpower needs should be filled from middlemen groups rather than agricultural workers, and that the government should devise some means of forcing experienced young agricultural workers back to the farms and ranches they had deserted. Nothing, however, ever came of the proposal.

Although the general trend of cattle prices was upward until after the armistice, the fact that market prices sometimes fluctuated a few dollars per hundredweight was also a matter of concern. Some attributed it to a deliberate attempt by the packers to fleece the producer, while others blamed the unsettled conditions that resulted from the conflict.

Those cattlemen who specialized in feeder stock appeared to be most subject to the whims of the market, especially towards the end of the war when they bought high-priced stock just before the onset of depression. But even before the postwar decline set in, many feeders were complaining that the prices of feed and other goods that they had to buy prevented them from making any money. In fact, some Kansas feeders claimed as early as 1918 that they were losing $10 to $30 a head on fed stock. This situation supported the view that one large feeder, Arnold Berns, set before a meeting of the Kansas State Board of Agriculture in 1918. Berns told the group that, with increasing costs, fluctuating prices, and the large number of feeders who got in and out of production, feeding had become a game of chance rather than a solid business venture.[10]

The relatively large capital investment that was required and the close profit margin in the feeding operation did make it the most speculative phase of the beef industry. A feeder in Marshall County, for example, reported that he had made a gross profit of $25,952 by fattening about 300 head of cattle each year between 1910 and 1919. Money had been made, he reported, only six of the nine years, and prices were high throughout most of this period. The three unprofitable years were not designated, but they probably fell toward the end of the period.[11] Many cattlemen today still feel that feeding is the most risky phase of the cattle business.

Weather also affected cattle production and profits during this period. While the war could not be blamed for drought and cold winters, these two factors contributed to the decline. The summer of 1916 was hot and dry in most of Kansas, and in the western counties prairie fires caused heavy property damage as well as the deaths of two Hutchinson area residents. It was so hot during the summer, said the Topeka *State Journal,* that the jackrabbits were "sitting in large groups under shade trees." The paper no doubt exaggerated, but these ever-present animals could be a curse or occasionally a blessing for ranchers. They ate precious feed, yet sometimes ranchers realized small amounts of money from the sale of their meat. There were numerous accounts all through this period of rabbits shipped to eastern cities, apparently for human consumption. This was especially true towards the end of the war—possibly because of the high price of meat—when one canning company wanted two million jackrabbits at fifteen cents each and offered twelve cents each for cottontails. Many Kansans responded to such offers.

Another weather phenomenon, the heavy winter snows of 1912, prompted stories about the abundant rabbits. A few tall tales, designed to relieve ranchers' anxiety, concerned the deep snow and its threat to the cattle. A Hutchinson paper noted, for example, that jackrabbits were knocking down the weak, wobbly cattle and eating their oil cake. "A dozen farmers are missing," the paper continued; "rabbits have carried them to their dens in the sandhills." Not to be outdone, another Kansan claimed to have killed 942 rabbits with a single shot after they had lined up to eat a trail of corn he had put out.

Heavy snows also fell throughout the early spring of 1918 and during the winter of 1918–19. Hundreds of thin cattle, shipped into western Kansas earlier than usual due to drought in Texas, were victims of the 1918 snows. Hide buyers were also busy during the following winter when heavy snows kept the western counties blanketed for several months. Sandwiched between these two severe winters was an extremly hot summmr that ruined some grazing land and forced a few stockmen to haul water.[12]

The early war years, then, were prosperous for cattlemen. Feed was usually abundant, once the effects of the 1913 drought wore off, and sometimes cattlemen had to struggle to find enough cattle to consume the supply of feed. But the tide of prosperity crested around 1916. High demand for meat and rising beef prices continued for a few more years; but production costs, the short labor supply, and periods of severe weather affected profits. The cost of living, up steadily since the war began, advanced markedly after 1916. Between July, 1916, and April, 1917, the cost of food increased by 46 percent, then advanced another 45 percent by the end of the year. Other prices reflected much the same trend. Yet, while conditions worsened toward the end of the war, cattlemen were hardly prepared for the drastic tumble of cattle prices that was to occur during 1920.[13]

Judging by farm values of selected Kansas products, the percentage of livestock's contribution to the state's agricultural economy slipped between 1900 and 1920 (see Figures 5–8).[14] Before the war, livestock and its products accounted for slightly over 30 percent of farm commodity values. A slight increase followed, then a decline to 27 percent after 1916, most of which ocurred as a result of reductions in livestock slaughtered. But the loss in relative value by the livestock sector after 1916, as Figures 5–8 indicate, was a decline only when compared to increases that occurred in crops, especially wheat. Livestock actually increased its total dollar value throughout the period after 1900, and between 1916 and 1920 the value of livestock slaughtered alone rose by over $100 million. This increase, however, was no match for the rise in the value of wheat, which more than tripled during the same period, and thus reduced the relative contribution of livestock. Corn also suffered a decline as wheat increased in importance. On the whole, the value of livestock and its products to the Kansas agricultural economy almost doubled between 1900 and 1920, while that for crops more than tripled.

Figure 5. Average Percentage of Farm Value of Selected Kansas Products,
1901–1905

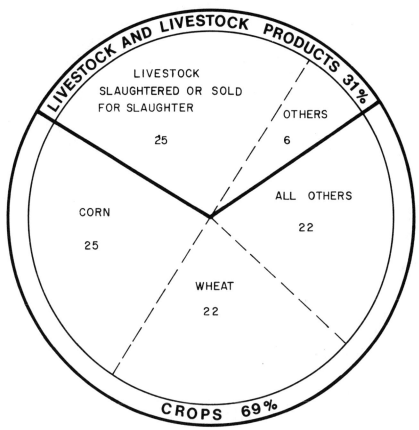

Source: "State Summaries," in *Repts., KSBA* (1901–1905).

Market prices, purchasing power, and the number of beef cattle were not the only things that concerned Kansas farmers and stockmen during the first twenty years of the new century. Other developments were also part of the agricultural scene, some of which were of great significance to the state's cattlemen. There was, for instance, a continuous influx of new settlers into the West throughout most of this period, many of whom were attracted by the siren calls of dry farming and wheat culture, both of which were considerably oversold by railroads, chambers of commerce, and others interested in population growth. A rainfall of as little as ten or twelve inches a year was advertised as sufficient for successful crop farming by some of the apostles of

Figure 6. Average Percentage of Farm Value of Selected Kansas Products, 1906–1910

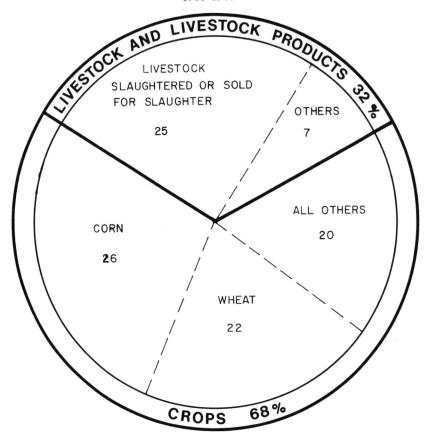

Source: "State Summaries," in *Repts., KSBA* (1906-1910).

dry farming. In the end, thousands were forced to retrace their steps to their point of origin, or move to towns that offered some means of livelihood. Serious droughts and the naturally small amount of moisture hastened many of the failures. The summer of 1913, as mentioned earlier, was dry throughout much of the grassland, with no general rain in Kansas between June and September. This was the most severe general drought in the state for over a decade.

The other drought periods of these two decades, most notably in 1901 and 1916, were also hard on producers but were of much shorter duration. These droughts were also noticed in the Flint Hills, where larger than normal

Figure 7. Average Percentage of Farm Value of Selected Kansas Products, 1911–1915

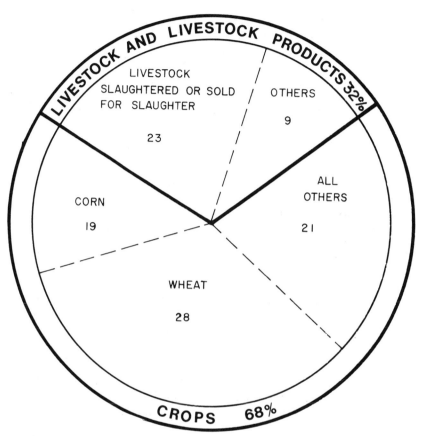

Source: "State Summaries," in *Repts., KSBA* (1911–1915).

inshipments of cattle from Texas, Oklahoma, and western Kansas were received during the spring and fall if adequate feed was available. Some Kansas stockmen also had to haul drinking water for their cattle due to the shortage. The drought and subsequent water deficiencies at this time prompted one of the first campaigns in the state to use tax money for building ponds. Governor George H. Hodges spoke frequently in support of the proposal, but there was also notable opposition. One Lyon County critic noted that ponds either disappeared or become poisoned during dry periods. The droughts and other impediments to successful agriculture on the Great Plains did not force all of the new crop farmers from the land, however; they, with the help of older

Figure 8. Average Percentage of Farm Value of Selected Kansas Products, 1916–1920

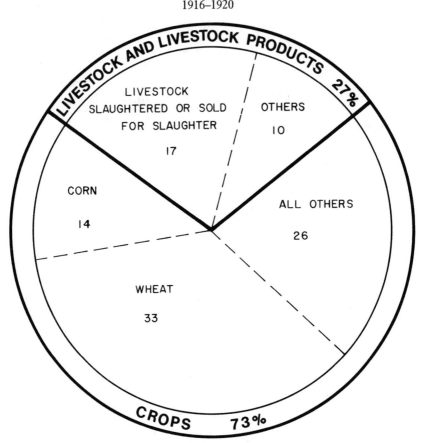

LIVESTOCK AND LIVESTOCK PRODUCTS 27%

LIVESTOCK SLAUGHTERED OR SOLD FOR SLAUGHTER

17

OTHERS

10

CORN

14

ALL OTHERS

26

WHEAT

33

CROPS 73%

Source: "State Summaries," in *Repts., KSBA* (1916–1920).

residents, had actually expanded crop acreage by 1920. Many of those who stayed also diversified their operations to include some livestock, often beef cattle.[15]

Expanded crop acreages often came at the expense of grassland. For example, E. E. Frizell, who was in the hardware business in Larned, bought and broke several thousand acres of sod during the early 1900s on what had been the Ft. Larned military reservation in Pawnee County. Frizell broke more sod during World War I and planted much of it to wheat. In Hodgeman and Ness counties just west of Larned, Frizell grazed cows and steers on several thousand acres of grass that he owned and leased. After the war Frizell and his sons continued to expand their wheat and cattle operation. They plowed under four thousand acres of grass and planted wheat in Hodgeman and Ness counties to complement their military reservation land. At the same time, the Frizells continued raising cattle on a large ranch in Colorado, as well as grazing Texas steers in Kansas.[16]

Others followed Frizell's example. Even some of the grassland in the Flint Hills felt the plowshare during this period. One local paper stated in 1912 that Emporia was as much a center for wheat and alfalfa as for cattle. During the first decade of the twentieth century the state's wheat acreage approached that of corn and actually exceeded it for the first time in 1907. It was, however, during the early twenties that many landowners increased their acreage under cultivation because of low prices for cattle and decreased income from grassland, and wheat became the state's major crop.[17]

Corn remained an important crop in Kansas throughout this period, even though its acreage declined from seven or eight million during the first decade of the twentieth century to a little more than five million in 1920. The importance of corn, as well as other forage crops, was enhanced in many cattle operations when the silo became more popular. Trench, cement, and brick silos were constructed to preserve feed and thus increase stock production. The "silo boom" became so evident that the Abilene *Reflector* reported that "if Kansas had the Tower of London it would probably tear it down to give room for a silo."

Expanded wheat planting and the use of gasoline tractors, however, received more press coverage than did silo development or corn production. In 1916 a dispatch from Hutchinson reported, "gas tractors are tearing the whole country upside down in western Kansas, and at the present rate the famous short-grass pasturage will be a thing of the past. Trainloads of tractors have been shipped into that part of the state and are turning the sod and getting the ground ready for cultivation. . . . One ranch in Morton county is plowing up 3,000 acres. Another in Ford county has eleven outfits on the Sherman ranch. Ten tractor outfits were unloaded at Satanta in Haskell county in two days. Montezuma, in Gray county, received five in one day."[18]

The urgency to expand food production was so great that tractors were sometimes equipped with headlights and used twenty-four hours a day. A Geary County farmer was reported to have "opened an old Indian mound, hauled off the artifacts as rubbish, and put the ground to wheat." The use of tractors rose to the point that the Board of Agriculture could boast in 1919 that more tractors were used in Kansas than in any other state.[19] Not all

Kansans, however, were readily convinced of the advantages of the gasoline engine. One expressed a popular objection when he pointed out that the exhaust from the tractor was not nearly as potent a factor in maintaining soil fertility as was the exhaust from the former source of power. Still, more and more tractors found their way to Kansas farms and ranches.

The Food Administration's campaign to increase food production encouraged much of this expansion. Production quotas were suggested for each state, and farmers who failed to cooperate were called "slackers." High prices also contributed. Wheat sold for an average of $2.12 a bushel in 1917 and as high as $3.14 at one time, while corn averaged $1.59 in 1918. This led to large demands for land, and the Emporia *Gazette* reported a year after the war began that there were far more tenants seeking farms than there was land available. But new cropland was added, and J. C. Mohler, secretary of the Kansas Board of Agriculture, noted that the state had eighteen million acres in crops in 1915 and about twenty-five million three years later.

After this expansion in cultivated land, cattlemen had more forage and grain available for feeding but they also had fewer acres for grazing. "Encroachment of tillers of the soil on cattle ranges calls for a new deal in the livestock industry and to keep up the production of stock 'intensified ranching' is the solution being preached in Wichita this week," was the message of the *Eagle* during the 1915 KLA convention. In other words, more pounds of beef had to be produced on fewer acres of land. Increased attention to cattle feeding, more silos to preserve feed, and the trend toward early maturation and fattening of cattle, all helped the stockmen augment the quantity of beef.[20]

Prompted by the interest of President Theodore Roosevelt on the national level and by the loss of grass to the plow at the local level, conservation of natural resources became a concern of cattlemen during the early years of the twentieth century. Discussions between western cattlemen and government officials about the use of the public domain was one result, but most concern at this time centered on the public forests rather than grassland. Some cattlemen wished to continue the free, unrestricted use that they were accustomed to; others favored a leasing policy; and a few agreed with the Forest Service's plan for a permit system that would have enabled government officials to control the number of cattle grazed.

There was little public forest land in Kansas in 1900, but over 300,000 acres were set aside in 1906 as a national forest reserve in five counties along the Arkansas River in the far western part of the state. Still, some residents of the state were concerned with forest policy, because cattlemen in Kansas

Breaking sod with a Hart-Parr tractor and moldboard gang plow, Finney County. During World War I and the 1920s, rigs such as this helped transform grassland into wheat fields. *Courtesy of the Kansas State Historical Society.*

paid full value for grass while competing in the marketplace with cattle producers in other states who had very cheap use of public land. Justin De Witt Bowersock, Republican from Lawrence, even introduced a bill into the 1902 Congress that would have permitted leasing of the public land for a few cents an acre.[21] Fortunately for the public and for the conservation of resources, however, the Department of Agriculture opted for a grazing fee system rather than the Bowersock Bill. This allowed greater control over the number of animals grazed.

More important to Kansas than the national forest reserve, and probably more significant than the outcome of the dispute over Forest Service grazing requirements, was the increased concern over the availability of grass that developed during the war years. This attitude and the conservation practices it stimulated were, in part, a response to rising land values, to the need for more intensive land-use, and to the periodic droughts. The droughts, disastrous as they may have been, had some redeeming value in stimulating an interest in the conservation of native Kansas grasses.[22]

Some of the state's journalists encouraged the new concern. In 1915 the Emporia *Gazette* noted that most Kansas pastures had responded well to increased rainfall, but also questioned the future of the grass in the absence of greater concern by graziers. Pioneers, the paper said, had talked of bluestem as high as a horse's back, but the "record-breaking drought of 1913 proved most disastrous for the native sod of our pastures, and now we are left with weedy grassless pastures." Greater efforts at conservation had to be exerted, the article warned, especially now that the war was stimulating more use, or "finally the point will be reached where we may record the passing of our prairie pastures."[23]

Other warnings, predictions, and tributes to Kansas grass, especially the bluestem of the Flint Hills, were made during the period, but the most interesting comments of the time were those of John A. Edwards. This Greenwood County cattle and hog producer was a popular toastmaster at many gatherings of Kansans and, frequently, the master of ceremonies at the annual KLA banquet. His wit was most appreciated, but he was also capable of more serious thoughts. Educated at the University of Kansas—he later claimed that he had played cards while his parents and classmates went to his graduation—Edwards had an abiding distrust of the large packers, and for the first three decades of the twentieth century he was usually a member of any group that investigated businesses associated with the beef industry. Spartan in his personal habits, Edwards as a state legislator had opposed the use of alcohol, authored the anticigarette law, and at one time offered $150 in prizes to clubs that made the best fight against the use of these "coffin nails."

Edwards' family had migrated to Emporia from the Denver area, where they had gone with a group of Welch people who were involved with mining. His father eventually became interested in banking and cattle, and at one time sent several shiploads of live cattle to England because American prices were too low. The higher prices he received, however, failed to cover the added expense of getting them there.

John A. Edwards, first with his father then on his own, began in the cattle business after completing his work, or possibly play, at the university. He acquired two large ranches in southwest Kansas where wheat and cattle were produced, and eventually married the daughter of C. D. Perry, whose large Claremont Ranch in Clark County was mentioned earlier. Edwards and his new bride, in fact, were with Perry when he was killed in an automobile accident.

Edwards owned a share of the First National Bank in Eureka, as well

92

as four rather substantial ranches in this bluestem area of the Flint Hills where he raised cattle, grain, and hogs. For fun he kept about a dozen elk and bred fine horses. Edwards made good money during World War I, and some of his expansion, including oil prospecting, occurred during or soon after the war. He was a plunger, and, unfortunately, many of his interests were built unsoundly on borrowed money. The postwar depression drove this robust cattleman out of ranching, much to the loss of his fellow producers. Neither KLA conventions nor the attacks on big packers were quite the same after Edwards retired from the arena. But this part of his story will be told later.[24]

In 1918 Edwards spoke to the KLA convention in Wichita on the value of the bluestem that he loved. With provincial and chauvinistic overtones— generated by the course of world events at the time—and to some extent with tongue in cheek, Edwards told the convention that bluestem "seems to grow and thrive over an area that is underlaid with oil." He continued with this statement:

> This Blue Stem of Eastern Kansas and Oklahoma is a wonderful grass. It is a flesh builder and a muscle maker and a nerve tonic. It is a fattener that has no equal. It needs to bow to no elixir of earth or heaven. It has grazed and raised and fattened and made sleek, not only our steers but the five greatest and most enormous and most corpulent bodies in America; and these fat bodies are the five great American packers and they got fat on our grass. And that's the kind of grass it is.
>
> Over in Kentucky they have grass, Blue Grass; a grass without a stem, and that character of vegetation only grows distilleries and Colonels; and they are lean. While our grass produces packers, and they are fat; and that's the difference financially and botanically between Blue Grass and Blue Stem.
>
> Over in Germany a hardy perennial grows which they call Neder Grasse. This grass makes soldiers and barbarians. Ours makes Citizens. There is a scanty, sickly grass which grows in Russia and Old Mexico. It is a hybrid. A cross between Wire, Sandburr and Buffalo grass. It is not a luxuriant herb like ours. It's the kind of grass which raises revolutions and repudiation. Ours is a peace producer and a debt payer.
>
> I have compared our grass with the Marsh grass and Bermuda of the South, and the Mountain grasses of the West and the Moss of North. I have found no grass, no fruit or vegetable, that produces

fat horses and cattle and fat contented people, like our Blue Stem. It makes a people so healthy and so hearty and so peaceful that they are willing to be robbed in daylight.[25]

Edwards' audience was enthralled, but if they accepted the gist of these remarks as well as that of the rest of the tribute they would surely have been encouraged toward greater conservation.

A bit later in time, but still illustrative of this increased awareness of grass, was a statement in the last will and testament of W. J. Tod, written sometime before his death in 1929. Tod said, in part: "It is furthermore my special wish and request that care should be taken to preserve the natural prairie grasses and that none of the natural grasslands should be plowed or broken up during the lifetime of my wife, Margaret, and that great care shall be taken to avoid their being overstocked at any time."[26]

Some of the techniques suggested to preserve or replenish the native grass were used during subsequent droughts and are popular even today. Reseeding with Kentucky bluegrass was suggested, but the adaptability of this and other eastern grasses was continually being questioned in many parts of the state. The practice of harrowing pastures, as well as repeated mowings to kill the encroaching weeds, was also advised. But the most frequently suggested technique—and probably the most effective—was some form of deferred grazing that allowed the grasses to replenish themselves. Delayed spring entry of cattle, alternate grazing areas, or complete removal of stock permitted grass a growing period free from the cropping of meandering cattle. The grass itself had remarkable recuperative powers if left undisturbed.[27]

The alarm over grass conditions in Kansas during the second decade of the twentieth century was, of course, not as great as that which would be experienced in the devastating 1930s. But the increased concern and growing respect for much of the natural covering of the state that resulted from the alarm was a far cry from the attitude of those nineteenth-century prognosticators who believed that all grass would eventually give way to other crops that were more productive. Those early views had been conditioned by experiences that their purveyors had had in the humid and timbered East that did not apply in the West.

The rising concern with grass during the war years reflected the progress of the state's cattlemen in adapting to the natural conditions of the environment and in learning to appreciate the value of the native vegetation. Unfortunately, sod was still being broken. Lessons learned during the war years had to be re-learned and more widely promulgated during the 1930s, when many "experts" riveted the blame for the dust storms wholly upon the plow and the abundance of cattle rather than the periodic droughts that were common to the grassland environment.[28]

By 1920 cattlemen could look back at two decades that, despite the sharp fluctuations in cattle prices and numbers and in the purchasing power of beef, had been relatively prosperous. Augmented demands for grain and meat as a result of the war and a growing population had also been characteristic. These developments, in turn, had helped cause the expansion of grain crops, more intensified land usage by ranchers, and their increased awareness of the need to protect the native grass. As the quantity of land available for cattle diminished, several expediencies were employed to help improve beef production. New feeds and better combinations of old feeds were used to produce faster gains, and some cattle were marketed at a younger age. But basic in enabling cattlemen to produce more and better meat, in spite of reduced land resources and sometimes fewer cattle, was the improvement of stock. More than any other factor, it was the upgraded animals that provided greater quantity and quality for the urban housewife. Herefords, already plentiful before 1900, became even more popular and highly developed during the opening decades of the twentieth century. In large part, this development was the work of several master breeders.

5

Herefords Triumph: Upbreeding, 1900-1940

Throughout much of the first half of the twentieth century, Robert H. Hazlett of El Dorado was the best-known breeder of purebred cattle in the state, if not the nation. This Flint Hills stockman, who died in 1936, left behind a legacy that included international fame as a breeder of excellent Herefords as well as established lines of cattle that were popular for another two decades.

Hazlett's efforts illustrated the methods used by many producers of purebreds, the care they took in matching sires with dams, the culling they found necessary to improve their herds, and the traveling they did in order to show and advertise the results of breeding programs. In a larger sense, the work of this Hereford breeder epitomized the tendency for wealthy individuals to develop model farms for purebreds with money they had made in nonagricultural businesses. This coincidence of wealth and fine cattle, rooted in the nineteenth century and even in Old World traditions, continues to the present time.

While rarely if ever stated, the motives of these suitcase breeders for entering this particular business were varied. Today, tax advantages may encourage, in part, investment in purebreds; but such was not the case during the nineteenth century or during much of Hazlett's career. Nor was the desire for profit the overpowering force, as profits frequently did not result. Usually, these men could have made more money in some other business. In some cases purebred breeding was a hobby, a mere diversion from regular chores, but it required a large infusion of capital. For many, the appeal of the competition inherent in building and showing a fine string of cattle, as well as pride in accomplishment, made the large investment worthwhile.

On another level, raising purebreds was often a nostalgic link with a youth spent on a farm—the fulfillment, as it were, of a longing to return. It was almost as if some accomplishment in agriculture was needed to crown an otherwise successful career. The legacy of an improved breed of cattle was a compelling force. While the rich competed with the many poorer cattlemen who used purebreds as their only source of income, the development of several breeds owes much to the willingness of moneyed investors to take up the trade. For many, like Hazlett, raising purebreds was the most exciting facet of the beef industry.

Far more important than excitement, however, or even the profits that some individual breeders made, was the help this improved blood gave cattlemen in coping with rising costs of production. Improving the country's stock had an added significance after 1900 because the demand for beef increased, the acreage allotted to the industry continued to decline, and the profit margin became narrower as production costs went up. Upgrading stock was the only way to boost production without enlarging landholdings. It became increasingly important that as much beef as possible be acquired from each animal, and that the cattle produce this beef with a minimum of feed. The eye appeal that enhanced sale prices and the ability to make better gains and to mature in less time were characteristics that could be bred into a herd of commercial cattle by careful selection of upbred or purebred stock. Not only were these qualities of great value to stockmen in terms of higher returns, they were also important in producing a better retail product, a higher quality meat that consumers were demanding more and more. Upbred stock paid dividends at market time, giving the owner some relief from the cost-price squeeze.

Purebred production and the upgrading of range stock after 1900 were based firmly on the work already accomplished in the previous century. By 1900 a number of producers were well along in their upgrading programs, but there was still much to be done. In this work, Herefords played the lead role; Shorthorn and Angus cattle were understudies. By 1920 the *American Hereford Journal* reported that 41 percent of the cattle in the West were whitefaces, while a decade later the same journal boasted that the "great range sections of our country are now at least 90 percent Hereford-using districts." Another claimed only 75 percent for the Hereford during the 1930s, but either figure represented a considerable change in the complexion of range cattle during the preceding few decades.[1]

Kansas continued to be very significant in the production of purebred and upgraded stock for the range country throughout the twentieth century. In

1920 Kansas had a greater number of purebred Herefords than any of the states that touched her borders, and it ranked third in the nation behind Texas and Iowa. The Kansas lead over contiguous states increased by 1930, and the state had moved to second for the nation as a whole. Kansas also led surrounding states in Shorthorn numbers in 1920, but fell behind Nebraska and Missouri ten years later. Kansas never led in purebred Angus production, although there were a few black cattle scattered across the state.[2]

Much the same position for the state becomes apparent from listings in the *American Hereford Journal* of breeders who registered the largest number of cattle in any given year. During the early 1920s, at least three Kansas firms or breeders were usually among the top ten, including the Miltonvale Cattle Company of Miltonvale, Jesse W. Greenleaf of Greensburg, and C. G. Cochran of Hays. In 1923 John A. Edwards of Eureka topped the entire list by registering 670 head. After the middle twenties, however, Kansas began to move down the register, not so much because production in the state declined but due rather to the increased numbers being raised in Texas and the Southwest. Clearly, the quantity, if not the quality, of Hereford production had shifted toward the Southwest by 1930. In 1936 Robert H. Hazlett was the only Kansan appearing on the list of thirty breeders, and he was twenty-sixth.[3]

Upbreeding and purebred production were stimulated most by high beef prices. The price levels during World War I had this effect, with the numbers of large and small producers expanding rapidly. Towards the end of the war, the first issue of the *Kansas Cattleman* expected the state soon to have 700 breeders of purebred Herefords. Then came the postwar depression and the disastrous declines during the 1920s. With their relatively large investments in highly bred cattle and with the prices not much higher than those for common grade animals, hundreds of producers of purebreds were eliminated from the field. Much the same thing occurred during the thirties. For comparison with the World War I period, the *Stockman* listed 450 breeders of purebred Herefords throughout the state in 1954.[4]

Those who used purebred stock or in some manner upgraded their commercial herds could do so in a variety of ways, using either registered purebreds, unregistered purebreds, or grade animals that carried improved blood. A producer might buy a whole herd of well-bred cattle at one time, but this was expensive and usually beyond the means of most stockmen. Instead, most took a more gradual approach. A few upgraded cows were purchased, or the poorer animals gradually were eliminated from the herd. Most often, herd sires figured prominently in the upbreeding process, as the prepotent blood of one bull could be spread to the offspring of more than a score of cows in a single breeding season. This was much the cheapest route, although quality sires were often expensive.

Some cattlemen tried to reduce the expense of buying good bulls by establishing their own purebred herds to produce sires for their commercial cows. These herds were usually small, although some grew to provide breeding stock for neighbors. This method was intended to be cheaper than continually purchasing large numbers of expensive bulls from those who specialized in purebred production, but it was also more trouble because the purebreds usually required better treatment than the commercial herd. Special care during the winter was often provided, and the purebred cows had to be protected from the overtures of poor-quality bulls. Many of the purebred sires from these herds were never registered, but it made little difference to the cows they serviced or to the stockman who dealt in commercial cattle.

In selecting males for upgrading, Hereford bulls stood at the fore. Their willingness to breed under adverse conditions and the potency of their seed in spreading desirable characteristics were unsurpassed. Dan D. Casement, a Kansas Hereford breeder who became one of the most renowned feeders in the nation, was only one of many to urge producers to be more concerned with their herd's display quality, character, size, scale, and uniformity. The right bull, Casement urged, was all-important, and this often meant a purebred Hereford sire from one of the many producers who specialized in this phase of the cattle industry.[5]

Robert H. Hazlett first began raising cattle at the turn of the century. Shortly, he improved his foundation stock, expanded the herd, and then rose rapidly to prominence. By 1920 the *Stockman* called him the "premier exhibiter and breeder in the state," and only a decade later he was equated with such master breeders as Robert Bakewell and Amos Cruickshank of Great Britain, and Gudgell & Simpson of the United States. Donald Ornduff, historian of American Herefords, may have said it best when he wrote: "It is not given to many men to achieve such success in breeding Herefords, or any kind of cattle, that the product of their herds becomes identified by the owner's name rather than that of the bovine family from which it sprang. Two such herds in the Hereford field come readily to mind, those of Gudgell & Simpson and Robert H. Hazlett."[6]

Hazlett had come to Kansas in 1885 from Illinois by way of Nebraska. Some said a fear of being persuaded to enter Illinois politics had prompted the move, while others claimed that he left to find cheaper land. He had also spent time in Leadville, Colorado, where he successfully engaged in mining. No one knew how much money he made; but, it was said, the El Dorado man never wanted for wealth after his mining venture. In El Dorado, Hazlett practiced law and sold real estate, and then when oil was discovered on some of his property he became active in oil and banking. In short, by the time he entered the Hereford business, capital was not a limiting factor.[7]

Hazlett's first acquaintance with Herefords came in Illinois as a young lad on his father's farm. Later, while in college, he helped champion the Hereford's admittance to the various state and county fairs when the Illinois State Board of Agriculture, dominated by owners of other breeds, refused to allow the whitefaces to compete as a beef breed. Hazlett continued to admire the breed, although he did not own any cattle until he bought a small herd of well-bred Herefords in 1898.

This first herd was strongly influenced by Gudgell & Simpson's Anxiety 4th breeding, but Hazlett had little thought of improving it at the time. Not until 1903, shortly after Will Condell began over three decades of work in managing the breeding program, did Hazlett become interested in improving his stock. He began with an outcross on the Anxiety 4th blood, but he soon gave this up when the issue proved unsatisfactory. He then decided to concentrate on the lines of Anxiety 4th. This decision set the stage for his greatest contributions. Next to Gudgell & Simpson, Hazlett's herd became more heavily concentrated with Anxiety 4th blood than any herd in the world.

About the time of World War I, the herd had improved so much that, at the strong urging of Condell, Hazlett entered the show ring, initiating over twenty years of unparalleled success. His herd was honored with 208 championships, 757 firsts, and about 1,000 other ribbons in almost all the major stock shows of the country.[8]

At his model breeding farm northeast of El Dorado, known as Hazford Place, Hazlett continued not only the principal bloodline developed by Gudgell & Simpson but also their method of linebreeding. He carried this method of closely mating those animals with a common heritage much further than did Gudgell & Simpson. And, as in the case of the Independence masters whom he had studied, the skepticism and advice from experienced breeders that met Hazlett's first attempts at linebreeding soon turned to amazement and imitation when the results became generally known.

101

Zato Rupert and Iza Rupert, full brother and sister, were the grand champion bull and cow at the American Royal and the Chicago International shows in 1933. These purebreds were developed, owned, and exhibited by Robert H. Hazlett, El Dorado, Kansas. *Courtesy of the Kansas State Historical Society.*

Beginning with four sons of Beau Brummel—a grandson of Anxiety 4th, through Don Carlos—Hazlett managed to concentrate the most desirable qualities of Anxiety 4th blood through carefully programmed breeding and rigid selection of calves to be retained in his herd. Some have said that Hazlett's selection policy could best be described as ruthless. Many calves that might have developed into excellent breeding stock were castrated and sold for slaughter, because, Hazlett believed, rigid selection was as important to the development of his herd as the concentration of blood through linebreeding. He felt that if a potential breeding animal showed the slightest deficiency it was not in the best interests of Herefords to perpetuate this fault by continued use. Hazlett's wealth enabled him to carry this ruthless selection much further than breeders who depended upon their cattle for their livelihood and often were compelled to sell cattle for breeding purposes that might have a slight imperfection. In a broader sense, independent wealth and the rigid selection that it allowed may be necessary ingredients to the final development of blood lines. For these reasons, wealthy individuals have frequently made the most significant contributions in the area of improved livestock.

The Bocaldo 6th and the Hazford Rupert lines developed by Hazlett exerted great influence in Hereford circles. Late in life, Hazlett believed that the greatest thrill he experienced during his many years in the purebred business was the production of the bull Bocaldo 6th, as he had also raised Bocaldo 6th's sire and grandsire as well as his dam. This famous bull was calved in 1914 and won his first major championship the following year. In 1916 Bocaldo 6th won seven grand championships in seven consecutive major stock shows, including those in Kansas City and Chicago, before he was retired from the ring undefeated. Because Hazlett had other bulls he wanted to use at this time, Bocaldo 6th was used sparingly at first. Then, unfortunately, the bull met an untimely death in 1922 as a result of swallowing a piece of baling wire which punctured his stomach and led to infection of his lungs and liver. There were descendants enough at the time of his death to perpetuate the line, however, although Bocaldo 6th failed to reach his full potential for improving the breed. It was the development of the Bocaldos and Ruperts that contributed more than any other factor to Hazlett's lofty reputation.

Hazlett cattle, according to Donald Ornduff, displayed excellent "fleshing qualities, smoothness, depth, and symmetry of form." Another observer referred to the type as the "stretcher," a large big-boned Hereford as opposed to the "short chunky dumpling type." Early maturity and a remarkable uniformity were also characteristics.[9] These cattle contributed more desirable qualities to the nation's Herefords than almost any cattle of their day.

Although Hazlett was sometimes criticized for his ruthless culling practices and for his reluctance to sell breeding stock to other purebred breeders, his restrictive selling policy was less the case with bulls for commercial herds. From Hazlett and from those herds owned by breeders who managed to purchase some of his stock, hundreds of bulls that carried the Hazford Place stamp found a home in leading commercial herds, including those of Walter Jones of Lebo, who ran cows on his ranch in Texas, and the Matador Land & Cattle Company. His influence also spread eastward. At his first public auction, residents of Missouri bought more cattle than breeders from any other state. Georgia, Virginia, Indiana, Kentucky, and Vermont were also represented.[10]

The kindly gentleman from El Dorado even saved a few purebred sires from anonymity by rescuing them from range herds. Early in his career

Hazlett was impressed with the progeny of a Gudgell & Simpson–bred bull named Publican. Learning of Publican through the work of his son, Bonnie Brae 8th, Hazlett unsuccessfully tried to buy the son. Failing this, he eventually located Publican contentedly working the ranges of the Matador in Texas. A trade was negotiated with Murdo Mackenzie, the Matador manager, about 1911, which brought the bull, now over seven years old, to Hazford Place. The El Dorado master figured that Publican had already given his best to the Matador herd, but still felt that his Anxiety 4th heritage should be preserved. In this Hazlett was correct. Publican's few years of service at Hazford Place resulted in several notable females for his owner's herd, as well as a number of bulls. Before his sale by Gudgell & Simpson to the Matador, Publican had sired the bull Domino, sire of Prince Domino 499611. It was through Prince Domino's many descendants that Publican made his most valuable contribution to the Hereford breed. Later, Hazlett also rescued Beau Santos, a son of Beau Brummel, from the John Adair ranch in Texas.[11]

At the ripe age of 90, after nearly four decades of Hereford breeding, Hazlett's health began to fail. He had remained physically active, though, up to near the very end. He had been honored by several agricultural societies, Kansas State University, and by a number of other organizations. While Hazlett's personal triumph was the production of Bocaldo 6th, his crowning success in the show ring was at the 1936 Chicago International. Unable to leave his wheelchair, he watched a bull and a heifer from his herd win the top two championships of the show. Then, a month later, the master breeder died. At this time his land holdings had grown to about 10,000 acres and his cattle herd to over 1,000 head, 600 of which were part of the purebred herd.

Hazlett's estate was the largest for which a will was ever probated in Butler County, up to that time. The bulk of his property—which included oil and bank stock as well as cash, land, and cattle—was willed to a nephew, while other relatives were granted large sums of money. The Condell family, Will and his son Frank, were rewarded for their many years of service with land, stocks, and cash. According to the will, the entire purebred herd was to be sold at public auction. Hazlett apparently wanted his improved cattle spread across the land, a step that he was reluctant to take while living.

The dispersion sale of the purebred stock in June, 1937, ranked as one of the all-time great sales of Herefords. It was even more spectacular than the sale of Sunny Slope cattle a few decades earlier. A crowd that at times numbered over 8,000 gathered for the three-day spectacular, although the circus tent erected at Hazford Place had a capacity of less than a third that number.

The high prices paid for the animals, at a time when prices were generally low due to the depression, marked the esteem in which Hazlett's herd was held. Ten show animals were sold as a group to F. E. Harper and Ray J. Turner for $18,800. Having failed to persuade the trustees to sell the whole herd to them before the scheduled auction, these two Oklahoma oil and real-estate magnates bought a total of fifty-six cattle for $56,530, easily the largest single purchase. Gross receipts for the 604 purebreds that were sold climbed to $305,250. This sum was paid by 133 buyers representing twenty-six states and three Canadian provinces.[12]

After buying Harper's interest, Ray J. Turner, later governor of Oklahoma, developed the Hazlett cattle for many years, combining the Hazford Ruperts and Tones with Prince Domino blood to produce the TR Zato Heir family. These cattle contributed much to the upgrading of Texas and southwestern stock.[13] In Kansas the Condell family kept one of the larger herds of Hazlett cattle. Will Condell had begun to develop his own herd of purebreds a few years before Hazlett's death. He bought a number of cattle at Hazlett's sale, which were mixed with stock acquired from the Wyoming Hereford Ranch. Eventually, the Hazlett lines lost their separate identity.

Frank Condell, who returned to El Dorado from Kansas City after Hazlett's death and established Dellford Ranch, started with Hazlett cattle and kept the lines mostly intact for two decades. Numerous sales were held to disperse the surplus stock from his herd. Then in 1958, pleading the absence of adequate help, Frank Condell decided to disperse the last of his Hazlett cattle and develop a commercial herd. It is an interesting commentary on the advance of purebred prices to note that this sale of only 349 head, about half the number Hazlett had sold two decades before, grossed $460,570, or about $160,000 more than Hazlett's original herd. Condell's dispersal ended, for the most part, more than a half century of Hazlett Hereford influence in the El Dorado area.[14]

For a decade or so after Hazlett's death the bloodlines he developed continued to be in demand. There were numerous advertisements by breeders of purebreds all over the country offering to sell Hazlett-bred stock. But with the development of new lines, the cattle lost favor by failing to keep up with the new trends. Compared to the Herefords in the 1960s, Hazlett cattle were finer boned. Inevitably, popular lines fade unless a skilled and dedicated breeder anticipates future demands and develops new qualities in his cattle. A few years ago an Iowa breeder dispersed a herd that had been kept close to Hazlett lines; but, for the most part, the Hazford Place contributions are

Hazlett's herd of show animals, sold in 1937 as a group to F. E. Harper and Ray J. Turner, both from Oklahoma, for $18,800. *Courtesy of the Kansas State Board of Agriculture.*

today hidden in the conformation of the new Hereford. The impact of Hazlett-bred stock on the development of the Hereford is preserved in the voluminous records that breeders keep on their sires and dams.[15]

Hazlett, of course, was assisted in producing improved stock for range upbreeding by many other Kansans who had either large, well-known herds, or small and relatively unnoticed collections of cattle. Not far from El Dorado, near the small Flint Hills town of Matfield Green, for example, lived the Crocker family. They had come to Kansas shortly after the Civil War; but it was not until later that two brothers, Edward and Arthur, began to build the family ranching enterprise into one of the largest in the state. With profits from grazing thousands of transient cattle, the brothers expanded their land and livestock holdings until they controlled some 40,000 acres in Chase County, the Riverview Ranch north of Hays, seasonal grazing in Greenwood County and the Osage Hills of Oklahoma, and an interest in the Double Circle Ranch in Arizona. The last leased nearly a million acres of Indian reservation land and supported some 25,000 cattle. Many of the stockers from the Double Circle were matured on the Crockers' Kansas grass. A 1920 visit by the editor of the *Stockman* led him to conclude that he had been shown

106

"what is probably the greatest ranch and the largest herd of pure bred breeding cattle to be found in Kansas."

The Crockers started their purebred herd around 1900 with Gudgell & Simpson sires, expanded it when beef prices were high, and disposed of their surplus stock with annual October sales. Sometimes buyers were offered as many as a thousand blooded animals at a single auction. Literally thousands of Crocker cattle helped upgrade western range herds.

The depression after World War I and the erratic swings of beef prices were unkind to Crocker interests, however, just as they were to many others. When the possibility of becoming "oil magnates as well as cattle 'Barons'" failed to materialize, their empire collapsed. The large purebred herd was dispersed, as was much of their land, including their interest in the Double Circle. Arthur Crocker had managed this ranch for many years and was largely responsible for its success. Some of their Flint Hills property was saved, and the family eventually reestablished their cattle trade, but not on the scale that it had reached during the early twenties.[16]

The Crockers certainly had a large herd during the heyday of purebred production that was stimulated by good prices during World War I, but it was not the largest in the state. That distinction belonged to C. G. Cochran of the Hays area. His herd included over 1,500 purebred Herefords when it was dispersed shortly after his death in 1926. Most of these cattle were registered. Cochran consistently filed papers on several hundred cattle each year during the middle twenties, which easily put him among the nation's top ten recorders, one year as high as fourth.

Cochran's breeding establishment, besides being large, was also unusual because it survived the postwar depression when others were having so much trouble. His other enterprises may account for this, as one of his principal interests from the time he migrated to Kansas during the 1880s was banking. By 1920 he was involved in several banks in western Kansas. His death prompted a large sale, but it was not the spectacular event occasioned by the dispersal of Hazlett cattle over a decade later. Prices for stock were low at the time, and many of the cows were sold in carload lots for $65 to $85 per head.[17]

About a hundred miles south of Hays was another large producer of purebreds during the golden twenties, Jesse W. Greenleaf. Located in the drainage basin of the upper Medicine Lodge River, Greenleaf lived in one of the best grazing areas of south-central Kansas. Rolling hills, excellent short grass, and dependable creeks characterized the region. Jesse and his brother Fred had come to Kiowa County with their father during the big cattle boom of the 1880s. They worked for stockmen in the area for a while, then began their own grazing operation for Texas steers with a large pasture—maybe as large as a hundred sections—north of Greensburg. Land was purchased from settlers who could not survive the dry years of the early 1890s for as little as $25 to $50 a quarter section. Other land was leased, and some land that was neither rented nor owned ended up behind the fence that surrounded the whole pasture. Toward the end of the 1890s, the Greenleafs sold their large pasture and invested in several thousand acres south of Greensburg. Today this beautiful ranch, nestled in a timbered creek valley, is still operated by Greenleaf's son, James O., and his two sons.

Jesse Greenleaf began raising purebred Herefords well before World War I. By the time the boom arrived, he was ready and anxious to capture his share of the market. His herd of up to 500 cows was of Gudgell & Simpson breeding as well as Hazlett, when the latter was available. The business was typically prosperous during the war. Carload lots of yearling bulls were shipped to Texas in addition to those that were sold locally. For a couple of years, Jesse sold bulls to the United States Department of the Interior for use by the Apache Indians around Flagstaff, Arizona. These bulls soon dispelled the government's reluctance to use purebreds in dry range country. The Fort Hays Agricultural Experiment Station also bought foundation stock from Greenleaf's herd.

Greenleaf had been one of the nation's top ten recorders of purebreds during the boom years of the late teens, but a sad day arrived in 1924. Faced with a declining market for bulls and low cattle prices generally, Greenleaf sold his whole herd. His 300 cows and calves, as well as a few herd bulls, were carried by special train to Wood Lake, Nebraska, where the Woods brothers were putting together one of the largest herds in that state.

The depression of the twenties also forced Greenleaf to give up ownership of the ranch, which passed to his wife's family. Since that time, the Greenleafs have leased the ranch. Jesse returned to raising commercial cattle—steers for summer grazing and a herd of cows. He had to ship the latter all the way to Atchison in 1934 to save them from the drought.

Jesse Greenleaf was not only a producer but also an active guardian and promoter of the beef industry. Most Kansas cattlemen knew the name Jesse Greenleaf. He spent fourteen years as a member of the State Corporation Commission, and after many years of serving KLA was honored with its presidency in 1938. His term on the State Corporation Commission was one of the longest ever served by one member. Because of his work in Topeka during the twenties and thirties and the desire for their children to have a college education, the Greenleafs gave up the ranch during the winter months for a home in Lawrence.

James O. Greenleaf began to assume the duties of managing the ranch during the early 1940s. He had graduated from the University of Kansas with a law degree in 1933, which was not a promising time to be looking for work. James returned to his first love after working for a while in the Kansas City stockyards and as an attorney in McPherson. He has been on the ranch ever since, following in his father's footsteps in more ways than one. Governor Avery, a classmate of James while both were at the university, appointed him during the 1960s to the State Corporation Commission.

After more than half a century of riding the crests of prosperity and the depths of depression in Kansas ranching, Jesse Greenleaf retired to Florida for a well-deserved rest soon after his son took over the ranch during World War II. But retire he could not, and he began to build a ranch outside of Sarasota not far from the winter quarters of the Ringling Brothers Circus. But land values were rising around Sarasota; and after a decade or so, he sold the 1,200 acres for five times what he had paid. Little did he know that in the next half dozen years the land would appreciate by ten times what he had sold it for.[18]

Greenleaf's career, like those of several others, illustrated the perils of raising fine stock. These breeders were subject to the same erratic cycles in beef prices as the rest of the industry, only more so because of the size of their investments. When depressions occurred, the fall was farther and harder. Many, who jumped in to take advantage of the boom prices during and shortly after World War I, failed to survive. Depressions, however, rarely discriminate, and some who had been in business for several years also went broke. A few years later the 1930s put more purebred breeders out of business, although the poor years the previous decade had not encouraged a large number of new entries.

Like the depressed years of the 1890s, those between the two wars changed the complexion of the state's entourage of purebred breeders. Gone were the Crockers and Greenleafs, and in their place came a few new breeders or expanded activities by those who managed to continue. And some, like Hazlett, did survive both depressions of the interwar period, but these successful breeders were often anchored with outside capital.

The bonanza farm and purebred herd of Benjamin B. Foster were among those that continued throughout the depressions between the wars. Foster Farms' Herefords had a staying power found in few Kansas herds, though the farm was not as well known in the state's agricultural history as a number of other establishments. They continued for almost fifty years, and at times were among the nation's most distinguished cattle.

While most businessmen-stockmen made their money in oil, real estate, or banking, Foster chose lumber. Foster's family had moved to Leavenworth from Kansas City during the 1850s, where his father freighted military supplies from Ft. Leavenworth to Colorado. In 1879, hoping to find other business opportunities, the elder Foster took young Benjamin with him on a trip in a covered wagon to find a place to establish a lumberyard. They selected Randolph, Kansas, a small town about twenty-five miles north of Manhattan and close to the Central Branch railroad that ran west from Atchison. Thus began a chain of retail lumberyards that was eventually spread throughout Kansas and a half-dozen neighboring states.

Benjamin Foster was only seventeen years old when he began managing one of the family's yards. He was a good businessman, neat and accurate in his bookkeeping, and scrupulously honest. By the early 1900s he was president of the family corporation, which by this time had over twenty yards. Not much later, the Fosters had accumulated more than seventy yards from which to retail the yellow pine lumber that was cut from thousands of acres of timberland they owned in Texas.

Foster grew to be a large, broad-shouldered man who dedicated himself to the family business. The retail headquarters were in Kansas City, where Foster spent most of his life. After marrying well, he and his family lived for twenty years in the Muehlebach Hotel in downtown Kansas City before moving to a suburban farm that his wife had inherited. Vivion Farm was a country estate, meticulously kept by numerous groundsmen. Today, it is the site of the Midwest Baptist Theological Seminary.[19]

Benjamin Foster, though a conservative businessman, was not averse to investments outside the lumber industry. During the few years prior to World War I, Foster speculated on western Kansas land. This led to the acquisition of a huge block of land near Rexford, a few miles northeast of Colby in Thomas County. Foster bought the land after droughts had turned the soil to dust and few people wanted it. He acquired about 16,000 acres in one contiguous plot near Rexford, 5,000 acres in Sherman County to the west, and over 9,000 acres just across the line in Colorado. The combined operation became known as Foster Farms, with its headquarters near Rexford. The

Elevator for storing grain and truck for transporting Foster Farms' show herd, Thomas County. *Courtesy of the Kansas State Historical Society.*

farms were Benjamin's personal enterprise, not that of the family-owned corporation.

Wheat and corn were the main products, with cattle grazing land that could not be farmed and consuming the forage catch-crops. Foster was a successful farm proprietor, applying many of the organizational techniques he had learned in business to his agricultural pursuits. The farm manager was required to keep detailed financial records and send daily reports to Foster's Kansas City office, as well as to report personally in Kansas City several times each year. Foster made infrequent inspection trips to western Kansas, but he knew well what was happening on his farms.

Foster's shrewdest move during the early years of his farming operation was to hire E. D. "Doc" Mustoe as manager. Mustoe, who loved to plant trees in that part of the state where few grew, was extremely capable. He was a good organizer, a fine public-relations person in the community, and a keen judge of livestock. The nickname derived from his esteemed ability to treat sick animals, although he had no formal veterinary training. Mustoe began with Foster in 1918 and continued with the firm until replaced by his son, E. D. (Dale) Mustoe, Jr., many years later. Dale was raised on the farms before attending college and serving in the United States Navy during World War II. After the war Dale returned to assist his father, then took his place when the older Mustoe retired. The two Mustoes were the only managers Foster Farms had prior to its sale in 1965, although there were superintendents over various parts of the operation before Doc Mustoe took over.

Thousands of bushels of wheat and corn were produced during most years, much of which was stored in Foster's elevators that towered above the land. Just after the First World War, some claimed that Foster was the largest independent wheat producer in the world. The farms were for many years a showplace in western Kansas for mechanized agriculture. Beginning during World War I, headers, binders, steam engines, and gasoline tractors were used for much of the work. One report noted that a steam engine pulled six binders that cut a 96-foot swath. More than a score of familes and the 282 men on the payroll for the harvest in 1919 were housed in the numerous buildings on the farm.[20]

Foster Farms had cattle almost from the beginning. A commercial herd of Shorthorns first populated the farm, until a gradual switch to Herefords occurred by using whiteface bulls on Shorthorn cows. Just after Warld War I a small herd of purebred Herefords was established to produce herd bulls for the commercial cattle. The collection of improved breeding cattle grew in size and quality as the outside demand for bulls accelerated. A few hundred cows, a top-notch show herd of ten to fifteen animals, and a total of about a thousand purebred cattle slowly developed.

A fortuitous event, not uncommon in purebred breeding, propelled the herd into the national limelight. Early in the purebred herd's history, Foster Farms purchased two expensive cows from Mousel Brothers, purebred breeders near Cambridge, Nebraska, with the understanding that the cows be with calf by the service of a promising bull named Young Anxiety 4th. One of the cows, Creamette 12th, had a bull calf that in a couple of years was responsible for introducing the quality needed for national fame. This bull,

Foster Anxiety, was the first in a long line of superb males in the Foster herd that included Promino, Beau Promino 25th, Valiant Stanway, and Beau Beauty. The last was the most successful show bull the farms ever had, dominating the circut during the early thirties.

Foster Farms began more than thirty years of show success during the early twenties after Foster Anxiety had bred quality into the herd. From the Cow Palace in San Francisco to the Bluegrass Show in Kentucky, as well as all the major shows in between, Foster Farms' Herefords won more than their share of top prizes. When in 1955 the purebred herd gave way to commercial cattle, Foster Farms had shown for twenty-six consecutive years at the National Western in Denver, one of the longest continuous showings on record for one herd under the same name.

The cattle business was complemented with other livestock. Beginning in 1931, several hundred horses and mules were raised and trained for farm work each year. Most of these animals were sold to farmers, but some were kept at Foster Farms to complement the other sources of power. The gasoline tractor eventually curtailed this segment of Foster's enterprise. Purebred Clydesdales were also acquired during the depressed 1930s. These large beasts were registered and shown well into the 1940s in some of the largest stock expositions in the nation. The Budweiser beer people bought Foster's lead team one year to add to their St. Louis stable of fine Clydesdales.

Foster Farms sold hundreds of purebred bulls to commercial cattlemen in more than a dozen states. A few large auction sales were held at the farms, but in most years return customers absorbed the surplus in private treaty purchases. While the farming and cattle operation was never strapped for money, as were many other operations that existed without outside help, Foster never lavished capital on the farm. Each division was supposed to show a profit each year, and usually did. Foster Farms' success during depressions, and even its expansion during the 1930s into the horse business, illustrated that the operation was economically sound. Excellent management by the Mustoes and their dedication over a long period to Foster's interests account in large part for the success. Foster Farms was a notable example of the combination of mechanized farming and fine livestock on a huge scale. It was a successful, diversified operation.

Today, Foster Farms is divided into a number of smaller operations, many of which are irrigated. While some of the land that was separate from the main plot had been sold earlier, the large farm near Rexford was not put on the market until 1965, several years after Foster's death. A consortium of local businessmen and farmers paid almost $2 million dollars for this large plot and several sets of improvements. The group began almost immediately to resell in smaller plots, retaining what they wanted for themselves from the original purchase. By 1970 most of the land was in the hands of smaller farmers.[21]

The Herefords discussed above had horns, but this is not true of all Herefords. Beginning around 1900 some breeders began to establish the Polled line, arguing that hornless cattle reduced production costs. They also pointed out that more cattle could be shipped in a single railroad car, that less space was required in the feedlot, and that injuries to both stock and owners were reduced. Although cattle were usually dehorned, the breeders of Polled Herefords argued that genetic elimination reduced considerably the work, cruelty, and expense.

Warren Gammon, an Iowa breeder, is usually given credit for initiating the organized development of Polled Herefords. About the turn of the century, Gammon collected a group of what was generally thought to be freak cattle. To this herd of hornless cows he added a polled bull, also a so-called freak, and began establishing the hornless trait in his whole herd.[22]

Breeders of horned Herefords have been slow to accept the polled cattle, especially in the West. There was a surge of popularity during the late 1940s and 1950s among smaller producers in states east of Kansas, but even today there are few polled commercial herds of much size. But their popularity grew as polled cattle improved. Today, Polled Herefords account for about half the whiteface cattle that are recorded, and many believe that their future is exceedingly bright.

The tradition and early acceptance of Herefords with horns reduced the appeal of the Polled Herefords, as did the difficulty of eliminating all horns by using a polled bull. Many cattlemen believed that, if they had to gear up to dehorn some cattle, a few more were little additional work. The principal objection, however, related to quality. "When you breed the horns off you breed the hind-end off," cattlemen charged, and it was true. In order to establish polledness firmly, quality was sacrificed. The surge in popularity in polled cattle followed hard upon the equalization of quality between the two Hereford choices that occurred during the forties and fifties.[23]

Kansas breeders were deeply involved in developing Polled Herefords. Pawnee County, around the small town of Larned, easily became the state's

Polled Hereford capital shortly after World War I. Almost a score of breeders were responsible, but most involved were John M. Lewis and his sons, Walter and Joseph, proprietors of Alfalfa Lawn Farms.

John M. Lewis wandered the country a bit before settling in Kansas. Returning to his home in Illinois after the Spanish-American War, the restless Lewis traveled to Colorado, where he fell in love with alfalfa. He returned to Illinois but could never forget the luxuriant forage crop he had seen growing in the West. When he arrived in the Larned area in 1908 and again found alfalfa growing abundantly, he bought a quarter section of land and stayed for the rest of his life. Alfalfa and Polled Herefords became his stock-in-trade.

Just before the outbreak of World War I, Lewis married the daughter of Wallace Libbey, a charter member of the American Hereford Association. Libbey gave the young couple a choice of $1,000 or ten registered cows as a wedding present. The couple wisely chose the latter, bought a bull named Polled Rollo, and began to develop a polled herd with their Anxiety-bred cows.

Progress was slow during the twenties, but by the thirties the Lewis herd was beginning to draw national attention. Walter and Joe, who were both educated at Kansas State Agricultural College, became more active in managing and running the farm, and the herd grew to several hundred head. Joe began a successful show career in 1939 that has been continued up to the present day and has brought Lewis cattle much publicity. Polled Rollo and his progeny were the early sires; then Victor Dominos became the Lewis hallmark. Walter barely saved this famous bull from passing unnoticed when he rescued him from a carload of young bulls his father was sending to a commercial herd in California. The Victor Dominos are today one of the most popular Polled Hereford families in the nation.

Today, Alfalfa Lawn Farms is a thriving enterprise. During the summer months, green fields of alfalfa surround the neat, stuccoed buildings. Not a blade of grass is out of place on this farm, one of the best-kept in the state. Polled Herefords graze nearby, awaiting buyers that arrive almost daily to select and carry away breeding stock. Most bulls are sold to producers in central and eastern Kansas, but a dotted map in Walter's office reveals that some have gone to almost every part of the United States, as well as to several South American countries and to Mexico, Australia, and New Zealand. The Lewis family is easily the top producer of Polled Herefords in the state and ranks high among the premier breeders of the nation. Joe continues the show herd, while Walter is sometimes called to judge international shows. Walter was also the first breeder of the polled line honored with the presidency of the American Hereford Association. The second generation of the family still controls the Lewis operation, but a third is waiting in the wings.[24]

More recent in gaining a reputation as noted purebred breeders in the state are J. J. Moxley and John Vanier. These two breeders began in the 1930s to fill the gap left by the decline or dispersion of other herds due to the depression. They continue today to fill orders for fine breeding stock. Interests outside the production of beef, especially in the case of Vanier, account in large part for their being able to move successfully into the purebred business during the 1930s.

J. J. Moxley, a beef cattle specialist at Kansas State Agricultural College during the early 1930s where he was involved in the government purchase of drought-stricken cattle, bought in 1935 a small Flint Hills ranch near Council Grove and began to raise cattle. Ten years later, Moxley retired from Kansas State and became more active in developing a herd of purebred Herefords that grew to around 200 head of registered cattle. Moxley is now retired, and his herd is being continued by the family. Many bulls from the herd thus continue to find homes in commercial herds across the state.[25]

John Vanier had a more varied career than did Moxley before he settled into the production of purebred stock. Born and raised in Nebraska, Vanier moved as a young man to Kansas City, where he became a stenographer at the Board of Trade. Thereafter, Vanier advanced himself carefully from flour salesman to the ownership of several flour mills in Kansas, and a meat packing plant.

Vanier's prosperity by the early 1930s enabled him to move easily into ranching and eventually into the production of purebreds. When he began, Vanier claimed that his purebred herd was not a hobby, but was intended to be a solid business in its own right, and in this he has not been disappointed.

During the early thirties Vanier purchased over 5,000 acres near Brookville, Kansas, southwest of Salina, which he called the CK Ranch in honor of central Kansas. In 1936, with cattle prices low and producers of purebreds falling by the wayside, Vanier started his purebred herd. The following year he added over fifty of the best breeding matrons that he could find from the Troublesome Valley herd owned by Fred Grimes in Colorado. This purchase catapulted him into the forefront of Hereford breeding, and in a year he was ready for his first public auction. A new sales pavilion at the CK Ranch was the site of the first auction, and many others followed in quick succession. The bull Onward Domino Jr., who descended from Publican, the bull that

Hazlett had rescued from the Matador, was an early herd sire. He in turn sired CK Onward Domino, a bull that became the fountainhead of several highly advertised Hereford families that were popularized by the CK Ranch. In 1952, for example, a descendant, CK Crusty 46th, topped the National Western sale in Denver at $41,500.

Vanier's herd grew rapidly. Over a thousand registered cattle were reported by 1943, while over a decade later the *Stockman* praised Vanier as the owner of the largest herd of purebred, registered Herefords in the nation. Up to 500 bulls were dispersed annually to cattlemen in Kansas and many other states. Vanier also encouraged many younger breeders by arranging special sales of fine calves to 4-H Club members. Throughout this period Vanier's wife played an active role in making their Herefords prominent, often buying and selling many of the purebred cattle. More recently, their son, Jack, has assumed managerial responsibilities for the family's wide interests. Presently, the family has numerous farming and ranching interests in a half-dozen areas of the state in addition to a large commercial cattle ranch in Wyoming. The headquarters for these far-flung interests, however, remains at the CK Ranch, where the production of some of the best Herefords in the country continues.[26]

Hazlett, Foster, and Vanier represented the large, successful Hereford breeders in the state who were able to survive depressions in order to reap profits when prices improved. And prices were sometimes high. Just after World War I the average individual price for purebred stock sold at auction was close to $500, which was an all-time high until World War II stimulated another boom and average prices rose to over $850 per head by 1951.[27]

But the large, rich breeders of purebred cattle, who could afford to buy the best cattle, to participate repeatedly in the large livestock shows, and to advertise heavily the results of their breeding programs, were responsible for only part of the fine blood that upgraded western cattle. Hundreds of other stockmen who raised only a few purebreds, or perhaps only upgraded common stock, also did much to improve the size, maturing time, and eye appeal of range cattle. These smaller operators raised their own herd bulls or traded with a neighbor who was also upgrading. The lesser-known breeders, who continually emphasized the need for good bulls, were scattered through many states, and Kansas was no exception.

Muriel and Charles Gregg of Coldwater, Kansas, for example, began a purebred herd of about twenty-five cattle in the early 1930s that produced herd bulls for their commercial stock. Fancy cattle for show was not their objective; so the purebreds received little special attention. The Domino line and then bulls from J. J. Moxley's herd and the CK Ranch supplied the outside blood for the purebred herd. The Greggs saved a good deal of money by producing their own herd bulls, and still received the benefits from the best Hereford blood available. A dozen or so of the fine bulls they had used for a couple of years in their commercial herd were sold each year to other cattlemen, reducing still further their expense for sires.[28]

One of the Greggs' neighbors, Clair Parcel, was another example of a small breeder of purebreds, only Parcel eventually became more interested in showing stock than were the Greggs. Beginning with an orphaned purebred heifer in 1937 as a 4-H project, Parcel and his father built a herd of well over a hundred Hereford cows by the early 1950s.

They began with Hazlett bloodlines and kept the herd relatively small during World War II. Much of the surplus was sold in the fine cattle country of southwest Kansas. The severe drought of the early 1950s had a disastrous effect on the Parcels' operation, forcing the sale of all but forty of their finest. When the rain and grass returned, however, so did the Parcels' fine Herefords. Today, using largely Line 1 bulls that were originally developed in Montana from the Advance Domino strain, Parcel has about 300 cows. He became more interested in showing and in a wider market as his herd grew, but still supplies many bulls for the local area.[29]

Though Herefords had no equal in upbreeding cattle in Kansas, as well as in other states west of the Mississippi River, they did have some competition from Angus and Shorthorn cattle. The latter had made their strongest bid for the range country during the nineteenth century, but a few Shorthorns are still used on the grasslands and on the small, diversified farms in eastern Kansas and the Midwest.

While a number of Kansans produced purebred Shorthorns, the Tomson herd southwest of Topeka became the most prominent during the twentieth century. It was during World War I and the postwar boom that James G. Tomson, the genius of the family as far as cattle were concerned, pushed the Shorthorn herd to national stature. Sometimes referred to as "the Hazlett of Shorthorn breeders," Tomson had a herd of well over a hundred cows and supplied many cattlemen with blooded sires. Although Tomson's Shorthorns were never popular in the large range herds of the state, they never lacked buyers. A few were sold as far afield as Australia and South America.

Tomson cattle were most popular during the 1930s and 1940s when they tended to dominate several of the large stock shows, including the American Royal. The Marygolds, Augustas, and Mayflowers, all originally from Scotland, were families of Shorthorns that were especially profitable for the Tomsons. These Shorthorn lines easily made the Tomson herd the best in Kansas as well as one of the finest in the nation during the period between the wars, although the Tomsons were never very aggressive in promoting their herd. As long as the cattle were medium-sized, uniform, quickly fattened, and easy to breed and calve, buyers were plentiful.

The head of the family was joined in the business during the busy 1930s by his son, James G. Thomson, Jr., who still is associated with the herd. James, Jr., was never as interested as his father in the purebred cattle, but was responsible for directing more of the Tomsons' energy into commercial Shorthorns, full and partial feeding of stock, and the production of hybrid seed corn.

A few years before the death of James G. Tomson, Sr., in 1964, the herd that he had worked so diligently to improve began to lose popularity. The fashion among breeders of Shorthorns had changed to a larger type, and the Tomsons were slow to adjust. Through private contracts and a large sale during the early 1970s, most of the herd was dispersed. At the time of the sale, it may have been the oldest herd in continuous ownership in the nation. Today, the Tomsons are not the premier Shorthorn breeders that they once were, but a fourth generation, sons of James G. Tomson, Jr., is still interested in cattle. Someday the present herd of seventy-five cows may produce the wonder bull that will drive the herd back to its former glory.[30]

Although George Grant had brought to Kansas during the 1870s the first black bulls known in the United States, Angus cattle were never as popular in the larger range herds as were the Herefords. Angus bulls were less available, which accounted in part for their being less popular, but the main reason was the overwhelming popularity of the whitefaces. Angus cattle were used some, however, usually in smaller herds in the central and eastern parts of the state.

There were also a few purebred Angus breeders in the state. Most began after 1900, although one of the earliest, T. J. McCreary of Highland, began late in the nineteenth century. McCreary imported his foundation stock from Great Britain, built a fine herd, and then became the source of stock for other herds that were established. Johnson Workman, from around Chapman, an astute Angus breeder, got his foundation stock from McCreary just before World War I. He continued to breed fine Angus stock for several decades and won the grand championship at the American Royal with a carload of his feeder steers in 1927. The Hollinger family of Chapman, the Laflins from Olsburg, and the Ljungdahl family from around Menlo were also prominent in the state's Angus circle, but their herds were usually small when compared to those of the large Hereford breeders.

Some believe that the greatest popularity of the Angus in range production is yet to come. Much improvement in the breed's size and ability to gain rapidly in feedlots has occurred since 1960. Crossbreeding Angus cattle with Herefords or some other breed has helped increase the popularity of the blacks. A few Angus bulls with a herd of Hereford cows is a relatively easy and rapid route to the hybrid vigor that many producers now insist upon.[31]

When many young people abandoned Kansas farms and ranches for service in World War II, they left behind herds of cattle that were often models of upbreeding. Their grandparents would have been amazed at the progress that had been made since the 1890s. Purebred producers were largely responsible for this by making fine herd sires readily available to range producers.

By the late twenties and early thirties the dominance of the east-to-west movement of fine cattle had passed into history, although some stock still moves in this direction. After the boom that was stimulated by World War I, fine cattle tended to move in all directions. Purebreds from Texas and Montana, for example, were sold in Illinois and Kentucky. The Wyoming Hereford Ranch dispersed cattle in all directions, as did many breeders in Kansas and other states. The movement of purebreds had gone full circle.

Kansas was a key state in the upbreeding process. Located at the crossroads of stock movements to and from the West, the state first transferred improved cattle from the Midwest to the range country, then joined in with its own good breeding stock. Some breeders became nationally and internationally famous for their work; but, most important, their improved cattle began to work their magic in the country's large commercial herds. This resulted in more and better beef, and helped keep production costs more in line with market prices.

But upbreeding was not the end of the struggle to reduce production costs and raise profits. During the early twentieth century, among other things, the loss from livestock diseases was reduced, and the state's cattlemen reorganized the association that expressed their collective voice on the economic issues of the day.

6

Mercer Takes Command: Organizations and Livestock Diseases, 1900-1940

Although Joseph H. Mercer owned relatively little livestock he was the most important single cattleman in Kansas for nearly three decades. His dual posts as livestock sanitary commissioner and as executive secretary of KLA were the principal avenues through which this dedicated stockman exerted a major influence on the beef industry in Kansas and throughout much of the West.

Mercer was born on a farm near what is today Batesville, Ohio, on September 7, 1864, the youngest of several children. His father was a farmer who served four years in the Union Army before deserting the family soon after the war. His mother's death left Mercer orphaned at the age of two. He lived the next decade with his maternal grandparents in Ohio before moving to West Virginia to live with Charles F. Mercer, an older brother.

After his own education in a small business college, Mercer taught school in Virginia and then moved to the Sunflower State in 1887, where he took up the grocery business in Cottonwood Falls. This small Flint Hills town and the surrounding area remained his home until duties with the Sanitary Commission and KLA forced a move to the capital. Mercer, when he came to Kansas, had little knowledge of the livestock industry, but friends like the Crocker brothers soon taught him the necessary fundamentals. Groceries then gave way to cattle and a little farming. Mercer retained a financial interest in cattle for most of his life, first operating a small leased ranch near Cottonwood Falls which he managed himself, then, after he moved to Topeka, simply by investing in livestock. Cal Floyd, one of the state's largest feeders and pasturemen, became not only a close personal friend but also an occasional partner with Mercer in investments. As it turned out, however, Mercer's enduring financial interest in cattle was more for love than profit.

Mercer was a little over five and a half feet tall, but his short-legged frame carried well over two hundred pounds. His broad, thick-set shoulders made him appear to be bigger than he really was. A friend once remarked that, when sitting down, Mercer was one of the largest men he had ever seen. His round, kindly face, adorned with glasses in later years, hid a determination that made him a fearless negotiator around a conference table or through his heavy correspondence. Contemporaries said that he was a sympathetic man who was honest, sincere, and tender; but he was a dedicated fighter for any cause that he adopted. As a result, railroad and meat-packing officials often saw him as bull-headed, and not without some justification.

Mercer first gained state recognition in 1906 when he was elected Chase County representative to the Kansas legislature. He served three terms in this position, throwing his influence into the camp of W. R. Stubbs, a progressive politician from Lawrence. Stubbs and Mercer formed a close friendship during these turbulent years in Kansas politics. When Stubbs plodded his way to the governorship in 1909, he appointed Mercer livestock sanitary commissioner. Mercer's influence, moreover, went beyond the area of livestock. A Topeka paper once reported that Stubbs ran his independent administration with the aid of the "Three-Joes'-Kitchen-Cabinet." Joe Mercer was one of the influential three.[1]

Mercer continued to have political ambitions throughout his life, but his seat in the house was the highest elected office he ever held. The gossip around the statehouse during the twenties indicated that Mercer was interested in the gubernatorial race at least twice, and he failed in a serious attempt at a United States senatorial seat in 1932. But it was not for want of ability that Mercer failed to rise in political circles. He would have made an excellent governor or senator, but he had little time to do the necessary spade work for political success. His duties with KLA and the Sanitary Commission kept him on the run continually. Overall, his extended service to the state through these organizations was probably greater than if he had been a higher official. Mercer's name became a household word with Kansas farmers and ranchers and was known in marketplaces throughout the West and Midwest. He was so important to the state's livestock producers that they persuaded him to refuse a presidential appointment to the United States Tariff Commission in 1926.

More than any other individual, Mercer built KLA into an effective state organization. He was the originator and implementor of most KLA activities between 1910 and 1937, and it was to his credit that the association grew to be one of the strongest in the West. He traveled repeatedly across the nation in the interests of the association, consulted personally with presidents and other high federal officials, frequently testified before House and Senate committees, and prepared evidence—which he usually presented himself—for Interstate Commerce Commission investigations. On the state level, Mercer performed many of the same tasks. He was the confidant of governors, occasionally their ambassador, and a persistent lobbyist at legislative sessions, always working through KLA in the interests of the livestock producer.

As sanitary commissioner, Mercer directed the machinery that monitored and protected the state's livestock, and lobbied for disaster payments when cattle disease did strike in the state through no fault of the producers. He directed livestock sanitary affairs for over a quarter of a century and, in so doing, made the Kansas commission one of the most effective in the nation. At his death in 1937, Mercer probably held the record for continuous service in a major appointive state position.

His work load was often overwhelming. Acording to the *Stockman* during the frustrating 1930s, it was more than a mere human "could bear-up under." Mercer's efforts were well spent, though, as the same journal claimed at the time of his death that his actions may have saved Kansas shippers $2 million a year in marketing expenses.

Mercer's ideas on problems associated with production, transportation, and marketing of stock, as well as his philosophy on the relationship of government to individuals and business, became the official position of KLA and of many of the state's producers. He was a loyal Republican in most of his principles, but never failed to support the small producer in his marketing battles with big business. His actions, but not always his words, supported an organized response from farmers and ranchers rather than the hallowed rugged individualism that some spoke of. He belonged to more than a half-dozen organizations that guarded the producer in his dealings with railroads, stockyards, packers, and the public. Mercer, along with many others, believed that a healthy agriculture was absolutely essential for a prosperous national economy. He was not so tradition bound, however, that he could not adjust to the idea of government aid to agriculture. Like many of the Democrats that he worked with, Mercer moved generally from advocating government price supports in the twenties to controlled production in the thirties. In short, he spoke frequently in favor of government support for agriculture so that it might compete better with other sectors of the nation's economy. In much of his thinking, Joe Mercer was ahead of most other agricultural

123

Joseph H. Mercer in his office in the state capitol, 1930s. As executive secretary of KLA and as the Kansas State Livestock Sanitary Commissioner, Mercer was one of the most important stockmen in Kansas and the Southwest for over three decades. *Courtesy of Bess Mercer Conley.*

producers in the state; but the majority, more often than not, fell into line behind him once he had explained his position.[2]

The first step in making KLA more effective was its reorganization, the stimulus for which came from a dispute in 1912 over the Kansas City Connecting Railroad.[3] While most stockmen favored the railroad's position in this dispute when they were compelled to testify before the Kansas Public Utilities Commission, there was enough division in their ranks to suggest that the small KLA needed to be revitalized. Reorganization, they hoped, might empower the association to speak with a unanimous voice for a larger number of the state's 40,000 major cattle shippers. Satisfactory funding of the organization was also a prime consideration in the efforts to reorganize. With reorganization in mind, T. M. Potter, a charter member and president of KLA at the time, appointed a committee of five active producers— Clyde Miller, Arnold Burns, John Hudelson, John A. Edwards, and Mercer— to formulate a constitution and draft by-laws. Balie P. Waggener, the cattlemen's old adversary in their disputes with the railroads, provided legal advice for this endeavor. After several meetings the group announced that the 1913 meeting of the state's stockmen would be for the purpose of ratifying or rejecting their recommendations. At this meeting, which was held in the legislative hall of the state capitol in Topeka, the modern KLA was born. The old, crisis-oriented association was discarded in favor of a more permanent organization which, it was hoped, would speak for a greater number of stockmen. The association claimed to represent all livestock producers in the state, but for the most part it supported sheep and hog men only when their interests coincided with those of the cattle producer. One of the committee's more important suggestions was that KLA hire a permanent, full-time secretary. The 200 shippers in attendance agreed, and Mercer, having served part-time since 1910, accepted the position at an annual salary that fell between $2,000 and $3,000, depending on how much money the association had. Offices for Mercer's work were established in Topeka, Wichita, and Kansas City. Thus began the longest term of any officer in the history of KLA, and the organization never regretted this decision.

Before the Topeka meeting to discuss reorganization began, however, stockmen were promised an exciting fight over the presidency of the association. The incumbent, state legislator T. M. Potter, was opposed by stockyard interests because of his support for the rail lines in the Connecting Railroad dispute. "They wanted Potter's scalp and would be satisfied with nothing less," the Topeka *State Journal* reported. This drew a number of stockmen to Topeka to witness the blood-letting, but the confrontation failed to develop. W. L. "Ironjaw" Brown, a cattleman, legislator, and newspaper editor who three years later disrupted the 1916 KLA convention in his eagerness to declare war on the packers, tried his best to provoke a showdown but to no avail. He nominated Potter for another term in spite of the stockyards people, but the convention chose not to follow Brown's lead. Instead, they settled on William J. Tod— a compromise candidate who was less controversial—and the promised fun was not forthcoming.[4]

Tod, noted earlier for his interest in purebred Herefords, was a wise choice at this time for the presidency. Few in the state were more respected than Tod, and few took a more profound interest in the affairs of the industry. Tod was a frugal, business-minded Scot, who never failed to cut expenses whenever possible. In this connection, his wife was fond of telling how joyfully Tod announced to her one day that the price of gasoline had dropped by a cent a gallon. "Why Willie, what difference does it make to you," she asked, "you've no gasoline buggy?" "Ah, but Margaret," Tod quickly replied, "I've a cigarette lighter."[5]

Tod had begun in the cattle business by managing the large Prairie Land and Cattle Company during the heyday of open-range ranching in the 1880s. He did well in this position and eventually purchased 5,000 acres near Maple Hill in partnership with George Fowler, the son of a meat packer. When the Prairie Land and Cattle Company dissolved, the partners acquired the 56,000-acre Crosselle Ranch near Folsom, New Mexico, a part of the land formerly controlled by the large company. Tod and Fowler insisted on Hereford bulls, some of which were produced at Maple Hill, and their New Mexico ranch became one of the first large spreads in the area to turn out high-grade, uniform calves in large numbers. Many of the steers were shipped to Maple Hill, where they were wintered, grazed on the early bluestem, then shoved into feedlots along Mill Creek for corn finishing.

The Tod-Fowler association continued for more than a decade, being dissolved before World War I, with Fowler keeping the Crosselle and Tod the Flint Hills property. Some believed that Tod's astute management turned his share into the finest small ranch in the state. He continued to buy and finish Crosselle stock for many years, much as his neighbors, the Adams family, were doing with their young cattle. Then, just before his sudden death, Tod purchased the Crosselle Ranch a second time. His son, James, was left with the responsibility after 1928.

Tod was a tall, handsome man who never dressed like a cowboy except for finely tailored boots, one of the few luxuries that he allowed himself. He had a natural dignity, and no one ever questioned his integrity. Fairness and honesty were his hallmarks. In 1913 he was the ideal person to team with Mercer at the head of a reorganized KLA. With Tod at the reins and Mercer in the harness, KLA was well equipped to lead stockmen into the era of the First World War.[6]

KLA's growth in power and influence over the state's cattle industry dates largely from the time it was reorganized. Its growth was reflected by an increase in membership during the first decade of Mercer's tenure as secretary. From the handful of stockmen who had constituted KLA from its origin in 1897 until its reorganization in 1913, the number grew to almost 1,500 in 1917, and to over 4,000 by 1918. The association failed to attain its objective of 10,000 members by the end of World War I but almost reached the coveted goal by the early 1920s. Tod's presidential address to the 1917 KLA convention noted in this relation that KLA was "now recognized as a power in this country, second only to the American National and Texas Association . . . [and] the greatest part of this Association's growth in numbers and in power, is due to the untiring energy, ability and unswerving loyalty of your secretary, Joe Mercer."

Membership, however, was not necessarily indicative of KLA's influence, for almost all the state's producers as well as many others throughout the West were affected by the association's work whether or not they participated in the decision making. Annual meetings were not limited to dues-paying members of the association, and attendance usually exceeded memberships by a large number. This was understandable, as the annual meetings filled several of the industry's needs. Meetings were an important part of the producer's continuing education, providing a relatively rare opportunity for stockmen and their wives to socialize with others in the industry, and serving as a clearing house for the many transactions necessary in the cattle business. Many cattlemen from Kansas and neighboring states left their homes for the mid- or late-winter meetings without a single steer or an acre of grass for their pasturing operation, yet returned having arranged for cattle and grass enough to satisfy their every need.[7]

In addition to hiring Mercer as secretary, one of KLA's more important accomplishments during this decade was the acquisition of an effective means of communication. This, too, was in large part Mercer's idea. After the tumultuous KLA meeting in Wichita in 1916, which gave approval to the scheme, Mercer began negotiations with a Manhattan publisher named Curtis L. Daughters for the publication of association news and general information of interest to stock producers. KLA paid twenty-five cents a year per subscription to have its news printed and sent to each member. The publisher was also obligated to keep one man in the field soliciting KLA members.

The first issue of the bimonthly *Kansas Cattleman* was dated November 1, 1916. In it the publisher noted that the *Cattleman* was to be strictly a livestock paper, a "valuable medium to the breeders," and of "great service to all stockmen." The journal was published in Manhattan under this heading for about a year, then the name was changed to *Kansas Stockman* with the May 20, 1918, issue when a number of sheep and hog producers complained that the paper appeared to be exclusively for the cattle interests. The first name, however, continued to be more descriptive of the paper's contents. Also in 1918 the publishing headquarters were moved to Topeka in order to be closer to KLA offices.

The increased cost for labor and materials as a result of the war proved to be as burdensome for the *Stockman* as it was for the state's producers. When the postwar depression settled down on the country, Daughters was faced with bankruptcy. KLA then purchased the paper and, although Daughters was retained for several years as the *Stockman's* editor, the responsibility for continuing the paper was added to those duties already resting on Mercer's shoulders.[8]

KLA had to its credit by 1920 a dedicated secretary, an expanded membership, and a bimonthly publication. It saved stockmen money by adjusting shipping claims, appearing at rate hearings and market investigations, and negotiating reduced rates for disease serums. It was a clearing house for many pasture contracts and cattle sales, an information bureau for general industry news, and a vehicle through which a large number of the state's leading cattlemen expressed their views. It also lobbied for favorable legislation on both the state and national levels. A 1918 issue of the *Stockman* claimed, "The Kansas Live Stock Association is the second largest state livestock association in the United States. It is the third largest livestock association in America. The Kansas Association has doubled its membership within the last year and with a little more effort on the part of its members it may easily become the most powerful in America within this year."

While a bit exaggerated, these claims were based on more than booming desires and local pride. Of the state stock associations in the West that have been written about by historians, only the Cattle Raisers Association of Texas appeared to have a larger membership. The associations in Nebraska, South Dakota, Wyoming, Montana, and Colorado apparently experienced declines in membership and influence during the war years while KLA was making significant gains. Declining membership and influence were often the result of crisis-oriented associations, as the few solid members of KLA remembered well. With the higher prices that cattlemen received during the war, many saw little need to absorb the added expense of a livestock organization. KLA might have suffered the same fate had members not reorganized and hired Joe Mercer. Finally, only the Texas-based association and the American National exercised more influence on the national level than did KLA, and this continued to be true throughout most of the Mercer era.[9]

Always on the minds of cattlemen to a greater or lesser degree is the problem of stock diseases. While disease was potentially the most costly factor in production, control and eradication of many diseases were often beyond the capabilities of individual stockmen. Consequently, federal and state agencies were created to act in the stockmen's interests. Texas fever, scabies or cattle mange, the dread foot-and-mouth disease, and blackleg—probably the most costly of all—were the ailments of most concern to cattlemen before 1920. There was also some interest in tuberculosis and brucellosis, but the major efforts at eradicating these two came after the First World War.

Mercer's second large responsibility was his position as livestock sanitary commissioner in Kansas. This state-financed agency promoted scientific research, issued quarantines, made regular inspections, and performed many other duties that were necessary for the health of livestock in the state. The work was critical in reducing the cost of production and in raising profits. While the commission had been in existence for some time, it often suffered from inept political appointees, controversies over its authority, and a lack of confidence in its decisions. Mercer soon corrected these faults.

Kansas, being the crossroads of much stock travel between the West and the midwestern feeding and marketing centers, was intensely interested in controlling livestock diseases. This interest had led the state to participate in some of the earliest quarantines against Texas fever, and also to the comparatively early formation of a State Sanitary Commission, now known as the Animal Health Department.

The Sanitary Commission had sprung from events that occurred during the 1880s. After increasing amounts of Texas fever and scabies appeared in the state—there was also a mistaken belief that foot-and-mouth was present—a few prominent stockmen in 1884 pressured Governor G. W. Glick into calling a special session of the legislature. Glick, the state's first Democratic governor and also a noted Shorthorn breeder in the Atchison area, was quite sympathetic to livestock interests. The special session created a joint committee to investigate conditions and recommend legislation. After a summer of hearings by the group in 1884, the regular meeting of the legislature in 1885 created the Sanitary Commission, which consisted of a three-member advisory board and a state veterinarian secretary. The legislature charged the new commission with establishing quarantines, examining cattle and issuing certificates of health to imported or exported stock, and diagnosing diseased animals. The three commissioners were required to be active producers engaged in farming or ranching. Later, it was learned that the members' private interests encroached too severely on their public duties. Thus, in 1905, the commission of three men was abolished in favor of a permanent livestock sanitary commissioner, a post that is still part of the state's administrative machinery.[10]

The Sanitary Commission achieved only moderate success in stopping the spread of disease into the state during the nineteenth century, as might have been expected, because the three commissioners served only part-time and governors sometimes used the agency to repay political debts. After 1915, Mercer was regularly reappointed as director, and his steady tenure was of great value to the commission and the state's cattlemen. Try as it might, however, the commission was unable to prevent periodic outbreaks of disease and severe losses to stockmen.[11]

Besides recommending a Sanitary Commission, the 1884 legislative committee also suggested that Kansas State Agricultural College could help livestock interests in the state. "We recommend," the group said, "that a chair of veterinary science be established in the State Agricultural College." The college's compliance with this recommendation proved to be of immeasurable benefit to producers in Kansas and throughout the West, although the graduation of veterinarians was delayed until the twentieth century.

The value of a department of veterinary science became most evident to stockmen when a preventive for blackleg was developed. Blackleg is an infectious disease, usually fatal, to which young cattle are especially susceptible if not vaccinated. A plague for cattlemen, blackleg was one of the most costly of diseases because it could sweep through a whole herd in a short period of time. Some estimates suggested that 10 to 20 percent of the yearly calf crop was lost to the disease in areas where it was prevalent. There was no cure and prevention was the only safeguard. Once infection began in an area, preventing its spread was virtually impossible. The blackleg-causing organism attacked animals during a vegetative stage, and when this form was exposed to air it produced tiny spores that lived in the ground for years. Animals in a pasture or feedlot might ingest the spores with their feed and contract the disease years after an earlier siege in the same area.

Many attempts at curing and preventing the disease had been made before an effective vaccine was developed at the Kansas college. Some of these supposed cures were folk medicine of the poorest sort, a few bordered on witchcraft, and a number were extremely cruel. All were ineffective. One cure during the 1890s that was advised for Kansas stock involved sewing "red precipitate and lard-soaked muslin strips" into the calf's hide until the disease passed or the calf died. In this case the cure was probably more deadly than the disease. Other cures involved the use of pellets or powders made from the processed meat of victims of the disease. Many of these attempts to produce vaccine derived from one that had developed in France about 1883.

By 1905 Kansas State Agricultural College was sending to western stockmen each year several hundred thousand doses of a serum made from the tissue of blackleg victims. The Bureau of Animal Industry even became involved in financing these early serums, but all proved ineffective. Some calves lived while others died, and cautious cattlemen often vaccinated several times and still lost stock. In processing the dead tissue, too much heat killed the disease-causing germs and rendered the serum impotent, while too little heat left a serum that killed the animals that were inoculated. A serum that was consistently strong enough to immunize yet weak enough not to cause the full effects of the illness remained undeveloped until the second decade of the twentieth century.

Oliver M. Franklin, a gangling, reticent Oklahoma farm boy who grew to maturity in Kansas, is usually given credit for developing an effective vaccine. Today his name is used as a hallmark of quality on many veterinary supplies. First educated at, then employed by, the Kansas college, Franklin was a young veterinarian when the serum was developed. Credit for this discovery, however, is due others as well as Franklin. As with most scientific developments, Franklin's remarkable breakthrough was based on much work that had gone before.

Dr. Francis S. Schoenleber, a man of brilliant intellect who came to the college from Chicago in 1905, established a veterinary curriculum and then began work to improve the serum that the college was already producing. Research progressed slowly until 1912 when Schoenleber managed to raise enough funds, some from other departments, to begin elaborate testing. He developed what was called a hyperimmune serum. Calves were injected with virulent blackleg germs; after the calves had produced antibodies, they were bled. The clear serum was filtered from the blood, and then used to vaccinate other cattle. The serum was more effective than earlier ones but still provided only temporary protection. What cattlemen really needed was a single dose vaccine to give lifetime immunity, or at least one that lasted until young cattle had passed the most susceptible age.

Thomas P. Haslam also shared in the development of medicines to protect against blackleg. He and Franklin were among the first veterinarians trained by Schoenleber at the Kansas school, and both were employed as researchers after completing their studies. Haslam worked principally on hog cholera, but he helped perfect filtering techniques in this country that were being developed simultaneously by scientists in Europe as well as researchers in Japan.

By the time of World War I the stage was set for Franklin's momentous breakthrough. Applying the fruits of research by others and discoveries already made at the college, Franklin perfected and standardized a pure vaccine that answered the cattlemen's prayers. Fortunately, the expensive filtering equipment that allowed the immunization properties of the blood from diseased animals to become part of the vaccine, yet excluded the living blackleg germ, was imported from Germany shortly before the war. At last, a one-dose, lifetime-immunity vaccine was available. The serum, which became known as the Kansas Germ-Free Vaccine, spread throughout the nation once its effectiveness was demonstrated.

Franklin continued to work with blackleg serums, acquiring new information and perfecting the original discoveries. In 1945, the *Stockman* claimed, a bit too exclusively for Franklin, that he had developed the "germ-free" liquid vaccine in 1916, as well as a "blackleg bacterin" in 1923. The journal claimed further, "History, verified by the U.S. Patent Office and the United States Courts, allocates to Dr. O. M. Franklin the distinction of contributing to mankind the two basic steps that led to the present control of Blackleg in cattle."[12]

Little excitement accompanied the first announcements of Franklin's new vaccine, but this was understandable. Cattlemen had heard of blackleg cures before. But with continued testing and Franklin's willingness to treat some well-known herds, acceptance was hastened. Soon after Franklin perfected his vaccine he received a frantic call from the Crocker brothers, whose large purebred herd was losing calves at an unprecedented rate. The herd had been reasonably clean of blackleg for many years, but somehow the disease had gotten started and the Crockers were threatened with financial disaster. Franklin had enough vaccine from a new batch when the plea for help came, but he had not had time to test its safeness. Undaunted, Franklin treated 600 of the calves with the untested vaccine. Some anxious moments followed but none of the calves died, and his success was noted far and wide.

A year or so later, Franklin had the opportunity to break a siege of blackleg in an Abilene feedlot owned by a Colorado banker-cattleman, Charles Collins. This time he used safety-tested vaccine. With demonstrations such as these, along with hundreds of other uses that resulted in no death, or very few, orders began to pour into the college so rapidly it was impossible to fill them.

Companies sprang up in Kansas, first in Wichita and then in a number of other cities, to produce the long-sought medicine. Franklin immediately moved into the commercial manufacture and sale of the vaccine, along with his continued research. He was involved in the Wichita venture, and when he saved much of the Charles Collins herd, he was able to entice the banker into the business. Collins invested heavily, building at once a large new plant in Amarillo, Texas.

Kansas cattlemen were aided by KLA in getting the new vaccine. Within a year or so of Franklin's disovery, Mercer negotiated a contract for the production and sale of the new vaccine to association members at a figure slightly above cost. The usual expense of fifty cents a head for immunization was reasonable for the time, considering the options, but even this price was reduced later as production techniques grew more efficient.

Before long the amount of blackleg vaccine used exceeded all other cattle medicines. The federal government helped some individual producers by providing free vaccine, but it was not until the twenties that most cattlemen accepted the necessity of vaccinating all calves. Widespread use of the serum helped to eliminate the cattleman's fear that he might "buy a disease" when he brought in new livestock. Thousands of cattle escaped the scourge, eventually providing more meat for the American table.[13]

While scientists at Kansas State worked on a blackleg preventive, Mercer was confronted with other disease problems. During the fall of 1912 Kansans experienced, for instance, what was probably the worst epidemic ever to affect the horse population. It certainly was the most serious situation that Mercer faced during his first term as sanitary commissioner.

About half the counties in western Kansas were struck at this time by what was commonly called "horse plague." It was, according to newspaper accounts, caused by a parasite that invaded the horses digestive system, then formed "palisade worms" in the animal's artery system. Death usually resulted. The only known cure at the time was the removal of horses from pastures that were infected and the application of a "laxative of some kind, say a quart of [raw linseed] oil and two ounces of turpentine to the dose, for a few days." Dead horses were burned in an attempt to destroy the parasite. These fires were so extensive, one paper reported, "the skies of western Kansas glow at night with the funeral fires of plague-stricken horses." Towards the end of the plague's visitation, Mercer reported that it had already killed over 4,000 horses, valued at close to half a million dollars. Mercer believed that it was the "most serious situation Kansas had ever faced" up to that time in the area of livestock diseases. With the onset of cold weather, the disease subsided and Mercer turned to other problems, although not as sanitary commissioner. A change in governors brought Sam S. Graybill and then Taylor Riddle to the post for two years before Mercer returned for his extended stay in office.[14]

Two years after the siege of horse plague, Kansas stockmen were alerted to another danger. In 1914 the worst outbreak of foot-and-mouth disease in United States history occurred in the Midwest. This scourge, endemic to Europe and the Orient, was extremely contagious; invariably killed the cattle, hogs, or sheep that it struck; and had no cure. Preventive measures were limited to quarantines and the destruction of infected animals. Foot-and-mouth had been known in the United States since the 1870s. There had been small periodic outbreaks, or the mistaken diagnosis of such, several times in the late nineteenth century. In 1902 and 1908 the disease appeared again, but in each case it was stamped out with vigorous slaughter campaigns costing thousands of dollars.

None of these outbreaks in the early 1900s apparently affected Kansas, but subsequent developments were another story. An epidemic in 1914 started from unknown origins in Michigan, where veterinarians first identified it as vesicular stomatitis before its true identity became evident. The latter was a less serious affliction that superficially resembled foot-and-mouth. Hogs shipped from Michigan apparently carried the infection to the Chicago stockyards, and from there it easily spread to some twenty-two states. About 200,000 animals with a value estimated at $7 million were infected and eventually destroyed. Stockmen, who had to bear most of the cost, were understandably reluctant at times to follow the destruction orders of federal agents. Before the disease was brought under control, most stock movements in the Midwest and East had been suspended, and the stockyards in St. Louis and Chicago were temporarily closed.[15] This foot-and-mouth epidemic did not reach Kansas until early the following year, as prompt quarantines by the sanitary commissioner against inshipped stock from the infected areas delayed its spread into the state.

On January 27, 1915, the Wichita *Eagle* carried a warning from Riddle to the state's stockmen and to the state veterinarian of Missouri that the Kansas quarantine was being circumvented. Cattle from states that had been infected the previous year were being sent to market in St. Joseph and Kansas City, then reshipped into Kansas as Missouri cattle. Three days after Riddle's warning, his worst fears were confirmed when foot-and-mouth was diagnosed in Cowley and Sedgwick counties among high-grade dairy cattle that had been imported from Wisconsin, apparently contrary to regulations. The disease was also discovered in Sumner County and among feeder stock in Butler County, but this appeared to be its limit within the state.

The Kansas legislature immediately appropriated $10,000 for eradication work, then later made as much as $300,000 available if it was needed. All stock movement within the state was suspended except for horses and mules, which were never affected, and other stock that was moving to market for immediate slaughter. By July the disease had been eliminated and the stock industry was slowly returning to normal. Over $76,000 was paid in equal parts by the state and federal governments for the stock that was destroyed, with the largest single payment of over $32,000 going to James W. Teter, an oilman and cattle producer from around El Dorado. The payments were not full compensation for economic losses but did make it possible for most of the affected producers to survive. A few stockmen lost several thousand dollars worth of feed, for which there was no compensation, and most incurred losses from delays in marketing and the temporary price slumps.[16]

This episode in 1915 ended foot-and-mouth in Kansas, although periodic threats occurred with a degree of frequency. One such scare materialized near Salina in 1916 when a federal veterinarian erroneously diagnosed foot-and-mouth among several cars of cattle shipped in from Nebraska. Confusion abounded, quarantines were issued, and about a hundred cattle were destroyed before the disease was correctly identified as vesicular stomatitis.[17] But for the most part, the sanitary commissioner was spared the press of emergencies like the foot-and-mouth alarms. Instead, he spent his time with more routine administrative tasks and the careful scrutiny of less contagious diseases. An exception was his continuous struggle with hog cholera.

The foot-and-mouth episode in 1914 and 1915 contributed to the appointment of Mercer as sanitary commissioner a second time to replace the harassed Taylor Riddle. Mercer had served a four-year term earlier during the administrations of Republican Governor Stubbs, but when the Democrats won the statehouse with Hodges in 1913 Mercer was replaced. Arthur Capper's gubernatorial success in 1915, as well as the foot-and-mouth debacle, brought Mercer back into the commissioner's office, although Governor Capper noted that Riddle had done an adequate job. Mercer was reluctant to add any public duties to those he was already performing for KLA, but finally accepted at the insistence of the governor and the state's leading cattlemen.

Mercer remained the commissioner until his death in 1937. This long tenure, in place of short appointments that tended to change each time a new governor took office, marked the most significant development in the commissioner's office in over three decades. For several years leading stockmen in the state had urged acceptance of the idea that livestock health was not a matter that should be subject to the whims of political appointees. Instead, they believed, the office should be taken "out of politics," and KLA should have the responsibility of nominating the person to be appointed by the governor. This plan came to fruition in 1915, when Governor Capper appointed Mercer, and became state law in 1919, when the legislature required that to qualify for his appointment the commissioner must have KLA endorsement and at least ten years of experience producing livestock.[18] As a result, the state's livestock producers had effective control of this important agency. The arrangement has continued up to the present day, although the posts of sanitary commissioner and KLA executive secretary were separated during the 1960s.

After World War I Mercer directed the Sanitary Commission increasingly toward the solving of other problems. The depressions and the narrowed profit margins, if profits existed at all, added urgency to the need to reduce the cost of disease. The nature of the Kansas industry, with its large inshipment of out-of-state cattle each year, also added burdens to Mercer's willing shoulders. Interstate movement of stock always increased the chances of spreading disease, especially if the state and federal agencies were not constantly alert.

Tuberculosis was a killer, as was brucellosis—sometimes called bangs disease or contagious abortion—and blackleg continued to kill for a few years after the war. The dreaded foot-and-mouth made no appearance in the state after the epidemic in 1915, due to the continued vigilance of Mercer and his immediate embargoes against Texas cattle when the disease appeared there in 1924 and 1925.[19] Embargoes against other states were never popular but were necessary for the state's livestock industry.

Blackleg and Texas fever continued to decline after the war; the former because of the greater acceptance and use of the Kansas blackleg vaccine, and the latter because the war on the tick was being won. By 1920 stockmen, government agencies, and several stock associations had exerted efforts that spanned more than three decades in their attempts to control the tick-induced Texas fever. Scientific developments spearheaded by the Bureau of Animal Industry, especially in discovering the cause and method of transmission, as well as the application of preventive dips, had reduced enormously the losses due to this disease. Constant vigilance and the various quarantine restrictions had also helped curtail the tick's movement throughout the West.[20]

In addition to improved livestock health and more meat for the consumer, the scientific work that was done to eradicate stock diseases had other implications for society as well. Some diseases were communicable to humans, and research on animal diseases sometimes led to breakthroughs in discovering preventives for diseases that affected people. Work on the tick is a good example. One historian has even claimed that in some ways the research on the tick was a great boon to humans. "Teddy Roosevelt," he said, "couldn't have completed the Panama Canal without it." Apparently, Texas fever was the first disease caused by a microparasite that was discovered to attack its victim after being carried by an intermediate host, namely the tick. Scientists later discovered that ticks and mosquitoes provided the same service to small organisms, and applied this knowledge toward conquering tropical fevers, an accomplishment that might have been delayed without the earlier work of the Bureau of Animal Industry.[21]

Although Texas fever was not a serious disease problem in Kansas between the wars, it did provide KLA and Joe Mercer with one of their proudest moments and, in the end, one of their best-advertised successes. During the late summer of 1919 several carloads of Texas cattle had been shipped into Wabaunsee County after they had been declared free of ticks by federal inspectors at Ft. Worth. In due course, several of the cattle sickened and died from Texas fever. The disease then spread to other fields. Almost immediately more than thirty cattlemen demanded nearly $270,000 in federal compensation on the basis of employee negligence. Mercer, ably assisted at times by John Hudleston, a member of a long-time ranching family in Pomona, Kansas, represented in Washington KLA's claim for over a quarter of a million dollars. Mercer was most effective through the pressure he was able to exert on the Kansas congressional delegation, and through his repeated testimony before several committees and the briefs and affidavits he prepared. Finally, after extensive maneuvering, Congress approved a bill in 1925 which allowed the claimants to bring suit against the government for negligence. A few months later a federal court in Kansas City found the claim justified and suggested the amount of compensation. The following year, almost seven years after the cattle were stricken, Congress awarded the thirty-three different claimants a total of $251,703. The *Stockman* joyfully announced that it was a "red letter day for the Kansas Livestock Association."

For its services, KLA received a percent of the claim—reported to be enough to finance its activities for 1927—as did a Wichita law firm, yet enough money remained to compensate adequately the claimants. After the local press reported that Mercer had returned from Washington with a quarter of a million dollars, his Topeka home was burglarized. The family guessed that the thief believed the payment had been made in cash.[22]

Because the tick was now under control, cattlemen became more concerned with other diseases. A relatively new disease, anaplasmosis, became clinically distinguishable from Texas fever, and it caused some problems in western states. Kansas had an outbreak of anaplasmosis in 1926, but it was soon brought under control. Cattle mange was a problem in the state during the early 1920s, especially in the western part, where quarantines and much dipping were necessary. Efforts of the sanitary commissioner and the local stockmen eventually curtailed the disease, but it was never completedly eliminated.[23]

The most costly diseases for cattlemen after Texas fever and blackleg declined, however, were tuberculosis and brucellosis. Eradication of both of these began with dairy stockmen, then spread slowly to purebred and range producers. Tuberculosis received attention first because of its greater incidence and the potential for humans to contract this cattle malady, although the human and bovine strains are different. Serious tuberculosis eradication efforts began with a joint federal-state program in 1917, but it was not until the 1920s that Kansas and many other states began extensive efforts. Once testing and slaughter had established that less than half of 1 percent of its stock were infected, a county was given a "modified free" rating. Early in the twenties Kansas efforts were hampered by small appropriations to match the available federal funds, as well as by the complicated and troublesome testing procedures.

Many range producers resisted testing efforts until they realized that cattle from modified free areas tended to sell better than those from unaccredited counties. By 1930 about half the counties in the state had been declared free of tuberculosis; then, with the slaughter of many diseased animals in 1934, the whole state was listed as free in 1935. Kansas was the nineteenth state, Mercer proudly announced, to be so honored. By 1940 the whole nation as well as Puerto Rico was declared to have less than half of 1 percent of its cattle infected with tuberculosis, down from a figure of over 4 percent in 1922. Federal and state governments had spent over $310 million in this cooperative effort, while cattlemen, it was estimated, saved over $150 million a year as a result.[24]

Serious efforts at controlling brucellosis were not begun until the 1930s. Then, with a more effective vaccine that was developed by USDA scientists and with the opportunity to slaughter large numbers of diseased stock because of the drought, dedicated attention was given to this costly disease, especially in dairy herds. In 1934 it was estimated that 11.5 percent of all the cattle in the country were infected, but after a decade of eradication work the figure was reduced to 2.4 percent. By this time, most of the diseased stock were range cattle; thus these stockmen became more concerned with vaccinations. Brucellosis was not completely eliminated, however. Even on the basis of the relatively low percentage of cases that existed during the middle 1950s it was estimated that the disease still cost producers $45 million annually.[25]

By World War II notable progress had been made in the area of cattle health. Texas fever, blackleg, tuberculosis, scabies, and foot-and-mouth, for example, had all been eliminated or drastically curtailed. Despite the notable efforts of this period, however, various parasites, brucellosis, anthrax, and shipping fever still afflicted cattle; but even in these areas progress was being made. How much money disease control saved cattlemen or returned to them in augmented profits is impossible to determine, but it certainly amounted to many millions of dollars. This was an important consideration when market prices were usually low. The health of humans was also improved. In Kansas the movements to improve and protect animal health were led by Mercer and the commission that he headed. This agency was effective and surprisingly free of controversy. Much of the commission's work frequently was done in conjunction with federal money and personnel, and this assistance represented no small contribution to the state's livestock industry.[26]

Mercer, the orphaned schoolteacher from Virginia, was the engine in the machine that made things happen in the Kansas beef industry. His work with KLA and with the Sanitary Commission was significant and fruitful, but controlling diseases and cutting losses from them were not the only areas to attract his attention or that of the state's cattlemen as a whole. Once producers had cut to the quick their home production costs, the only other way to raise profits was to reduce marketing expenses. This they attempted to do by working for better rates from the railroads.

7

David and Goliath in Kansas: Cattlemen and Railroads, 1900-1920

Cattlemen, when their stock was ready for market, encountered large corporate interests—first the railroads, then the stockyards and packers. Cattlemen in the early part of the twentieth century were necessarily dependent on the rail lines, just as they had been during the nineteenth. Driving their cattle to market, of course, was no longer possible, and only during the war years did trucks begin to provide an alternative to rail transport. Even then, only a few stockmen chose this method. Consequently, most producers found the railroads essential, and their only recourse was to change or modify those railroad policies that they disapproved of.

Most of the disputes between shippers and transportation lines that had surfaced during the closing years of the nineteenth century continued into the early twentieth. As far as cattlemen were concerned, forestalling higher shipping rates was by far the most important concern in their dealings with rail lines. After an increase in rates during the early years of the new century, stockmen were generally successful in maintaining stable tariffs until the government took over the lines toward the end of the war.

Kansas cattlemen continued to employ several techniques in their dealings with rail lines. Approaches by individuals and small groups were made, the young KLA became active at times, and the established state agencies that were charged with regulating the carriers were frequently called upon to represent the shipping interests. Regulatory measures at both the national and state levels, which were in part stimulated by the Progressive movement, also affected the relationship of cattlemen and railroads during this period. The new regulations, much to the cattlemen's delight, were all designed to limit what stockmen believed to be the arbitrary power of the carriers. Several

141

of the state's cattlemen figured prominently in getting legislation that was designed to curtail railroad power.

As the Populist element in Kansas politics faded during the early twentieth century, a new progressive group took up the banner of reform. Operating within the Republican Party—a party that had been dominated by conservative factions that fed, to some extent, on slush funds provided by the offices of the state's treasurer and printer—the reform politicians were led by such men as Walter R. Stubbs, Victor Murdock, Edward W. Hoch, and William Allen White. These reformers engaged in "boss-busting," forced several realignments in political circles, controlled the legislature and the governorship at times, and were responsible for some significant legislation affecting the shippers' continuing fight with the railroads.[1]

Walter R. Stubbs, the fighting Quaker contractor from Lawrence, was particularly significant in this progressive movement. After almost a decade of leading the reform group in the Kansas house, where he demonstrated repeatedly that he was skilled in political maneuvering, Stubbs won the gubernatorial race in 1908. He served two consecutive terms as governor, then lost his bid for a United States Senate seat in 1912. Another drive for the same office was turned back in 1920, as were gubernatorial attempts a few years later. Stubbs was also a stockman, active in KLA and other stock associations for many years, but he is most remembered for his political activities.

Stubbs was one of the most colorful politician-cattlemen the state has ever had. Born in 1858, the second son in a brood of twelve children, Stubbs moved with his family to a small Quaker community near Lawrence shortly after the Civil War. There the young, freckle-faced Stubbs, not "a bit handsome" by some accounts, began his meteoric rise to fortune. Displaying great energy and enthusiasm, he advanced from selling hedge plants to trading horses and eventually to farming. He was not yet twenty years old when he bought a grain binder and began custom harvesting, sometimes working far into the night with another person carrying a lantern ahead of his rig.

During the 1890s, Stubbs developed a commissary car business to service construction workers who labored on canals and railroads. From this he moved easily into railroad construction. He also won contracts to build canals and to construct the Republic Steel and Iron mills in Chicago and two additional stories to the Marshall Field & Co. wholesale house in the same city.

By the time he entered Kansas politics and turned his financial interests more toward farming and ranching, he was already a rich man. That fortune, incidentally, was wiped out in the postwar depression.

Stubbs was an imposing figure, six feet tall and two hundred pounds of dynamic energy, with a mop of unkempt reddish-blond hair that looked as if it was seldom touched by a barber. His speeches were often as entertaining as they were informative. Beginning with the unfashionable broad-brimmed hat of Quaker tradition, Stubbs discarded articles of clothing as fast as he sent barbs toward his political opponents. Continually speaking on the evils of big business and political influence, he sometimes punctuated his addresses by dispensing with his handkerchief, peeling off his coat, and throwing away his shirt cuffs and vest, all timed and calculated to emphasize a particular point. Finally, amid shouts of approval from his audience, Stubbs rolled up his sleeves and revealed a red woolen undershirt, a mark of his humble beginnings. The crowd loved the speaker's showmanship, if not always the substance of the speech.

Like many progressives of his day, Stubbs was not an advocate of equal rights for women. "No women stenographers for Governor-Elect Stubbs," a Topeka paper reported. "Their place is at home making salt-rising bread." The governor, it was said, "won't have 'em." Although women were the foundation of the family and the country, Stubbs believed, their support should be rooted in the home.[2]

Stubbs and his progressive associates committed their maximum effort to reducing the influence of railroads on Kansas politics, which would be to the advantage, they felt, of the state's shippers. During the nineteenth century, declared the anti-Populist William Allen White, the railroads had meddled in the state's political affairs in order to "defend their own interests against unscrupulous demagogues." White generally blessed the railroads' efforts at this time, although not all agreed with his analysis. It was true, however, that the railroads' interest in politics was visible well before 1900. When the influence persisted into the next century, a reconstructed White and a number of other state leaders who had opposed populism found the situation intolerable.

The Union Pacific, Missouri Pacific, and Rock Island railroads were most active in political circles, according to White, while the Santa Fe was usually exonerated of any serious transgressions. Free passes were considered the railroads' major source of influence, a favor that was used to pressure both the delegates to conventions and the members of the state legislature. Influence over legislators, it was said, enabled the railroads to "steal taxes [and] continue the inequalities and injustices of rates." Railroads also attempted to influence the choice of judges, United States senators, and members of state regulatory agencies. In short, railway lobbyists were a dominant force at this time in the Grand Old Party in Kansas.[3]

Cattlemen, like the railroads, also worked to influence the state legislature, but their power was small compared to that of the roads. As a result, stockmen wanted stronger railroad laws and a direct primary in order to reduce the power the roads had in state nominating conventions. Two Flint Hills cattlemen, along with Stubbs, were as effective as any in pushing the legislature along these lines. George Plumb and C. A. Stannard, respectively the secretary of KLA and the owner of Sunny Slope farm, were both elected to the legislature in 1904 and continued to represent the stock interests in one capacity or another for several years. Joe Mercer and John A. Edwards, both of whom served about the same time, were also influential stockmen-legislators.[4]

State railroad legislation in Kansas during the early 1900s roughly paralleled the Elkins, Hepburn, and Mann-Elkins Acts at the federal level, all of which were designed to end rebates, regulate freight and passenger rates, and increase the powers of the regulatory agencies. The first Kansas legislature of the new century faced immediately the task of establishing a new regulatory agency, since the state supreme court had declared the Court of Visitation unconstitutional the previous year. They responded by recreating the old Kansas Board of Railroad Commissioners with powers to supervise service and to investigate and fix rates subject to judicial review. The new law provided that an executive council of the legislature, rather than the governor, should designate the three commissioners. In general, the board was somewhat stronger than its nineteenth-century counterpart, but it still remained inadequate from the shippers' point of view. They wanted the board to have enforceable rate-making powers, and they demanded the right to elect the commissioners at large.[5]

In 1903 the legislature again attacked unsuccessfully the rate-making powers of the board, but did establish the popular election of the commissioners. The latter provision was important to stockmen. It led to the election of James W. Robison, president of KLA, to the board in 1905, establishing a precedent regarding representation that cattlemen were inclined to press in subsequent years.[6]

The progressive 1907 legislature, dominated in large part by Stubbs, accomplished more toward diminishing railroad influence in the state than did any other session during the early years of the twentieth century. Among other things, the legislature provided a fine of $100 a day for any railroad in violation of maximum rates set by the board. More importantly, it established a bill to limit passes and set in motion the move toward two cents per mile passenger fares. George Plumb, along with Stubbs, deserved much credit for the lower fares.[7]

Though rate setting by the board remained a nebulous power, the antipass bill was a major step toward reducing the railroads' use of passes for political purposes. When the prohibition against passes was linked to the law requiring a general primary in Kansas, which Stubbs and the progressives forced through a 1908 special session, White commented, a bit prematurely, that "the oligarchy of politics—like the lords and nobles of feudal times—is passing away under the enlightenment of the people." He also noted that "with the passing of the primary law the title to the governor, to the congressmen and to the two United States senators, passed from the railroads to the people of Kansas forever."[8] The state legislature in enacting these laws had, in effect, legislated practically the whole Populist program that was so much scorned during the 1890s.

Despite White's early optimism, opinion was divided on the effectiveness of the new regulations. When George Plumb ran successfully for a place on the Kansas Board of Railroad Commissioners, the Emporia editor noted that this agency, "if a good one, can perhaps do more for Kansas than any member of congress or the governor. If a bad board, it can certainly do more harm." A letter to the *Gazette* and several complaints by shippers to Stubbs while he was governor indicated that supervision of the railroads left much to be desired.[9]

Most difficult was the setting of freight rates, because there was no basis from which to work. In the case of litigation over rates, the courts generally sided with the roads. Shippers agreed that rates should provide a fair return on the actual investment of the railroads, but no one knew exactly how much capital investment was involved. Just prior to World War I the Interstate Commerce Commission was directed to assess the true value of railroad property, but due to the war and the complicated nature of the question, no system of equitable rates based on capital investment resulted from the work of the ICC.[10]

Federal and state legislation by World War I had made some progress in regulating the carriers, but problems remained. The railways' political influence in Kansas had been curtailed somewhat. General fregiht rates had not advanced significantly but neither had they been reduced, as most shippers demanded. It may be that added expenses for the railroads justified their refusal to reduce rates. State taxes across the nation per mile of rail line, for example, increased 140 percent between 1900 and 1916, and the total number of workers went up by 50 percent. On the other hand, increased expenses did not mean that the railroads were going broke. The Santa Fe claimed in its annual reports that total taxes advanced roughly parallel to net income during the period and that total expenses, including taxes, rose only from 63 to 66 percent of revenue. Net corporate income for the period more than tripled from $11.0 million in 1900 to $38.1 million in 1916.[11]

The state regulatory agency had also been strengthened during this period. In fact, when the Public Utilities Commission was created in 1911 to replace the old Board of Railroad Commissioners, state supervision was extended to include stockyards and commission merchants. Rapidly, and often at the urging of railroads, however, the ICC was usurping many of the activities of state agencies that related to freight tariffs, even in relation to intrastate rates. This tendency became more pronounced after World War I.[12]

In addition to the general leglislation affecting railroads that cattlemen and most other shippers called for during the early 1900s, cattlemen continued to battle the roads on other levels. They occasionally used KLA as a tool for prying concessions from the lines, but for the most part the association remained relatively inactive until a real or supposed crisis sparked new interest. This was true until its reorganization in 1913. No record, for example, was discovered of any KLA gathering for the period between the third meeting in 1899 and a Wichita convention of stockmen in September, 1903. But a crisis that developed in 1903 brought the association to life temporarily and sent stockmen scurrying across the state.

Under the sensational headline "Raise in Tariff Means Ruin of Cattle Business," the Topeka *Daily Capital* for August 26, 1903, announced new rates that were scheduled to take effect September 1, and reported that many cattlemen were in the capital to protest them. Among those present were sixty members of KLA, with more expected momentarily. George Plumb, still secretary of the association, had initiated a hearing before the railroad commissioners by filing a complaint against the railroads operating in Kansas.

Plumb's action was necessary because the commissioners could act only after there were formal complaints.[13]

Balie Waggener, a Missouri Pacilc attorney, took the lead in presenting the railroads' case. He first argued that the board had no jurisdiction because it had been constituted to review existing rates, not those merely proposed. In addition, he suggested that there was a critical question of whether interstate or intrastate commerce was involved because the Kansas City stockyards and the railroads' business offices were on both sides of the Kansas-Missouri line. After the board rejected Waggener's jurisdictional argument, the railroads' attorneys attempted to justify the rate increase on the basis of the roads' failure to show a profit on stock shipments. The greater chances for costly injuries, the fact that stock cars deadheaded 60 percent of the time, and the increased cost of labor were cited as reasons why stock shipments were not profitable when compared to other freight.

There may have been some justification in the position that stock shipments failed to show as much profit as other freight. Three years after this particular struggle, the *Gazette,* praising the effectiveness of KLA but without providing statistical support, noted that "to this association the shippers of the state are indebted for the rates on live stock. They are much lower than on any other commodity in the state and are due to the work of the Live Stock Association."[14] The railroads claimed that the rates proposed for 1903 tended to equalize the freight charges on cattle with those on lumber and wheat and, in a larger sense, that the new schedule put Kansas rates on a par with those in surrounding states. In retrospect the latter of the dual claims was hardest for the rail lines to justify. Tariff schedules were infrequently published in the board's reports, even though a provision by the 1905 legislature required the roads to submit them; but a study published in 1906 placed Kansas rates consistently above the average tariffs in surrounding states, and Texas, Iowa, and Illinois. Kansas rates beat the average somewhere between .03 cents per hundredweight for a 350-mile haul and 3.12 cents on a 200-mile carry.[15]

Cattlemen, on the other hand, argued that they could not afford to pay higher rates and that the poor service did not merit an increase. A decline of $2 per hundredweight in cattle prices and rising feed costs were cited in support of the cattlemen's claim of impoverishment. They also pointed out that a raise was unwarranted in view of the added efficiency and the larger carrying trade of the lines. Some purebred stock breeders were also upset with the new rate schedules. They often shipped in small quantities; but due to the railroads' determination of what constituted a full or partial load, they had to pay what they felt were exceedingly high tariffs. One said that rates were the largest obstacle in his fine stock business.

Cattlemen talked of several alternatives during the several days that the Topeka meeting continued. Some suggested driving cattle to market, while others favored a cooperatively financed packing house that would raise cattle prices to a point where the producer could afford higher rates. There were for the cattleman, however, few alternatives. He could either win the rate case, or, losing this, adjust his operation, possibly by going out of business.[16]

The hearing was continuing into its second day when suddenly the railroads withdrew their proposed increase. "The giant Goliath on one side," the September 11, 1903, Topeka *Daily Capital* noted, "and the youthful David with his sling shot on the other" had fought each other and David had won again.

Various explanations were given for the railroads' abrupt decision to withdraw their proposed schedule. Balie Waggener boasted that he had persuaded the lines to withdraw in order to preserve the Kansas cattle industry. The board suggested that the railroads' realization that they had provided poor service, due to the heavy rains and floods during the spring of 1903, was the reason. The Topeka paper implied that the threatened enactment of a Kansas law, similar to the Texas requirement that the roads pay $500 for each day they were in violation of a directive from the railroad commissioner, encouraged the lines to stop their attempt to raise rates. Mercer was probably closest to the truth, however, when he suggested that "David's victory" was something less than the honored Biblical triumph. Writing some ten years after the 1903 dispute, Mercer noted that the cattlemen and the railroads had struck a bargain. The lines would maintain the 1903 level of rates, according to the agreement, if cattlemen ceased agitation to return to the old carload system of charging freight rates that had been eliminated a couple of years before.

Several references were made to a contract that was negotiated between cattlemen and railroads about this time—probably the result of the bargain that Mercer noted—but an extensive search of available records failed to produce a copy. The casual references that were encountered implied that shipping rates, the permanent abandonment of the carload system, and several other requirements affecting railway service to stockmen were part of the contractual obligations. This agreement lasted, according to Mercer, well into the second decade of the twentieth century.[17]

The struggle in 1903 over rates was larger than the borders of Kansas, encompassing the whole range country and several stock associations in Texas and the Southwest. The incident was also a factor in coalescing several dissident elements into a stronger national association. "Judge" Sam H. Cowan, long-time legal representative of the Cattle Raisers Association of Texas, the national associations, and sometimes KLA, led the cattle interests in this instance on the national level. He was ably assisted by such men as the Scottish manager of the Matador Land and Cattle Company, Murdo Mackenzie, who was later instrumental in turning control of the national association back to the producers. These two men, along with Mercer and several others, trekked to Washington to petition lawmakers for federal relief from the dominance of railroads. Cowan, it was said, eventually helped write the main provisions of the 1906 Hepburn Act, which grew, in part, from the attempt of the roads to raise livestock shipping rates in 1903.

The Hepburn Act, with its provisions that allowed the ICC to set "just and reasonable maximum rates," upon the complaint of a shipper, was a mild victory for stockmen. The American National and the Texas associations filed more than a dozen complaints with ICC within a decade after the passage of the Hepburn Act. However, a provision for broad judicial review of ICC actions, the requirement that complaints had to be originated by shippers, and the failure of the law to modify the railways' power to classify freight modified the stockmen's victory. The triumph in 1903 over increased rates may have been greater than the Hepburn victory, as it demonstrated again that cooperation on the state and national levels in organized protests was one of the cattlemen's most effective weapons.[18]

After 1903, Kansas cattlemen were not generally aroused over rail tariffs until the roads proposed a general increase of both inter- and intrastate rates in 1910. This stability in tariffs was one reason that KLA was largely inactive during the 1903 to 1910 period. During that time only one meeting of KLA—an Emporia gathering in 1906 devoted to recommending "reasonable, equitable and non-discriminatory freight rates"—was held. In 1910 another KLA convention was held in the same town. By 1910, Robison had died and Plumb had resigned in hopes of obtaining a seat on the Board of Railroad Commissioners. An Osage City stockman, H. B. Miller, became the second president of the organization, and Mercer began his twenty-seven years as secretary.

The real purpose of the Emporia meeting in 1910 was to prepare for a conference of shipping and commercial interests called by Governor Stubbs.

Over 150 delegates representing states from the Great Lakes to the Rocky Mountains were invited to Topeka for the purpose of petitioning ICC to refuse the advance in rates proposed by the railroads. Addresses by the Kansas governor and by Murdo Mackenzie outlined the shippers' favorite arguments. Their lengthy speeches said, in effect, that railroads, in view of their present high profits, did not deserve higher rates, and that about 30 percent of a steer's value was already invested in transportation costs by the time it was carried from the Southwest to Kansas, then to a midwestern feedlot, and eventually to market. Legislation requiring a physical evaluation of railroad property was also urged. After extensive hearings and innumerable petitions from groups like the one Governor Stubbs had organized, ICC refused most of the railroads' requests, keeping the record of success for western cattlemen in this area almost unblemished for the early years of the new century.[19]

According to some railroad historians, the roads by 1910 deserved higher tariffs. In the face of numerous shippers' associations, like KLA, general freight rates had remained essentially at the seventy-five cents per ton mile level since 1897. Not until 1913 did the ICC allow a "modest 5 percent advance" in all freight rates. This record of stability in rates prior to 1918 compared quite favorably, from the shippers' standpoint, with the massive 28 percent increase that William G. McAdoo instituted in 1918 while the government controlled the roads.[20]

On the other side, there was also merit in the argument of cattlemen and other shippers that greater efficiency and a rise in business guaranteed railroads a reasonable profit even though operating costs had increased and rates had remained the same. An investigation of western railroads in 1914, for example, revealed that the returns on the "book cost" of the roads—which no one outside the industry knew for sure—fell somewhere between 4.9 and 5.6 percent. Net returns, according to the study, were sufficient to cover interest charges and operating expenses and still pay dividends on capital stock ranging from 10.4 percent in 1911 to 7.0 percent in 1914.[21] Nor did the stability of rates as a whole necessarily compensate shippers for short-haul and freight classification inequities that were continued by the lines. An adequate physical evaluation of the railroads and more restriction on classification practices may have helped the contending interests decide the rate issues fairly, but this was not available at the time.

Cattlemen had other complaints during the early years of the twentieth century. Some objected to dirty stock cars, inadequate loading facilities, and a shortage of cars. The *Gazette,* ironically at the same time that there were complaints of high freight rates, noted that stockmen "will 'tip' the trainmen as high as $10 a car for unordered stock cars" when there was a pressing need. Cattlemen were also critical of delays in service, and some advocated repeal of the federal law that required detraining for feed and rest after twenty-eight hours.[22] Although there were other complaints, nothing equaled the cattlemen's concern over stock tariffs; and, to their credit, they had much success during the years before the First World War in blocking higher rates.

Freight rates and the general relationship of the cattle industry to transportation continued to be important for stockmen and the activities of KLA throughout World War I. Tariffs by 1914 had remained at much the same level for over a decade, except for the modest 5 percent increase in 1913. The lines, of course, continued to be interested in changing this situation. In 1914 cattle-shipping rates in Kansas varied from 24.5 cents per hundred pounds for 450 miles to 7.5 cents for a 50-mile trip. This represented an average of $58.80 per car for the longer and $18.00 for the shorter haul. Rates for shipping hogs from various points in Kansas were consistently 2 to 4.5 cents per hundred pounds higher than cattle rates, and sometimes amounted to as much as $10.00 a car more. The additional charges for hogs resulted not from any additional weight but rather from the larger amount of work required for handling more animals per carload of stock, and because the traffic would bear additional charges. Hog producers were never as well organized as cattlemen.[23]

On at least two occasions between 1914 and 1917—when the government assumed control of the nation's rail lines—the roads attempted to raise the published tariffs on livestock. Partly as a result of organized lobbying before the Kansas Public Utilities Commission and ICC, stockmen defeated these increases. Despite this, railroads continued to show large profits even though expenses had gone up. Cattlemen claimed repeatedly throughout the war and during the early 1920s, with little dissent from the rail lines, that the period before the war was one of the most profitable in railroad history. Santa Fe, for instance, reported a $15.8 million increase in net corporate income between 1914 and 1917, or a rise of 71 percent. During the same period, however, the carrying trade for all the western lines rose by only 41 percent. The Santa Fe example may not be typical of all western railroads, but it does suggest that roads did not suffer a decline in profits at least for the first few years of the war.[24]

There was, then, some justification for the cattlemen's insistence that tariffs remain unchanged, and for the most part they were successful until after the government assumed control of the lines. There were significant increases after that.

Railroads, however, could raise charges for shipping stock without changing the published schedules, if they chose to do so. Livestock tariffs were based to a slight extent on the estimated value of the stock that was carried. By enhancing the estimated value of stock, rates were automatically increased. Cattlemen agreed to this sliding scale for tariffs—actually they probably demanded it—and it became a provision of the elusive uniform contract. Cattlemen agreed to this provision because their reimbursement for stock that died in transit was also based on the estimated value. While a higher evaluation raised rates, it also increased the amount that the lines paid for dead stock. Before the general rise in cattle prices at the beginning of the war, each head of mature cattle was valued at $50.00. With the rise in prices, this figure rose to $75.00. At the time, Mercer told Kansas cattlemen that "under present conditions, a steer valued at $75.00 is shipped under the uniform freight rate now in existence, but if valued over $75.00, the carriers have a right, under the Interstate Commerce order [of August, 1915], to increase their rate 2 per cent on each 50 per cent increase in valuation, or fraction thereof."

Mercer claimed that the sliding scale was costing some cattlemen as much as $8.00 a car more than the published rates, but it is doubtful that many shippers were actually affected. Most apparently allowed their stock to be moved at the estimated value of $75.00 rather than increase it to a level more representative of actual value. Shippers then enjoyed the standard rate but suffered a loss above $75.00 on any dead stock. The gamble usually paid.

After experiencing this sliding tariff in conjunction with rather sharp fluctuations in cattle prices, stockmen began advocating that the estimated value clause be eliminated from the contract, a provision they were successful in getting in 1917. From then on shippers paid only the published rates, and payments for dead stock were related more to the actual rather than the estimated value. These new provisions probably did not apply to purebred cattle, which were usually shipped under special conditions.[25]

Another way that railroads might increase shipping charges was through the mutually beneficial practice of disinfecting stock cars after each use. This practice was required by a new federal regulation that came about the time the European war began, and was, no doubt, caused in part by the foot-and-mouth epidemics that had occurred. The lines asked the shippers to pay disinfecting charges of $2.50 a car and $4.00 for double-decked cars, in addition to the regular tariffs. When the announcement was made, Mercer asked the Public Utilities Commission to stay this railroad order on intrastate shipments, and he urged the American National to petition ICC for the same privilege on interstate traffic. Cattlemen were not so much opposed to helping defray the cost of disinfecting—they realized that it was primarily for their benefit—as they were to the level of the charges. They felt that disinfecting could be done more cheaply, and wanted a delay to allow time for an investigation. The railroads finally agreed to a six-month trial period so that actual costs might be assessed, but there was no evidence that Kansas cattlemen were ever successful in getting the charges reduced or that they continued their fight for very long. After Mercer's brief encounter with the roads in 1915, the state's stockmen were content to allow the American National to continue the battle on the disinfecting issue.[26]

The question of free transportation for shippers who accompanied their stock to market was also an issue at this time, and had been a periodic source of disagreement for a long time. Cattlemen claimed that it was not only a well-established tradition but also a requirement of state law that the lines provide free transport for the owner of stock or for his representative. Large shippers rarely had any problems in extracting transportation from the lines, but the various state agencies charged with regulating lines were continually besieged with complaints from small shippers who felt that they were not receiving adequate service. The issue became more complex in 1907, when the legislature enacted an antipass law. Cattlemen favored the antipass restriction, and had helped get it established, but they were careful to see that the provision did not exclude their right to free transportation. The accommodations for these free rides were also subject to regulation. Each caboose attached to a stock train, for example, was "to be equipped with seats and water-closets, and suitable drinking water necessary to accommodate the number of stockmen properly on such train." Noncompliance with these stipulations was to result in a $20 per day fine for the road. Cattlemen viewed any refusal by the rail lines to provide attendants with transport or adequate facilities as a mere subterfuge for increasing profits.

By the second decade of the twentieth century, the railroads usually accommodated shippers accompanying their cattle, although small shippers still occasionally found it difficult to obtain free transport both to and from the destination of their stock. Generally the lines did not balk at carrying one attendant for each two to five cars of stock or up to three men as the number of carloads for one shipper increased. What the railroads did justifiably object to was the inordinately large number of "floaters" who inhabited the cabooses, claiming to be caretakers but actually having little or no official relationship to any stock being carried. A representative of the railroads told the 1916 KLA convention that cattlemen were largely responsible for the floaters and that some drastic action might soon be taken. The situation was especially taxing on the lines' facilities during the busy shipping seasons.

The dispute was finally settled towards the end of the war, at least for a time, by including in the uniform shippers' contract guaranteed transit privileges that were acceptable to both the shippers and the carriers. A limited number of attendants were assured of transport, but only *bona fide* owners of stock and their employees qualified.[27]

Mercer and KLA again represented Kansas stockmen in this negotiated settlement with the railroads, but KLA was not the only organization that the state's stockmen depended upon during this period. In 1915 a group of Kansas cattlemen met in Chicago with other stockmen from across the nation to form the National Livestock Shippers' Protective League. The purpose of this new organization was to coordinate and extend the activities of state and local associations in the area of freight rates, or, in short, to frustrate any increase in interstate livestock tariffs. The league obtained the necessary finances for its operation by assessing each carload of stock five cents, a fee that was collected by the commission firms at the central markets. It was a voluntary payment, however; and, though local associations urged shippers to contribute, there was often a deficiency of funds.

The league functioned for over seven years, but its success is difficult to assess. There were several notable rate increases after 1918; yet, Mercer—the league's president for a few years—wrote in the late twenties that it had been notably successful.[28] In any event, the league offered stockmen another avenue for organized response to real or imagined injustices on the part of railroads. To some degree it also overshadowed for a time KLA's work in rate disputes, especially in the area of interstate rates.

The more or less unblemished record of western stockmen in preventing major increases in livestock tariffs was spoiled soon after the federal government assumed control of the rail lines in December, 1917. There had been much speculation early in the war as to what would happen to the railroads in the event that the United States became more actively involved. Even before President Woodrow Wilson sent his war message to Congress, the increased traffic was becoming difficult for the roads to handle. The lines had tried voluntary cooperation; but with the large increase in freight and a degree of labor unrest, it became impossible to coordinate the schedules of the many individual lines. Delays and monumental traffic jams resulted, while snow and freezing weather towards the end of 1917 aggravated the difficulties.

Wilson's solution was probably necessary and inevitable in view of the circumstances. Under the provisions of the Federal Railroad Control Act, the president established the United States Railway Administration for the purpose of assuming control of the nation's rail lines. The administration was also given absolute rate-making powers. William G. McAdoo, Wilson's overworked and much-harassed secretary of the Treasury Department, was appointed director general of the new government agency. These new duties, not slight by any means, were in addition to those McAdoo continued for a time to have in the Treasury Department. Under the provisions of the government takeover, all antitrust and pooling restrictions were suspended, and the lines were guaranteed an annual profit equal to an average of what they had earned between 1915 and 1917, plus government-financed repairs and improvements. The railroads preferred to eliminate 1915 from consideration of average income, as it was a relatively unprofitable year, but there were no complaints about the last two years, as they had been very rewarding.

One of the first actions taken by McAdoo that affected the vital interests of stockmen was a 25 percent across-the-board increase in freight rates, something the rail lines had been attempting—with only limited success—for almost two decades. All special tariffs, such as the feed-in-transit rates, were eliminated, and passenger fares were returned to 3 cents a mile. On stock shipments the increase was 25 percent on all existing rates below 28 cents per hundred pounds—this included most points in Kansas, Colorado, and Oklahoma—and a flat 7 cent increase on all rates that were at the time above 28 cents a hundred. In Kansas this amounted to a raise from 24.5 to 30.5 cents per hundred—or from $58.80 to $73.20 per carload—for a 450-mile haul, and from 7.5 to 9.5 cents per hundred—$18.00 to $22.00 per car—for a 50-mile run. Tariffs for hog shipments also went up and were usually $8.00 to $12.00 per car more than those on cattle.

The government apparently felt that the war-induced inflation and the generally increased operating costs justified the new schedules. The most convincing argument, however, was the rise in the cost of labor. The Adamson Act had already pushed up labor costs, then the railway administration increased wages again shortly after the takeover. By 1918 total wages for railway employees were more than 40 percent above what they had been only a few years before.

KLA and the American National, as well as several other associations, protested the new tariffs, maintaining that the railroads were already producing a fair return on the invested capital and that a 5 percent raise would have been adequate for the additional labor expenses. Some stockmen even advocated government subsidies for the lines rather than higher rates. But, in all, there was surprisingly little objection to the government's action either in assuming control of the lines or setting the new rates. There was probably more protest in Kansas over a proposal that former governor Stubbs had made only three years before in an article published in the *Saturday Evening Post* than there was over Wilson's action. Stubbs had proposed that the government take over the railroads and operate them as a public utility—in short, much the same thing that happened in 1917.

Comparatively little opposition from stockmen resulted from Wilson's action, and, indeed, circumstances had changed considerably between the time of the Stubbs proposal and that of the Wilson takeover. The declaration of war was, of course, the major difference; and this was bolstered by an unprecedented propaganda campaign to persuade Americans to support the war effort. Stock prices were also up, which made it at least appear that cattlemen could afford higher rates; and, most importantly, stockmen knew that they had little recourse but to accept the governmental fiat. Many cattlemen were also ready for government control of the industry that they had been confronting for several decades; at least this seemed to be the implication of the Stubbs article. Only after a couple of years of experimenting did the cattlemen decide that they preferred private control of the railroads.

Government involvement with the rail lines during World War I ultimately resulted in more centralization of regulatory powers in the federal government in this area as well as in most other sectors of the economy. State agencies were not as yet ready to admit this, but it became increasingly clear during the early 1920s. Government control, according to the Kansas Public Utilities Commission, lost sight of the agricultural shipper; rates were up and service was down. This no doubt contributed much to the tendency of stockmen to become very critical of government-controlled railroads during the postwar depression. For the nation as a whole, however, many felt that the takeover was successful. It ended car shortages for the most part, and supplied much of the coordination that was necessary in a time of crisis.[29]

While cattlemen continued to combat the railroads during the war, the amount of energy they expended was decidedly on the wane. Regulation, from the ICC down to the various state agencies, had become more effective, but more important in the cattlemen's case was the fact that livestock rates did not change significantly for more than a decade. Stability of rates induced a calmer relationship between stockmen and railroad men. When stockmen were hit with a substantial rise in rates toward the end of the war, the circumstances that usually stimulated shipper opposition to rising tariffs had changed, and there was little they could have done to prevent the advance in any event. Some unrest among shippers reappeared around 1920, but even then it was not as intense as it had been in earlier decades. The tendency to get along with transportation lines during these first two decades of the new century did not mean, however, that producers were becoming more satisfied with the big businesses with which they came into contact. Much of the antagonism that cattlemen had formerly reserved for rail lines was transferred to the large meat-packers. While processors had never been exempt from producer criticism, they began to feel its full force during the early decades of the twentieth century, especially after the beginning of the war in Europe.

8

Monopoly and Confusion: Stockyards and Packers, 1900-1920

Farmers and ranchers spent the years prior to 1914 raising production to fill the demands of consumers. But thereafter, production generally moved ahead of the growth in urbanization and total population, and only the accelerated demands of the First World War prevented the build-up of surpluses and a drastic downturn in agricultural prices. Instead, prices moved upward and production was stimulated to even greater heights. The scarcity of shipping facilities and the relatively short trip across the Atlantic favored the United States, which, for example, temporarily displaced Argentina as the principal supplier of British beef.

Agricultural producers were generally satisfied with their economic situation throughout the first two decades of the twentieth century. There were, of course, short periods of unrest, but it was not until around 1916 that large numbers of producers became unhappy. This disaffection grew as the war came to a close, and took a sharp upturn during the immediate postwar years.

Basic to the discontent among farmers and ranchers after 1916 were a number of factors beyond anyone's control. Drought and black rust invaded the wheat fields. More importantly, production and living costs rose even faster than the prices ranchers and farmers received for what they sold, a situation which was at least partly caused by the European conflict. But agricultural producers often did not blame the abnormal conditions of the war, the droughts, or the diseased crops and stock, but rather the marketing system. The increasing complexity of the general economy, the impact of droughts and disease, and the effects of the war on production costs and market prices were not fully understood by farmers and ranchers, while marketing, they felt, was something they did understand. Because farmers and ranchers frequently used marketing agencies, they believed that profits would be enhanced if inequities perpetrated by the businessmen engaged in the marketing process were corrected. Many of their complaints about marketing practices were well founded.

Dissatisfaction with an inadequate marketing system, which had been part of the agrarian scene for several decades, reached a climax about the time the United States declared war on Germany. Increasing demand and rising prices for livestock—prerequisites that would guarantee larger profits, stockmen believed—failed to deliver what cattlemen expected. Something must be out-of-joint, producers reasoned. Adjustments were needed somewhere, and the marketing process seemed the best place to begin. Stockmen had support from other quarters, too. Arthur Capper, for instance, as governor and then as United States senator, crisscrossed the state deploring what he considered to be an antiquated and unfair system for the marketing of livestock. This unrest among producers and their representatives brought several investigations of both the stockyard and packing interests, culminating toward the end of the war with an extensive probe by the Federal Trade Commission (FTC) into the operations of the packing industry. Packers were most frequently held responsible for marketing problems and generally received the brunt of the stockmen's disaffection; but other middlemen, such as stockyard operators and commission men, were also held accountable. Government regulation, first at the state and then at the national level, proved the most effective means of improving the situation, but stockmen experimented with other options before demanding government help. In general, the lion's share of the ill will that farmers and ranchers had formerly reserved for railroads gradually shifted to packing houses and stockyards.

Kansas City, the western stockman's gateway to the East, continued to develop as an important central market, receiving far more than half of its receipts from points west of the yards. The number of cattle and calves marketed in Kansas City, though reflecting the cyclic fluctuations described earlier, varied for most of the period between two and three million head. The yards' specialization in the stocker and feeder trade continued, with almost half of the cattle received leaving the market for additional growing.

The physical facilities of the Kansas City yards were expanded and improved during the early 1900s. Hampered somewhat by the great flood in 1903 and a smaller one five years later, the Kansas City yards acquired more land and built additional pens and a new Exchange Building, which served as the nerve center for all business transacted in the yards as well as for many of the affairs conducted in relation to the whole western industry. The new structure, as it was slowly pushed some eleven stories above the surrounding yards, became the source of much pride. When it was completed in 1911 it was advertised as the largest livestock exchange building in the world. By 1920 the yards covered an area of over two hundred acres.[1]

Kansas stockmen, particularly cattlemen, were not completely happy with the Kansas City yards, however, and demanded that the state's lawmakers correct some of the inequities that they experienced. In 1907 the Kansas legislature bowed to the cattle interests by initiating the first investigation of the yards in over a decade. The 1907 inquiry, moreover, had the advantages of precedents set during the nineteenth century, when stockmen had also turned to the government for help in redressing their grievances against stockyards, just as they had done in their battles with railroads.

In an investigation in 1895, for example, the "bewhiskered Kansas Legislature" had been concerned with what cattlemen considered to be excessive yardage fees. As a result, Kansas lawmakers forced a reduction in maximum charges for cattle from twenty-five to fifteen cents per head. The reduced rate, however, proved worthless to shippers, as the stockyards company merely built quarantine quarters for the inspection of cattle suspected of having or carrying Texas fever and required that most cattle be inspected, adding for this service a charge of ten cents a head to the maximum allowed by the Kansas law. Two years later another investigation resulted in a Kansas statute—comparable to one passed by the Missouri legislature—allowing the owner to sell dead stock to whichever rendering company he chose, and providing for a 30 percent reduction in feed and yardage charges.

Stockmen calculated that reduced feed charges would save Kansas shippers $350,000 a year, but their hopes were thwarted again. A year after passage of the 1897 law the Emporia *Gazette* reported that "the farmers of Kansas haven't got a dollar out of the stock yards legislation, and what's more they never will get a dollar." The stockyards company contested the law in the courts for several years and, in the meantime, operated outside its requirements. Eventually, the state tired of the legal battle and the yards continued to operate virtually unrestricted.[2]

Prompted by generally depressed cattle prices—much like the condition that had existed during the middle 1890s—and by continued protests from stockmen, the Kansas legislature looked into the Kansas City yards again in

Kansas City stockyards. *Courtesy of the Kansas State Historical Society.*

1907. This time, one of the state's leading cattlemen, John A. Edwards, was in charge of the investigative team. George Plumb and state senator H. B. Miller, the second president of KLA, were also members of the five-man group that again cooperated with a similar Missouri committee.

The final report to the Kansas legislature by the Edwards committee failed to reveal the sources for the information it contained, but it was apparent that both stockyards personnel and commission men had testified and that there must have been some access to the company's records. If accurate, the report revealed several interesting facets of the Kansas City business. In 1898, according to Edwards' report, the stockyards company had escaped the full weight of the 1897 regulation by reorganizing as a Missouri company. This maneuver placed the company outside Kansas jurisdiction, or at least made the state's power questionable. In addition, the newly organized Missouri company removed itself further from Kansas' scrutiny by not obtaining a license to do business in the state and by neglecting to file annual reports with the attorney general. Edwards strongly recommended that the Kansas attorney general continue the investigation that his committee had initiated, with forced licensing in view.

162

The investigative team also disapproved of what they considered high yardage charges—as high as $8 for some carloads of stock—and the inadequacy of weighing facilities. The principal complaint, however, dealt with the prices that shippers paid for the feed their stock consumed in the yards. "Millions of dollars have been stolen—literally stolen from the farmers of Kansas, and have gone into this corporation whose stockholders and managers are doubtless church-going Christians," according to the Emporia *Gazette*, and the Edwards report substantiated much of the claim. It noted that shippers were habitually given short weight and charged high prices for feed. Since 1900, for example, shippers had paid $175,000 for 10,000 tons of hay that they never received, and the company sold about 7,000 tons more than they purchased from their suppliers. To correct this situation, the report suggested fines be levied for not delivering full weight when selling feed.

The stockyards company defended its various price levels on the basis that they were necessary to guarantee a reasonable profit on the capital invested; but Edwards' report also disputed this claim, especially for the period of the yard's existence prior to 1900. For the twenty-six years before 1900, according to the study, the company paid an "average of 32½ per cent annually in cash dividends to stockholders and 34½ per cent in stock and real estate dividends to stockholders" each year. For the period between 1904 and 1907 a comparatively slight 9 percent a year was cited as the dividend on the companys $9 million capitalization. The committee failed to account for the wide divergence in profits between the nineteenth and twentieth centuries. Increased operating costs as well as the inadequacy of the records supplied by the company were possible explanations. The company was also accused of avoiding legitimate taxation by paying property taxes on only about 16 percent of its valuation. Neither the high profits nor the avoidance of taxes, however, encouraged the committee to recommend any specific measures to correct the abuses. It could have been argued that licensing the company might be expected to correct the tax situation, and that the comparatively low profits during the few years prior to the investigation suggested that the fees of the yards were appropriate.[3]

The only tangible result of Edwards' investigation was a resolution by the Kansas lawmakers to the effect that "the legislature of the state of Missouri be requested to unite with the legislature of the state of Kansas in the passage of a uniform law governing stock-yards." However, no progress was made in this area throughout the next decade, although an open letter to both the Kansas and Missouri legislatures in 1909 called again for regulation that might "bring to justice that corporation which has practiced extortion and robbed the livestock shippers and dealers of the West for the past thirty years." The author of the letter had been the company's "Feed Master" for several years but had lost his position, he claimed, because he had "made an honest effort to give full weight, and measure . . . and had not been a party to the crime of stealing nearly $30,000 from the patrons of the yards." The legislatures, though, were unmoved by either this letter—which appeared to be largely a personal vendetta against the president of the stockyards company, G. F. Morse —or the complaints of shippers. The jurisdictional problem and the difficulty of coordinating the laws of two states were major obstacles to regulation. Around 1911, the stockyards company did admit that it was subject in some instances to the regulations of the Kansas Public Utilities Commission; but only generalities and vague references to "reasonable and just rates" emanated from the commission. Stricter regulations of stockyards had to await the federal regulation that came after World War I.[4]

Kansas cattlemen and the state regulatory commission did, however, get involved in a struggle between the yards and the railroads that began around 1912. As the confrontation also involved the packing interests, a discussion of this industry is in order before treating the three-cornered dispute of 1912.

Between 1880 and 1920 the large packing companies acquired heavy financial interests in the stockyards at most central markets. Cattlemen, for the most part, only guessed at this relationship until the FTC investigation in 1917 made it abundantly clear. Had the cattlemen been certain that the buyers of their stock also controlled most of the yards and that this relationship led to collusion on prices, their interest in legislation to control the consolidations in the meat trade would have become acute much sooner.

The packers' principal entrée into stockyard ownership before 1900 had come from being offered a financial interest in yards as an incentive for locating a meat-processing plant in the vicinity. The original developers of the yards— often the railroads—gradually gave way and the packers became the dominant influence. This occurred in Kansas City to a slight extent during the early 1890s, when Armour was given a half-million-dollar stock bonus for locating a plant there. After 1900, however, several new yards were begun in or around the beef-producing area almost wholly with packer money.[5]

The effects on producers of packer-controlled stockyards, according to the FTC study, were entirely bad. Though facilities were sometimes expanded, they were usually inadequate for the natural growth in receipts and were habitually understaffed. Exorbitant charges for yardage and feed resulted, and deficient weighing facilities abounded. Most harmful to the producers, however, was probably the "extreme and unwarranted fluctuation in the daily prices paid for live stock," a condition that was attributed to the packing interests. A commission man from the Wichita market revealed to FTC one method that he believed packers used to force prices down. Cudahy and the much smaller Dold concern divided most of the receipts, and they might refuse to buy anything if not given first choice.[6] Commission men felt that competition was subtly being eliminated and prices lowered by such threats.

In Wichita it was about 1906 before a major packing concern gained an interest in the yards. At this time a contract was negotiated between the Wichita Stock Yards Company and Cudahy that gave the latter a sixth of the $700,000 worth of capital stock in exchange for a guarantee that the plant would continue to operate in Wichita for at least ten years and continue to buy all the livestock necessary for the local plant from the Wichita yards. Over the next few years the capitalization of the yards was increased, and each time Cudahy's portion was augmented. By 1917 the packing company admitted ownership of over a third of the $1.4 million worth of stock. Cudahy did not, however, use its interest to drive out all the small, independent packers from the Wichita area. Jacob Dold continued to operate under a contract with the yards similar to that of Cudahy. This became the basis for the FTC assertion that these two packers agreed to divide most of the receipts, with the subsequent possibility of the price fixing that was described above.[7]

In Kansas City control of 67 percent of the Boston-owned stockyards plant passed to Edward Morris around 1912. This large packer gained control of the $8.2 million company through a complicated plan that involved reincorporating the firm in the state of Maine, a $2 million increase in capitalization, and his purchase of much of the company's voting stock. The remaining four large packers in the Kansas City area owned a total of only 5.6 percent of the voting stock in the reorganized company.[8]

Complaints of stockmen over the charges and service of the Kansas City yards increased about the time Morris initiated his move to take control of the yards, but so did efforts to improve facilities. Better weighing, yarding, and unloading equipment, however, precipitated the involved dispute between the stockyards company and the rail lines that was noted earlier.

In its simplest form the dispute centered on the yards' desire to construct a few miles of what they called a terminal or connecting rail line in addition to new unloading docks. The railroads opposed entry of the yards into what they considered to be "their business," while the yards refused to allow the rail lines to construct facilities on stockyards' property. After much debate, the Kansas Public Utilities Commission landed in the middle of the controversy, as did several of the state's cattlemen. The fact that the allegiance of stockmen was divided on this issue was instrumental in developing a stronger livestock association that could speak with a unanimous voice on issues such as this. The fact that the Kansas City yards were spread over an area served by two different state governments and the fact that the Missouri Public Service Commission had fewer qualms than its Kansas counterpart about issuing a charter for a terminal rail line allowed the stockyards company to maneuver a victory. After obtaining permission in 1915, the stockyards company purchased more land in Missouri and built a connecting line wholly within that state.

By 1917, the yards claimed, all the improvements demanded by cattlemen had been completed without additional freight rates or handling charges to antagonize the shippers. And this claim was generally true; most shippers, though they continued to complain about high yardage fees, found that the new facilities did provide better service. After the war the state of Kansas again attempted to regulate the Kansas City yards, but this effort failed too. The yards came under effective regulation only when the federal government took up the task in the Packers and Stockyards Act.[9]

Monopoly and meat packing, in the minds of many producers, were hand and glove, and this belief helped stimulate inquiries into the packing industry much like those related to stockyards. By the time of the First World War, when the FTC conducted its extensive and significant investigation, there had already been two federal examinations, several more by individual states, and a judicial ruling that had exonerated the packers of any wrongdoing. Ironically, while Kansas cattlemen expressed much concern over the prices that packers paid for stock, they apparently concerned themselves little, if at all, with working conditions and wages in the large packing plants. By the early 1900s the deplorable conditions had been well advertised in such books as *The Jungle,* but Kansas stockmen failed to admit publicly that they were aware of the situation.

The first public investigation of the packing industry had occurred during the late 1880s when five United States senators—from Missouri, Kansas, Nebraska, Texas, and Illinois—spent two years scrutinizing the activities of Swift, Armour, Morris, and Hammond. Their report, published in 1890 and called the *Vest Committee Report* after the Missouri senator who chaired the inquiry, concluded that there was "collusion with regard to the fixing of prices and the division of territory and business." The packers, however, admitted to no price fixing, claiming that they set only the wholesale price of dressed beef. Depressed prices for livestock, they said, were the result of overproduction. Though producers were not convinced by the claims of unrestricted competition in the marketplace, the committee's work resulted in no corrective legislation except insofar as it contributed to the passage of the Sherman Antitrust Act.[10]

Neither this investigation, the Sherman Act, nor the possibility of other federal legislation retarded the packers' tendency to combine their operations. Three years after these four large companies were investigated, they joined with Cudahy to form what came to be known as the Veeder Pool. It took its name from Swift attorney Henry Veeder, who functioned as secretary and statistician at regular Tuesday afternoon meetings of the members. Representatives at these weekly meetings apparently assigned beef-purchasing territories and apportioned to each participant quotas for the movement of dressed meat into consumer channels. The pool operated from 1893 until 1902, except for a couple of years, enlarging its membership in 1897 by adding the firm of Schwarzchild & Sulzberger. Producers only guessed at the pool's existence, and even a federal grand jury that was convened in 1895 failed to bring any indictments against the large packers for violations of the Sherman Act. Later, when the activities of the pool became generally known, the packers claimed that its effects had not been harmful to the producer but rather beneficial in that the demand for beef at the central markets had been greatly stabilized.[11]

The Veeder Pool was abandoned in 1902 when the Department of Justice asked for an injunction against the large packers for violating the Sherman Act. Armour, Swift, and Morris then attempted a gigantic merger, before forming a holding company known as the National Packing Company. Proportionate to their assets, the parent companies purchased stock in the holding company and divided the cost of absorbing smaller independent packers. At weekly board meetings, consisting of representatives of only the three large companies, officials decided upon the prices to be paid in the central markets and established buying and distributing quotas. This holding company, which proved to be a highly effective and profitable arrangement, was terminated in 1912 only in the face of a government threat to initiate a civil suit.

Relatively low prices were the producers' lot when most of the receipts at the central markets were divided according to a prearranged plan among two or more large packers. With this situation in mind, the *FTC Report* concluded that market prices tended to be "the lowest price which will keep the producers raising cattle, hogs, and sheep and sending them to the stockyard."[12]

The discontent among producers during the early 1900s was often reflected, and at times even stimulated, by journals and newspapers. The Topeka *Daily Capital,* for instance, charged in 1903 that the high price of dressed beef showed "how well in hand the beef trust has the market and incidentally how remorseless this trust is in squeezing both consumer and producer." The stockyards and packing house combination, the paper said, "gets its rake-off at both ends and has pretty well milked the cattle industry dry. . . . That it fixes prices now and holds the market in the hollow of its hand nobody will dispute."

In western Kansas some of the newspapers were singing much the same song. "What has happened to the price of meat under the manipulation of the Chicago combine?" one small community paper asked. The price of meat, it responded to its own question, has doubled and "cattle on the western plains must sell at starvation prices, and every eater of meat must pay monopoly prices to enable the few men who make up these six companies to pile up money by the billion." While assessing the conditions of the beef industry at this time, the *Gazette* added that the Kansas farmer was "on the grouch" and that it was up to packers and railroads to "jolly him into a cattle growing humor."

Efforts to eliminate the controlled prices in the central markets stimulated talk of a cattlemen-owned packing plant. On the whole, however, this proposal was naïve, failing to account for most of the intricacies of the packing industry, especially the necessity of an efficient system of national distribution. Slaughter of the animals by packing plants was only the first step in putting large quantities of meat into consumer channels. Many cattlemen must have also understood this, as little more than talk ever came from the proposals to establish a packing house. Instead, the producer and consumer combined to demand another government investigation of the industry, a demand that was met in 1904.[13]

Encouraged by protests over livestock and dressed-meat prices and by some early muckraking attacks on the industry, President Theodore Roosevelt ordered James R. Garfield, commissioner of corporations and son of the former president, to investigate the meat trust to see if it was the cause of the violent price fluctuations. Garfield's 1905 report astounded cattlemen, angered consumers, and confused the muckraking press. The six largest packers, the report said, accounted for 97.7 percent of the beef cattle killed at the principal western slaughtering points but only about 45 percent of the total number of cattle butchered. This, it implied, was not nearly enough to establish a monopoly. In addition, the high beef prices were caused by the short supply, as the packers' average price for dressed beef was lower than what they paid for livestock. Their small profit margin—amounting to an average of eighty-two cents per head or a mere 2 percent on sales—came from by-products. This report, according to Rudolph A. Clemen, an employee of the packing industry, produced facts that were of "such comprehensive and voluminous form that any intelligent person who examined the material could not question their authenticity or their representative character."[14]

Many, however, did question the report, and Garfield was roundly criticized in beef-raising areas. One local newspaper in Kansas was astonished to learn that "the beef trust is a benevolent sort of thing and for years has been buying steers and slaughtering them at a profit of less than 2 per cent . . . and part of the time at a loss." The Kansas City (Mo.) *Journal* published several long articles based on research by Cuthbert Powell, its commerce editor. Powell claimed that he had made as detailed an investigation of the local situation as was possible without complete access to the packers' books— a deficiency, he suggested, that also existed for Garfield.

The large meat-packers, Powell claimed, controlled the industry through a "community of interests system" that included their control of all leading stockyards in the West, except those in Kansas City and Chicago; their controlling influence in many of the stockmen's banking facilities; their control of refrigerated cars and distribution systems; and, finally, their collusion through holding companies and pooling agreements. Powell did not necessarily dispute the packers' claim of making only 2 percent on their dressed-meat sales but claimed that this was an inappropriate figure to consider. Compared to the eighty-two cents per head profit claimed in the Garfield document, Powell found a net gain that approached twelve dollars per head when by-products were included, and a profit of 43 percent on capitalization when refrigerated car and stockyard profits were considered. Garfield had been "humbugged," and his report was being "laughed at [and] ridiculed," Powell believed, as the packers could shift money around in various departments and grow rich while showing a loss on butchering.[15]

Although they did not accept the Garfield report, cattlemen were hesitant to call for any federal legislation. Many did, however, call for yet another investigation. The Kansas legislature, with a number of cattlemen-legislators participating, urged the president to throw the Garfield statement away and begin a real investigation. Although this was not to be for over a decade, federal action against the packing industry did not terminate with Garfield's work. The government brought suit against Swift and ten other packers in 1911 for alleged antitrust violations. A jury trial exonerated the accused. The action did, however, appear to initiate the demise of the National Packing Company, whose combined assets, including the several small packing concerns that had been absorbed, were now sold to Swift, Armour, and Morris. The "real" investigation and the meaningful legislation, which cattlemen failed to call for at this time, did not come until after 1917.

Thus, during the first decade and a half of the twentieth century the large packing interests continued the concerted actions that they had begun during the previous century. These moves toward association within the packing industry had much in common with those occurring in other industries except for one significant difference. In many industries, such as the railroads, consolidation and the subsequent elimination of much competition was motivated by defensive considerations—the industry was not able to cope with severe competition. In the packing industry, consolidation was not so much a defensive as an offensive action, a means of increasing already substantial profits. Largely as a result, the few large packing families built in a short period of time an amazing system for processing and distributing the nation's meat supply. The extensive reinvestment of what cattlemen considered to be excessive profits accounted for much of this expansion. Growth occurred, however, at the expense of many small packers, who were not privy to the councils of the large packers, and at the expense of the nation's livestock producers, who believed that they received lower prices and poorer service when the small packers were driven out of the field. By the early years of the twentieth century, packers were so entrenched that they could demand special favors from railways, stockyards, and sometime even the cities in which they operated. Cattlemen and other livestock producers often suffered from these special privileges. They had little voice in the deals made among cities, stockyards, and packers; yet they received lower prices and poorer service as a result. Producers might have spared themselves some anguish had they demanded and received more government intervention at an earlier date, but nineteenth-century myths about the nature of the cattlemen and the prevailing convictions on the role of government forestalled the demand for legislation until after the war.

Farmers and ranchers reacted to the large packers as well as to the marketing process as a whole in a variety of ways during the first two decades of the new century, but most frequently they opted for joint efforts through an organization. The relatively slow growth in Kansas of the new agrarian organizations—the American Society of Equity, the Nonpartisan League, and the Farmer's Union, for example—and the dearth of cattlemen in the ranks of those organizations that did exist left many of the state's stockmen little recourse but to rely upon the older organizations for any collective action that they might desire.[16] For cattlemen this meant that KLA remained the principal instrument for attempting changes in the marketing situation. After steady growth since its reorganization, KLA was in a position to help improve conditions. Its efforts during the war years became increasingly significant.

Displeasure with marketing conditions, for example, dominated the 1916 KLA convention almost to the exclusion of other considerations. This particular meeting also provided a good example of the cattlemen's temper after the prosperity of the early war years began to wear thin. At the time, though, other factors were also affecting stockmen, making the time ripe for "war on the packers," as it was called.

The American National's meeting in El Paso a few weeks earlier had initiated this recent explosion of discontent with the marketing system by venting many of the stockmen's complaints. The American National appointed a committee to investigate marketing conditions and called on Congress to remedy all abuses. Then, just a few days before KLA's meeting, Congressman Borland of Missouri introduced into Congress a strong resolution designed to force the FTC and the Justice Department to move against the packing industry.

With these previous developments in mind, Kansas stockmen journeyed to their annual meeting. As a result, the 1916 convention in Wichita was more turbulent than any other gathering of the state's stockmen. The convention was described at the time as one of the largest meetings of cattlemen ever held in the United States—larger, it was said, than the American National's gathering the month before. It was estimated that almost four thousand "rank and file" cattlemen attended the three-day affair held in the spacious Eaton Hotel.

The convention began on a relatively calm note with an address by H. J. Waters, president of Kansas State Agricultural College, in which he expressed his ideas about the benefits of eating meat. The college president deplored the government's campaign to cut high food costs during the war by decreasing meat consumption. "Meat makes brawn, a healthy body and a fertile mind," he told the convention. Americans eat more meat than any people in the world, Waters continued, and it "makes a dominant race . . . [and] when we advocate economy on the meat bill, we are striking at the very thing that makes American people the greatest dominant race in the World." Cattlemen applauded the allusions to the "barbaric Hun" and the concept of the superiority of the American people. Similar sentiments later became popular themes in efforts to increase meat consumption.

Governor Capper followed Waters to the stand, presenting the convention with more germane issues. His speech directed attention toward the packing industry for the remainder of the meeting. "There is not the slightest doubt in my mind," Capper announced in an often repeated speech, "that the live stock markets are systematically controlled by factors other than supply and demand. . . . When the profit in feeding steers is so painfully absent, as it has been in the last year, when we have raids on the hog market as we had last fall, it is plain . . . that there are abnormal forces controlling the price of farm products, and I believe that powerful interest to be the big packing houses." The governor urged, among other things, expansion of cooperative marketing and a thorough investigation of marketing conditions by the federal government.

Cattlemen awoke the next morning to read in the Wichita *Eagle* that "Kansas feeders, breeders, ranchers . . . say packing houses are cornering all the profits," and that there was a "conspiracy" of middlemen to rob the producer. Several of the speakers for the second day continued to heap abuse upon the packers, one claiming that profits had doubled for the meat processors the last few years while feeders were losing money. George E. Tucker, KLA vice-president and editor of the Eureka *Herald,* added to the general accusations by charging that the Kansas City packers controlled the market newspapers to the disadvantage of the producer and suggested that KLA establish its own market information service.

Not all the sentiment, however, was antipacker; a couple of speakers defended the industry. The president of the Wichita Cattle Loan Company, for example, cautiously suggested that it was not the railroads, banks, or packers that were adversely affecting the beef industry but rather the practice of keeping cattle too long before marketing them, thus increasing the cost of production. J. C. Swift, commission man with the Kansas City Live Stock Exchange, also defended the meat processors and the independence of the market news agencies in Kansas City. What the Kansas association needed more than its own newspaper, he said cryptically, was "a Moses to lay down new laws, a Jefferson to write a new declaration of independence, and an Abraham Lincoln to write a new emancipation proclamation." While cattlemen scratched their heads at this puzzling statement, Swift continued that it was extremely unfair to criticize the packers without giving them an opportunity to speak.

The prevailing sentiment, however, was against the packers. As the *Eagle* reported the next day, "cattlemen were standing up in the aisles . . . cheering themselves hoarse over speeches denouncing the [marketing] system." Willis L. "Iron Jaw" Brown, a stockman and former Populist editor from Kingman, brought the row with the meat processors to a climax by demanding in no uncertain terms that federal authorities investigate the industry immediately. Brown, also a progressive legislator, introduced a resolution that strongly supported Congressman Borland's attempts to force action against the packers for alleged antitrust violations. Brown's resolution received much vocal support, but before a vote could be taken another faction introduced a resolution that simply called on the packers to divest themselves of ownership and management of the central stockyards.

The debate over the two resolutions was loud and disorganized. Finally, President Tod suggested that both resolutions be sent to a committee for further study. Brown, who insisted on "action not words," was persuaded to accept this compromise, but shouted that if the "resolution don't come out of that committee room by noon tomorrow, the hair is going to fly in this convention." At this point Edwin Morris—grandson of the late Nelson Morris, the packer—brought the delegates to their feet by racing down the aisle of the hall demanding to be heard. By this time, however, it was late in the afternoon, and the packers' side of the dispute was delayed until the following day. Cattlemen imbibed satisfaction with their steak and ale that night, confident that they had won the day.

J. A. McNaughton, a representative of Cudahy, was the principal spokesman for the packers the next day. Somewhat illogically and apologetically, he argued that the packers had made their fortunes during the "good old days." Now, because of growing specialization, the rising cost of live animals, and shorter hours and higher labor expenses, packers were making little profit on dressed meat, and were able to stay in business only because they had a fair margin on by-products.

McNaughton used the example of a thousand-pound steer, shipped three hundred miles to a central market, to illustrate his point. In this case, he said, the rail line received over $2.50 for transporting the animal, the speculator who financed the buying and selling 25 cents, and the commission firm about 60 cents. The poor packer, meanwhile, who did all the processing and distributing, received less than a dollar.

The packers also invited a representative group of stockmen to examine their books in an effort to quiet charges of excessive profits. An investigation of the books of Kansas City packers by the state's cattlemen was planned and possibly even attempted, but no report of their findings ever surfaced. But even if an investigation did occur, the time and the accounting expertise that would have been necessary for an accurate evaluation were probably beyond the capabilities of most cattlemen.[17]

How influential Kansas cattlemen at the exciting Wichita convention were in persuading President Wilson to order the FTC investigation of packers is difficult to assess. They claimed to have had a great deal of influence and even insisted that it was KLA officers who initiated the call for federal action within the American National. On the other hand, antipacker sentiment was common throughout the beef states, and a large number of producers were demanding some kind of government action. The packers' opposition to an investigation by either the FTC or the Justice Department indicated their fear of resolutions like that of KLA. President Wilson, with all the publicity on the subject that was available, must have been aware of the unrest that existed in stock-producing circles, but it is doubtful whether he realized that some stock interests were in favor not only of raising their profits by reducing those of the packers but also of forcing federal regulation of the whole marketing system. Stockmen's complaints, including the emotional outbursts of the Kansas producers in 1916, probably did have an effect on the president, but the final decision for a thorough investigation came out of circumstances that were much broader than the unrest among stockmen. Producers of almost all food products were demanding a hearing, and consumers—spurred by a 46 percent increase in food prices between July, 1916, and April, 1917—were also clamoring for the president's ear. Something must be done, these groups claimed, about the atrocious actions of the "food gamblers," who were causing high prices and reaping all the profits from food production.

Wilson found himself on the horns of a dilemma. He sympathized with producers and consumers, as well as with the charge that food speculators, including packers, caused much unrest. On the other hand, he hesitated to take any action that might impair food production and shipment to the Allies or thrust the government into the position of setting food prices. The importance of the 1916 presidential election was also on his mind.

In the end, Wilson delayed action until after the election and then ordered an investigation. The Borland resolution was still alive throughout most of 1916, but it was eventually killed when Congress refused to appropriate adequate funds. The way was thus cleared for new action. In December, 1916, the president announced that the Justice Department would begin an investigation of the food trades, but before any of the work began Congress passed a bill that transferred the investigation from the Justice Department to FTC. The food processors actually favored the transfer to FTC—and were instrumental in getting it—but had the packers been given a choice, they would rather have had the USDA in charge, as the latter did not have the authority to subpoena certain records. Wilson refused to support the transfer until convinced that it would not impair food production or shipment overseas. On February 7, 1917—four days after the United States severed diplomatic relations with Germany, and a full year after the tumultuous KLA convention in Whicita—Wilson approved the transfer. Five months later, funds were appropriated and FTC began its work, the results of which were published in five parts from 1918 to 1920.[18]

The *FTC Report* on the packing industry provided a more complete body of information on profits and the various other activities of the large packers than had any of the previous inquiries. Three commissioners—including the former progressive congressman and Wichita newspaperman Victor Murdock —and a host of field representatives launched an extensive investigation of Armour, Swift, Morris, Wilson, and Cudahy. These men analyzed hundreds of documents from packer files, over nine thousand pages of sworn testimony, and thousands of pages of field reports before compiling their final report. Many obstacles were encountered. The packers had business interests in fields where the commission's "inquisitorial powers" were limited and some preliminary evidence was unreliable due to deceptive methods of bookkeeping. The packers, according to the report, also falsified records and coached employees in the proper responses to the investigators' questions. But even with these handicaps, the commission claimed that the extensiveness of the investigation and the careful sifting and piecing together of the available evidence rendered an accurate report, marred only by its tendency to understate the actual situation.[19]

Most producers agreed wholeheartedly with the findings of the commission, as it confirmed many things they already believed. The packers, on the other hand, denied not so much the raw data but rather the conclusions that FTC deduced from the vast number of facts. Historians seem to be in general agreement that most of the factual information was accurate, although Rudolf A. Clemen, who published a major work on the meat-packing industry a few years after the conclusion of the FTC investigation, defended the packers. But Clemen's research, and possibly even his manuscript, was well under way before FTC began its work. Clemen has taught economics and history at Northwestern University and, at the time his book was published, was on the editorial staff of *The National Provisioner,* the trade journal of the packing industry.[20]

The Big Five, according to the FTC, held such a dominant place in the meat industry "that they control at will the market in which they buy their supplies, the market in which they sell their products, and hold the fortunes of their competitors in their hands." In the dressed-meat business alone the five large packers killed "70 per cent of the live stock slaughtered by all packers and butchers engaged in interstate commerce." By way of comparison, only one independent packer in the United States slaughtered over 1 percent of the beef, and only nine independents slaughterd as much as 1 percent of the pork that moved into interstate commerce. The Big Five's control of by-products was even greater than that of fresh and preserved meats, as many of the smaller packers were unable to utilize the by-products from slaughter and thus destroyed or sold them to the larger packing interests.

The packers in question denied that they controlled the dressed-beef trade to the extent that was implied by the FTC. Instead, they made a concerted attempt to convince the public that their portion of slaughter did not "exceed one-third of the total meat production of the United States." This was pretty much the same argument that big packers had used during the Garfield investigation in the early 1900s. According to the method they used to compile their figures, it may have been true. The Big Five omitted from their slaughter figures all the animals killed by their affiliated companies, yet they included all the stock still butchered on farms for home consumption in their tabulation of the nation's total slaughter. By figuring one-third of the total slaughter on this basis, the FTC countered, "monopoly could not be considered to exist in the meat industry, even if every pound of meat consumed in towns and cities were handled by a single company, so long as farmers continued to kill their own hogs and cows."[21] The FTC might also have pointed out that the relatively large percentage of stock still slaughtered on the farm did little to change the situation of the commercial stock producer, who still had to sell on the market to relatively few buyers.

Nor was the Big Five influence limited to the domestic stock trade or just to meat processing and distribution; according to FTC, they also had large interests in foreign slaughtering plants and in the distribution of almost all foods. The large American packers, for instance, owned or controlled more than half of the meat exported from Argentina, Brazil, and Uruguay, and also had large investments in other countries having surplus meat. "Under present shipping conditions," FTC noted, "the big American packers control more than half of the meat upon which the allies are dependent." The Big Five also handled more than half of all the interstate commerce in cheese, poultry, and eggs, and about a third of all cottonseed oil. In addition they had rapidly growing interests in the distribution of canned fruits and vegetables.[22]

The principal method, according to FTC, by which this small group of packers gained and increased their monopolistic domination of the food business was through their control of the distribution system. The instruments of control in this area included ownership of 91 percent of the refrigerated cars in use, as well as immense holdings of cold storage plants and branch houses used in wholesale distribution.

In addition the Big Five had interests in several central stockyards. FTC established to its satisfaction that of the twenty-eight central markets in which the large packers had financial interests an average of over 80 percent of the stock in each yard was controlled by one or more of the Big Five. The percentages ranged from control of about 23 percent of the stock in the west Philadelphia yards to total ownership of the yards in Denver. In Kansas one or more of the Big Five controlled almost 60 percent of the Wichita yards, 68 percent of those in Kansas City, and 85 percent of the St. Joseph yards.

In addition to controlling the yards *per se*, the major packers had large interests in collateral institutions including terminal rail lines, market newspapers (though packers did not appear to be financially involved with the market paper in Kansas City), and banks for stockmen. Strength in the financial area was based not so much on actual ownership as it was upon the influence that the Big Five exerted by reason of their large patronage of the banks and the large number of their representatives who sat on the boards of directors. In Kansas the Big Five had members on the boards of five banks in St. Joseph, three in Wichita, and three in Kansas City. Finally, the above interests led to a large amount of packer influence in "live-stock exchange buildings where commission men have their offices; control of assignment of pens to commission firms . . . control of yardage services and charges; control of weighing facilities; control of the disposition of dead animals and other profitable yard monopolies; and in most cases control of all packing-house and other business sites."[23]

The packers' influence at central markets was more threatening to stockmen than any other of their activities. Not only did it give packers the opportunity to fix prices, it also allowed them to cheat the producer in a multitude of exchanges, not least of which were short weights and excessive charges for feed and yardage.

The multiple and diverse interests of the large packers outlined above had been developing for over a generation. By 1917 the FTC believed that the existence of a conspiracy was abundantly clear. The Big Five, they said, intended to "monopolize and divide among the several interests the distribution of the food supply not only of the United States but of all countries which produce a food surplus, and, as a result of this monopolistic position, to extort excessive profits from the people not only of the United States but of a large part of the world."[24]

While President Wilson was especially interested in the Big Five's possible impairment of the flow of food to the Allies, the stock producer was more concerned with price fixing, excessive profits, and other unfair practices in the central markets that FTC attributed to the large packers. This, too, harmed the war effort, many cattlemen said, by discouraging production.

One of the most annoying and costly difficulties faced by producers was the violent fluctuations in prices at the central markets, which were caused, cattlemen believed, by the Big Five's dominant influence. A letter from a Kansas banker to Joe Mercer in 1918 illustrated how price fluctuations hampered producers and robbed them of just returns. The banker was financially involved with the large Kansas feeding firm of McCready & Shroyer, near Miltonvale. One day, according to the letter, the feeders responded to a call from the St. Joseph yards to ship fat cattle, as the receipts were expected to be light. The feeders responded immediately by shipping four carloads, but, due to the difficulties of sorting and loading, the remaining thirty-three loads were delayed in reaching the yards by twenty-four hours. They received $14.85 a hundredweight for the first four cars and $13.00 for the remainder, for exactly the same quality of cattle. The fluctuation represented a difference of over $20.00 a head, which caused the banker to question the advisability of continuing his support for so risky a business.[25]

The FTC investigation supported the belief that packers were manipulating stock prices. The Big Five employed "a vicious system of . . . price cutting," FTC said, to keep small competitors out of the market. In addition, FTC found evidence that stock prices sometimes depended upon whether the large packers were "overstocked with fresh and cured meats and want[ed] to sell in a high market or . . . understocked and want[ed] to buy in a low market."

Another practice that affected the producer was "wiring on," as it was called, which amounted to a packer informing a second stockyard of the price offered at the first yard if a shipper decided to take his stock beyond the initial point. Not only did the practice eliminate competition, it deprived the shipper of the chance to find higher prices at another central market. Also, the shipper had the added freight cost and loss from shrinkage if he decided to try another market. John A. Edwards reported a classic example of this practice. He said that he had sent a "train load" of fat cattle to Kansas City where he was offered $1.50 a hundredweight below what he thought he should have. He decided not to sell and went on to St. Louis where he was offered 75 cents below the Kansas City price by a representative of the same large packer, after, Edwards claimed, the buyer had checked with Kansas City. From St. Louis, Edwards went on to Chicago—usually the top market for fat stock—and was offered the same price that he had been offered in Kansas City. Edwards was also advised that he should have sold in Kansas City and saved himself all the additional trouble and expense. In this case, Edwards claimed, he eventually sold to an independent packer for the price he had expected in Kansas City, but most shippers, especially the many small stockmen, were unable or unwilling to go to this much work or expense to market their stock.[26]

The section on profits probably contained the most disputed conclusions of the *FTC Report*. The veracity of this section—in the minds of FTC, producers, and packers—was critical in establishing motives for the numerous unfair practices of which the packers were accused, as well as a basis for a judgment on "excessive profits." Basic to the dispute were two different methods of figuring profits. The large packers referred to profits in terms of a percentage of sales dollars or a certain amount per head of stock slaughtered, while the FTC and the producers cited profits in terms of a percentage of net worth. The packers' point of view, for example, was illustrated in advertisements in livestock papers and journals claiming that they were operating at a margin of $1.22 per head for cattle, and only 66½ and 15 cents for hogs and sheep, respectively. "How many local butchers," the advertisements asked, "would be content with less than fifteen cents profit upon a sheep which he has slaughtered?" Throughout much of the time that the investigation was in progress Swift sponsored advertisements that claimed profits of only 3 cents on each dollar of sales. By 1919, when producers and consumers were even more upset with high food prices, advertisements claimed that profits were down to 2 cents per dollar.[27]

FTC's report, which was as comprehensive as available records allowed, cast doubt on the accuracy of the packers' method of figuring profits and questioned the veracity of their advertisements. The report dealt with several areas related to financial operations, including a survey of the Big Five's development, a comparison of the large packers' earnings before and during the war, a study of their accounting systems, and a comparison of the profits of the big packers with those of several independent packers. An added concern of the investigators was to discover whether the controls established on profits by the Food Administration were effective.[28]

After showing that the remarkable growth of the large packers had come largely from reinvested surpluses, the report turned to the question of net profits during the second decade of the twentieth century. According to FTC, they totaled $251.7 million for the six years between 1912 and 1917— $59.5 before the war, and $192.2 million after the war began. In terms of a percentage of capital invested—defined as the net worth of capital stock and surplus—this represented an average of 13.6 percent profit, 7.8 percent for the prewar years, and 19.4 percent after the war started. In summary, the report noted that there was no doubt

> that the packers' profits, particularly since the beginning of the European war, have been enormous, both in the United States and in the foreign countries. Measured by prewar profits, the 1917 profits were 350 per cent greater than in the average of the three years before the European war; measured by the amount of sales, they averaged, in 1917, 4.6 cents on the dollar, which was sufficient to produce for the five companies a total profit of $96,182,000; measured by the net worth of the combined corporations (capital stock plus surplus), they aver-

aged, in 1917, 21.6 per cent; measured by the capital stock outstanding, as an indication of the dividend possibilities, they averaged, in 1917, 39.5 per cent; and measured by the packers' actual investment of new capital, they amount to several times even this last figure.[29]

The implication of this conclusion was not lost on stockmen. Considerably higher prices could have been paid for livestock without endangering a reasonable profit even though the packers may have made only a few cents on each dollar of sales. Profits subsequent to the 9 percent restriction ordered by the Food Administration were especially difficult to ascertain, but the commission believed that they approached 15 percent in 1918. The figures cited by the report, however, were admittedly incomplete; but, in the opinion of the commissioners, they had erred on the side of conservatism in their estimates. Yet, the commission realized that the failure of the packers to follow "well-recognized and fundamental principles of accounting" rendered it impossible for the FTC to "ascertain accurately either the total profits of the great companies or the profits per head or per pound for the principal meat products." The report implied that the packers' profits were considerably higher than they reported.

It was unfortunate that the financial records kept by the industry, especially cost accounting, were inadequate for a definite appraisal of the profits made in meat slaughter. The FTC might have put the dispute over profits to rest had they been able to establish beyond any doubt a definite profit level. The commission, however, was certain that packer profits per pound of meat did not exceed a few cents and sometimes may have been even less than a cent. But the commission was equally certain that the advertised claim that profits were only a few cents per unit—a small amount in the public mind—was wholly misleading and tended to obscure the real facts. "As a matter of fact," FTC concluded, "a profit of a cent per unit far from being a small profit, may be an exorbitant profit measured in terms of return upon capital invested." For example, the Big Five reported to the Food Administration a figure of 2.2 cents for each dollar of sales as their profit in 1918, a figure equivalent to 15 percent on capital stock and surplus. "Thus while the packers' profits per pound may appear to the public to be small," FTC noted, "they are in reality large, due to the enormous tonnage produced on the basis of a relatively moderate investment."[30]

The FTC also reported that the big packers had invested money in other businesses related to meat slaughtering as well as some completely unrelated to food processing. Cattlemen saw these investments as an outlet for excessively large profits and another example of the packers' growing influence. In Kansas City the large packers were reported to own all of the stock of the Fowler Packing Company, the Fowler Serum Company, and the Standard Rendering Company. The last company was used by the large packers, along with the Fowler Desiccating and Rendering Works, to dominate the collection of waste material from the city's retail meat markets. In addition the packers owned 50 percent of the Aaron Poultry and Egg Company. In businesses unassociated with food processing, FTC reported that Swift and Armour either owned outright or controlled a majority of the voting stock in the North Kansas City Land and Improvement Association and the North Kansas City Development Company. The latter, in turn, owned the North Kansas City Light, Heat, and Power Company, as well as a company concerned with the area's water supply. Armour also controlled 30 percent of the National Bank of North Kansas City.[31]

The FTC failed to make much of their discovery that independent packers were also making large profits, possibly because the commission questioned the implications of their own findings. After analyzing the earnings of 117 large independent packers for 1918, FTC concluded that they had earned 18.1 percent on net worth—"a manifestly high return"—compared to the Big Five's 15 percent, and that there were similar profits for every year since 1914.

There were, the commission hastened to add, other circumstances to consider before any conclusions could be drawn. The independent packers that were studied, for instance, were a "selected group" that kept clear and reliable tabulations of their business activities. It was apparent that the large independent packers were more profitable than the smaller ones, and that the business activities of the independents and the Big Five were not strictly comparable. The latter had wide-ranging business interests, some of which were far removed from meat slaughter, while the independents were almost exclusively meat packers. In fact, the lower total return of the large packers might have indicated that they were actually making considerably more on the meat part of their businesses than the independents were, as there were indications that some of their investments outside of meat slaughtering were disastrous. The commission concluded:

> If it can be assumed that the great packers made as much on the meat-end of their business as do the independents, it would follow that they must make considerably less on the nonlive-stock end, in order

to get a lower average rate on the whole business. . . . In other words high profits on meat may be used to finance new activities pending the establishment of the latter on a firm basis, meanwhile keeping down the average return on the total business to a level less than that shown for the larger independents.[32]

FTC noted that if the Big Five were actually earning less, then their asserted operating efficiency and the practicality of large industrial conglomerates should be seriously questioned. One might also note that if the disparity of earnings discovered by FTC actually existed, then the larger earnings of the smaller plants help explain the eventual breakup of the larger packers, and, to some extent, the decentralization of the whole packing industry.

During the early period of FTC's investigation, a few Kansas cattlemen expressed little faith in the agency's work. Results were not published for almost a year, and some stockmen grew impatient. The timing of the investigation was poor, cattlemen said, as rising stock prices tended to take the sting out of the stockmen's discomfiture.

Other cattlemen, however, worked to keep the stockmen's attention focused on the supposed evils of the packing industry. Walter R. Stubbs, for instance, scolded cattlemen at the time the investigation began for losing the fervor for reform that had been expressed at the 1916 KLA convention. He said that only the power of the federal government could correct the abuses and that the cattlemen themselves were responsible for the lack of government action. The large packers, Stubbs believed, "were poor as Job's turkey thirty or forty years ago and all the money they have got, they have gotten from the producer. . . . When you ship your hogs and cattle down there to the stock yards, you have to pen them in a packer's yard; you have got to send them right to his home to get them penned up. . . . [you pay] two or three times the right price for feed. . . . [and] that is your fault. I am not blaming the packer a bit." When FTC issued a preliminary report in 1918, however, the cattlemen returned to their antipacker stance. Many of their charges were supported, and it appeared that the investigation, if followed by appropriate legislation, might well eliminate many abuses experienced by the producer.[33]

The FTC had little doubt after completing its study that legislation was needed. The large packers had grown to immense proportions since their origins in the nineteenth century, primarily through reinvesting profits from the industry. About the only change that FTC noted in large packer operations since the 1890s was that the monopoly had become broader and more inclusive. Their "monopolistic control of the distributive machinery" had enabled them to move almost at will into the whole food and by-product business. There was no possibility, the commission said, of effecting fundamental improvements "short of the acquisition by the Federal government of the distributive utilities now controlled by the Big Five." With this in mind, FTC recommended that the government acquire through the railroad administration ownership of all rolling stock used for transporting livestock and all refrigerated cars. In addition the commission suggested that the government buy enough branch houses, cold storage plants, and warehouses to ensure competitive distribution. To ensure fair marketing, the commission recommended that the government take over all the principal stockyards of the country, as well as other facilities located in the yards that were necessary for marketing operations. In short, FTC suggested a large step toward nationalizing the nation's marketing system for livestock, a step that many cattlemen were hesitant to take.[34]

So cattlemen obtained the extensive investigation that they had been urging for over a generation, but some were unwilling to approve the resulting suggestions. Throughout the postwar depression, no action was taken to put the full package of FTC recommendations into effect. Most cattlemen were convinced by this time, though, that federal action was necessary. Only the type of action or role that the government should assume was a matter for debate. The FTC recommendations, although reminiscent of some proposals made by the Populists during the 1890s, went beyond what most congressmen considered to be a proper relationship between government and private business. Congress eventually responded with a considerably milder form of government involvement than was urged by FTC. Its recommendations were, in large part, in line with the desires of producers.

It would be a mistake to leave the impression that the Kansas stockman was a chip-on-the-shoulder sort of fellow who did little during this period but criticize the various elements of the marketing system. He was, in fact, often very happy with the railroads and stockyards, and sometimes sent a few congenial sentiments toward the large packers. And he always recognized the importance of these businesses to the beef industry. One issue of the *Stockman,* for example, noted how fortunate Kansas producers were to have the "great Kansas City yards" close at hand, yards that many stockmen in

Texas, Oklahoma, and the Southwest paid higher freight rates and endured larger stock shrinkages in order to patronize. The fact that Kansas City had the largest stocker and feeder market in the world was also appreciated. Many cattlemen also realized that the packers' extensive storage facilities and national and international systems of distribution were of great benefit to the stock industry. Others believed that the storage facilities of the large packers tended to equalize the supply of animals in the central market and, to some extent, modify price fluctuations.[35]

Not all of the producers' responses, then, were as negative as the literature sometimes implied, because grievances were probably given more coverage in newspapers and journals than expressions of satisfaction. But there were significant grievances and negative responses among stockmen, and these were destined to increase before they declined. Ultimately, federal legislation laid to rest some of the producers' complaints against stockyards and packers, but Congress was not prodded into action until FTC's findings were joined to the unrest of the 1920s.

9

Depressions and Low Prices:
Beef Production between the Wars

Producing agricultural products after World War I was a different proposition than it had been earlier in the century; frustration, failure, and depression were the common fare. There were a few good years, enough to generate hope and keep many producers in business; but on the whole it was an era that was prosperous for only a few, a continual struggle for most, and a period of failure for many. Although beef producers generally fared better than dirt farmers, especially those wedded to a single crop, they too suffered many of the same depressed conditions. A severe decline, followed by a slight recovery during the middle twenties, confronted the beef business even before the combined impact of drought and depression sent agriculture reeling in the following decade. Recovery began only in the late thirties when the cycle of drought was broken; then World War II finally brought some prosperity back to the stricken industry.

The unexpected depression after World War I affected most of the nation's industries, but its effects were most severely felt for the longest period of time by the agricultural sector. Although stock prices had not yet declined nearly as much as they would, Joseph H. Mercer was one of the first Kansans to describe the depressed conditions when he announced early in 1920 that the previous year had been the most abnormal one ever chronicled in the history of KLA. He cited as causes of the abnormality the extreme winter of 1918–19 and the late spring that followed, the high cost of feed, and the unsettled marketing conditions. While 1919 had been a banner year for KLA growth, he said, "its members have probably suffered greater financial losses throughout the year than have ever before been recorded in the history of the live stock industry in this state." He estimated that Kansas cattlemen had lost an aggregate of over $75 million in depreciated herd value. Thousands of stockmen, he said, "have had their all swept away—savings of a lifetime scattered to the four winds—and will never again have sufficient credit to again enter the business."

No one in 1920 expected the economic plight of farmers and ranchers to deteriorate still further, but it did. In 1922 Mercer made observations similar to those he had made earlier, only this time he crowned 1921 with the dubious honor of being the worst in agricultural history, with scores of Kansas farmers "hopelessly bankrupt." Conditions began to improve slightly after 1922, but the whole period between 1919 and 1926 was depressed. Then about three years of relative prosperity followed, sandwiched neatly between the postwar depression and the general economic collapse that hit at the close of the decade.[1]

Even the *Stockman* had its problems during the depressed twenties with unpaid subscriptions and advertising bills. Then, as reported in the May 15, 1921, issue, an internal problem arose: "The Honorable printers, the Reverend pressmen and the Estimable binders," were on strike, the paper noted, "they seek to labor but 44 hours per week, whereas they have been working 8 hours per day."

Surviving the twenties did little to prepare farmers and ranchers for the disaster that confronted them and the nation during the thirties. All sectors of the economy suffered, but the persistence of the postwar agricultural depression rendered the agricultural sector even less able to cope with the new calamity. Agriculture's plight was reflected in net farm income figures, which declined from $10 billion in 1919 to only $2.5 billion in 1932 (Table 1). By 1936 national farm income was back up, but it was still low and did not reflect conditions in parts of the Great Plains. Annual cash receipts from the marketing of Kansas farm products, for example, declined from an average of $476.6 million during the last half of the 1920s to $271.3 million during the 1930s, a reduction of over 43 percent. Kansas farm income did not again approach the average of the late twenties until 1941.[2]

The general economic depression of the 1930s was complicated by droughts, especially on the Great Plains. In Kansas rainfall had not always been adequate in every part of the state during the twenties, but there was an annual average of at least twenty-eight inches before the decline in the thirties. The state's average, for instance, was only twenty inches in 1934 and just slightly over eighteen inches in 1936, one of the driest years on record. Although the greater amounts of rainfall in eastern Kansas kept the state average relatively high, the central and western sections were consistently dry, receiving only ten to twelve inches of moisture in 1934 and not much more than that in 1936. Then, though spring and summer rains—when the grass and crops needed it the most—were scant, nature ordained that the parched and hot summers of 1934 and 1936 be followed by winters with almost no snowfall.

The legendary dust storms followed hard on the heels of the drought, to the dismay of housewives. The blinding dirt of the 1930s generated considerable literature—some from the USDA—which tended to blame the plow that broke the plains and the irresponsible overgrazing allowed by cattlemen for the dust as well as the soil erosion that resulted. Some of the literature even predicted complete loss of productivity on much of the Great Plains as some areas became a man-made "Great American Desert." This view, however, should be seriously questioned. The dust storms were obviously related to vegetation cover, which in turn was related to the quantity of rainfall. Not the plow, some historians suggest, but the periodic droughts endemic to the Plains caused the dust storms, and not even the native grass would have prevented the blowing dirt. Breaking the sod may have even increased the ground cover, and thus the much-maligned plow may have reduced the destructiveness of the storms. When rainfall increased during the 1940s, bumper wheat crops and native grasses returned to the same Kansas lands that had eroded so severely during the 1930s, supporting the view that dust storms did not seriously harm productivity, exonerating farmers and ranchers, and disproving the predictions of prophets who foresaw only deserts and doom for the Great Plains.[3]

While dust and drought prevailed, however, reports from Kansas understandably became increasingly pessimistic as the 1930s wore on. According to Mercer, 1930 was a catastrophic year due to financial deflation and dry weather. The following year was worse. Then, he wrote, 1932 brought "even greater disaster to the livestock industry than the preceding year." Each year thereafter, until the late thirties, was reported as being worse than the preceding one. The *Stockman* noted in 1934 that "there is not an old-timer in the cattle country whose memory runs back far enough that he can relate any early day experience which in any way compares with the hopeless conditions that face the cowman today." Hot temperatures and scant rainfall forced many stockmen to operate trucks around the clock hauling water and feed, if available, to their famished stock. Many springs, creeks, and wells that had never in anyone's memory failed before dried up during the early thirties.

In 1934 a report from southwestern Kansas noted that "the highways and

Table 1. Farm Cash Receipts and Income, and Indexes of Prices Received and Paid by Farmers, and Parity Ratio; 1919–1940

		Indexes of prices received and paid by farmers (1910–14 = 100)						
		Prices received by farmers[2]			Prices paid by farmers			
Year	Net income to persons on farms from farming[1]	All farm products	Crops	Livestock and products	Living	Production	Prices paid including interest, taxes, and wage rates	Parity ratio[3]
1919	10,061	217	230	206	202	195	197	110
1920	9,009	211	235	190	228	195	214	99
1921	4,131	124	121	127	164	128	155	80
1922	5,081	131	136	126	153	127	151	87
1923	5,895	142	156	128	156	138	159	89
1924	5,681	143	159	128	156	140	160	89
1925	7,575	156	164	149	161	145	164	95
1926	6,810	145	139	151	158	141	160	91
1927	6,569	140	134	146	155	141	159	88

1928	6,844	148	142	155	156	148	162	91
1929	7,024	148	135	159	154	146	160	92
1930	5,060	125	115	134	144	135	151	83
1931	3,981	87	75	98	124	113	130	67
1932	2,510	65	57	72	106	99	112	58
1933	3,012	70	71	70	108	99	109	64
1934	3,428	90	98	81	122	114	120	75
1935	5,858	109	103	114	124	122	124	88
1936	4,954	114	108	119	124	122	124	92
1937	6,754	122	118	126	128	132	131	93
1938	5,101	97	80	112	122	122	124	78
1939	5,189	95	82	107	120	121	123	77
1940	5,299	100	90	109	121	123	124	81

[1] Realized net income of farm operators plus value of inventory change plus wages paid to farm laborers living on farms, in $1,000,000.

[2] Base, August, 1909–July, 1914 = 100

[3] Ratio of prices received by farmers to prices paid, including interest, taxes, and wage rates.

SOURCE: Adapted from information in U.S. Bureau of the Census, *Historical Statistics of the United States, Colonial Times to 1957*, p. 283.

canyons are lined with weary famishing herds, including every age and size, and not a cow, steer or calf has a value except that put on by the government appraiser." Conditions worsened in this area before they improved. Two years later it was estimated that 12 percent of the state's cattlemen were out of water, while 13 percent were out of feed. A letter to Senator Capper in 1937 lamented that most of the livestock in the western part of the state was gone, that 90 percent of the farmers were bankrupt, and that dust storms occurred three to five times a week. The following year a traveler through western Kansas saw as many tractors as cattle and not "enough native grass to fill an overcoat pocket."[4]

Government purchases of cattle in 1934 helped conserve feed supplies, but cattlemen were forced to try everything to save their remaining stock. Anything available with nutritional value was used for feed. James Tod, president of KLA and the only son of former KLA president William J. Tod, experimented with burning the thorns off the "tree cactus" that grew on his New Mexico ranch as feed for 1,700 starving cows. It worked well, he said, as long as the cactus held out. Tod used kerosene burners for this work and noted that a man working ten hours could burn enough to satisfy 110 cows and calves for a day. It took calves only a few days, and cows a little longer, to acquire a taste for the cactus, which, according to Tod, reminded one of the avocado pear.

Eventually, Tod was forced to move his herd to Mississippi, but this provided no salvation either. Unaccustomed to the climate and the diseases in the area, many of Tod's weakened cattle soon died. In the end, Tod's losses forced him to sell the model ranch near Maple Hill that he and his father had so carefully built.[5] The buyer was his brother-in-law, Horace G. Adams, Jr., who already owned a large ranch near Maple Hill.

Many cattlemen had to sell or move stock during the thirties. Some took a leaf from Tod's notebook and sent cattle to southern states where moisture and feed were more plentiful, while others moved cattle to the Flint Hills or eastern parts of the state. Wherever there was a little extra feed, cows from the dry West soon appeared. Jesse Greenleaf saved much of his stock—by this time only a commercial herd, because the postwar depression had forced him to dispose of his purebreds—by shipping them to the Atchison area to graze the marshy flats along the Missouri River, where they often kept company with bootleggers tending hidden stills, as well as hobos who were also trying to survive. Feed was also shipped into the state when it was available, with KLA serving as a clearing house to coordinate the distribution of surplus feed to needy cattle.[6]

The causes of the depressed state of American agriculture between the wars were many and varied. In the 1930s the economy was generally depressed, and agriculture had the drought to contend with besides. But in the 1920s the long depression in agriculture was due in part to the producers themselves. Writing in the New York *Times,* William Allen White noted fairly accurately that the farm problem during the twenties was not the result of any organized or insidious plot by other economic groups, but rather the consequence of agriculture's relatively slow adaptation to changing times. The slowness, White added, was partially due to the nature of the industry and the extended period of time that was required to change basic operations.[7]

The inability of producers to adapt rapidly to changing conditions was illustrated well by the agricultural surpluses that existed after World War I. The war had stimulated a large demand for foodstuffs, and farmers and ranchers had happily responded. They gave little thought to the prospect of decreasing demands with Europe's recovery after the war, or to the time it would take to adjust their farming and ranching operations to lower demands. Yet, while producers can be criticized for lack of foresight, they were often following during the war the best advice of Food Administrator Herbert Hoover, who cajoled, pressured, and praised the willing farmers and ranchers to greater heights of production. Even after the war, Hoover believed, a devastated Europe would continue to demand American farm products in increasing quantities. He was wrong, and slow to correct his error. Europe failed to maintain its demands, let alone increase them. With the reestablishment of prewar shipping patterns, other nations cut into the outlets recently acquired by the United States. Europe's recovery after the war was relatively rapid, which again defied Hoover's predictions.[8]

Some American producers even contributed to Europe's rapid recovery and thus, indirectly, to reduced markets. J. O. "Jake" Southard, a Kansas raiser of purebreds, exemplified not only America's contribution to postwar Europe's beef production but also the fate of some who expanded their beef cattle production during the wartime boom. Southard, known as the "Comiskey Hereford King," was a former employee of Swift & Company who had entered the cattle business just before the war began. The Monarch family of purebred Herefords became his trademark. Thousands of dollars

J. O. Southard's sale pavilion where his Monarch Herefords were sold. *Courtesy of the Kansas State Historical Society.*

were made during the war, Southard noted later, and were as easily spent. After the conflict, Southard became the first American to earn a contract with the Belgian and French governments to assist in restocking cattle lost or butchered during the war. More than 15,000 milk and beef cattle were called for, which were reported to have grossed Southard over a million dollars. But the flush times this Kansas cattleman enjoyed changed late in 1921. When the full force of the deflation hit the industry, Southard nearly went broke. He soon announced that he was retiring from ranching in order to promote community sales, where he would "turn anything from a ratskin to a ranch into money on a few days notice." His sons continued in ranching, but even this enterprise ended two years later with a complete dispersion sale. The relatively profitable years of the middle twenties brought Southard back into ranching again, but this time he wisely retained his interest in the Southard Sales System to supplement his income.[9]

As a result of Europe's recovery, small quantities of agricultural produce were marketed overseas during the twenties and thirties. At the same time, developments on the domestic scene, such as unemployment and altered buying patterns, militated against using as much as could be produced. Per capita beef consumption, for instance, declined from 75.8 pounds in 1918 to an average of 65.2 pounds during the 1920s. This level remained fairly constant between the wars except when government relief agencies provided large quantities to the unemployed in 1934.

Wheat and corn producers also faced a declining demand for cereals. Early in the twenties, government attacks on the high cost of living and the

continued practice of "Hooverizing" the food budget that had been patrioti-
cally adopted during the war reduced demands for food, as did the changing
patterns of consumption that resulted from new dress fashions and health
fads. The slim-look of the twenties, however, was not as detrimental to the
beef producer as it was to those who raised grain. Unemployment, especially
during the early twenties and thirties, and the increased number of manufactured goods that consumers needed, or at least thought that they needed, also
cut into food budgets.[10]

More specific information demonstrates that the general rural depression
discussed above was much more than a figment of farmers' and ranchers'
imaginations. The rising number of beef cattle in Kansas, for instance,
reflected more than the character of agricultural production during the war.
Over 2.7 million cattle and calves were reported in 1919, representing a 47
percent rise since 1914, or more than double the increase of cattle in the
nation as a whole (see Figure 1, p. 21). One expected, however, the cattle
in a western beef state to increase more than the national average. The distribution of these cattle remained much the same, although a slight shift
toward the western and southwestern part of the state had occurred by 1920
before the drought of the thirties pushed cattle back into the Flint Hills (see
Maps 2 and 3, pp. 71 and 72).[11]

The high number of beef cattle in 1919 declined to an average of about
2.2 million head during the 1920s. The following decade the average was
almost 2.6 million head, until 1935. The combined forces of depression and
drought, as well as a greater realization that overproduction depressed prices,
drove the cattle population below 2 million by 1937. Because there was enough
feed available, except during droughts, there were generally more cattle than
the markets were able to absorb.

The easy credit that was available had encouraged the growth in cattle
numbers during the war, and there was a similar situation during the late
1920s. John Clay, long-time ranch manager, commission man, and cattle
financier, blamed packer money for much of the boom in cattle financing. It
began with P. D. Armour, Clay said, and "his example was followed till every
big packer, his associate banks, his imitators in the search for wealth, promoted loan companies that sold their securities freely in every part of the
country." Cattle financing became, according to Clay, a race for "greed,
glory, and power." But the packers were not alone in lending capital. Most
banks, especially those near producing areas, urged their customers to claim

a slice of the war bonanza. Almost anyone with cattle for collateral could get money, contributing further to the oversupply.

The speculative boom was not limited to cattle; investment in land also occurred at inflated rates, and eventually made the postwar depression more severe than it might otherwise have been. In some cases, land values rose by 70 percent during the war, and much of the land that changed hands at these inflated values did so with a down payment of as little as 5 to 19 percent. Farmers and ranchers also bought other goods—radios, bathtubs, and even more costly items like trucks, automobiles, and tractors. Some of these articles were, of course, necessary for efficient operation, but they were also expensive and added much to the agricultural debt. The general absence of rural prosperity during the 1920s had a redeeming feature, however, as it kept overspeculation in agriculture at a minimum.[12]

As production remained high and other conditions depressed the nation's economy, prices of farm commodities and the purchasing power of farmers and ranchers plunged downward and remained low for most of the interwar period. While general price levels remained adequate on most farm products throughout 1919, they had declined 43 percent by 1921 (see Table 1). Prices that farmers paid, for the most part, showed no such decline. The purchasing power of corn was a graphic example of this relationship of prices. In 1919 about a fifth of a bushel of corn bought a gallon of gas, while six bushels of corn purchased a ton of coal. Two years later the ratios had increased to two bushels for the gas and sixty bushels for the coal. Some farmers wisely substituted corn for coal. Cattlemen had similar experiences with their products. In 1913 the USDA claimed that seven cattle were worth a wagon, grain binder, or gang plow. By 1921, seventeen cattle were required for the same purchases.

Farm parity figures, reflecting the uneven correlation in prices farmers and ranchers paid and received, declined from 110 in 1919 to 80 in 1921. Farm parity averaged just over 90 for the remainder of the decade; but grain prices remained low, and the rise was due largely to products like cotton and meat. The price situation for agriculture deteriorated further in the 1930s as the nation's economy became depressed, and farm prices fell more than did those of nonfarm goods and services. The parity ratio in 1932, for example, was down to 58, a decline of 34 points from 1929. Wheat was thirty-two cents a bushel in 1932, and fifteen-cent corn was again used for fuel.[13]

Low profits and high costs during the twenties spelled high debts for many farmers and ranchers. Those on the Great Plains had the most severe problem; 9 percent of all Kansas farmers and 28 percent of those in Montana reported losing their farms or other property. Mortgaged indebtedness for Kansas farmers and ranchers reached an all-time high for the interwar period in 1924, when the figure was reported to have reached $535 million. Not even during the depressed thirties—when Kansas farm mortgages amounted to $411.7 and $429.2 million in 1930 and 1932, respectively—was the figure as high as the 1924 figure, but it probably would have been higher had other factors been comparable to the twenties. By the thirties many marginal operators had already been forced out of business, there had been no war boom to encourage investment, and the financial institutions were increasingly unable to loan more money to farmers and ranchers.

Although the raw totals do not necessarily reveal the fact, farm and ranch indebtedness was probably a more serious problem for those still in business during the 1930s than it had been the previous decade, and credit amelioration was one of agriculture's most pressing needs. During the early thirties one estimate reported that 50 percent of the nation's farm and ranch owners were debt free, 33 percent would have no serious debt problems if prosperity was restored, and 17 percent were confronting a hopeless situation. Almost a million ranchers and farmers lost their land during the four years following 1930, and some were Kansans. According to Roy S. Johnson, a Federal Land Bank official, the number of mortgaged farms and ranches in the state decreased between 1930 and 1935 from 78,496 to 69,939, or from 47 to 40.1 percent of the total number. But one must approach this decline cautiously. As foreclosures reduced the number and percentage of mortgaged farms and ranches, they also made the situation appear better than it actually was.[14]

The market levels for cattle also revealed the depressed state of American agriculture, although beef prices made a better recovery during the 1920s than did grain prices. In 1919 Kansas beef cattle were selling for $10.40 to $11.25 a hundredweight and sometimes higher. Two years later prices had been cut by half. Once under way, the drop was exceedingly steep. The experience of E. T. Anderson towards the end of 1920 illustrated the rapidity. Anderson sold forty carloads of cattle in November, 1920, for an average of $13.00 a hundred. Three months later he sold the same quality of cattle for $7.75; and while Anderson was upset with the low price, he had actually received about $2.00 a hundred more than beef prices averaged for the whole year of 1921. The rapidity of the decline in prices, as well as the extent, put a number of cattlemen out of business.

After reaching bottom in 1921, beef prices began a tortuously slow advance of a few cents a hundredweight each year until 1925, when the average price jumped about a dollar. From $7.00 a hundred in 1925 the average price moved up to $10.00 by 1928, then turned downward again. By the time they reached bottom during the early 1930s, stockmen had had a real education in low prices. From an average of around $10.00 per hundred during the late twenties, Kansas beef prices fell more than 50 percent by 1932 and to the phenomenally low average price of $3.95 in 1933. Not since the first decade of the twentieth century had beef prices dipped so low, and then they were part of a considerably lower structure for all prices. After the bottom was sounded in 1933, yearly average prices for Kansas fluctuated some but generally moved upward along a course between $4.30 in 1934 to $7.60 in 1939. It was 1942 before beef prices again reached the 1919 and 1928 levels.[15]

The deflated prices, especially the sharp declines during the early twenties and thirties, were especially hard on feeders. Many of them were confident as World War I ended that the market would maintain some stability; thus, they purchased relatively high-priced feeder cattle. By 1921 they found themselves with large investments in stock and high-priced feed, and extremely low market prices. Some claimed losses as high as $60.00 a head, but most were probably not as high as this. Many feeders were, however, forced to get out of the business or sharply curtail their operations. A 1921 study of twenty-two widely scattered counties in Kansas revealed that investments in feeding cattle had been reduced by 65 percent from the 1920 level, and it estimated that investment was down at least 50 percent throughout the whole state. There was little profit in feeding cattle at current prices.

Feeders experienced a similar situation, only worse, during the thirties when they were caught with relatively high-priced stock that had been bought in 1929. Meanwhile, during the early part of this decade, the drought-induced feed shortages were added to the feeders' woes; and in Kansas the number of cattle that were full-fed during the early 1930s was negligible. Mercer noted, for example, that the number being fed in 1934 alone was close to 80 percent less than the preceding year.[16]

Yet the agricultural producers, despite their plight, were better off than many city folk. Most were employed, had places to live, and could raise some of their basic food needs. And the price situation did improve after 1932, apparently more as a result of the drought and short crop situtaion than anything else. The parity ratio of 58 in 1932 improved slightly to 64 the following year, then climbed more rapidly to 93 by 1937, the high for the decade, before another decline in the late thirties.[17]

198

The economic plight of cattlemen between the wars naturally took its toll of individuals. Out in western Kansas the severe winter of 1918–19 combined with the early stages of the depression to strike a death blow to one of the state's most enduring ranches. Peter Robidoux, an adventuresome French Canadian, had worked his way to Wallace County on the railroad shortly after the Civil War. Searching for greener pastures, Robidoux gave up railroad work, bought a barrel of whisky and a box of cigars, and launched a merchandising career. He prospered for twenty years in the small town of Wallace, especially during the boom years of the 1880s. His initial commercial venture, housed in a small tent, grew to be the largest general merchandise store between Kansas City and Denver. Goods were high-priced at Robidoux's place, but they continued to sell until the decline of the 1890s, when his competitors began to cut prices. More obstinate than wise, Robidoux refused to cut his prices during the depression, and eventually closed his doors after spending a whole day without a single customer. He never returned to the store, some said, allowing more than $20,000 worth of inventory to rot on the shelves.

Merchandising, however, was not Robidoux's only calling. As profits had accumulated, he gradually purchased 32,000 acres of real estate, much of it good bottom land along the Smoky Hill River, and became a rancher. After the severe winter following World War I killed thousands of his cattle, Robidoux subdivided his land and sold parcels to eager buyers during the early summer of 1919. The *Stockman* reported that several hundred prospective buyers—who had arrived in over a hundred automobiles—followed the auctioneer and a spirited band from plot to plot as the land was auctioned. Unmindful of the faint glimmer of depression that clouded the horizon, buyers paid $30 to $42 an acre for the bottom land, while the upland pasture sold for $15 to $20. The exaggerated demand for land, as well as Robidoux's advancing age, no doubt influenced him to sell, and the serious deflation that followed proved the wisdom of his decision.[18]

John A. Edwards, mentioned earlier for his work as a progressive legislator and stockman in western Kansas and the Flint Hills, lasted a little longer than Robidoux, but his end as a rancher was much the same. Edwards had plunged deeply into cattle and land investments during the flush war years before the low cattle prices of the early twenties left him unable to meet his payments. When oil speculation failed to make up the difference, the bank foreclosed the mortgage on his ranches. One misfortune followed another in the Edwards household; their home was partially destroyed by fire just as the other disasters became apparent.

Near desperation as his fortune continued to decline, Edwards scraped together a paltry $50 in 1927, split it with his wife, and set out to find work, leaving his family behind in the half-burned house. He finally landed in the small town of Paola and, with the help of friends, began a second career as a supplier of natural gas. Here he remained until his death in 1958, regaining part of the prosperity that had accompanied his cattle operations up to 1920. The postwar depression, coupled with his overexpansion, had ended his sparkling career as legislator, stockman, and prominent representative of livestock groups in their disputes with railroads and packers. The cattle business in Kansas was never the same without Edwards. He had been a popular speaker at KLA conventions and other gatherings on special hoildays, where he critized the cattlemen's adversaries as forcefully as possible. All this ended, too, when the depression drove one of the state's most popular cattlemen from his favorite endeavor.[19]

One of the largest cattle operations and fortunes to disintegrate during the twenties, however, was that of former Kansas governor Walter R. Stubbs, the fighting Quaker from Lawrence. As Stubbs disengaged himself from contracting during the early 1900s to allow a free hand for politics, he also invested in land. A few years later, after his two terms as governor had ended in 1913, Stubbs turned most of his attention toward his rural properties.

Stubbs bought and sold several large ranches in the West. By 1920 he was reported to have the largest dairy in Kansas, near Mulvane, in addition to large ranches in Kansas, Colorado, New Mexico, and Texas. He initiated his Texas interests by purchasing the right to lease sixty sections of XIT land from the father of O. C. Hicks. The Hicks family eventually moved to Kansas after the depression of the twenties, and ranched near Garden City for more than forty years. Stubbs, meanwhile, was a great favorite in Texas for a few years, overcoming disastrous cattle losses during the severe winter of 1918–19 and dazzling the locals with his prohibition speeches.

Stubbs' ranching interests in Kansas included 3,200 acres near Plainville, as well as thousands of acres of leased grassland farther west in the state. Most of his 15,000 cattle were at first Angus, but he gradually shifted to Herefords. At the time of his last senatorial race, a newspaper said of the former governor that "his ranch and ranch land holdings are among the largest in the West and Southwest and are probably as well managed as any in the United States."

Despite his astute management and large fortune, however, the postwar depression struck down Stubbs' empire just as it did many smaller operators, and he ended his ranching days as the manager of a large ranch and irrigation project in Colorado. This prominent cattleman died in Topeka in 1929, only a few months before the stock-market crash ushered in a depression even more severe than the one that the governor had struggled with.[20]

The newspapers and journals of the 1920s identified only a few of the large operators who failed during the postwar depression. But there were others, as well as many small operators—some of whose operations were marginal to begin with—who were also forced out of business. A few failures during the twenties were caused in part by overexpansion during the war, when it was hard not to be optimistic, because cattle prices were high and the government was demanding more and more goods from agricultural producers. In contrast, the depression of the thirties was not preceded by a flush period that had encouraged overinvestment. Fewer producers had over-expanded, but many still suffered ruin because of other conditions.

Depressions like those in the twenties and thirties naturally spurred producers to attempt to raise profits, but the avenues through which they could act unilaterally were limited. They sought higher prices for farm produce and lobbied for government subsidides. They examined the retailing end of the food industry to see if there were excess profits that might be directed back to the producer. Improved merchandising techniques were sought by producers, as well as expanded capital. These and other avenues were explored, but none bore much fruit. Writing in 1929, William Allen White said that the farmer "turns to the government, and gets only more taxes . . . to the banker . . . and finds his interest rates soaring . . . to the industrial worker and finds him pounding farm prices down that he may have cheaper food." In general, White was accurate. The agricultural producer, for example, never received the prices for his products that he needed or desired. On the other hand, new developments in agriculture helped to reduce production and marketing costs. Progress was not, however, in proportion to the effort expended by farmers and ranchers.[21]

In the realm of production, forces beyond the producers' control determined many fixed costs, but there were others that could be affected. For the rancher, land continued to be his largest investment, followed by his foundation stock. After that there were numerous additional items—feed, labor, fences, buildings, maintenance, taxes, death losses, and interest on a cattle loan, probably. With all of these expenses in mind, the USDA and the Kansas Agricultural Experiment Station reported in a joint study in the early 1920s that a cow-calf operator had an average of almost $28 annual carrying costs per cow, and that the gross cost of a weaned calf was over $33. Though these figures applied to the Flint Hills, they were no doubt representative of most Kansas production.[22]

Pasturing calves into grass-fat beef was also expensive. In the Flint Hills grazing aged steers and cows cost $17 per head per season in 1919, almost triple the expense for the same services before the war. The figure declined to around $8 or $9 for most of the twenties, but even this level was higher than it had been before the European conflict. By 1931 lease prices had declined to $7 or $8 for aged cattle and went as low as $3 to $6 a head in 1933. After this, the drought and shortages of grass tended to push rates up, as the bluestem region provided better grazing than other areas of the West even though conditions were far from normal. Grazing rates for the last half of the thirties averaged around $7 to $8, and this included allowances for more acreage per animal than was required during a period with average rainfall. Young cattle were pastured more cheaply and the rents outside the Flint Hills were usually lower. These rates often seemed exaggerated during the whole period when compared with prewar years or the market price of cattle.[23]

There were other expenses in addition to grazing fees in preparing cattle for market, so many that most of the cattle studied by the USDA during the early twenties lost money for their owners. The period of the study, of course, encompassed the worst years of the postwar depression, but during the late twenties a report by Mercer also demonstrated that production costs remained high. After several of the state's ranchers had provided him with figures that included all expenses for beef animals from birth to delivery at the market, Mercer reported that it cost between $11.75 and $12.25 per hundred to produce marketable beef. Cattlemen, in short, made little money between the two wars except for the latter years of each decade. Survival, not profits, was the goal for most.[24]

Yet the Flint Hills continued to accommodate large numbers of cattle throughout most of this period, as did the state as a whole. According to reports in the *Stockman,* the number of cattle shipped in between January and June averaged 250,000 each year between 1922 and 1927, and 233,000 between 1928 and 1937. Texas, Oklahoma, and the other sections of Kansas still furnished the bulk of these cattle. Additionally, there were considerably more cattle grazing the Flint Hills' bluestem each year than appeared on in-shipped records. Some of these were locally owned cow herds, some were feeder stock, while others were cattle shipped in at times other than the January to June period. Railroad shipping records provided some evidence of this additional stock when 100,000 more cattle were shipped out of the Flint Hills in the fall of some years than were brought in during the spring. Some estimates placed the total number of cattle in the area at close to a million each year.

Depressed conditions during this period encouraged an interest in chang-ing the traditional practice of basing pasture rents in the Flint Hills on a fixed fee per head. Some Texas cattlemen suggested that pasturemen install scales, then charge according to the gain made by the cattle. This, they believed, would force landowners to "take a little more interest in seeing that pastures are not overstocked and that the cattle receive proper attention." Others proposed various profit-sharing plans between the owner of the cattle and the pasturemen that tied rents directly to market prices or to the net profit for the whole operation. Owners of stock were especially prone to seek new bases for payments during hard times to reduce some of their risks as well as their investment, if the pasturemen could be persuaded to help finance the herd. But changes in the methods of contracting Flint Hills grass were not extensive. The old methods of charging by the head or acre remained domi-nant, and there was usually no problem in finding customers for the superb grass.[25]

Labor and taxes were also expenses that appeared high for much of the interwar period. In 1919, largely as a result of the war, Kansas farm wages were 253 percent above 1913 levels. Labor costs, however, did not involve large cash outlays for many ranchers. Their profits, if any, were frequently derived from the exploitation of their own and their families' labor.

Taxes were a different story. Farmers and ranchers complained through-out this period, with much justification, that their land taxes provided a dis-proportionate amount of the state's revenue. While Kansas taxes were lower than the national average, they were still high for a depressed sector of the economy. Between 1910 and 1925 state taxes rose 159 percent, with most of the increase occurring before 1921. By 1929 Kansans were paying fifty-eight cents per acre in land taxes, with 75 percent of this revenue going toward education and roads.

Rural residents protested this inequitable taxing system, but with little success during the twenties. Some proposed reduced spending on roads, or a

high tourist license to pay for it, while others suggested less money for education, especially teachers' salaries, which were "far in excess of real worth."
Some also suggested reducing real estate taxes by initiating a tax on state
income, sales, or intangibles. A number of Kansas cattlemen favored sales
taxes, while dirt farmers tended to oppose them, apparently because they
believed a sales tax added to the cost of machinery and repairs would be an
unfair burden. At least one cattleman believed that schools should be financed
by a luxury tax rather than local property taxes; then the state, he believed,
could "tax hell" out of luxuries like silk stockings and hotel rooms that cost
more than $1.50. Many others also favored heavier taxes on luxury items.
But all of these proposals fell on deaf ears during the twenties, and owners
of land and cattle continued to carry more than their share of the tax load,
along with all their other expenses. In view of their power in the state legislature, however, most farmers and ranchers were apparently unwilling to
reduce property taxes if it meant sacrificing the additional services to which
they had grown accustomed or initiating new taxes to fund the services.

Property taxes per acre were lowered during the depressed 1930s, but
new taxes were added. From a high of fifty-eight cents in 1929, tax levies
in Kansas declined to thirty-six cents per acre in 1933 and 1934, and to an
average of a little over forty-one cents an acre during the whole decade. But
lower property taxes did little to lighten the tax load carried by rural residents,
and tax delinquency increased at an "alarming rate." By the early thirties
many farmers and ranchers had reconsidered their opposition to a state income
tax, and the farm lobby became an important factor in persuading the Kansas
legislature to initiate such a tax. The new law also taxed a number of intangibles, but the increased revenue did not alleviate the landowners' tax
burden as much as they had expected.[26]

Of special interest to a number of stockmen was the tax on inshipped
cattle. By 1930 this assessment had been on the books for over thirty years,
but had always been erratically collected, if at all. Cattlemen who happened
to use pastures in counties where officials conscientiously collected the tax
became disgruntled, and shortly after World War I several Texans contested
its constitutionality, though unsuccessfully.

Towards the end of the twenties the tax was more generally collected in
an attempt to find added revenue, and out-of-state cattlemen joined some of
the state's own in calling for repeal. Pasturemen in the Flint Hills, convinced
that the tax decreased their business, were especially vocal in repeal efforts.
In 1929 they formed the Bluestem Pasturemen's Association for the purpose

of promoting their business interests, notably the repeal of the tax on foreign cattle. Late the same year their efforts were successful when the state legislature provided that cattle shipped into the state between March and September required no Kansas assessment if taxed in another state. Judging from the available records, however, there was no noticeable rise in the number of in-shipped cattle as a result of the amended law, although out-of-state cattlemen did profit from the change.[27]

Cattle mortality was another factor on the cattleman's expense account, an item that could sometimes be reduced with better management practices. Annual death losses during this period were irregularly reported, but appeared to range from around 1 to slightly over 2 percent of all the state's beef cattle during those years that might be considered normal. Deaths from severe winter storms were least avoidable, although increased winter feeding and better care of cattle in general helped reduce these losses. With the advent of the radio, stockmen were better informed on weather conditions and could often take precautionary measures.

Cattlemen had more control over losses from disease, especially after cures and preventives like the blackleg serum were developed at Kansas State Agricultural College. Thousands of dollars were saved by spending only a few cents a head for treatment, and this was important for producers who were living with marginal profits.

In addition to reducing the cost of disease, cattlemen could sometimes enhance their income by improving other production methods. Better care and more winter feeding—which decreased deaths, improved calf crops, and reduced winter weight losses—were basic improvements. Feed for fattening stock could also be improved, and experiments were carried on at Kansas State Agricultural College along this line. In 1913 the college inaugurated an annual Feeders' Day for stockmen of Kansas and surrounding states in order to facilitate the dissemination of the latest scientific findings. Feeders' Day is still part of many cattlemen's yearly agenda. By the late thirties Kansas State College—called such after 1931 in recognition of the fact that the institution was "not only to make men better farmers but also to make farmers better men"—had provided much information on such things as the relative values of roughages, the fattening qualities of various grains, and the proper mixtures to use. The contribution of various protein supplements to feeding diets was also studied, as was the proper method of caring for grass.

Well before the end of the interwar period experts at the college had reported a number of times on what they believed to be two of the "soundest

Baling alfalfa, Finney County. *Courtesy of the Kansas State Historical Society.*

and most practical methods of handling beef cattle in Kansas." One of these, known as the Kansas deferred full-feeding plan, consisted of purchasing yearlings in the fall, wintering them well enough to produce two hundred or more pounds, then summer grazing without grain until the first of August. After this, the plan called for 100 to 120 days of full-feeding in a dry lot before marketing as finished beef. The whole process involved ownership of the cattle for thirteen to fifteen months.

The second method recommended by the college experts involved ownership for three months longer. Sometimes referred to as "growing, grazing, wintering, and selling as fleshy feeders," this plan consisted of purchasing steer calves in the fall, wintering for a hundred pounds of gain, summer grazing without grain supplement, and, finally, a second wintering to produce two hundred pounds more. The cattle were sold in the spring as "fleshy feeders," after the rush of slaughter stock and before the large movement of stockers and feeders in the fall. Many Kansas producers who were not wholly committed to the production of calves used these methods, exactly as suggested or with slight variations.

C. W. McCampbell, a teacher in the animal husbandry department between 1910 and 1945, was instrumental in advertising these methods as well as many of the other conclusions of the college research staff. McCampbell was ably assisted by others, one of the most widely known in relation to beef production being A. D. "Dad" Weber, an expert livestock judge, who spent some thirty years at the college working to improve agriculture.[28]

The Adams family of Maple Hill had one of the better-known operations that used the Kansas plans for feeding stock. With one of the largest ranch enterprises in the state, Horace G. Adams started feeding cattle during the

Baling alfalfa, about 1926. *Courtesy of the Kansas State Historical Society.*

1920s, about the same time that Kansas State began to test and advertise the new plans. Several thousand acres of Adams' bottom land near Maple Hill were devoted to corn and forage crops, which eventually filled the battery of silos that towered above the ranch headquarters. The Adams family fed annually for many years as many as 5,000 of their own cattle.

Besides feeding, the Adamses participated in several other aspects of the beef industry. The large operation was begun shortly after Horace G. Adams came to Kansas with his father in 1881. The father was a banker, but Horace bought bluestem pasture and began to ranch. He bought over 10,000 acres around Maple Hill, then acquired an interest in over 60,000 acres along the Cimarron River in Meade County. Some of the ranch spilled over into Oklahoma. The combined acreage became known as the XI Ranch. When Horace Adams died in 1933, he left his seven children around 85,000 acres, said by some to be the largest quantity of land owned by any one person in the state. Only the Robbins family of Belvidere, who owned nearly as much land and leased considerably more, had an operation comparable to Adams' in size.

Two of the sons, Horace G., Jr., and Raymond E. Adams, managed the ranching empire after the father's death. Raymond was especially active, buying shares from his brothers and sisters and expanding the original holdings. Horace G., Jr., retained part of the XI Ranch, while Raymond bought most of the family's remaining land. Today the fourth generation of the Adams family operates the large spread.

The Adams operation always included some of the best Herefords raised in the West. Upbreeding began early with Gudgell & Simpson stock, followed by Hazlett bulls and those from the Turner ranch in Oklahoma. The Adams

Filling pit silo with winter feed. *Courtesy of the Kansas State Board of Agriculture.*

family was among those ranchers who had their own purebred cattle for raising breeding stock for the range herd. When the purebreds were finally dispersed in 1940, they numbered well over a thousand head. Raymond Adams also kept highly bred quarter horses for many years, dispersing them finally during the early 1950s.[29]

The Adams cattle-feeding operation during the twenties, as well as the operations of other producers, revealed a trend to marketing younger stock. This was an attempt to cut costs by reducing the time that cattle spent maturing and fattening. "The day of the four-year-old steer is almost past," James Tod noted about 1920. He and his father had a similar cattle-feeding operation next door to the Adamses. Along the same line, McCampbell reported as early as 1922 that only 20 percent of the butcher stock purchased by packers weighed over 1,300 pounds, whereas this class had dominated the slaughter market before the war. Packers now preferred, he said, finished stock at 800 to 1,100 pounds. Many of these lighter cattle were around two years of age when butchered. A year after McCampbell's observations, the *Stockman* noted that 44 percent of the cattle on feed in Kansas were under 700 pounds and only 1 percent were above 1,300 pounds. Although there was much variance in the use of the term, the younger stock were often referred to as baby beef

Filling a "corn crib" silo, Greeley County. *Courtesy of the Kansas State Board of Agriculture.*

and, with growing frequency, were being creep-fed a grain supplement while still running with their mothers.[30]

The emphasis on younger stock developed in response to a number of factors, but chief among them were the need to cut production costs through feed and grain savings and the evolving consumer demand for smaller cuts of meat. The war had contributed to the changing consumer preference, because much of the large, aged beef—considered most desirable at the time— was shipped abroad for military consumption or for the Allies. The smaller animals were relegated to the domestic table, and American consumers began to develop a preference for them.

Cattlemen also learned that the four-year-old steer not only used more feed but also wasted time in the fattening process. During the first two or three years, much of the summer gain was lost during the winter months unless a grain supplement was added to the roughage diet. Then, if too much gain occurred during the winter, it might be lost the first part of the grazing season. Stockmen were happy to adapt to a trend in the consumer market which resulted in lower production costs, as most were convinced by this time that, in the words of one cattleman, "it takes two pounds of gain to replace one pound of shrink." By the thirties some Kansas cattlemen kept their older stock no more than two years, marketing it at 800 to 1,200 pounds, while others, especially those in the Flint Hills, continued with their three-year-old steers.[31] Upbreeding, as noted earlier, was essential to the trend of marketing younger beef, because the ability to finish quicker was to a large degree bred into cattle.

While cattlemen adopted many of the practices that promised to reduce costs, there were always risks involved. Improved methods that reduced operating expenses were welcomed, but those that increased numbers of cattle contributed as well to lower prices by creating surpluses. This enigma was not uncommon for agricultural producers.

Certain costs were also reduced through cooperative action. KLA was increasingly called upon during this period to assist with problems that related more specifically to the production phase of the industry. KLA proved to be a handy outlet for the stockmen's frustrations, an avenue through which stockmen could conduct some of their business, and a source for much of the advanced scientific thinking on production techniques.

Kansas cattlemen reacted differently toward their organization during this depressed period than did stockmen in other parts of the West, as KLA grew in strength while other associations declined. To the north, the associations in Nebraska, Wyoming, and South Dakota struggled to survive, especially during the 1920s. The Nebraska association may not have even met during the early twenties; the South Dakota organization almost died; and in Wyoming the cattlemen's group reported only 262 members in 1930. The state associations in Colorado and Texas were somewhat stronger, but the one in Colorado was preoccupied for much of the period with internal problems. The Texas and Southwestern Cattle Raisers Association, created in 1921 by the consolidation of two smaller organizations, was the only state association in the West that rivaled KLA in strength.

The American National was active during this period, although there was some indication that its policies tended to favor cow producers over feeders and that it was not as concerned with marketing problems as some cattlemen believed it should have been. In 1933, for example, a new organization known as the United States Livestock Association was founded. It was almost exclusively concerned with marketing problems and appeared to be primarily representative of midwestern stockmen, especially feeders. This association claimed 15,000 members by 1934. Mercer and James Tod represented Kansas cattlemen, and had advisory positions in the new organization.[32]

Kansas cattlemen, then, had the help of one of the strongest stock associations in America during the interwar period. Mercer was still "the engine in the machine" that kept KLA going and its membership expanding. About the time the postwar depression was being generally felt, KLA claimed that with 10,000 members on the rolls "the Association is now the strongest live stock organization in the United States, and we think we say without being boastful that it is most effective." The Texas group, by comparison, reported 4,766 members at this time.

Membership, however, was not necessarily the most significant barometer of strength. More important was the claim made midway through the interwar period that KLA represented some 85 percent of the Kansas beef industry. And there is no reason to question this claim. Mercer himself referred to KLA in 1920 as "one of the few really effective producers' organizations in our country," well recognized in other states. A few years later he gave much the same evaluation of KLA, but added that it "is representative not only of Kansas livestock interests, but those of all mid-western and cornbelt states."[33]

Many of the same sentiments were aimed toward KLA during the 1930s. An official of a Kansas City commission firm noted, for example, that "the Kansas Live Stock Association has probably done as much or more than any other association for the live stock interests not only of Kansas but of the entire Southwest." Judging by the many activities of the organization—especially in the marketing area and in the stockmen's relations with the government—this claim was well founded, although the association did suffer a severe loss in 1937 with the death of Mercer.[34]

William G. West, long-time friend and associate of Alf Landon and Mercer, became the new executive secretary of KLA, a critical position if the organization was to continue to be effective. But his tenure was cut short by death less than a year after he had assumed the post. William J. Miller, who served KLA as secretary for the next ten years, followed West.

Miller, who was also a close friend of Mercer, represented a family that had long been active in Kansas politics and business, as well as farming and ranching. Two brothers, William W. and Hiram B. Miller, had migrated to Kansas after the Civil War and had gone into the mercantile business in Osage City. As the business prospered, they purchased land. Hiram B. eventually became active in cattle politics. He was a charter member of KLA and in 1910 was instrumental in its reorganization. By the time William J. Miller, son of William W., became KLA executive secretary, descendants of the two brothers controlled an insurance agency, a farm and grassland near Osage City, a ranch and feeding plant near Miller, a farm near Topeka where hogs were fattened on city garbage, and a hog serum plant in the same city—all of which, acording to the *Stockman,* were minor businesses compared to large ranch holdings in Colorado, New Mexico, and Texas. Neither of the secretaries to follow Mercer, however, made any significant changes in the work of KLA. The hard-working former schoolteacher had established the pattern, and the organization carried on in much the same way for many years.[35]

In addition to educating readers through its journal; providing cattlemen an annual opportunity to meet, learn, and negotiate business; and serving as a continuous broker to match cattle with feed, KLA made a concerted effort to stop cattle thefts, which increased during this period. Thefts increased during the interwar period for a variety of reasons, the most important of which were the general economic slump, unemployment, and the availability of the truck. The last had the most significant impact. With a truck for transportation, or even the back seat and trunk of a car, "backseat butchers" could easily slaughter several animals and spirit them away under cover of darkness to an unscrupulous meat dealer, butcher, or community sale, sometimes located in another state.[36]

The economic cost of rustling for some producers was serious. A few Kansas cattlemen reported losing more than fifty head in a single year, and it was estimated that the state as a whole lost over $100,000 worth of cattle in 1937. Most years, however, losses were not as severe as this, but they were still significant when profit margins were small. Preventive measures supported by KLA included offering rewards for the arrest and conviction of thieves, support for the McCarran Bill, and brand inspection at the central markets. The McCarran Bill, which proposed to make interstate transportation of stolen cattle a federal crime—was first vetoed by President Franklin D. Roosevelt, then finally passed in 1941.

Mercer also attempted to prevent any pardons being given to imprisoned cattle thieves. Stockmen as a whole supported legislation to establish a statewide brand registration statute, a relatively late move to acquire such a law. The legislature finally complied with their wishes in 1939, requiring that brands be registered by the state rather than the county. The sanitary commissioner was charged with administration of the law until a state brand commissioner was created during the late 1940s. Cattle thefts had declined by World War II, but they did not stop.

The new brand law had not required branding, only state registration of brands if they were used. Nor did the law compel sellers of cattle to prove ownership with a brand registration or bill of sale. Small sale rings across the state opposed the latter requirements because of the added paper work. About two hundred people were convicted of rustling during the first decade of the law's operation, but stockmen again experienced a rash of rustling during the early 1950s, perhaps because of poor economic conditions. The KLA and the Kansas Bureau of Investigation (KBI) were both responsible for reducing this profit-robbing activity, even though it was never eliminated. The KBI, in fact, was organized largely because of agitation by stockmen during the thirties for more state aid in preventing stock thefts.[37]

KLA also performed a valuable service for producers during the interwar period by helping to establish the National Live Stock and Meat Board, the first significant entry of the association into the retail dimension of the meat industry. This unique organization—one of the first joint efforts by producers, commission men, packers, and retailers, who were often considered rivals in the meat trade—popularized meat-centered diets and expanded markets through new merchandising techniques.

The idea that eventually led to the establishment of the Meat Board was first presented at the 1919 KLA convention in Hutchinson by Thomas E. Wilson, then president of Wilson & Company. He suggested that producers cooperate with packers in organizing a committee to study marketing conditions. If successful, the cooperative group was to become permanent. KLA, especially Mercer, was largely responsible for forming the Producers' Committee of 15, and for urging it to accomplish its work. But the committee, now supported by several other stock associations in the West and Midwest, found many disagreements between range men of the West and feeders of the Midwest. For almost three years the group languished in uncertainty as to the direction it should take. Henry C. Wallace, the secretary of agriculture and chairman of the committee, preferred to concentrate on marketing ills rather than those in retailing, and was largely responsible for blocking any action until the present Meat Board was finally decided upon in 1922.

Extremes in the literature published by those who either opposed or advocated meat diets did much to encourage action by the Meat Board. Some writers of the time denounced meat because of the ill effects it supposedly had on the public's health, while others made ridiculous claims in their defense of meat. One Kansas producer, obviously prejudiced, insisted that every "great man we ever produced was a great meat eater or consumer, from George Washington down to Joe Mercer." His enthusiasm grew as he warmed to his subject: "If you want to look like real men and women," he said, "eat meat. But if you want to look like a pig-tailed Chinaman, just live like one, don't eat any meat; eat rice. Show me a nation on the face of the earth that amounts to anything that doesn't eat meat." Frank W. Atkinson, KLA president at the time, expressed similar sentiments a few years later. After reminding his listeners that the strong ate meat and not "prunes, sardines and grapes," Atkinson suggested that "if the hard boiled Irish could only have been taught to raise more beef and less hell and potatoes, the British Empire today would be calling their Prince of Wales, Mike, and their King, Patrick the 27th."[38]

The new board immediately launched a number of research and education programs in an attempt to protect meat from adverse publicity. Financial support came from a voluntary five-cent contribution from producers for each car of stock sold along with the same amount from the buyer of each car. The assessment was later advanced to twenty-five cents a car, and eventually to a few cents per head when railroads were no longer the principal carriers of livestock.

It is impossible to evaluate precisely the contributions of the Meat Board, as no one knows what meat consumption would have been without its services. Almost certainly, though, consumption of meat was increased by the board's efforts. Serious research projects, educational endeavors, and other promotional activities have characterized the board's work for over half a century. Mercer, who was chairman of the board for several years, Dan Casement, John A. Edwards, W. R. Stubbs, Will Miller, and A. G. Pickett are only a few of the Kansans who served the board that KLA had such a large part in founding.[39]

The individual cattleman, then, could lessen a few of his production costs, but not many to any significant degree. Most remote from his influence were such factors as the total number of stock on the market, feed costs, market prices, and land values. Those factors that were generally beyond the influence of producers were frequently the most important. Prices, for example, both those paid and received, always remained beyond the producers' influence. Yet cattlemen came through the two severe depressions of this period as well as any other agricultural producers, and maybe better than most. Times were hard and some producers were forced out of business, but the price of cattle always seemed to rally before that of many other agricultural products. The consumer's preference for meat, and his inability to find an acceptable substitute, played a large part in this. When he could afford it, he ate meat, especially beef.

Some of the state's cattlemen who had reasonably stable operations even used this generally depressed period to expand their holdings. If his ranching enterprise did not have large debts held over from World War I, a cattleman was in a good position to seek new capital from outside the cattle industry. The Robbins family, for example, had neither large debts nor a shortage of capital when the beef industry turned sour between the wars. They expanded their operations and by the 1940s had become the largest cattlemen in the state. The Robbinses were certainly some of the best managers of ranching property in Kansas.

William Webster Robbins, a Connecticut Yankee from near Wethersfield, had migrated to Kansas in 1883 to help establish the small town of Norwich, southwest of Wichita in Kingman County. The family was already prominent in Connecticut, having migrated to America in the 1680s, and had money for investment. Robbins used his capital first for a bank in Norwich, then a small ranch near the old English settlement of Runnymede. Edward Denmore Robbins, a brother of William Webster and chief counsel for the New York, New Haven, and Hartford Railroad, sent additional capital for buying land. When William Webster, the youngest of the Robbins brothers, died in 1916, the partnership had some 20,000 acres of good range land around Norwich and near Belvidere in Kiowa County. The expansion that was to follow, however, dwarfed these already significant holdings.

Edward Chester Robbins, son of William, returned from World War I in 1919 to manage the property for his uncle. Here was the ranching genius of the family, the man most responsible for expanding the 20,000 acres into a ranching domain that came to be owned by a half-dozen sons and daughters of the original two brothers. Although most of the other Robbins men were Yale graduates, Edward did not graduate from the university. He did have two years at the revered institution and often prided himself on having several Yale graduates on his payroll. No dilettante rancher was he, however. Edward Robbins was a practical man with good sense about cattle and land, popular in cattle circles, and patient enough not to expand more rapidly than the family's fortunes allowed.

Edward Robbins was joined in the ranching business by two brothers, Martin H., during the early thirties, and Richard W., a few years later. The latter had recently retired from the presidency of Transcontinental and Western Airline, now TWA. Richard was also a long-time director of the Santa Fe Railroad, as well as of several other large companies. When Richard became actively involved with ranching, he purchased for his headquarters the beautiful Rockefeller ranch near Belvidere, which had been established by the industrial family several decades before. The Rockefeller ranch was only a few miles from Edward's home.

By World War II, after two decades under Edward's guiding hand, more than 70,000 acres of grass were owned by the Robbinses in the Belvidere area and in the Flint Hills to the east, much of which was purchased when small ranchers were forced out of business by the depression. They also rented some land in the state, and had a long-term lease on 75,000 acres of the Anchor D Ranch in the Oklahoma Panhandle.

The Robbinses had begun ranching with grade cattle mixed with fine Shorthorns, but turned to Herefords during the twenties. By using the best purebred bulls available, the family was soon producing some of the best commercial whitefaces in the state, cattle that were eagerly sought by feeders in the area and in the Midwest. Herefords remained the hallmark of the ranch until Robbins initiated crossbreeding with Angus cattle during the 1940s, but a large number of straight-bred Herefords still remain on the ranch today.

The normal procedure while Edward managed the property was to keep most of the cow herd in Oklahoma, carry yearlings for a year on the grass near Belvidere, then send two-year-old stock to the Flint Hills for a few months of additional maturing. From the last area the cattle were shipped to market for slaughter or for additional fattening in a feedlot. For a long time a few carloads of Robbins cattle were shipped each year to Lancaster, Pennsylvania, where one or two at a time were bought and carefully fattened under the watchful eyes of Amish farmers.

A maximum of 6,000 cows and a total cattle population of over 15,000 grazed the short grass of the Robbins spread during the late forties, although fewer cattle were usually kept, especially during times of drought. Grass in the Flint Hills, however, enabled the Robbinses to survive the dry 1930s and 1950s in reasonably good shape. Before the hard times of the thirties forced Edward to devote all his energy to saving the cow herd, he also had other

216

livestock interests—he had kept three large flocks of sheep in addition to raising several thousand turkeys and several hundred hogs.

In 1958 the Robbinses' operation experienced a significant change when a natural gas field, eventually consisting of over thirty wells was developed on their Kansas land. The family then consolidated its land interests, dropped their lease on the Oklahoma property, and reduced their cow herd considerably. With income from sources other than cattle, their Kansas grass was carefully protected from overgrazing.

A number of ranchers would probably have expanded still further with the added wealth of gas production, but not the Robbinses. Edward and Richard were both getting older and beginning to disengage themselves from managerial duties. Edward died in 1967, Richard a few years later. Today many of the family's interests are managed by Evan Koger, a grandson of the founder of the Kansas ranch and nephew of Edward and Richard. Koger, a Yale graduate with a passion for scuba diving, grew up on the ranch, learning the finer points of the business from Edward. All of the Kansas land that was acquired by the Robbinses is still in their possession. The outside capital that was available at critical periods and the superb management of Edward Robbins were indispensable for the rapid expansion that occurred during the abnormally depressed period between the wars.[40]

Although few ranchers were as successful as the Robbinses, the growth that did occur helped to make beef the single most important agricultural product in the state by 1940. An examination of the cash receipts for Kansas farmers and ranchers from the marketing of major farm commodities during this period supports the increasing importance of cattle to the Kansas economy, as well as the stockman's advantage over the grain farmer (Figures 9–12).[41] During the period 1920 to 1940, cash receipts from all livestock and its products averaged over 61 percent of total farm income for Kansans, compared to only about 32 percent for all field crops. Government payments made up the remainder, averaging a little over 12 percent of the total in 1935 and 1940. Cash receipts from marketing cattle and calves alone averaged almost 29 percent of the total income, while that from wheat was about 23 percent. The percentage of income from beef actually increased during the depression and drought of the 1930s, while that from wheat and crops as a whole declined significantly. Moreover, income from beef cattle became even more dominant in the Kansas farm economy after 1940.[42]

217

Figure 9. Percentage of Farm Cash Receipts from the Marketing of Major Kansas Commodities, Plus Government Payments, 1925

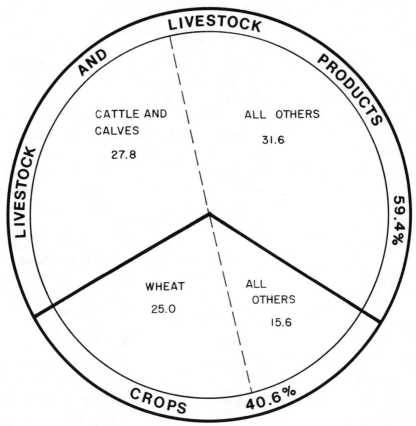

Source: *Fiftieth Rept., KSBA* (1966–1967).

The acreage devoted to wheat expanded somewhat between the wars; but when the whole period is considered, the state's cattlemen lost relatively few acres of grass to expanding crop lands. The grass lost in the twenties was partially regained in the thirties. During the whole period, grazing land totaled between eighteen and twenty million acres, or roughly 40 percent of the state's fifty-two million acres. The expansion of wheat during the 1930s came mostly as a result of decreases in other crops; corn acreage, for instance, declined over four million acres.[43]

Nor was the expansion of wheat necessarily detrimental to the beef industry, which actually expanded along with wheat during much of the time.

218

Figure 10. Percentage of Farm Cash Receipts from the Marketing of Major Kansas Commodities, Plus Government Payments, 1930

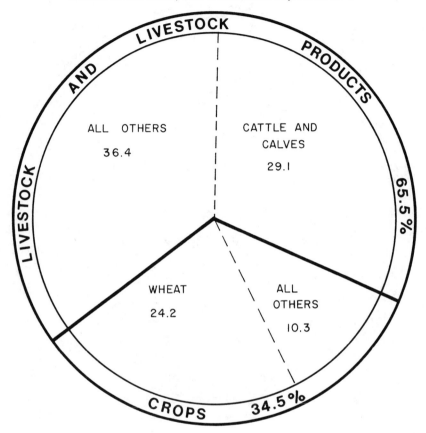

Source: *Fiftieth Rept., KSBA* (1966–1967).

When prices were low, wheat was sometimes fed to stock; but more important was the growing practice of grazing cattle on fall wheat. Large numbers of cattle were actually shipped into the state for this purpose, then sent on to grass during the early spring. Other crops were also grazed, and an increasing number of acres were devoted to forage crops for livestock. The increased grass and feed that became available as the tractor replaced the horse also aided the cattlemen. The number of tractors in the state shot up from 17,177 to 95,139 between 1920 and 1940, helping to produce enough additional feed for a million head of cattle or more.[44]

The lessons of the drought and depressions of the 1920s and 1930s were

Figure 11. Percentage of Farm Cash Receipts from the Marketing of Major
Kansas Commodities, Plus Government Payments, 1935

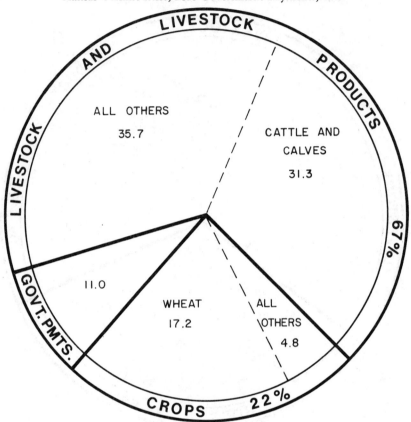

Source: *Fiftieth Rept., KSBA* (1966–1967).

taught in a hard school, but they were important. Improved tillage and soil
conservation practices were encouraged, corn tended to give way to wheat in
parts of the state, and stockmen became more concerned with conserving feed
and building reserve supplies. The government was instrumental in some of
these developments. There was also more diversification in Kansas agriculture
as a result of the drought, and many farmers who had depended almost exclusively on crops began to keep a few beef cattle. Although the lessons were
hard, most farmers and ranchers learned them well. When the time came
for high-geared production during the 1940s, Kansans were ready to meet the
challenge.[45]

Figure 12. Percentage of Farm Cash Receipts from the Marketing of Major Kansas Commodities, Plus Government Payments, 1940

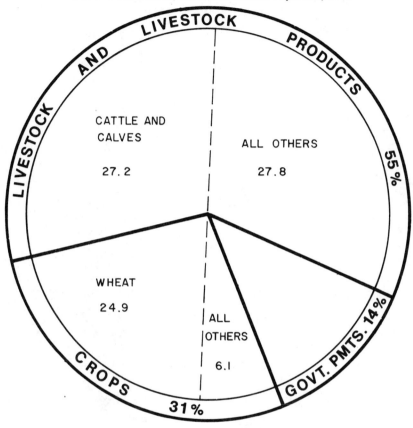

Source: *Fiftieth Rept., KSBA* (1966–1967).

10

Outside Help: Cattlemen
Look to Washington, 1920-1940

Some historians see the depression after World War I as a watershed in the history of American agriculture. During that time, technology, among other factors, enabled producers to supply far more than could be consumed, but the cost of production was much greater. Society began to question more than it ever had before whether rural life was actually superior to an urban existence, as many people had thought it to be. But most important in making this depressed period a landmark was the increased willingness of farmers and ranchers to seek government relief. The war had taught agricultural producers that government action could change economic conditions during an emergency in wartime, and many producers came to believe that the government might also deal with economic emergencies in a time of peace as well. As a result, rural folk spent more time and energy attempting to persuade the government to abandon its *laissez-faire* attitude toward agriculture.[1]

Kansas cattlemen were among the first organized rural groups to seek government help during the postwar period. As early as the fall of 1919 a group gathered at the Muehlebach Hotel in Kansas City, Missouri, to plan strategy for a Chicago meeting with the Big Five Packers and for a visit with government officials in Washington. Walter R. Stubbs was elected chairman of the group, which also included Joseph H. Mercer, George Donaldson, Dan D. Casement, John A. Edwards, and some forty others, all prominent in the Kansas beef industry.

In Chicago the delegation questioned the meat processors about declining livestock prices. To account for the decline, the packers cited the FTC investigation, the government-encouraged unrest over food prices, and the fear of restrictive legislation. They finally passed the buck on to Washington.

223

The cattlemen, although not necessarily convinced of the packers' innocence, departed the following day for Washington, where they eventually met with Kansas legislators, USDA officials, and Attorney General Palmer. Stubbs, with obvious contradiction, criticized the secretary of agriculture for failing to obtain both higher meat tariffs and more foreign markets, while KLA President George Donaldson berated Palmer for his stand against the packers' supposed hoarding of meat. After some debate, the attorney general promised that there would be no prosecution for the alleged hoarding; thus, the packers should not fear government intervention in slaughtering for storage. But, he added, his office would continue to urge regulation of the large meat processors.

Before returning to Kansas the disparity between livestock and retail meat prices was graphically demonstrated to the disgruntled cattlemen at a local eating establishment. "Thin slices of roast beef cost more in Washington for the delegation than a cow would cost in Kansas," Edwards snorted, and many of the Kansas cattlemen protested by eating a fish supper. "They couldn't afford beef. Stubbs took soup," Edwards added. Then Edwards turned his wrath toward retailers, claiming that they added 100 percent to the carcass price of meat as their gross profit. "It is disheartening to realize," Edwards continued, "that the charge from the butchers' block to the consumers' kitchen is as much per animal as the cost of raising, grazing, feeding, fattening, and marketing the animal, plus the freight, the commission, the packing house expense and profit, plus freight to the retail shop."[2]

After returning to Chicago to report that the packers were safe from prosecution for hoarding, the Kansas delegation returned home. Nothing significant resulted from the expedition, but the protesting delegation from Kansas was part of the larger movement that worked for the adoption of the Packer Consent Decree and eventually the Packers and Stockyard Act. The trip to Washington illustrated the growing recognition by Kansas cattlemen that government action was an essential part of the solution to their difficulties.

After their success in getting the Packer Consent Decree and the Packers and Stockyards Act, stockmen turned to other areas in which they believed government action could aid the industry, concentrating first on higher tariffs, then on agricultural credit.[3] Most farm representatives were convinced that high protective tariffs were necessary for agriculture to prosper. Industry, they reasoned, prospered behind tariff walls; why not agriculture? The

Democrats' Underwood Tariff, they believed, was based on the folly of free trade.

Likening agriculture to industry was a delusion, however. The two sectiors of the economy were not comparable in all respects, agriculture's inability to control production being the most notable difference. What United States agriculture really needed at the time was not the reduced foreign markets that resulted from higher tariffs, but rather low tariffs to encourage larger exports. The simple fact that before foreign countries bought they must first sell was passed over in favor of the clearer lesson—at least in the minds of producers—that was gleaned from the growth of manufacturing as a result of high duties. The delusion, of course, was understandable; yet, the success of agricultural interests in getting higher tariffs probably worked to their ultimate disadvantage.

In 1921 Congress passed the Emergency Tariff Act, which, at the urging of the farm bloc, included prohibitive duties on twenty-eight agricultural commodities, including wheat, corn, meat, sugar, and wool. This temporary protectionist measure was made permanent by the Fordney-McCumber Act the following year. Both tariffs included duties on manufactured goods, which farmers and ranchers increasingly realized caused them higher production costs; but they were willing to trade rising tariffs on manufactured goods for the right to set those on farm products about as high as they wanted them. Imported beef was taxed at three cents a pound and lamb at four cents, compared to one and a half cents and two cents in 1909, a relatively high tariff year itself. Live cattle were taxed at an ascending rate, depending upon their weight, ranging from $1.50 to $2.50 per hundred.

Kansas cattlemen applauded these duties, as did most other stockmen, although some midwestern feeders complained about the high tariffs on imported stockers and feeders when the domestic supply began to appear inadequate. Kansas stockmen, however, were unsympathetic toward lower tariffs on live cattle. When fifty-four carloads of Canadian feeders arrived in the state during a single week in 1927, Mercer fired off letters to Senators Arthur Capper and Charles Curtis demanding much higher duties.[4]

Agriculture did not respond to the high tariff rates as well as producers had hoped, and shortly after the Fordney-McCumber Tariff became law, they began advocating additional rates. Imported hides were an article of special concern, as the tariffs of the early twenties had left hides on the free list. Duties were added later, but many cattlemen believed that they were too low. Over 35 percent of the hides used in the United States, Mercer claimed in

1925, came from Mexico and South American countries. This was an outrage to the domestic cattle producers, he felt, and it had caused cattlemen to lose $225 million over the previous five years.

Nor did the high tariffs exclude all canned meats. A 1926 issue of the *Kansas Stockman* reported that Rodney Edward, a Kansas stockman-farmer, was recovering "from the shock of learning that for some time he had been eating Argentina and Uruguay canned beef." Fresh meat and livestock from South American countries were excluded, due to the fear of importing hoof-and-mouth disease, but canned meats and cured hides were allowed to enter. The low South American production costs, cattlemen believed, were unfair competition. They were especially outraged when some of them discovered that they were eating the lower-priced, imported product without knowing it. "Here am I," Edward grumbled, "a cattleman in the heart of the cattle country, buying and eating South American beef."

The effect of imports on domestic prices, however, was not nearly as great as cattlemen generally believed. According to one study, the quantity of imports was so small compared to domestic production, and the amount of beef consumed was so elastic, that tariffs could not be blamed for declining prices. It also revealed that complete exclusion of foreign beef would have done little to raise prices.[5]

Despite this study on the effects of the tariff, however, most stockmen demanded higher and higher tariffs. Mercer made several trips to Washington during the second half of the decade to spur Congress toward that goal. In 1928 he advocated tariffs levels three times higher than the existing duties; a year later he testified that over 206 million pounds of meat and meat products were being imported each year, to the decided detriment of American cattlemen. Congress failed to act, however, until the 1930 passage of the Hawley-Smoot Tariff. This pushed protection to an all-time high with *ad valorem* rates estimated to be up 30 to 40 percent. Over seventy farm products were included among the protected items, including a 10 percent *ad valorem* rate on hides and shoes.

Mercer proudly remarked that it was "the best tariff agricultural and livestock interests have ever had," and that stockmen finally had what they wanted with this new tariff—except, one might add, higher stock prices. But by this time their problems were more serious than the threat from imported meat, and the long-sought tariffs did nothing to improve the declining state of agriculture.

Mercer had worked hard to sell Congress on higher duties but, curiously, had passed up a Coolidge appointment to the Tariff Commission, where he might have been influential in effecting higher rates sooner than 1930. Mercer's refusal—at the urging of the KLA executive committee—illustrated the value they placed on his services to the industry as a whole in many areas besides tariffs. Mercer and a number of other agricultural leaders continued to work for still higher duties, even after the Hawley-Smoot Tariff helped set off a wave of increased duties throughout the world. In the end, agricultural prices remained low, and United States exports declined over 75 percent between 1929 and 1933.[6]

When the Trade Agreements Act was considered in 1934, cattlemen and most other agrarians labored diligently to defeat the new thinking on import/export trade. They were unsuccessful, however, and a tradition of almost forty years of rising tariffs was reversed when Congress authorized the executive branch to raise or lower duties through reciprocal trade agreements. Tariffs, of course, could be raised, but many farmers and ranchers knew that the trend would be toward lower duties. The most-favored nation principle of the new agreements was also anathema to many rural groups.

By 1939 some twenty-two reciprocal agreements were in force. Average duties had declined from 46.7 to 40.7 percent, and the quantity of United States imports and exports had gone up. The value of United States crop exports, however, remained about the same throughout the whole period from 1932 to 1938, although quantities increased when conditions allowed surpluses. Low prices kept the total value stable. Beef exports remained essentially the same throughout the whole decade of the thirties, never exceeding 1 percent of domestic production and usually staying closer to 0.5 percent.[7]

Cattle and beef imports were slightly higher than exports, amounting to 2.8 percent of home production in 1930. They declined from that the next few years, but then climbed to 3.3 percent in 1935 and 4.8 percent by 1939. Rising imports were triggered by lowered tariffs, by decreased domestic supplies, and by rising cattle prices toward the end of the decade. Much of the canned meat reportedly came from American-owned packing companies in South America. The live imports were principally the stocker-feeder class from Mexico and Canada, after both countries had negotiated reciprocal treaties with the United States. Combined imports from these neighboring countries amounted to over 744,000 live cattle in 1939.

Most cattlemen were enraged over the imports, and had few kind words for Secretary of State Cordell Hull and his reciprocity schemes. "The cattlemen and sheepmen have been sold down the river by a bunch of brain trusters," one Kansan remarked; but, in fact, the imports had little effect on the industry. Midwestern feeders were usually happy that the foreign cattle were available, and it is doubtful that enough stock or meat was imported to affect market prices seriously. In addition, a meat embargo continued to protect cattlemen against large shipments from Argentina, one of the world's leading beef-producing countries. World War II and disruptions in world trade occurred, however, before any accurate measure of the effects of these increased imports was determined.[8]

Throughout the decades following World War I farmers and ranchers sought additional government programs to assist agriculture. Marketing was their principal area of concern during the twenties, but there was much demand for programs that would aid them in production as well. The McNary-Haugen proposal, which resulted in a long and sometimes bitter fight, is a good example of the kind of aid they sought. Originated in large part by George N. Peek and espoused by the "red-headed, pipe smoking Secretary of Agriculture" Henry C. Wallace, the McNary-Haugen proposal called for a two-price system for basic agricultural commodities, including cattle, sheep, and swine. Cattle, however, were dropped as a basic commodity after a temporary rise in prices around 1926. Behind protective tariff walls, high prices were to be set for domestic agricultural products, while surpluses were to be purchased by the government and dumped on the international market at whatever price they might bring. The proposal, however, was never given a trial. It was defeated in Congress during the early twenties, then failed twice to get President Coolidge's approval during the last years of the decade.[9]

Coolidge, of course, held the trump card on the McNary-Haugen proposal and used it, but dissension within agriculture's ranks also contributed to its defeat. While the Plains cattlemen generally favored the bill as long as beef was considered a basic commodity, there were some who advocated its defeat. William J. Tod, former president of KLA, and Dan D. Casement were two Kansas cattlemen who were much opposed to this particular type of government intervention. Most cattlemen in the state, however, appeared to favor the McNary-Haugen idea, especially before cattle were excluded as a basic commodity. Mercer repeatedly argued for direct government support. To critics who cried "socialism" and "class legislation," he replied, "Why not?" Other sectors of the economy, he said, profited from government help. Now it was agriculture's turn for aid in its time of crisis. McNary-Haugenites even received support from the bastion of republicanism at Emporia headed by William Allen White. He had made a study of local indebtedness early in 1922 and concluded that "the mortgage records in Lyon County indicate that in a few years we shall have a peasantry instead of an independent manhood upon the western farms" unless the government became more involved with agriculture. But support from Kansas was insufficient to carry the day.[10]

While the McNary-Haugen Bill was being debated, Mercer and others advocated an agricultural commission with power to balance production and consumption as well as to make desirable changes in marketing and distribution. Organizations like the trade associations and large business combinations of urban industries served as the pattern. The consolidation in nonagricultural sectors of the economy resulted in less competition, Mercer and others pointed out, and had a large effect on their successful existence. In a letter to President Coolidge in 1924, Mercer noted that the country had sufficiently catalogued and discussed the needs of agriculture. "Hence our conclusion," he continued, "that a permanent federal agricultural commission with authority of law would be of far greater consequence in solving the perplexing and difficult problems of agriculture than continued investigations." Marketing problems, Mercer believed, were the key to most of agriculture's difficulties. He also proposed that the commission be empowered to establish what he referred to as systematic production. Few details of what systematic production meant were supplied to the press, but Mercer appeared to have in mind a vague notion of production controls.

Once Mercer's letter to the president was published in the *Stockman,* there was much response from cattlemen in the area. Judging from letters that were published, Mercer's idea was favored by about eight to one. Some of the letters suggested various modifications, but essentially they all favored some type of government control of production, price fixing, or systematic marketing. One perceptive writer even suggested that a producer's attitude toward government aid was based not so much on philosophy as it was on his degree of financial solvency. "The greatest foe of agriculture," wrote John S. Hill, a Kansas hog producer, "is in the ranks of the farmers themselves, and consists of the man who has made his, while land was cheap and easy to get, and refuses to see [that] the younger man [is hampered] by reason of modern conditions."

A few letters in opposition to Mercer's proposal were also published, and, in accordance with Hill's reasoning, several of them were from well-established producers. Tod, for instance, wrote Mercer, "I dread to think that you have inhaled some of the dust from such a deadly fungus as the McNary-Haugen bill." Another view illustrated that some stockmen had already despaired of ever getting any government aid and questioned its effectiveness even if it should materialize. Charles E. Collins—Kansas farmer-stockman, Colorado banker, and manufacturer of veterinary supplies—who had supported earlier efforts for government aid, now wrote to Mercer that he had "about reached the conclusion that the thing for the producers to do is to just stay at home and work like hell and not know anything, and he will think things are alright." Collins continued, all "we know about agriculture, economic questions, agronomy, astronomy, astrology, bacteriology, butrology, pessorallgy, plokfhiechanisjehanbosne [*sic*], and every other damn thing that one could know [has not been] worth a five cent piece. . . . The less you know, the less you worry." He failed to explain, however, how ignorance and less worry might raise prices.

The Manhattan stock feeder and showman Dan D. Casement was also among those who condemned government-aid proposals at this time. Casement had been educated at Princeton University—he was said to be the only stockman in the country who recited Browning to his cattle and Horace to his horses—before he assumed control of a ranch in Colorado, a farm in Ohio, and a spread a few miles north of Manhattan known as Juniata Farm. It was reported that he would spend days riding the ranges of the Matador Land and Cattle Company looking for a "wonder calf" to be fattened and sent to stock shows. Frequently, Casement's feeder and fat stock won top prizes at the nation's major stock shows.

Throughout his life Casement was unalterably opposed to what he called government handouts to agriculture. He opposed the McNary-Haugen Bill, Mercer's proposal for an agricultural commission, the Agricultural Adjustment Act (AAA), and any other plan that appeared to compromise what he considered to be the traditional values of rural America. In 1926 Casement wrote that "the farm is the last fortress of individualism in a new social order, governed by group interests and complicated by the complexities of modern mass life." Legislation could not reverse the laws of nature that sent or withheld moisture, nor, he believed, could it affect the economic law of supply and demand. This opposition to government aid during the twenties proved to be only a warm-up for the vast opportunities that Casement would have to oppose such aid during the following decade.[11]

There was, then, some opposition in Kansas to almost all the proposed aids to agriculture, including Mercer's agricultural commission. But Mercer's plan generally had wide support within the state, even though it implied much more control over production than many other proposals did. How much Mercer's thinking influenced the shaping of the Farm Board, which was eventually created by the 1929 Agricultural Marketing Act, was not completely clear. Most likely it had little more influence than most of the other proposals that came to Washington during this decade, and the suggestions for agricultural relief were legion. Will Rogers once remarked during the twenties that "farmers have had more advice and less relief than a wayward son. If advice sold for 10 cents a column, farmers would be richer than bootleggers." Rogers was not far off the mark.[12]

The postwar financial situation also illustrated that farmers and ranchers encouraged a larger government role in their industry. As the bottom dropped from under wartime prices and the easy money for agricultural expansion began to dry up, many producers believed that the federal government was obligated to provide credit and debt relief. The government, they noted correctly, had encouraged much of the expanded debt, yet obligations contracted during the heady days of the war were almost impossible to repay once deflation began. To make the situation even tighter, there were stepped-up demands by a number of banks for the repayment of existing loans. Even the Federal Reserve made credit more difficult to obtain in 1920 by temporarily imposing progessively higher discount rates for larger loans. Farmers and ranchers naturally and legitimately began to desire government relief.

Agricultural credit needs varied a great deal. Land purchases, for example, required loans for as long as forty years, while loans on cattle were needed for from three months to four years. All loans, according to borrowers, should be at low interest rates.

Credit for the beef industry at this time, as in the past, came mostly from private sources. The Federal Reserve Banks were of little help, as the six-month limit on discounted paper helped only feeders. Stockmen complained that the Federal Reserve kept interest too high—around 6 percent during the 1920s—and was too restrictive in making loans. The Federal Land Banks were not of much help in the area of long-term credit, as the amount the banks loaned even to their select clientele was usually quite small. In 1923 the maximum was increased from $10,000 to $25,000—at 5.5 percent—but even this failed to alleviate the scarcity of credit, as few borrowers qualified for the maximum amount. In 1924, for instance, the average Federal Land Bank loan in Kansas was only $4,198, hardly enough to buy much of a farm or ranch. Just as important was the absence of intermediate credit, a system that provided loans for the several years that they were often needed.

The first attempt to correct the credit situation for cattlemen was a cooperative effort by the Stock Growers' Finance Corporation, which discounted its first cattle paper in 1921. Almost $50 million, including $1.3 million from seventeen institutions in Kansas City and $150,000 from twelve in Wichita, was pledged to a pool for discounting loans. The rate was 7 percent, but the loans were renewable for up to thirty months in order to provide capital for herd owners who were breeding cattle. M. L. McClure, a former Kansan with Federal Reserve experience, headed the institution. Kansas cattlemen were optimistic at first, but when they realized that prospective loans still had to qualify under Federal Reserve standards and that discount rates were 1 percent higher than those of the Federal Reserve, their optimism evaporated. And this was the case across the nation, as only about $20 million of the available money was ever loaned.

Stockmen continued to press for government action, and finally in 1921 Congress authorized the War Finance Corporation—replaced by the Agricultural Credit Corporation in 1924—to rediscount the cattle paper of private lending institutions. This paper was discounted at 5.5 percent for a six-month loan and at 6 percent for an advance that lasted a year. Most important for a large number of borrowers were the practices of granting loans that did not qualify under Federal Reserve standards, of loaning nearly the full value of a herd, and of accepting feed as part of the collateral.

Over $300 million was pumped into the cattle industry by the War Finance Corporation by the middle twenties, and this no doubt saved a number of stockmen from disaster. Some banks and a few cattlemen, according to Mercer, complained of the red tape—the initial application was thirteen pages of detailed items—but the major complaint was that these efforts were also too small for the need that existed. By the end of 1922, for instance, Kansas stockmen had received $3.5 million from the corporation, or, according to Mercer, only 20 percent of what was actually needed. But, in view of the declining market for livestock at this time, additional capital might have resulted in unnecessary expansion and even lower prices.

Congress in 1923 also created twelve Intermediate Credit Banks in an effort to satisfy long-term capital needs. Loans to cooperative marketing agencies were also a prime consideration of these institutions. They provided some relief, but they became of more importance during the next decade.

When cattle prices improved after the middle twenties, the pressure for government-secured loans declined as private sources again became willing to satisfy much of the demand. In the end, the government venture, notably that of the War Finance Corporation, had been only moderately successful. Producers suffered at the end of the decade from much the same lack of long-term, low-interest credit as before. But they did not forget the government's efforts during the early twenties. When the severe depression of the next decade settled down upon their mortgaged farms and stock, they again turned to Washington for relief.[13]

The government's involvement in agricultural credit during the thirties became increasingly complicated and even more extensive than it had been before. Most important to the producer was the fact that the involvement became permanent. Credit for farmers and ranchers became critical after the crash in 1929, although bankers were slow to admit it. Many lending institutions, some capriciously and others to protect their depositors, not only refused to make loans for agricultural purposes but also called in existing loans or refused extensions. The *Stockman* noted in 1931 that the large banks in Kansas had "their vaults filled with money," yet refused to grant loans that they would have readily accepted only two years before. During the early thirties, there was little doubt that immediate and long-term credit was one of agriculture's greatest needs, but many banks were slow to agree. Mercer polled most of the state's bankers during 1930 and found that nearly half of those polled said no to the question asking if there was a need for long-term agricultural credit, or failed to respond. Freight rates, in the bankers' view, were the most serious problem confronting producers.[14]

Along with calls for general inflation—one stockman-banker, Charles E. Collins, suggested that the government print and issue $100 milion in greenbacks each month and then recall them at a rate of $50 million per month after the depression—Kansas producers turned increasingly to governmental agencies for credit. Until the New Deal period they were continually disappointed. Federal Land Banks did not compensate for the decline in commercial credit, even though Congress during the early thirties tripled the money available to them. The Intermediate Credit Banks had never been very effective, although some $64 million was dispensed or discounted between 1929 and 1933 in the whole Tenth Federal Reserve District, the unit which includes Kansas. There was some additional help from the Regional Production Association which was created in 1932. Using funds from the Reconstruction Finance Corporation, the Production Credit Association that was located in

Wichita had loaned about $10 million by April, 1933. A prominent Kansas banker-cattleman, Cal Floyd, directed the Wichita institution and believed that it was "one of the greatest movements the government had ever undertaken." There was criticism, however, because many applicants were turned away. Those who received loans complained of the slowness with which the paperwork was done.[15]

Although inadequate, as far as farmers and ranchers were concerned, all the government efforts in the field of agricultural credit from the time of President Wilson were important as a foundation for subsequent programs. The desperate financial condition of American agriculture compelled President Franklin D. Roosevelt to take speedy action soon after he took office. Within a few months of his inauguration the president had created the Farm Credit Administration (FCA) by executive order, and Congress had passed major agricultural legislation, including the Agricultural Adjustment Act and the Emergency Farm Mortgage Act. These measures combined the government programs providing credit to agricultural producers and placed the various institutions under the governor of FCA.

The FCA supervised and coordinated several major efforts to supply more credit. To aid the Federal Land Banks, Land Bank Commissioner Loans were created, primarily to assist with a second mortgage those farmers and ranchers who were already obligated. Foreclosure of farms in the Tenth Federal Reserve District declined from 167 to 94 the first two years the commissioner loans were available. Production and marketing loans were also made by the Intermediate Credit Banks. By discounting the paper of the Production Credit Corporation, the ICB supervised local associations of producers and made loans to local marketing and purchasing cooperative agencies. Later, they began to discount loans made by the Farm Security Administration—now called the Farmers Home Administration—which proved to be especially helpful to small ranchers.[16]

Most cattlemen were delighted with New Deal efforts in this area. Among the advantages in the new system were relatively low interest rates, expanded rather than reduced credit during emergencies, and local management for the production and cooperative associations. An indirect benefit was the fact that ranchers and farmers were forced to keep better records of their operations. Since the thirties the federal system has generally satisfied a large part of the credit needs of range stockmen. Feeders, however, have depended more on commercial institutions; but they, too, have indirectly benefited from the government's efforts. Several Kansas cattlemen publicly lauded these aids to the beef industry, and just a few months before his untimely death Mercer noted that "probably the greatest aid government has rendered agriculture as a whole has been in extending financial help to distressed farmers and stockmen."[17]

Despite all the government aid, however, commercial lending institutions were still the dominant source of agricultural credit in 1941, holding 62 percent of the farm mortgages and 70 percent of the outstanding short-term credit. More convenient locations, less red tape, and the traditional patterns of rural borrowing helped account for this. Private institutions obviously served a vital need, but because of their obligations to depositors and shareholders their effectiveness was limited during the thirties. One historian has written that commercial banks have tended to be "fair-weather friends, ready to supply credit when it was easy to get and to people who had little difficulty getting it anywhere; but were conspicuously absent in times of stress or for the person who was not the choicest client." The government system created during the New Deal did much to correct this situation.[18]

President Hoover, the last Republican president until after World War II, made a final attempt to aid the agricultural sector, but those ranchers who advocated a larger government role were disappointed with his Agricultural Marketing Act. Although stockmen were better off than dirt farmers during the late twenties, they still expected help. The act, for the most part, was designed to assist cattlemen in marketing their stock through cooperatives. A lot of talk about production controls and price setting emanated from the Farm Board that was created by the act, but little was accomplished by what some referred to as the Republican 4-H Club of Hoover, Hyde, Hell, and High Taxes.[19] Hyde was secretary of agriculture in Hoover's Cabinet.

Mercer and a number of Kansas cattlemen parted company with the Farm Board over its decision to aid stockmen only through *bona fide* existing or newly created cooperative associations rather than established livestock organizations. The board's proposals for orderly marketing, the expected but undefined effects that this would have on production, and the establishment of an agency to provide more marketing information were not foreign to Mercer's thinking. In fact, he claimed early in 1930 that "the Kansas Livestock Association was destined to take a major part in the new evolution of the livestock industry which is being sponsored by the government." But Mercer and KLA, like many other agricultural representatives, wanted more than the board offered, and at the very least expected KLA to participate on an equal basis with cooperative associations in any decisions related to the state's livestock industry.[20]

Despite the Farm Board and other government agencies, the economic condition of stockmen declined rapidly during the early thirties. When the new Democratic administration took over in 1933, demands for government action increased conspicuously. Washington responded in kind, which led former United States senator Henry J. Allen of Wichita to compare Roosevelt and the New Deal to the new preacher that a deacon had just heard. "He is the most powerful man in prayer I have heard," the deacon reported, "he asked the Lord for things that the old preacher didn't even know that Lord had."[21]

By 1933 few producers were unwilling to "ask the Lord" for help, and the urgency was illustrated by the frequency with which calls were sent out from Kansas. At a KLA-sponsored emergency conference in Emporia in 1932, Mercer addressed the group on the causes of the depression. Expressing a principle of agricultural fundamentalism, Mercer told his listeners that agriculture's plight was the basic cause of the depression and that the government must secure a more equitable system of income distribution. Two months later, Mercer said that the government was "morally obligated to aid in effecting an economic readjustment in livestock production and farming generally."[22]

The AAA, created in 1933, provided producers with one of their first real opportunities for government help from the New Deal. Basically, the AAA intended to raise farm income through production controls, the nemesis of agriculture for over a decade. The AAA also had power to purchase surpluses, to withdraw land from production, and to make marketing agreements. The wheat program, which included payments for diverted acreage, eventually proved to be one of the most popular AAA practices in the state.

Rural participation in the formulation and administration of AAA programs was also stressed. In the livestock sector, participation first appeared in the National Corn-Hog Committee of Twenty-Five, a group that represented the producer and advised AAA of aceptable programs. This committee eventually recommended an emergency program for government purchases of surplus hogs, then suggested that a permanent system be devised that included reductions in corn-hog production and a two dollar per hundredweight processing tax. The AAA accepted most of the recommendations, although it did make the hog reduction program more stringent than had been recommended.

Mercer represented Kansas corn and hog raisers at several meetings in Washington and Chicago, but before departing he met with some of the state's leading producers to discuss possible plans. Those attending meetings were divided on specific proposals, but all favored a definite program and expressed their willingness to cooperate. Throughout the discussions of the National Corn-Hog Committee, Mercer opposed the processing tax, as well as the particular type of imposed limits on production that most other committee members supported. He believed that the corn-hog problem could best be solved with price supports, marketing agreements, and higher tariffs.

Kansans were divided on the corn-hog program throughout AAA's few years of operation. When Mercer polled KLA members on whether the hog program should be extended into 1935, judgments varied. One thought it was "the first time . . . an intelligent effort has been made to help agriculture to be put on a parity with industry," and another said he knew "of no words to express my contempt for such an idiotic, senseless, unworkable scheme to usurp the American farmers' freedom." Arnold Berns, past president of KLA, believed the problem was too technical for the average farmers' consideration. Berns supported his stand by noting that, if he went to the Mayo Clinic, he would not solicit the opinion of the whole Rochester population. In the end, Kansas was the only state to vote negatively on the 1935 program, although many of the state's producers participated in the program after it had been ratified by a large margin nationally.[23]

The relationship of the AAA to the cattle industry also indicated the government's desire to please the producers. Throughout the first few months of Roosevelt's administration and while AAA was being debated, cattlemen found themselves in the dilemma of wanting aid but opposing production controls and processing taxes like those being suggested for the corn-hog program. Their failure to appreciate the significance of the 15 percent rise in cattle population since 1929 and the fact that cattle prices had not yet fallen as low as other farm commodities accounted for much of the opposition to government production controls. The fear of higher retail prices and reduced consumption kindled their opposition to processing taxes. Additionally, many cattlemen believed that a government-enforced marketing agreement with packers was adequate to curtail production, along with government-financed elimination of diseased animals and selected spaying of females. A Texas cattleman, according to one historian, even suggested that Secretary Wallace equip the hind legs of all bulls with roller skates, rather than subject the cattle producer to planned production. Beef purchases for relief, higher tariffs, and public money for financing a campaign for more consumption were also suggested.[24]

As a result of the producers' opposition, cattle were written out of the AAA program as a basic commodity, but this was acceptable to cattlemen for only a short time. As prices continued to fall, as the drought became more severe, and as they learned that other AAA programs hurt them—cotton, wheat and corn reduction, for example, raised feed prices—cattlemen began to agitate for more consideration. During the initial phases of this campaign, leading Texas cattlemen—notably Dolph Briscoe, who was president of the Texas and Southwestern Cattle Raisers Association—spearheaded the drive to get cattle accepted as a basic commodity. Though KLA failed to support the movement until after its southern neighbors had got the ball rolling, it did throughout this whole period lead the fight against a processing tax.

Although cattlemen were unsuccessful throughout 1933 in restoring cattle to the basic commodity list, other measures were taken to help them, including beef purchases by the Federal Surplus Relief Corporation (FSRC). Then, at the Albuquerque convention of the American National in January, 1934, those who favored cattle as a basic commodity forced a vote on the issue. The result was indecisive even though about 90 percent of the Texas delegation favored the proposal. The American National did, however, appoint a committee of five to study and recommend further actions.[25]

Shortly after the Albuquerque meeting of the American National, Secretary Wallace called more than a hundred cattlemen to Washington to discuss proposals for the beef industry. From this number, seventeen were selected as a manageable working group. They, in turn, recommended that cattle be made a basic commodity, and that a committee of twenty-five cattlemen—later reduced to five—be appointed to devise a plan for production control, a requirement before Wallace would approve AAA money for the beef industry. Mercer was a member of both groups and had by this time accepted the necessity for production controls, although they were contrary to his preference for limiting production through marketing agreements.

The Jones-Connally Cattle Act of April, 1934, resulted from the long agitation for government aid. It made cattle a basic commodity, authorized $200 million as compensation for reduced production, and provided an additional $50 million for the purchase of diseased stock. A definite plan for production control, however, had to be worked out before any funds were

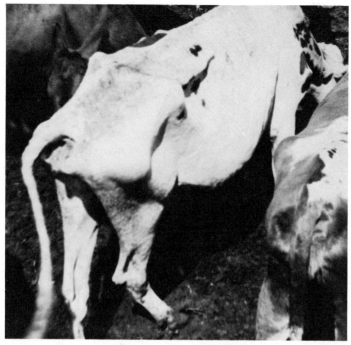

Cattle suffering from the drought, Cloud County, 1934. *Courtesy of the Kansas State Historical Society.*

allocated. While cattlemen and AAA officials debated a permanent plan, they realized that the severe drought of 1934 had changed many of the circumstances. Immediate relief, not long-range planning, became the order of the day, and all thinking and action turned in this direction.[26]

While producers described conditions in the most extreme terms—and there was, no doubt, some commercial value in this type of rhetoric—the 1934 situation certainly merited immediate governmental consideration. In Kansas feed was scarce in many sections and water was in even shorter supply. Governor Landon aided the stockmen by persuading some of the state's oilmen to lend deep-well pumps, pipelines, and tank trucks for use in distressed areas. This was repeated in 1936, which was as severe a drought year for Kansas as 1934. Landon and Mercer also labored to find feed that could be shipped in from other states. Railroads transported the feed at reduced freight rates and provided reduced tariffs on cattle that were shipped to feed. Still there were more cattle than there was feed and water, and something had to be done to reconcile the differences.[27]

On June 19, 1934, President Roosevelt signed an order to create the special Drought Relief Service, and purchases of drought-stricken cattle began two weeks later. The Drought Relief Service worked through state and county representatives in determining drought areas and the cattle to be purchased. Eventually, every state west of the Mississippi River except Washington was declared a primary or secondary drought area, as were counties in several other states east of the Mississippi.

Cattle were usually inspected by local men assisted by Bureau of Animal Health officials. Inspectors first determined whether the animals were fit to be shipped to other feeding areas or to slaughter, or whether they had to be killed in the immediate area due to weakness or disease. After the cattle were appraised, benefit payments to the owner amounted to $3 to $6 per head in addition to a purchase payment that ranged from $1 for young calves to $14 for stock two years or older. If the owner chose to sell, he was required to share the purchase money with the mortgage holder, if one existed, who in turn waived any claim to benefit payments. Payments were made, for the most part, from funds provided by the Jones-Connally Act and other emergency appropriations, and from money available to the FSRC.[28]

Many years after purchase of drought-stricken cattle in 1934, a Kansan told an apocryphal story that he claimed had been popular in the southwest part of the state. The urgency of the situation, the story went, pressed a young biologist into service as an appraiser. He did well, it was reported, until he encountered several goats in the district where he was working. He had never seen goats before, so he wrote to Secretary Wallace that he had been "executing your orders here in the Southwest, but I have discovered a new and unusual animal. I have never seen any thing like it before," the young man complained. "The animal seems to have a very sad face, has whiskers on its chin, and its hindend is worn slick. Would you advise I shoot some of them?" Wallace was greatly disturbed when he received the communication and immediately wired back: "For God's sake, don't shoot any of the animals described in your letter, those are ranchmen."[29] Regardless of whether the story was true or not, it did illustrate the skepticism with which some producers viewed government agents and the new directives from Washington; but in the end, cattlemen were forced to admit that the program had been helpful.

Purchases of cattle in Kansas were typical of those in most other states, although the Kansas Emergency Relief Committee (KERC) provided better organization than some areas had. The KERC was begun in 1932 to administer Reconstruction Finance Corporation funds; but before the emergency of the thirties was over it directed a multitude of activities, including work relief projects, service to transients, and food distribution, in addition to operations related to cattle purchases. John G. Stutz directed KERC, but as much authority as possible was delegated to local officials. In the cattle program Stutz was assisted by Dean Harry H. Umberger of Kansas State College, V. L. Morrison, E. M. Evans, and dozens of local officials.[30]

The month of July, 1934, was the hottest month on record in Kansas. The average temperature during the whole summer broke a forty-eight-year record, and this after four successive years with hot temperatures and little rain. Cattle purchases began in July, the first in Meade County. By the end of the month so many cattle were pouring into Wichita awaiting reshipment to southern states, eastern Kansas counties, or slaughtering plants that private feeders had to be contracted temporarily. Seven months later, 521,164 beef and dairy cattle had been purchased from every county in the state except Allen. Heaviest purchases were in counties just west of the Flint Hills in central Kansas, while the lightest buying occurred in the eastern part of the state. By January 15, 1935, purchasing was completed.

Kansas producers received payments that totaled over $7.5 million, an average of $14.44 a head. Of all the states that supplied cattle to the government, the $14.44 a head was one of the highest payments made, and the 3 percent condemnation rate in Kansas was one of the lowest, a credit to the efforts of the Sanitary Commission to eliminate diseased stock during the twenties.

While it was not always possible to do so, the government purchasers made a concerted effort to eliminate all diseased animals from herds, as well as to preserve the better breeding stock from slaughter. Some 15,000 registered cattle from several states, for instance, were sent to Indian reservations as foundation stock, and their owners were compensated by an average of $45.00 per head. Most producers appreciated the opportunity to eliminate the poorer quality or diseased stock from their herds, but by the same token many were also reluctant to sell their better stock. About 10,000 sheep and a few angora goats were also purchased.[31]

If cattle fit for human consumption were not shipped to other pastures, they were slaughtered and the meat distributed to the needy by the FSRC or some other designated agency. Much of the slaughtering was done by major packers, but many smaller plants were also used. In Kansas the KERC negotiated contracts with eighteen plants for this work. In addition, it allowed counties that had adequate local butchering facilities to slaughter a few of the cattle for the immediate distribution of fresh beef to needy families. Local butchers in about thirty-five counties in the state slaughtered over 8,000 head, with a considerable savings in transportation and storage.

The KERC also established nine beef-canning plants in the state for the dual purpose of processing the beef purchased and providing work relief. Existing or remodeled plants were used to process 102,231 cattle into almost 13 million cans of meat. For the short time they were in operation, about 9,000 men and women worked in the plants. Many of them gained experience that was utilized later in private concerns after the KERC plants had closed.[32]

In all, over 8.3 million cattle were purchased, with almost half of these coming from Texas and the Dakotas. Only about 18 percent of the purchase was condemned, the remainder being used for food. The belief that many would not survive shipment to feed or slaughter was the most frequent reason for condemning cattle. The government purchases, in conjunction with heavy commercial marketing, reduced the 1934 cattle inventory by 11 percent. Producers were paid a total of $11.7 million by the government, and it was estimated that they received $120 million more from their commercial marketing than they might have without the government program. The effect of the government's purchases on cattle prices following 1934 is difficult to determine, however, as the surplus was reduced by commercial marketing as well. But it was evident to producers all over the country that prices during the fall of 1935 were over 50 percent higher than they had been in 1934. For many, this spoke for itself.

Nevertheless, a number of people complained about the program. Producers wanted higher prices, even though they were paid more than the stock would have brought on the open market. They also demanded larger purchases, and called frequently for the abrogation of the promise to participate in future government controls on production. There were also complaints on administrative procedures. The American National once charged that the program was in the hands of economists and theorists, all "qualified" by the fact that they knew nothing about the real situation. Some saw the purchases as the first step in the government's takeover of the industry, which would lead to the cattlemen's loss of independence, or as an insidious vote-getting scheme.[33]

There were also many who supported the program. On the whole, most producers were happy with the sale of their cattle. Widespread approval

Drought cattle purchased by the government and shipped to the Kansas City stockyards, 1934. *Courtesy of the Kansas State Historical Society.*

encouraged one Texan to report to *The Cattleman* in 1934 that "President Roosevelt is much greater than Moses, because he is leading millions of people out of the depression and Moses only led a relatively small number of people out of the Wilderness." Others talked of the government "saving" the industry, or preventing a "complete demoralization" in beef-industry circles. But, in fact, the program neither saved nor destroyed the industry. Rather it protected many cattlemen, bought their stock when there was no other market, and prevented a great deal of unnecessary suffering on the part of starving, thirsty cattle. Additionally, it provided work relief for a short period, and a lot more beef for relief recipients than they would have otherwise received.[34]

Kansans' reactions to the cattle purchases were similar to their response to most AAA measures. The corn-hog plan was least popular, while cattle and wheat plans received the greatest support. Kansas, in fact, led the nation in the number of wheat producers who participated in diverting acreage and in the amount of payments received. By the time the Supreme Court dispensed with the AAA, Kansas had received a total of $87.5 million in government payments, third highest behind Iowa with $94.2 and Texas with $148.2 million.[35]

Stockmen have traditionally had a poor reputation as conservationists, and drought condition focused much public concern on ecology. Even before the thirties many accounts of the practices of nineteenth-century cattle and sheep producers stressed their overgrazing grassland and destruction of vast areas of public domain. Certainly, some destruction resulted as stockmen hurried to use as much of the public's grass and water as possible before others did. Not all stockmen failed to conserve the national resources, but the public generally viewed stockmen as destroyers of the natural environment. New Deal conservationist efforts, however, helped not only to improve the cattlemen's deplorable reputation but also to change many of their wasteful practices. The government, for instance, established guidelines for more efficient use of the public grassland, and made payments to help develop water-saving ponds and to establish grazing practices that preserved the native grass. Although stockmen sometimes resisted governmental guidance, they came to appreciate the efforts after a while and in the end became known for their conservationist work.

The Taylor Act of 1934 was the first major thrust of the New Deal into the area of conservation. Designed to correct past evils, the act withdrew from possible settlement most of the unappropriated public land in the West and organized much of it into grazing districts. Kansas stockmen did not profit directly from the Taylor bill. Rather, they probably suffered some loss in the marketplace in competing with stockmen who grazed cattle on public land at low fees, but only on rare occasions did they object to the inequity.

The Soil Conservation and Domestic Allotment Act of 1936 was the most important piece of New Deal legislation related to conservation. This act, largely an expedient to circumvent the 1936 Supreme Court ruling that voided much of the first AAA, kept federal funds flowing into the agricultural sector of the economy by paying farmers and ranchers to shift to soil-conserving crops and to adopt other conservationist practices. With the Supreme Court in mind, Congress now provided funds directly from the United States Treasury rather than from a processing tax. Payments for shifting away from soil-depleting crops—which were said to be surplus crops like wheat—averaged $10 an acre, while cattlemen benefited from the 35 cents per animal per month payment that was made for allowing range land to reseed itself through deferred grazing. Cattlemen were also paid $1 per linear foot for digging additional stock wells, 10 cents for every hundred linear feet of contour ridging of the range, and 50 percent of the cost of some pond construction. A number of cattlemen felt that contouring was as advantageous to landowners as any practice to come out of this period.

In all, Kansas received by far the largest payment made to any state during the first year that the Soil Conservation and Domestic Allotment Act was in force, but the largest portion of this went toward diverting wheat acreage. Payments remained high for the rest of the thirties, although a limit of $10,000 to any one farmer or ranchman was set in 1939.[36]

In addition to the several federal agencies that were involved in conservation work in the state during the thirties, the KERC sponsored work relief projects related to conservation. Much of KERC funding eventually came from the federal agencies created to provide relief, although some early efforts had been paid for by the state. Some of the CCC camps in the state exemplified KERC's activities, being administered by the state and paid for largely with federal money. Towards the middle of the decade KERC's work was taken over by other agencies, especially the Works Progress Administration.

Practical conservation work that directly affected stockmen related primarily to grass and water. Because it was impossible to reduce herd strength rapidly without severe economic loss, some of the state's grassland suffered intensely as rainfall diminished. A few stockmen predicted that much of the grass was gone forever, but others were more realistic. A. E. Aldous, an agronomist at Kansas State College, estimated that the grazing capacity of the Flint Hills had decreased 30 to 40 percent by 1935. Aldous said little about the short grass in the central and western parts of the state; but in view of even greater shortages of moisture there, the grazing capacity in these areas must have declined even more, especially after the 1936 drought.

The grass, though sparse, was not dead. A lack of moisture rather than deliberate overgrazing was the basic cause of the poor crop. On the other hand, there were practices that stockmen could readily adopt that would help them not only to replenish the natural vegetation but also to weather the periodic scarcity of rainfall in the future. Various methods of deferred grazing that allowed the grass to reseed itself appeared to work best in the short-grass areas, although there were attempts to seed buffalo grass artificially in the western part of the state. In this connection and after considerable study, the Ft. Hays Experiment Station concluded that harvesting short-grass seed was impractical. But it could be reseeded by scattering hay that had gone to seed over bare spots. A manure spreader could be used for spreading the cured hay before pressing it into the prepared soil with a packer. Reseeding seemed to prove more successful with the long grasses of eastern Kansas, however, and here too the hay method was frequently used. By 1938 the *Stockman* reported that 7,563 of the state's cattlemen were deliberately applying a deferred-grazing program; and thousands more, no doubt, were employing the concept to a greater or lesser degree. Ranges could also be protected by distributing salt, water, and feed so that stock would not continually gather in only one area for feeding. Weed and brush control and contour terracing also improved range land. But, even though all of these practices were beneficial, rainfall was most important. When sufficient rain fell, the grass that had become largely dormant during the drought began its slow recovery. As early as 1938 the *Stockman* noted that the bluestem was coming back in many Flint Hills areas. In 1946 Kling L. Anderson reported to the Board of Agriculture, "Many [acres] once thought to be destroyed, now have a cover of grass nearly equal to that before the dry years." Nature and intelligence had contrived this great change, which disproved many ominous predictions that had been made along the way.[37]

The drought also motivated farmers and ranchers to construct more ponds. These were intended to conserve available water and store it for future use, reduce soil erosion, and provide more stock-watering locations. If stock gathered at only one place for water, the grass was destroyed by their frequent trampling. John R. Brinkley, the colorful doctor who claimed to restore virility with his goat-gland operation, and a part-time politician, was one of the first Kansans to suggest wholesale pond building at public expense. But pond building was not significantly expanded until government agencies became involved in work relief.[38]

Pond building was also encouraged by government officials and various state and federal conservation agencies. Governor Alf Landon, for example, was a strong advocate of pond construction and encouraged it at every opportunity. Early in his first term as governor he persuaded the legislature to grant a tax reduction to those farmers or ranchers who constructed water-conserving dams. Then, motivated by his concern for water conservation and by the desire to "pry more relief money from the federal government," Landon held a special conference on Kansas water problems in 1934. Detailed plans for 50,000 ponds—along with designs for numerous large lakes for storage and for flood control—were submitted to the federal government. It was soon announced that Kansas would begin receiving half a million dollars a month for construction. Some of the larger, more expensive projects were shelved;

but a year later KERC was supervising the building of 2,391 ponds and 26 lakes.[39]

The number of ponds and windmills that were constructed in Kansas during the thirties is still a matter of speculation. Various agencies sometimes gave progress reports on their individual efforts; but these were only partial lists at best, and no one seems to have included the numerous individual efforts of farmers and ranchers that were unrelated to any of the government relief projects. One of the best estimates, however, indicated that at least 7,000 dams, pits, and ponds had been constructed by 1940. Conservationist groups encouraged the erection of additional windmills to provide more water and help distribute stock more evenly over the range land. Several relief agencies provided much of the labor and money for many new wells constructed during the thirties. But the figures for new wells are as speculative as those for ponds.[40]

The Morton County Land Utilization Project was another government attempt at conservation that affected Kansas cattle producers. Morton County, located in the far southwest corner of the state, usually has about seventeen inches of annual precipitation, but during the thirties rainfall dropped to around eleven inches. Dust storms and soil erosion naturally followed, and the government acted. Land purchases in Morton County began under the Resettlement Administration in 1935, at which time 53,590 acres were bought. Rehabilitation began immediately, principally through efforts to arrest the blowing sand. In 1938 an additional 42,800 acres were acquired under the authority of the Bankhead-Jones Act. Other purchases and exchanges followed until the project included almost 107,000 acres of sandhill land on both sides of the Cimarron River, or about 23 percent of the county. The project has remained pretty much the same size up to the present.

Under supervision of the federal Soil Conservation Service—the project has been administered by the Forest Service as a National Grassland since 1954—the area was reseeded to grass and developed for pasturing. By 1943 some of the land was judged sufficiently recovered to allow grazing, and less than a decade later the whole area was being utilized as pasture. The land was leased to the Morton County Grazing Association—formed in 1944 specifically to handle this project—then subleased to members of the association, with some 25 percent of the grazing fees being allocated to the county in lieu of taxes. The association handled many of the routine administrative duties, decided on the number of stock each member was allowed to pasture, and provided range riders, salt, and fences. The Forest Service, however, determined the grazing fees, the length of the grazing season, and the total number of animals allowed on the land.

Under the expert management of George S. Atwood, the Forest Service's representative for almost twenty-five years, this cooperative effort by the government and local stockmen was an unqualified success in returning much of the land to high productivity. More rainfall during the forties, of course, was also instrumental. Stockmen in the area have generally approved the project, although they frequently disagreed with what they considered to be unnecessarily low limits on the numbers of stock allowed to graze, or complained of a short pasturing season.[41]

Thus cattlemen have demonstrated their interest in conservationist practices throughout the twentieth century, sometimes reluctantly, and often only with the encouragement and leadership of government. Yet the controversy over the cattleman as conservationist continues. The fact that almost all the land in the state is privately owned accounts in large part for the environmental concerns of Kansas stockmen. This is not to say that Kansans did not learn and profit from the extensive government efforts at conservation, especially after the droughts of the thirties focused much attention on the matter. Most of them did profit, and not a few of the younger stockmen probably appreciated for the first time the delicate balance that must be struck between nature and human activity. Many learned the necessity of adapting to the environment. With nature's cooperation, the government's encouragement, and their own unquenchable optimism, they became not only better conservationists but better cattlemen as well.[42]

Throughout the New Deal period there was always some disagreement among the state's cattlemen on the methodology of individual projects sponsored by the government. The same discord was apparent when cattlemen discussed government aid as a single concept, a practice that became increasingly popular as the New Deal wore on. Most Kansas cattlemen welcomed the government's efforts in their behalf, although there were a few who maintained that the agricultural sector had no room for government subsidies.

Dan Casement, noted earlier for his opposition to government involvement during the twenties, exemplified opposition to New Deal programs better than anyone else in the state. Sent by his parents to Princeton, where he learned individualism and self-reliance, Casement then went to western Colorado to graze cattle and incidentally to illegally fence in some of the public domain. Eventually he became the most widely known Kansas cattleman in the nation. More has probably been written by and about Casement than any other stockman in the state. Unparalleled success in the show ring with his feeder stock, wide appeal as a public speaker, and his undaunted willingness to say what was on his mind largely accounted for his popularity. Casement also had a charismatic personality. Equally at home in the farrowing pen or the lobby of the Waldorf-Astoria, the Manhattan stockman had a wide circle of friends. Some said he made an art of profanity. He was, for example, fond of calling a person with whom he disagreed a "prismatic S.O.B.," which translated into "a son of a bitch from any angle one cared to look at him." Some of his other well-chosen vocabulary was unprintable.

Casement, with his brightly colored vests, fashionably tailored jackets, and ever-present pipe, was usually at the major stock shows and other gatherings of stockmen, spewing his feedlot philosophy to all who cared to listen. He was equally comfortable with Thomas Jefferson's agricultural fundamentalism and Andrew Carnegie's Social Darwinism, changing his message little throughout his life. Speaking at a meeting of the American National, for example, Casement told cattlemen, "You do not represent a business system or a political organization. You are a social class, typifying a way of life, a fraternity of ideals, that preserve the best in American lore, that unify in a single code of citizenship the traditions of our forefathers for freedom, independence, opportunity, resourcefulness, and rugged individuality."

This was the same simplistic message that Casement dispensed for three decades. Shortly after AAA went into effect, for instance, Casement wired Secretary Wallace that the new program had caused hog prices to decline almost a dollar in five days. The program, he said in the wire, "is universally condemned by leading farmers and supported only by professional farm leaders in whom real farmers place no trust. It is axiomatic," he continued, "that neither the laws of nature, economics nor evolution can be repealed by human agencies. Your program aims at the impossible. . . ."[43] There was no acceptable method to regulate production, he believed, and to attempt to do so "spells the suicide of democracy," while "to do so by force would invite revolution."

Casement believed further that producing food was "the foundation of our national economy, the base on which the whole structure should rest, the center from which all of its elements should radiate." In answer to New Deal plans that attempted to help the poor farmers and stockmen, Casement replied, in excellent Carnegie fashion, that "poverty and underprivilege are ordained by the law of life and vital to its design. No human authority can ever abolish them." The solution, he said, was not government aid but rather "an unspeakably slow attrition." Depressed farmers and ranchers were happy to believe that agriculture was the most important sector of the nation's economy, but they were not sure they agreed with the ideas of inevitable poverty and necessary attrition.[44]

Casement was not merely an armchair philosopher, content to damn the New Deal from afar. He also had the courage of his convictions. In 1935 the ultraconservative Farmers Independent Council of America was formed, ostensibly to disseminate among farmers accurate information concerning agricultural ills and the true intents of the AAA. Although the council was established primarily by Stanley F. Morse, Casement became the president of this agrarian counterpart of the American Liberty League, and he did as much as anyone to advertise the organization's views. The council thought even Alf Landon was too liberal for its full support in the 1936 election, and the Roosevelt landslide dealt the council a mortal blow. While it continued to exist for a time, it never became the large movement of farmers in revolt against government aid that its founders had envisioned. Eventually the council died, "having become little more than it had been in the beginning, a propaganda organ for industry, the meat packers, and some large cattle interests."[45]

Casement, like most of those he represented, carefully selected the government interventions upon which he heaped abuse. Little if any opposition from Casement or any others was expressed toward high protective tariffs for cattlemen, the millions of dollars of public money that the USDA spent to improve the cattle industry, or the various laws that regulated for the producers' benefit the businesses that were tangential to beef production. Nor did Casement see any inconsistency in his beliefs and the relatively low fees that he and others paid to graze cattle on the public lands of the West.[46]

Although Casement never altered his views on government aid throughout his long association with the Kansas cattle industry, the views of hundreds of others were not at all consistent, nor were they in line with those of the Manhattan feeder. As noted above, government aid did not come to cattlemen against their will; stockmen demanded help and at the time were usually appreciative of it. The methods and extent of government attempts to aid agriculture were, however, sometimes criticized. Mercer, for instance, remarked at one time that the New Deal was like the farmer who had "too much hay down," and the *Stockman* once published this ditty:

> Little Boy Blue, come blow your horn
> There's a government agent counting your corn;
> Another one lecturing the old red sow
> On the number of pigs she can have and how.

Although some criticized the methods, few were critical of the principle of aid itself. KLA president W. H. Burke, for instance, noted in 1935 that one could get few farmers and ranchers in central and western Kansas excited about opposing government help, as the AAA "has provided a great many of them with the only incomes they have had in the last three years. Their bonus checks have been the only money they have had for food and shoes."

Later the same year Burke chided two of the most prominent members of the Farmers Independent Council by noting that he would shortly visit Charles Collins, who now opposed government aid in all forms, where he would price calves at 8 cents a pound, "a similar crop of which he [Collins] could not sell for half the money before the government, under the AAA, bought at fair prices, some 8 million surplus cattle." Burke then reported that he would also stop at Dan Casement's farm to see his large pig crop, "made possible by his personal sacrifice in refusing to sign a control program, now selling at 10 cents per pound." Dan was a fine host, Burke said, and he would "not remind him that a previous crop of pigs, before the government reduced the surplus was begging for a buyer at 3 cents per pound." R. J. Laubengoyer, another Kansas stockman, told the KLA convention in 1938, "I practiced so-called rugged individualism in farming and ranching until I discovered that it was useless to buck a braced game." Most other business and labor groups, he said, were being subsidized in one way or another.[47]

Joe Mercer probably best summarized the thinking of most agricultural producers in the state during his unsuccessful bid for the United States Senate in 1932. Mercer traveled the state telling his listeners,

I am not an advocate of government in business, yet as I study the situation it does appear that the true function of government is in serving its citizens in acute emergencies by directing its business af-fairs so as to prevent unnecessary suffering and property loss. . . . Government alone can direct in controlling production . . . control credits and prevent wild speculation . . . stop bank failures. . . . How unnecessary and ridiculous it is for millions of our citizens to tramp the streets, hungry, poorly clad and cold, looking for means of livelihood, because we have too much food, too much wool and cotton and too much fuel.[48]

Although willing to demand and accept aid during the thirties, a number of Kansas stockmen soon forgot the position they had taken during the depressed interwar period. Judging by the popular literature that emanates from the industry today, many cattlemen talk as if they are opposed to government aid, and some even believe that this sentiment is based on a long tradition. Well-chosen elements of Casement's philosophy, for example, are honored today by many as typical of the views cattlemen have always had toward government support. At a KLA convention in 1950 cattlemen yielded to the general hysteria that was characteristic of the times and proudly adopted a "Freedom Resolution" that condemned the "socialized state." In a supporting statement the *Stockman* waxed eloquent in its description of the conventioneers, referring to cattlemen who "disdained the dole" as "those men who take their winnings and their losings in stride [like the] pioneers who made America great. . . . They asked no favors . . . those cowmen, who are the bravest, most rugged individualists, the most forthright characters to band together."[49]

Ten years after adopting the Freedom Resolution, the *Stockman* continued to beat the same drum. Under the heading "Livestock Producers Don't Like Government Help," the journal intoned again, "Historically the cattle business has been through repeated experience of boom and bust coinciding with the ups and downs of the cattle cycle. At times it might seem pleasant for the cattlemen to unload these problems onto the taxpaying public. But cattlemen have a long and proud history of insisting upon carrying their own problems of natural and economic hazards."[50]

Thus, the myth of complete independence and self-reliance, which had been generated long before and perpetuated by men like Casement, persisted beyond the middle of the twentieth century. In reality, as the interwar period revealed, it was a strange position for the livestock sector in view of its generally advantageous relationship with government at both the state and national levels. It is probable that opposition to government aids increased during the prosperous World War II period, but prior to that many successful—and unsuccessful—attempts were made by the government to assist producers of beef. And these came, largely, at the request of farmers and ranchers. Nor was the producer through asking for help when he managed to get aid for the production phase of the industry. Petitions for government regulation of marketing institutions and transportation were also on his crowded agenda between the wars.

11

Beginning a Revolution: Markets, Packers, and Trucks, 1920-1940

After maturing the cattle, producers turned their attention to transporting the stock to market and processing the beef for consumption. Marketing, the middle state in the long process that put beef on the American table, was significant in determining profits. Marketing was of special importance to producers during the twenties when many believed that improvement in this area was essential for raising income and thus profits. Then, during the chaotic thirties, cattlemen returned their attention largely to production and government aid, as it was hard to work for improvements in marketing when many cattlemen were simply trying to survive. Ironically, though, it was during the thirties that the most notable changes in the transporting and marketing of stock occurred.

The cost of marketing, which had edged upward during the inflated World War I period and had failed to retreat as rapidly as did stock prices during the postwar deflation, was the fountainhead of discontent. Many suggestions for reducing these charges surfaced, but few were actually attempted and fewer still were successful in achieving their objective. First in time came renewed interest in closer government regulation of transportation facilities, stockyards, and packers; then more concern for cooperative marketing developed. Still, producers were dissatisfied, and when a combination of factors—primarily the increased use of the truck—forced marketing and packing facilities to begin decentralizing, many producers were happy to accept the amended system.

Some change in producers' attitude toward big business also became evident during this period. Cattlemen, for example, had become less critical of the large packers by the late twenties, and these processors became more

255

friend than whipping boy. The intense struggle over railroad freight rates had also lost much of its fire by 1940, as cattlemen turned more and more to motor transport. All these developments had great significance for the beef industry, much of it lasting far beyond World War II.

Almost as soon as the emergency in Europe had passed, shippers began debating whether the railroads should continue under strict government control. Joseph H. Mercer and a number of Kansas cattlemen, remembering the rise in rates and what they thought was poor service, believed that the lines should be returned to private direction as soon as possible. Shippers of agricultural products as a whole, however, were divided on the issue, and the split contributed to the passage of the Transportation Act of 1920. This piece of legislation returned the lines to private control and, more importantly, ordered that the Interstate Commerce Commission approve rate increases to the extent that lines received a "fair return" of about 6 percent on their aggregate value. State regulatory agencies were instructed not to interfere with any tariffs that were designed to produce the 6 percent return. This, in effect, reduced significantly the state's power to regulate the carriers.

In the western district the ICC established an average value of $60,000 per mile of track and, subsequently, allowed a 35 percent rate increase. While westerners believed unanimously that this advance had been excessive, some tariffs in the eastern district were raised by 40 percent. As a result of the substantial advance, Kansas intrastate rates for cattle advanced from 30.5 to 41.0 cents per hundredweight for a 450-mile haul, and 9.5 to 13.0 cents for a 50-mile journey, representing over $98 and $31 per car, respectively, for the longer and shorter hauls. Sam H. Cowan, legal representative of several western livestock associations, estimated that the two substantial advances since the beginning of the war had increased all rates by 75 percent of their prewar levels, not too far removed from the 60 to 70 percent actually experienced in Kansas intrastate tariffs.

The disparity that existed between freight rates and livestock prices at this time was exemplified by the account of a westerner who shipped several carloads of sheep to the Chicago market. The sheep, supposedly, sold for less than the freight bill, so the commission company wired the owner for additional money to make up the difference. "Don't have any money," replied the shipper, "but I'm sending more sheep."[1] Many Kansas cattlemen, faced with rising freight rates and declining stock prices, understood well the sheepman's plight.

The rise in freight tariffs in 1920 was one of the most significant increases in railroad history. Coming at a time of severe deflation in agricultural prices, the large advance reversed sharply the tendency for rates to remain somewhat proportionate to agricultural prices. Furthermore, for the first time an alternate source of transport was becoming available to shippers and would eventually reduce the gains the railroads made in the Transportation Act more than any action of shippers or groups that represented them.

Kansas stockmen, and agricultural producers as a whole, wasted little time in protesting the new 1920 rate schedule. Lengthy ICC hearings followed, with Mercer and other KLA members figuring prominently. The cattlemen argued that the railroads' evaluations had been set too high and that shippers, faced with the depression, were unable to pay the higher charges. They had limited success in 1922, when the ICC revaluated some railroad property and subsequently lowered rates, but the new tariffs hardly approached the prewar levels that were desired by cattlemen. In general, the rollback in Kansas intrastate tariffs amounted to only about 10 percent.[2]

After the decrease in 1922, the rates in Kansas, as well as most of the western district, remained essentially the same for a decade and a half, except for emergency reductions in response to the drought of the thirties. But the stability of rates did not end the controversy between the shippers and rail lines that had existed sporadically for over two generations. Railroad petitions for higher tariffs arrived at ICC offices simultaneously with shipper demands that rates be reduced. The carriers, for instance, petitioned ICC for a 5 percent increase in 1925 while KLA asked for a 25 percent reduction. Both were denied. Repeat performances occurred in 1931 and 1932, with much the same result. Then, much to their credit, the rail lines yielded to pressures from political leaders and shipping interests for emergency drought rates. These lower tariffs were a significant factor in adjusting to the drought and depression as they allowed stockmen some flexibility in deciding upon a course of action to meet the emergency. Kansas cattlemen could, for example, ship in hay at half the regular rate. Or they could ship cattle out to available feed at 85 percent of the fat stock rate, then return them at 15 percent, which represented only half of the published schedules for the round trip. The lowered rates enabled many cattlemen to cope with the disastrous feed shortages and to save breeding stock from the government-sponsored canning factories.[3]

Stockmen also objected to other items on the rate schedules. Mercer, for example, reported to the annual Feeder's Day Convention in 1927, "our entire freight rate structure is a most complicated affair, filled with inconsistencies, irregularities and unfair rates." He apparently had in mind rate discrepancies on cattle shipped into Kansas from the Southwest, all with similar origins but some with unloading points some fifteen miles beyond the point where rail lines were competitive. The absence of competition, Mercer claimed, allowed railroads to raise shipping charges by $11 to $35 a car.

Although cattlemen protested some preferential rates, they strongly defended others that were to their benefit. Reduced tariffs on purbred stock, feed-in-transit, and sale-in-transit rates, for example, were all matters of dispute. Cattlemen wanted lower purebred rates and the continued practice of reducing the charges for cattle sold or fed while in transit to a central market. The lines, on the other hand, desired to keep purebred tariffs the same—there was more profit in carrying a telephone pole than a purebred bull, one railroad official claimed—and to move special tariffs generally toward a single, uniform charge for all cattle. In the end, purebred rates were reduced to half the regular fare in 1924, sale-in-transit tariffs were continued, and the interwar period ended with railroads still attempting to modify the feed-in-transit rates.[4]

Just before World War II, cattlemen were again confronted with rising freight tariffs. The ICC allowed advances on specific commodities in 1937, but livestock interests avoided this increase. Their success was short-lived, however, as ICC permitted another advance the following year, subject to the approval of state regulatory agencies. The Kansas Corporation Commission first refused but then acquiesced to the higher tariffs, both actions at the request of cattlemen. Livestock interests apparently accepted increased intrastate rates in 1938, because they feared that continued opposition might result in higher interstate charges.[5]

By 1939 the *Kansas Stockman* claimed that average rates for farm products were 163 percent higher than they had been in 1913. Two years later they were even higher. On the eve of the United States' entry into the war, Kansas cattlemen were paying over $100 and $40 per car, respectively, for 450- and 50-mile hauls. This represented several dollars a car more than shippers had ever paid to transport their stock by rail, and about double what they had paid during World War I. The general success that cattlemen had had before World War I in keeping rate hikes to a minimum contrasted sharply with the rising tariffs they experienced between the wars. By then, however, higher tariffs were being balanced somewhat by an alternate means of transport.[6]

While rail lines continued to carry the majority of Kansas livestock, a new development that eventually revolutionized stock transport appeared on the horizon. Trucks began to make inroads on rail transportation, slowly during the twenties, then much more rapidly during the following decade. By the beginning of World War II the revolution in livestock transport was well on its way. Trucks, or trailers pulled behind the family automobile, began to interest livestock shippers for the first time during World War I, but it was a decade later before they carried a significant number of stock to central markets. Because large numbers of hogs were often raised in the immediate area of the large markets, this species led others in turning to truck transport. In 1919, for instance, the *Stockman* noted that "trucks frequently bring hogs a distance of from 50 to 75 miles in good condition" to the state's larger markets. Moreover, some stockmen began suggesting that trucks would eventually solve the producers' short-haul problems, but it took two decades to prove these views correct.

In 1920 it was estimated that 10 percent of all farm produce was carried to market by truck, but still only 3 percent of the hogs and cattle were carried in this manner. Then, during the twenties, the number of trucks on Kansas farms increased eightfold, and the construction of hard-surfaced roads followed in due course. Yet, even with improved roads and the new trucks, the vast majority of livestock still arrived at the central markets by rail (Table 2).[7]

During the following decade a major shift began to occur. With trucks in mind, Mercer noted midway through the 1930s that "possibly at no time in history have shipping conditions changed so rapidly as during the past recent years." Over 97 percent of the hogs arrived at St. Joseph by truck in 1936, although the percentages for sheep and cattle were lower. The shorter distance from shipping point to market apparently meant that hogs were most easily shipped by motor transport at this time. Many cattle and sheep, coming from a much wider area, were still shipped by rail. By the end of the interwar period, however, the *Stockman* reported that at sixty-seven of the principal markets in the country 66 percent of the cattle, 62 percent of the calves, 69 percent of the hogs, and 22 percent of the sheep arrived by truck.[8]

The figures showing the large increase in truck transportation to central markets, significant though they were, did not reflect the even greater num-

REO truck delivering a cow to the Stuart Commission Company, Wichita. *Courtesy of the Kansas State Historical Society.*

bers of stock that were transported to the many local marketing points that sprang up during this period, especially during the thirties. The truck, in fact, was a significant factor in the whole decentralization process that occurred in livestock marketing and packing facilities. The figures do show, however, the reciprocal influence of available railroads and the quantity of stock brought in by truck. Wichita had the fewest railroads and the largest percentage of stock delivered by truck, while Kansas City was just the opposite.

A number of reasons accounted for the growing popularity of truck transportation, not least of which was the persistent belief that rail tariffs were too high, especially charges for short hauls. Many argued that additional charges by the railroads only reduced their livestock-carrying trade. After experiencing less business, many stockmen believed, rail lines attempted to maintain their profit levels by raising rates for the livestock that was carried rather than reducing rates and becoming more competitive. This, stockmen held, only encouraged the vicious circle of more trucks and higher railroad freight rates.

The Kansas experience during the thirties, however, does not completely support these judgments, as the large growth in truck use during the early thirties coincided with a period of stability in published rail tariffs. Railroads

Table 2. Percentage of Cattle and Calves Trucked to Central Markets,
1925–1936

Year	1925	1930	1936
Kansas City	3.0	11.0	40.8
St. Joseph	8.8	27.8	74.4
Wichita	16.6	32.5	80.6
Averages	9.5	23.8	65.2

SOURCE: Exhibit C-1, Ex Parte No. 123.

would probably have had to reduce their rates in order to maintain their livestock-carrying trade at its former level, as it remained more costly to ship by rail than truck on short hauls. Only the large commercial truck lines were supervised to any degree by state regulatory agencies, and not until after 1933 did the Kansas Corporation Commission make any attempt to establish uniform rates between the two different modes of transportation. Equal rates did not result, however, as this attempt applied only to commercial trucking concerns; much of the stock was hauled by owners or by neighbors who were not subject to state regulation.

Factors other than lower costs contributed as well to the large shift to truck transport. Trucks were more convenient, as shippers could readily adjust the shipping schedule to their personal needs, set their own departure and arrival times, and more effectively select desirable marketing days. Trucks serviced all areas of the country, and provided direct ranch-to-market transport without any intervening loading and unloading. This factor, along with the fact that livestock in trucks usually received better care, resulted in fewer injuries and deaths. Trucks also provided faster service in most instances, which resulted in less shrinkage. All these factors were significant considerations in the shippers' choice of transportation, as was the fact that once trucks were purchased they became indispensable machines around farms and ranches, performing a multitude of chores other than transporting stock to market.[9]

The truck was welcomed first by small shippers, those who usually marketed less than a railway carload, and especially those who lived within fifty to a hundred miles of a market. But before the period had ended, large producers who usually shipped long distances were also turning to motor transport. Those with good access to rail lines were slowest in converting to the truck. The Robbins ranch, for example, which was close to the Rock

261

Modern truck unloading at the Herrington sale barn, 1977. *Courtesy of the Kansas Stockman.*

Island as well as the Santa Fe lines, did not switch to trucks until after a squabble with the Santa Fe during the middle 1950s over rates and labor. Stockmen in the Flint Hills turned completely to trucks during the late 1950s and early 1960s. For shippers who always had a carload or more to be shipped a long distance, railroad freight rates were not much of a factor in the shift. Most likely, truck transport cost more during the early period, due to the small vehicles and the poor roads that slowed delivery.[10]

Today, trucks have supplanted rail lines almost completely. The long lines of pungent rail cars that snaked their way across western states have given way to huge trucks that thunder down the highways night and day, sometimes decorating the approaching traffic with the shrink that shippers hoped to avoid. While railroad rates were a compelling reason for small shippers to ship by truck, there were others that were more important to the transition. The convenience of having the stock picked up at the farm or at loading pens in the pastures and the greatly reduced time in transit were, and are today, the most significant reasons. These advantages continue to keep stockmen happy with the truck.

Throughout the interwar period Kansas livestock producers, as well as many others throughout the West, continued to patronize heavily the three terminal marketing facilities in or adjacent to the state. About 1930 a report noted that 67 percent of the Kansas cattle marketed at the public terminals went through the facilities at Kansas City. Wichita and St. Joseph received around 12 percent each, and all other markets accounted for only 9 percent. Receipts at Kansas City during this period averaged around 5.7 million head annually. About 2.2 million of these were cattle and calves, and most of the remainder were hogs. While Chicago continued to be the largest national stock market, especially significant for fat cattle, Kansas City was in second place in total receipts and was the largest trader in the country for stockers and feeders. Early in the twenties Kansas City was receiving almost double the number of stockers and feeders that were received at Omaha, the second largest market for this class of stock.

The other terminal markets readily available to Kansas producers, at St. Joseph and Wichita, received a total annual average of about 3.3 and 1.0 million head of stock, respectively. Of the total, cattle and calf receipts averaged over half a million at St. Joseph and somewhat less than that in Wichita. Like Kansas City, both were also important hog-marketing centers, especially St. Joseph. All these markets tended to show their highest receipts during the early twenties, then experienced steady declines for the remainder of the period. Decentralization of packing and marketing largely accounted for this.[11]

The large companies continued to dominate meat packing throughout the interwar period, but their relative importance declined in much the same proportion, and for similar reasons, as that of the terminal stockyards. The World War I period had been unusually profitable for the large packers because of the immense demand for meat and the disrupted trade patterns that allowed the United States to satisfy more of Europe's need. But the flush times turned sour when the kaiser's armies surrendered. The demand for meat then declined and prewar trade patterns were reestablished. Several business ventures by large packers that were unrelated to the meat trade also fell victim to the general depression and affected their overall prosperity.

The large packers blamed much of their misfortune on the government. The Food Administration, they claimed, had encouraged them to process all the livestock produced while the European conflict continued. F. Edson White, a representative of Armour, told Kansas cattlemen that the packers' cellars were stacked high with meat at the end of the war, and hides were stacked wherever there was an available spot. While this may have been an exaggeration in order to account for low stock prices, the big packers did, apparently, have large inventories of meat in 1918; and production remained high while the whole economy slipped into the postwar depression. Some packers cited the government's restrictions on their auxiliary enterprises as a reason for their decline. After the early twenties, however, the large packers recovered along with most other industrial sectors, then continued to prosper for the rest of the interwar period except for the early thirties.

The dispute over the packers' profits, so volatile during the war, failed to abate during the twenties but did subside to a large extent during the following decade. Most of the same offensive and defensive arguments used during the war were repeated by producers and processors throughout the postwar period. Cattlemen claimed the packers had excessive profits on their investment, yet the processors insisted that they made only 1 percent on sales. Both may have been correct, although the cattlemen's charge appeared less well founded than it had during the war.

The large packers lost part of the meat slaughter business to smaller packing plants. Between 1916 and 1929 their percentage of the meat slaughtered for interstate commerce declined from over 70 to about 58 percent. It was true, however, that some of the smaller plants were owned by the large packers. While their percentage of the total slaughter was down and they may have experienced a lower margin of profit, the large packers remained a dominant influence in the meat industry throughout the whole period.[12]

While the packers struggled with the postwar depression, the producers' agitation for a larger government role in marketing finally came to fruition. The first in a series of moves was the so-called Packer Consent Decree of 1920. It developed after officials in the Justice Department had studied the *FTC Reports,* then initiated a suit to prosecute the Big Five packers for violations of the Clayton Antitrust Act. In order to escape prosecution and severely restrictive legislation, to avoid damaging publicity, and, possibly, to forestall a closer look by the Justice Department into their operations, the Big Five agreed to relinquish their interests in stockyards, terminal railroads, market newspapers, and some cold-storage warehouses. Additionally, the packers promised to dissociate themselves from the wholesaling and retailing of all groceries except meat and related items and dairy products. Those producers who were eagerly awaiting startling revelations and vindication of their many charges from the prosecution were shocked at the agreement and not a little dismayed. Many of their efforts were then turned to supporting one or the other of the legislative proposals that were designed to regulate livestock marketing.[13]

Even before Attorney General Palmer had negotiated and the Supreme

Court of the United States had confirmed the Packer Consent Decree, Congress made a number of attempts to regulate the marketing and processing of livestock. Most of these bills died in committee for lack of support, usually because packers and many producers considered them too "radical" if they attempted to implement any of the FTC recommendations for government ownership. A bill sponsored by Senator William S. Kenyon came closest to passage. It provided a system of licensing for all interstate slaughterers, stockyards, and commission firms, as well as some other agencies associated with the meat trade. The Kenyon Bill was debated at length throughout 1919, but eventually failed.

Nevertheless, almost 80 percent of the producers polled by the *Stockman* in 1919 favored some type of federal regulation of stockyards and packers. The 1920 KLA convention even featured a formal debate on the issue. "Resolved, that Federal Supervision of Stock Yards and Packing Industries Is Necessary to Restore Confidence in Live Stock Business" was the topic of the formal discussion. Mercer and John A. Edwards upheld the affirmative side, emphasizing the monopolistic practices of the packing industry, the packers' manipulation of market prices, and their excessive profits. Representatives of Swift and Wilson argued that the evils attributed to the industry did not exist, that cooperation between packers and producers was essential, and that curtailment of packer operations with restrictive legislation would be harmful to the producer. The audience, mostly Kansas producers, enjoyed the confrontation immensely. While the packers presented the "facts" and the most logical arguments, the efforts of Edwards and Mercer were more colorful and emotional. There was little doubt which side won the debate as far as the audience was concerned.[14]

While Congress debated regulation of stockyards and packers throughout 1918 and 1919 but produced no bill, the attention of Kansas producers shifted to the state level, where similar legislation was being considered. Early in 1920 during a special session of the state legislature, Mercer and a few lawmakers wrote a bill designed to regulate the state's livestock trade. Known as the Burdick Bill after a legislator from Atchison, it provided for a Kansas Live Stock Bureau with power to establish and put into effect "reasonable rules, rates and charges" for packers, stockyards, commission men, and rendering plants. Protection of the public's interests was the basis for the proposed legislation, which was to be enforced through licensing and the newly created Court of Industrial Relations.

The bill received little outside attention until the legislature indicated that it might pass a measure that would satisfy KLA demands. Following this, the *Stockman* reported, the Kansas City packers came to Topeka with "blood in their eye." Long-winded opposition followed, Mercer was called "bull-headed," and KLA was accused of having "conspired to deprive the packers of their rights and ruin them." Nonetheless, the bill passed and the packers had to carry their fight into the courts in order to prevent implementation. This they did, and escaped conforming to the new Kansas statute until federal legilslation finally paralleled the state's effort and rendered it unnecessary. The Burdick Bill, however, would have been ineffective in regulating the firms in Kansas City in any event. Many of the operations were or could easily become Missouri-based and thus outside the jurisdiction of Kansas statutes. The episode did indicate, however, the strong producer support for regulation, and this hastened the advent of the Packers and Stockyards Act of 1921.[15]

This long-awaited regulation of the central markets and meat processors materialized when packer sentiment for legislation combined with that of producers and, to a lesser degree, with that of consumers. Not since the passage of the Meat Inspection Act in 1906 had public sentiment for regulating packers reached such proportions. One of the large packers, Thomas E. Wilson, expressed the general position of the industry in 1921 when he told Kansas cattlemen that producers and consumers were so hostile toward the meat processors that something was needed to restore public confidence. This the Packers and Stockyards Act was expected to do, and besides it was far less "radical" than some of the earlier proposals.

In addition to general pressure for legislation KLA had a specific role in getting Congress to approve the Packers and Stockyards Act. Several years after passage a representative of Swift & Company listed KLA's pressure on Senator Arthur Capper as the principal reason the measure was adopted. It was true that Mercer and other KLA members provided the senator with much advice concerning the proposed legislation, but Capper was not difficult to convince.

The act attempted to prevent those packers engaged in interstate commerce from engaging in any unfair, discriminatory, or deceptive practices such as giving undue preferences, apportioning supplies, dividing territories, and manipulating prices. Packers were also required to keep uniform accounts and records that would accurately reflect their business operations. Stockyard owners and commission merchants were required to publish and charge reasonable nondiscriminatory rates, as well as to submit their other activities to scrutiny. The secretary of agriculture was charged with the enforcement of the Packers and Stockyards Act, subject to review by the courts. And, in practice, so many precautions to protect packers from arbitrary regulation were provided that they could, if they chose to do so, keep most rulings tied up in the courts for several years.[16]

As a result of the Packers and Stockyards Act and the Packer Consent Decree, some of the practices that shippers complained of were eliminated. Among producers, the decree was the least popular of the two measures, especially after it had been in force for a decade. Strenuous efforts were made during the middle of the interwar period to have the decree set aside in order that the large packers might enter the retail food business. The meat processors led the movement, but it received strong support from many groups of producers, including KLA. Mercer testified several times before USDA investigative groups to the effect that packers were regulated sufficiently by the Packers and Stockyards Act and that packers could be an effective competitor of grocery chains if they were allowed to participate in retail meat sales. Lowering the price of meat and a subsequent increase in the quantity consumed were Mercer's primary goals in getting packers into the retail business. But USDA recommended and the courts confirmed only a partial nullification of the decree. In 1931 packers were allowed to deal in most foods at the wholesale level but were generally denied entry into retail sales.[17]

While producers were sucessful in obtaining more government regulation, the cost of marketing remained high and continued to agitate stockmen. There was no large reduction in the charges of commission merchants or stockyards as a result of the new legislation, although during the early 1930s the USDA conducted a prolonged investigation of marketing expenses and reported that charges had been reduced, with an expected savings to shippers of several hundred thousand dollars annually. Despite these claims, however, producers felt that marketing costs were high compared to livestock prices.[18]

Because they believed that marketing was too expensive, stockmen made several additional moves in their continuing effort to increase profits. Kansas cattlemen first encouraged small packers, like the Ruddy Packing Company in Kansas City, to compete with the large stock buyers. Then, Mercer and Edwards became deeply involved in a scheme to raise enough money from Kansas and southwestern cattlemen to purchase the bankrupt Drover's Packing Company, also located in Kansas City. They expected a plant owned by cattlemen to allow producers to reap some of the rich rewards that they claimed were common for the large packers. All of these attempts, however, either folded as individual enterprises or failed to affect the producers' share of the meat industry's profits in any significant way.[19]

Another proposal for reducing marketing charges and increasing profits materialized during the early twenties in what was called the conference plan for selling stock. Cattlemen had been advocating a conference system with middlemen for several decades. Under Mercer's leadership, KLA repeatedly called for the establishment of a permanent routine that would enable shippers to come face-to-face with middlemen to resolve grievances. Finally, in 1922, the Kansas City Livestock Exchange agreed to a plan proposed by Mercer. Stockmen first suggested reducing the number of commission firms plying their trade at the Kansas City yards, believing that with fewer merchants commission charges that reached $18 to $20 a car for cattle might be reduced. Mercer claimed that there were twice as many firms on the Kansas City scene as were needed and that the high commission charges were a direct result. Cattlemen believed that a larger volume for fewer merchants might enable the charges to be lowered. After repeated attempts to reduce the number of commission men and to make the conference plan work, cattlemen had to admit defeat.

Far more effort was devoted to a similar practice that had also been suggested a number of times, usually under the rubric of orderly marketing. Basically, this concept involved proportioning daily receipts to the expected packer demand through the cooperation of all the middlemen in the marketing process: railway officials, commission merchants, stockyard managers, and packers. It was thought that advance estimates of receipts by the USDA market news service and the lengthening of the marketing week to five or six days would be essential for orderly marketing. With supply geared to demand, Mercer often proclaimed, prices for livestock would be higher and more stable. But much to Mercer's disappointment, stockmen were unable to establish a permanent system of orderly marketing during this generally depressed interwar period. It had worked effectively, many producers believed, not only after a fire at the Kansas City stockyards in 1917 but also when it was urged by the government towards the end of the war. But too much cooperation was needed, apparently, for orderly marketing to be achieved without a central authority to compel it. Mercer, however, was slow to give up the idea, and it became during the late twenties the cornerstone of his proposal for an agricultural commission. It was the basic suggestion that KLA made to the Farm Board when it became a reality.[20]

Cooperatives were another attempt to reduce marketing costs that largely failed to help the state's cattlemen. The number of Kansas cooperatives had increased slowly until the latter part of World War I. By 1917 the state reported 553 cooperative concerns, 59 of which were livestock shipping associations. No terminal cooperatives were reported at this time, and it is likely that none existed, although attempts had been made to establish them. Towards the end of the war the Farmers' Union, after doing business successfully in the Omaha yards, spread its operation to other central markets, establishing cooperative commission houses at St. Joseph in 1917 and Kansas City the following year. The yards in Wichita and Parsons acquired Farmers' Union branches in 1925 and 1935. These terminal cooperatives received stock from any producer who cared to pay the small membership fee. In 1923 the American Farm Bureau Federation added a cooperative commission house to the Kansas City exchange. While this provided stockmen a choice of cooperative firms, it also resulted in more competition for the new, struggling firms.[21]

Statistical data, while sparse and inconsistent, indicates that in 1929 there were cooperative commission houses at twenty-two of the nation's central markets, handling over twelve million head of stock annually at receipts of $314.5 million. In Kansas City receipts by cooperatives rose from zero to over 10 percent of the total by 1924. A larger percentage was handled by the Farmers' Union agency in St. Joseph, where 20 percent of the total receipts in 1923 and an average of almost 14 percent for the whole decade of the twenties passed through the cooperative firm. Large hog marketings helped account for the proportionately larger patronage of the St. Joseph cooperative. The cooperatives in Kansas City and St. Joseph claimed an annual savings for producers of almost $40,000 and $78,000, respectively—perhaps an exaggeration—throughout the decade after World War I, in addition to providing better services.

During the early 1930s the relatively small influence of cooperatives in the marketing of Kansas stock declined considerably and then recovered slightly toward the end of the decade. By the middle thirties only fourteen cooperatives were reported to be in the Kansas livestock trade, doing an annual business of $1.2 million. Growth had been hampered by the lack of cooperation between the Farmers' Union and the Farm Bureau groups, by the large number of small lots that had to be handled, and by the producers' tendency to dump their inferior stock on the agencies. As a result, the influence of the cooperatives was limited by their inability to control enough of the marketings to raise prices.[22]

For the most part, the producers' conscious efforts to reduce marketing expense came to naught, but other developments did reduce somewhat the cost of marketing stock. One of the most significant was the decentralization of the nation's marketing points and packing industry. Usually referred to collectively as direct marketing, decentralization of the traditional marketing facilities involved both an augmented number of community auctions—often called sale barns—and a rise in the quantity of stock sold directly to the packer, either by the producers themselves or by country buyers who represented a particular packer. Consequently, larger numbers of producers sold their stock without sending them to central stockyards. Decentralization of the packing industry involved simply an increase in the number of small packers that operated outside the immediate area of the terminal stockyards. During the interwar period, marketing decentralization was the most pronounced of the twin developments, and by World War II the facilities that allowed large numbers of producers to avoid terminal stockyards were in place. Only the beginning of packer decentralization was accomplished at this time, however, with the most significant development delayed until after the Second World War.

Some observers thought that decentralization was a revolutionary development for the livestock industry, something entirely new for the thousands of livestock producers across the nation. In one sense this was true, but decentralization was also, in part, only a continuation of the movement of packers and stockyards toward the source of supply that had begun well back in the nineteenth century. In another sense, although decentralization was revolutionary in the minds of most twentieth-century producers, it was reminiscent of the relationship that had existed between producer, marketing point, and processor before the Civil War and the subsequent development of large, regional marketing and packing centers. The twentieth-century version of moving meat into consumer channels, however, was done on a much larger scale and was considerably more sophisticated than its nineteenth-century counterpart.

Exact figures are unavailable for the percentage of Kansas beef cattle that was marketed through community sale barns or directly to packers without passing through central stockyards. Some indication of the growing popularity of direct marketing in the state, however, can be inferred from the national trends that developed, from the widespread interest in the new marketing practices, and from the increased number of auction houses in the state by 1940.

The *Stockman* occasionally referred to the growing number of community auctions in Kansas during the year immediately following World War I, but there were relatively few of them until the early 1930s. Though the increase in Kansas was not as large as some midwestern states experienced, a considerable number of new local auctions were established in the state. The number was estimated to be somewhere between two hundred and three hundred by the late thirties, enough to provide each county in the state with at least two.[23]

Development of community sales presented the beef industry with new dimensions of the old problem of protecting livestock from diseases and stock thieves. Central markets had long ago provided for regular sanitary inspections, treatments, vaccinations, and brand inspectors, who determined whether the consignees actually owned the stock being sold. Most of the same procedures eventually developed at the community level. Regulation along these lines was begun in Kansas when the legislature passed a KLA-sponsored bill in 1937 that required the licensing of markets and charged the sanitary commissioner with the responsibility of controlling the spread of diseases.[24]

Stock was also sold outside the central markets directly to packer buyers. This practice avoided the competitive bidding of community auctions and, more than any other method of direct marketing, incurred the wrath of cattlemen. With the cooperation of the railroads in permitting the use of their pens and loading facilities, packers established concentration yards in some parts of the countryside where stock was collected and sent directly to the slaughtering plant. This practice was especially popular in marketing hogs, and thus was more common in the heavier hog-producing areas of the Midwest, but the *Stockman* reported that it was also becoming popular in Kansas. This method was roundly criticized by several Kansas producers, primarily because it delayed the passage of other stock that was destined for terminal marketing. Producers also believed the method lowered prices. To fill these concentration yards, packers sent buyers to the countryside to negotiate private sales—some said with favored producers. A few stockmen even claimed that the large packers secretly divided the country into territories, each having an area in which other packers would not compete.[25]

Another controversial method of direct marketing involved the establishment of packer-owned yards near those of the central stockyards. Mercer blamed the Packers Consent Decree, with its prohibition of packer-owned yards, and the regulations of the Packers and Stockyards Act for this development, but in fact a few of these private yards existed before the postwar government regulations.

Private yards in Kansas City, called the Mistletoe Yards and owned by Armour, constituted one of the major burs under the KLA saddle for over two decades. The Mistletoe Yards had been built during the early 1900s when the Fowler Packing Company failed to get the Kansas City Stockyards Company to build runways to its plant, located about a mile from the main yards. Armour fell heir to the yards when it bought the Fowler plant, and, according to John A. Edwards, maintained the yards and the older Fowler processing plant at the expense of the modernized Morris house, which it absorbed during the early twenties. Throughout this interwar period the number of livestock sold through these private yards increased rapidly. Although hogs constituted the principal and possibly the exclusive species of stock passing through the Mistletoe Yards, many Kansas beef producers were concerned with the precedent that was being set for marketing outside the terminal centers. Despite repeated attempts by KLA either to close down the yards or to have them placed under the supervision of the USDA, the Mistletoe Yards continued to exist.[26]

Although it is impossible to determine the exact quantity of Kansas livestock involved in direct marketing between the wars, the large increase in community sale barns and the great concern that the *Stockman* expressed regarding direct sales indicated that marketing shifts in Kansas were at least as great as those that occurred nationally. In fact, direct marketing may have been even more popular in Kansas due to the large number of stockers and feeders that were produced. Nationally, about 10 percent of the marketed cattle and 15 percent of the calves were sold by direct marketing methods throughout the twenties. By 1939 the percentage of cattle and calves passing to new owners outside the central markets had grown to 23 and 34 percent, respectively, and by 1956 the percentages had risen to 30 and 63. While this change in terminal market patronage was quite evident in the stocker and feeder class, the marketing of fat cattle ready for slaughter continued to depend heavily on the central markets, even as late as the 1950s. Even though the movement of cattle outside the terminal marketing centers during this period was significant, that for hogs was even more startling. By 1940 as much as 50 to 60 percent of the hogs marketed were sold outside the major terminals.[27]

Marketing of livestock outside the terminal exchanges, then, was well established by 1940 with both the community and direct-selling methods.

Direct marketing developed because of a variety of factors, not least of which was the stockmen's persistent desire to reduce marketing expense. To a large extent direct marketing accomplished this end. Commission charges at local auctions were, for example, less than those at the large terminal markets. But a more important advantage enjoyed by patrons of community sales was in escaping railroad freight rates. Reduced transport charges operated most effectively in the exchange of stocker and feeder cattle, and the transfer of this class of stock became one of the more important functions of community sales, especially if the cattle were destined to be fed in the immediate area. Cattlemen also saved freight charges by using community sales to market stock when they finished the fattening process, although this was usually not what was done. Marketing stockers and feeders through community sales was one of the few forms of direct marketing that received KLA's unqualified blessing, and savings on freight rates was the principal reason for the association's support.

Low market prices and the consequent decline in the producer's ability to pay freight rates were also important in encouraging direct marketing. The developments during the early thirties, when market prices were extremely low and direct marketing experienced a rapid growth, demonstrated this relationship. But whether the lower commission charges and the savings on freight rendered the producer larger profits remained a disputed matter. The lower prices that were paid for livestock—and prices were usually a dollar or so a hundredweight lower than at the central markets—prevented higher profits, according to some, and the absence of a wholesale shift away from terminal markets supported this view.

Other reasons for the popularity of direct marketing, however, may have been more significant than the real or supposed enhancement of profits. Technological developments—the radio, telephone, teletype, and especially the truck—enabled local sales not only to keep abreast of the latest developments in marketing but also to have an hourly account of price fluctuations at the central markets. It was an advantage for producers to know the price levels at the terminal markets and an inducement for them to market directly if the local price was not too much below that at the larger market. The increased use of trucks, though, was the most significant technological factor in encouraging direct marketing. Conversely, opportunities to market locally encouraged the use of the truck. This new mode of transport, along with the many new and improved roads, not only reduced transportation charges but greatly facilitated the movement of stock at the community level. In the

end, the widespread use of trucks served to link the local and terminal marketing centers, to the producers' advantage. They had a choice as to marketing
points, and the competition resulted in better service even if not in higher
profits.

Many producers perferred marketing closer to home because they could
save time, watch their stock weighed and cared for, and often deal with
people in whom they had greater confidence. Local marketing was also an
economic boost to the whole community, as farmers and ranchers who brought
livestock to sales often bought many of their supplies and other necessities
before returning home. Chambers of commerce, however, learned quickly
that a sale barn located in or near a town might prompt unfavorable comments from those who happened to reside downwind from the holding pens.

While most direct marketing was adaptable to all species and lot sizes,
producers with hogs or small lots of cattle most often used the community
sales method. Larger stockmen supported selling direct to a packer representative or feeder. Producers also used local sales for dumping their inferior
animals, while the choice stock was shipped to the larger markets. Although
this was not particularly good for the reputation of the local market, it did
enable producers to market more uniform bunches at the major terminals
and save railway tariffs on inferior stock. Consequently, the opportunity to
sell the poor stock locally incurred the displeasure of local auction operators,
but it likewise increased the profits of producers.[28]

Doubts about the advantages of direct marketing were common during
the early period. KLA, for instance, fought tooth-and-nail against direct
selling and only reluctantly condoned community sales, except for the transfer
of stockers and feeders. M. W. Borders, who was billed as a farmer, believed
that direct marketing was evil and the "gravest question that has ever confronted the livestock industry of this country." His support for this position
was steadfast, if not necessarily justified. Immediately after making the
accusation, he delivered the longest talk ever given at a KLA convention.
His audience, although tired by the long ordeal, was generally sympathetic
to his diatribe against direct marketing.

Heading the list of KLA complaints against marketing direct was the
depressing effect it supposedly had on prices. Mercer reasoned—when he was
not accusing packers of arbitrarily setting prices—that the free and open
competition on the large central markets determined the price that producers
received. It followed then, he believed, that if packers went outside the
central markets for some or most of their supply, prices were forced down.

274

Community auction barn, Dodge City. *Courtesy of the Kansas State Historical Society.*

Some producers, including Mercer, believed that packers were engaging in direct purchasing deliberately to lower prices. The KLA secretary also claimed that direct purchases in the countryside by packer buyers skimmed the choicest animals from herds, leaving only the poorer stock to depress even further the price levels on the large public markets.

According to transcripts available in KLA files, direct marketing prompted the most serious dispute between packers and Kansas producers that occurred between the wars. Reportedly, charges and countercharges, threats and counterthreats, and much "'offensive language"—not included in the transcripts—were part of confrontations in Kansas City and later in Chicago that had been arranged by Mercer. At one time, the packers walked out of the meeting in disgust. Somewhat later, after Mercer had smoothed their ruffled feelings, Gustavus F. Swift vowed never again to sit down with producers if the threats and abuse continued. Though stormy and exciting, the meetings accomplished nothing. KLA's strong opposition to direct marketing continued for a few years, then declined as it became apparent that the organization was losing the battle.

Before giving up, however, KLA led a movement for passage of legis-

Inside the Dodge City auction barn. *Courtesy of the Kansas State Historical Society.*

lation that would have authorized the USDA to supervise most livestock transactions—especially those that were conducted in places like the Kansas City Mistletoe Yards—just as the government looked after the large public terminals. But after more than a half-dozen years of periodic debate in Congress on what was usually called the Capper-Hope Bill, the legislation failed. The opposition from states farther removed from large central markets and thus more interested in direct marketing was instrumental in defeating Capper's proposal. Packers also opposed the bill, arguing that they preferred to use the central markets for their necessary supply, as this method burdened the producer rather than the packer with risks and expense of shipping. They were forced to buy direct, the packers claimed, because there was not enough livestock being sent to the central markets to keep their plants in full production. Competitive buying by packing plants on the West Coast and by small plants in the area served by the terminal markets was cited as the reason for declining receipts.[29]

After a long and sometimes bitter fight, KLA and other producers who opposed direct marketing were unable to reduce its popularity. Selling hogs directly was always the most urgent concern, but KLA was also troubled about cattle that were exchanged in this manner and even more fearful of the long-range implications on livestock price-setting policies if the central markets ceased to exist. As far as the effect of direct marketing on livestock prices during this period was concerned, however, KLA's strenuous opposition may have been largely a wasted effort. Direct marketing continued to increase in spite of KLA, and a USDA-sponsored study by the Brookings Institution concluded that there was no evidence to support the charge that packers lowered general prices by directly purchasing stock. Producers in general and KLA in particular, it seemed, were always willing to blame almost anything but overproduction and the often depressed state of the whole economy for what seemed to be small returns from their stock.[30]

During much of the time that direct selling developed, there was a parallel movement toward establishing small packing plants outside the immediate area of the large stockyards. Kansas, however, did not respond to this development in the same manner that it had reacted to the decentralization of marketing points. While some decentralization did occur, the relative importance of the packing industry in the state temporarily declined.

There had always been, of course, some packing outside the large terminal centers, as well as processing that was divorced from the large packers. The big packers sometimes established their own small plants or bought those established by others. Kansas had a few packing plants scattered across the state, serving mostly the demands of the immediate area. As early as 1868 Edward W. Pattison established a packing plant in Junction City, for instance; and by the beginning of World War I several towns, including Pittsburg, Hutchinson, Manhattan, and Topeka, all had plants that were divorced from the terminal packing centers in Kansas City and Wichita. Most of these plants were concerned primarily with hog slaughter, but a few cattle were killed, and the only government-inspected horse-meat packing plant in North America during the early 1900s was the Hill Packing Company in Topeka.[31]

The ownership of the nation's packing businesses and the plants themselves were decentralized to such an extent during the first postwar decade that the proportion of the meat slaughtered for interstate commerce by the big packers declined from over 70 percent in 1916 to around 58 percent in 1929. The large packers' response to these decentralized plants was generally to buy them, or to build plants of their own that were outside terminal markets. During the two decades following 1927, Swift, Armour, Wilson, and Cudahy absorbed about sixty-five smaller plants in addition to the new ones they built for themselves. By the 1940s the percentage of slaughter performed by the large packers was back up, although the location of the processing plants had been diffused.[32]

The tendency of packers to decentralize during this period had a strange effect on the packing industry in Kansas. Always among the leading states in livestock production, Kansas might have been expected to profit from the movement of packing towards the source of supply, but such was not the case. Instead, the importance and size of the industry declined throughout the interwar period. Excluding agriculture, packing was the largest industry in Kansas during the twenties, and the state as a whole ranked second behind Illinois. A decade later Kansas was third, and had declined to sixth by 1939. The value added by Kansas packing revealed much the same pattern. In 1919, $40 million worth of value was added, $33 million a decade later, and only $20 million in 1939.

One of the major reasons for the slump in Kansas packing between the wars was the drought-induced decline in hog production. Hog slaughter, like the direct marketing of hogs, was often the stimulus for decentralization. The diffusion of cattle and sheep slaughtering locations was less rapid than that for hogs. Cattle and sheep came from a wider area, and to be economic the slaughter of cattle needed to be on a scale sufficiently large enough to utilize all the by-products. Scale was especially significant for those by-products used in the manufacture of pharmaceutical supplies. The effects of New Deal crop-limitation programs, which reduced the amount of corn raised in Kansas and then encouraged its production in diverted cotton acreage in a few states like Texas, also affected Kansas packing. Not only was hog production discouraged in the state, but other areas were encouraged to increase their feeding of livestock and, subsequently, their slaughtering of these animals.[33]

In addition to declining hog production and the problem of scale, the distribution system of the larger plants was also involved in the decline of Kansas packing. As the distribution system reached almost all areas of the country, the importance of local slaughtering was reduced accordingly. After World War II, however, the Kansas packing industry was to regain and even surpass its former prominence.

Nationally, other factors were important in encouraging packers to decentralize. Shifting and growing population centers, the relatively high costs from congestion at large terminals, the increased cost and complexity of labor relations, and the desire to exchange obsolete old plants for more efficient new

278

ones, all had some bearing. But the most significant stimulus was related to transportation. The truck was beginning to reduce the packers' dependence on railroads, not only for the delivery of livestock but also for the distribution of meat, especially after the refrigerated truck came into use. The use of trucks for distribution and also for delivery of livestock to processing plants, to a large extent, was a development that had a much greater impact after 1940.

Despite the truck, however, railroad transportation remained vital to packers throughout this interwar period. But here, too, freight tariffs played a significant role in decentralization. Theoretically, freight rates on live animals were fixed so that they were equalized with rates for shipping meat, even after the reduction of bulk and the transportation of by-products at a lower rate were figured in. But this was usually not the case in actual practice. When all shipping expenses were figured, rates tended to discriminate against the shipment of live animals from central states eastward. Cattlemen often opposed rates that favored the shipment of meat because they believed that eastern buyers might be driven out of the central markets in the Midwest by these inequitable rates, thus reducing competition. Mercer occasionally opposed reductions on meat tariffs before the ICC, because, he said, comparable rates on live animals and meat enabled "order-buyers from the East to liven the Kansas City market." Yet Mercer also favored locating packing plants as close to the source of supply as feasible in order to reduce shipping expenses for producers, a stand contradictory to his position on meat tariffs.

While tariff schedules favored the shipment of meat from central states eastward, they had just the opposite effect on shipments to the West Coast, where the transporting of live animals was encouraged. The railway tariff situation, then, tended to influence central states to ship meat to the East and live animals to packers on the West Coast. Either way, decentralization of the traditional packing locations was encouraged.[34]

Considerable decentralization had occurred by 1940 in both the nation's marketing and processing facilities for livestock. It was the beginning of a revolution. Railroads had built the large stockyards during the closing decades of the nineteenth century, enabling meat processors to centralize and still distribute their products nationally. Now, trucks were tearing the system apart. As a result, cattlemen were given options in the marketing of their stock. Stockmen were also successful in getting the government to regulate the stockyards and packers during this period, but failed to find the large decline in marketing costs that they had expected. A variety of interrelated forces contributed to these movements, forces that continued and multiplied after World War II, when even larger accomplishments in the same areas were to occur. Establishing the foundation during the interwar period, however, was important in its own right.

12

Postscript: A Glance beyond 1940

During the early 1940s, as many young people in Kansas exchanged their overalls and blue jeans for the uniforms of the armed forces, they left behind a mature beef industry. Some of the state's cattlemen marketed calves from their large and small cow herds, others specialized in producing younger cattle on grass, and a few fattened the grass-matured stock on grain. Cattlemen had upbred their herds beyond the wildest dreams of their nineteenth-century predecessors; science had mitigated the evils of many livestock diseases; and technology had solved many of the problems involved in producing beef. Stockmen had responded to the evolving economic situation first by organizing the Kansas Livestock Association and then by building it into one of the nation's strongest state organizations. The KLA, in turn, provided cattlemen with the collective power to deal with big business and to win from government the concessions they needed for improving the industry's health. In short, the Kansas beef industry was well prepared to make its contribution to the country's war effort and to develop still further after the conflict ended.

From a national perspective the Kansas industry, like that in states surrounding it, was transitional in beef-producing techniques. Here, in a state located strategically at the threshold of the Great Plains, were stockmen engaged in full-feeding cattle on grain, a practice that dominated the Midwest, and those involved in more expansive grazing operations that characterized the cattle industry to the west and south. This transitional character reflected to a large degree the state's environment and its agriculture as a whole. As one moved from east to west, rainfall declined, long grass gave way to short, and corn yielded to wheat as the basic field crop. Kansas producers, who had chosen to specailize in calf production, maturing of stocker cattle, or grain fattening of feeder stock, had adapted well to their environment.

After almost a decade of drought, adequate rain returned to the Great Plains during the 1940s. Thirsty pastures again grew green and lush, demand for beef rose substantially, and cattlemen smiled on their newly found prosperity. Although troubled somewhat during World War II with ceiling prices, transportation and labor shortages, rustling, blackmarkets, and rationing, cattlemen adapted to these difficulties along with an increase in number of cattle and greatly improved prices. In Kansas, the number of beef cattle and calves rose from 2.0 million in 1940—with an average selling price of $7.95 per hundredweight—to 3.4 million in 1945, bringing $12.41 per hundredweight. Prices had not been as good since the First World War, nor had cattlemen had as many cattle to market since 1903. In larger numbers than ever before, cattle moved away from their traditional marketing locations to help meet the growing demands of the West Coast, especially California. The higher ceiling prices there, railroad rates that favored live animals, and the concentration of military personnel and defense plants, all contributed to the change.

The prosperity and optimism that characterized the beef industry during the war continued into the postwar period. Although the number of beef cattle in the state declined—remaining, for the most part, below three million head until 1951—and despite the fear of many that a repeat of the post–World War I depression was in store, prices climbed to unparalleled heights. An average of $23.29 in 1948 was the highest for any year of the decade. The demise of ceiling prices, full employment with high wages, aid for European recovery, and the desire of American consumers for more beef contributed to the higher prices. Cattlemen enjoyed unprecedented prosperity and needed no direct government subsidies. As a result, they loudly rejected Secretary of Agriculture Brannan's plans for increased aid. It was time for "rugged individualism" again, although cattlemen still demanded high tariffs and disaster relief.[1]

A severe blizzard toward the end of the forties was one of the few things that dampened the spirits of Kansas cattlemen during this period. Sweeping in from the northwest during November, 1948, and with a repeat performance in January, 1949, heavy snows, strong winds, and bitter cold blanketed that part of Kansas west of Salina. By late January, 1949, the *Kansas Stockman* estimated that 50,000 sheep and 10,000 cattle had perished and that hundreds more were unaccounted for. Losses sometimes reached 40 to 50 percent of individual herds. Hundreds of young cattle died as the calving season arrived before the snow and cold had passed. It was the worst storm for the

Great Plains since the legendary winter of 1886–87, with the final count in April, 1949, approaching 200,000 cattle deaths in the whole region.[2] Many of the cattle and sheep that perished in western Kansas were pasturing on wheat, a growing practice in that part of the state after the drought of the 1930s. The return of normal rainfall and the advent of the tractor encouraged raising more winter wheat. As the rains increased during the forties and fall wheat got a better start, pasturing livestock on wheat had increased in popularity. Over 300,000 cattle, but occasionally as many as 600,000, and over a million sheep were grazed commercially—about half by nonresident operators—when moisture and the growth of wheat were favorable. While the practice added a few coins to the pockets of farmers and ranchers, it proved disastrous for some during an unusual winter like that of 1948–49, when feed reserves were inadequate and it sometimes was impossible to transport to the fields the feed that did exist.[3]

Despite some adverse weather, however, the 1940s were good to cattlemen, especially when compared to the difficult struggles of the previous decade. One observer has noted, "The whole story, briefly told, came to this: Prosperity deadened all pain, and few cattlemen felt any pain anyhow."[4]

Phenomenal weather patterns and fluctuations of over $10.00 per hundredweight in cattle prices perplexed Kansas stockmen during the 1950s. In 1951, to begin with, the state experienced the wettest year since records were begun in 1887, culminating in heavy and severe floods in the eastern part of the state. With the Korean War in full swing, an all-time high average price of $29.69 per hundredweight for beef cattle accompanied the unusual amount of rainfall. The next year, beef prices dropped $4.00 a hundredweight and rainfall also declined to below normal. By August the Topeka *Daily Capital* reported that trucks were hauling hay and other cattle feeds into the western section of the state because of drought. Drivers kept their trucks running twenty-four hours a day, hauling feed from as far as Iowa, Minnesota, Illinois, and Indiana. At times, water also had to be hauled, but the many farm ponds that had been constructed since the 1930s helped alleviate this shortage.[5]

Beginning in Texas in 1951, the drought hit most of the Great Plains before it had run its course by the late fifties. Consequently, dust storms that reminded older residents of the 1930s struck western Kansas in full force. Herds were reduced but the state's total beef-cattle population was not affected by the drought nor the decline in demand after the Korean War ended until 1957. Beef cattle, which numbered 3.3 million head in 1951, rose rapidly by half a million before 1956, then declined to below 3 million by 1957. The

283

decline in numbers was brief, however, and by 1960 the state had over 4 million beef cattle and calves. Beef prices fell as a result of the drought-induced marketings and the end of the war, forcing the government, with machinery that had been established during the New Deal, and also the Farmers' Home Administration established in 1946, to enter the marketplace and credit outlets to help support prices and profits. The lowest price occurred in 1956 when beef cattle averaged $16.34 per hundredweight before a slow climb to almost $24.00 in 1959, and to just under $22.00 in 1960. In all, according to John T. Schlebecker, "Times were not bad, but neither were they good." Some of the prosperity of the forties carried into the early fifties; then drought, inflation, and rising production costs eroded the profits in raising beef. Ironically, a severe blizzard struck western Kansas during this generally dry period. This 1957 storm caused estimated losses of 15,000 cattle, 6,000 sheep, and 2,000 hogs. As was true during the winter of 1948–49, many of the sheep and cattle that died were grazing winter wheat.[6]

Notable progress also occurred after World War II in the area of disease control, although the large battles against the tick, blackleg, and tuberculosis had almost been won before the war. Brucellosis control moved forward, but not until the 1950s were serious measures taken by range producers to eradicate it. Vaccination of calves was the main means, but there were also expanded testing programs and some slaughtering of stock. In 1949 Kansas restricted sales of cattle without brucellosis tests unless they came from a herd certified to be free of the disease. A few cases of anthrax appeared in the state during the fifties, but immediate quarantines effectively stopped its spread. Vesicular stomatitis and anaplasmosis also appeared in the state on occasion, but not in epidemic proportions.

One of the major accomplishments of scientists was the elimination of parasites. The cattle grub, caused by heel flies, was especially troublesome, affecting a third of the range cattle on the Great Plains in 1945, with millions of dollars lost as a result of damaged hides and inferior meat. Nor did cattle that were continually annoyed by heel flies gain as well as they might have. By 1947 Kansas was in its third year of a DDT-spraying program to rid herds of the heel fly. Better weight gains followed, but the spraying affected only indirectly the grub that ruined hides and damaged meat. By the middle 1950s, however, USDA scientists, working with the large chemical companies, had developed effective chemical treatments that spelled doom for many costly parasites, including the destructive grub. The new vaccines and chemical treatments were expensive and pushed up production costs, but the investment was more than repaid at market time.[7]

Many other changes also occurred in the Kansas beef industry during the dramatic twenty years following World War II. Most of the prewar concern over packers, stockyards, and railroads disappeared, as more and more of the stock found markets outside the terminal centers. Trucks and pickups continued to replace the railroads, who made little effort to retain their livestock-carrying trade. In their attitude toward the government, cattlemen, as might have been expected, displayed much inconsistency. While opposing the likes of social security, and price and production controls, they demanded at the same time disaster relief, high tariffs, government purchases of beef, and much aid in the area of disease control.

The most visible changes in producing beef in the state after the war, however, did not occur in marketing, in the cattlemen's attitude toward government, or in disease control, but rather in developments related to irrigation and feedlots. To many, the unprecedented rise in irrigation and the full-feeding of cattle in large commercial lots amounted to a revolution. As it happened, these spectacular developments also affected most of the other aspects of the business of raising cattle.

Feeding cattle on grain before slaughtering has been a part of the American beef business almost from the beginning and has always had some role in the Kansas industry. With few exceptions, single family operators before World War II fattened the cattle that were full-fed or partially fed. Most frequently, a cattleman bought a carload or even several carloads of older steers and fed them throughout the winter. The work provided the feeder profitable employment during the slow winter months, kept some of his equipment in use, and often supplied a better market for his grain. Fattening with grain also occurred in conjunction with the use of forage crops or the roughage left over from harvesting grain. A few Kansas cattlemen fed several thousand head a year, but they were exceptional. Before the war, most of the state's cattle were still marketed as grass fattened and ready for slaughter, or as "warmed up" feeders destined for cornbelt feedlots.[8]

Although most cattle marketed from Kansas before World War II were not finished on grain, there was a slight increase in feeding toward the end of the 1930s. After a short burst of feeding during the early forties, however, the ceiling prices and the rising demand for beef brought many cattle directly to slaughter from grass, interrupting the trend toward more feeding that had begun earlier. But after the war Kansas participated in the growth of feeding that occurred throughout the Great Plains and the Southwest. The expansion occurred when more of the state's farmers and stockmen began feeding, when those who already fed cattle expanded from 50 or 60 head to 150 or even as many as 500, and when the large commercial lots developed.

Large commercial feedlots—usually defined as operations with a thousand-head capacity or more, feeding cattle that are owned by the operator or are fed on contract for others—were the most visible development in the postwar revolution but, until after 1960, not necessarily the most important. The spectacular growth of feeding in Kansas came after the middle 1950s and was initiated by the smaller feeders, usually one man and his family. Many of today's urban dwellers, who are struck by the pungent odor emanating from the large commercial feedlots dotting the highways, sometimes located just outside a city, may conclude that most of the beef in their supermarkets comes from the large lots. But this was untrue of Kansas beef as late as 1960. Although the Board of Agriculture failed to tabulate the number of small feeders during the fifties, it did report in 1960 that "in spite of the remarkable development of large commercial feed lots in many areas of the state, it was significant to note that more than 75 percent of the 1960 Kansas cattle feeding was still in smaller farm operations." The most remarkable development before 1960, then, was not the large commercial lots that dealt exclusively in cattle, but rather the significant rise in the number of smaller lots that were only a part of the total farm or ranch operation.

The percentage of cattle being fed in large commercial lots, however, rose dramatically soon after the Board of Agriculture made its report. From 26.7 percent in 1960, the portion of cattle fed in commercial lots with a capacity of a thousand or more rose to 57.5 percent five years later, and to 87.6 percent by 1975. The number of commercial lots in the state also increased, but not as dramatically as did the percentage of cattle fed in them. In 1952, for instance, there were 7 large feedlots in the state and only 22 by 1960. Five years later the number had grown to 88 and to 140 by 1974. As the large lots grew in size, many of the smaller feedyards went out of business, reducing the total number of lots in the state from 13,500 in 1965 to only 6,300 in 1975. By the 1970s the number of large commercial lots had stabilized at around 135. The many smaller feeders who responded to market conditions by going in and out of business, however, caused fluctuations of more than a thousand a year in the total number of feedlots in the state. As a result of the revolution, Kansans by the 1970s marketed around two million head of grain-fed cattle each year, up from less than half a million in 1955.[9]

Many reasons account for the remarkable postwar development of feedlots in Kansas. Most of the reasons apply to similar developments throughout much of the Great Plains. The relatively dry climate reduced the diseases that feedlot operators had to deal with and led to fewer environmental problems; and the area was close to large supplies of feeder cattle and grain, and near several good markets for fat stock. The postwar period brought a rising demand for meat, especially the smaller cuts from quality beef that could be produced efficiently in feedlots. Economic factors, such as the rising cost of grass-fattening cattle and the desire of cow herd owners for income at times other than their traditional fall marketing of calves, also encouraged feeding. Science and technology played a role. Growth hormones, like stilbestrol, in addition to the many antibiotics that were mixed with feed, not only produced healthier cattle but also larger gains at a more profitable rate of growth. Mechanical loading, feeding, and mixing devices saved much labor in the fattening process and added to profits, once the initial investment had been retrieved.[10]

The large supplies of grain and forage in the immediate area of the feedlots, however, encouraged expanded feeding on the Great Plains more than any other factor. Access to these raw materials eliminated the prohibitive expense of shipping grain into the feeding area. Irrigation, which provided the increased yields of grain and forage, thus became the second basic element in the postwar revolution in beef production. Few travelers through the semi-arid western part of Kansas today can remain unmoved by the sight of thickly planted corn towering alongside the highways, the lush fields of green alfalfa, and the millions of bronze and heavily laden heads of sorghum, waving gently in the summer breeze. Somewhere, often hidden during the late summer by the tall corn, is probably an aluminum pipe, almost a quarter of a mile long, supported and moved along by a half dozen or more giant, wheeled towers. With a single rotation around a center pivot, at the operator's command, this amazing device spreads several inches of precious moisture on thirsty crops that formerly had to beg the heavens, often unsucessfully, for a taste of rain. Even the Sand Hills around Garden City, relatively rough land for irrigating, now feels the tread of the towering center-pivot systems. The first settlers in western Kansas learned painfully that corn was not the best crop for the environmental conditions; now irrigation has circumvented, at least for a while, the laws of nature that send or withhold rain.

Although irrigation had been a part of Kansas agriculture for a long time, its growth at first was slow. A little over 50,000 acres were artificially watered in 1920, less than 90,000 by 1940, and only 100,000 by the end of World War II. Then a rapid expansion began. The number of irrigated acres in 1945 had more than doubled by 1950 and had risen to 900,000 by the time the drought ended a few years later. By the late fifties over 90 percent of the irrigated acreage was located within twenty counties in the southwest corner of the state.

The increase in irrigation during the 1950s, however, proved to be only a shadow of the explosion that occurred the following decade. From fewer than a million acres in 1960, the number shot upward to over two million by the early 1970s. Drought encouraged some of the expansion, as did the scientific advances that were made in crops, fertilizers, and watering techniques. Extremely important in the growth of irrigation, however, was the large demand for grain and forage that developed as cattle feeding increased, a demand that farmers, with the greatly improved irrigation equipment, easily filled. In all, the rapid and large increase in cattle feeding and irrigation proved to be concomitant developments with significant reciprocity. Sorghums, especially after hybrids were introduced in the 1950s, rivaled wheat in importance. The state's cornbelt shifted from the northeast to the southwest, and the yields of the crops under irrigation more than doubled the dry-land production. Feedlots fostered and then consumed the added production. In many ways feedlots made farmers and ranchers partners in the beef business rather than adversaries, if, indeed, they had ever been anything else.[11]

As a result of the developments in feeding and irrigation, the number of beef cattle and the amount of red meat packed in the state rose significantly. The western one-third of the state had more cattle than ever before (see Map 4, p. 73). The count of beef cattle in Kansas grew from 4 million in 1960 to over 5.8 million by 1970, and to 6.8 million by 1974. Numbers fluctuated with market conditions, but the last figure represented two and three times the number of beef cattle the state had kept before the feedlot industry expanded. Between 1.6 and 2.8 million of these cattle came from other states, some for grazing, but most for the large feedlots that dotted the countryside. Oklahoma and Texas, as in the period before World War II, provided about half the inshipped cattle, with the balance coming from more than a dozen other states.[12] Meat packing also expanded as many packers moved closer to the supply of butcher cattle. In 1961 Kansas packers slaughtered enough livestock to produce over a billion pounds of meat with a value of $432.8 million. By 1974, slaughter was up to 2 billion pounds at a value of $1.5

billion. Beef and veal accounted for 61 percent of the total poundage of red meat packed in 1961 and over 82 percent in 1974. By the 1970s the packaging of red meat was one of the state's leading industries, generating six or seven times its dollar value in other business activities. The growth of feedlots with their large concentrations of fat cattle had helped make it profitable for the packing houses to move from the congested cities to the small towns near where the stock was produced.[13]

The extraordinary growth of feedlots and irrigation did not occur without difficulties, especially in the area of the environment. Despite many unknowns, such as the rate of recharge and the quantity of available water, for example, farmers plunged into the irrigation era full force. Slowly, the Water Resources Division of the Kansas State Board of Agriculture caught up with developments and began to impose more rational planning in the use of water. When many owners located feedlots near urban areas, citizens complained of the offensive odor that rose from the lots, especially during wet weather, and the many flies that were attracted by the manure. The lot operators, on the other hand, pointed out the numerous economic advantages that cattle feeding provided the communities. Both groups had viable arguments. The most serious problem for feedlot owners, however, was not the offensive odor but rather the disposal of waste without polluting surface and underground water supplies. Natural conditions—a lower water table, as well as less surface water—helped solve most of these problems in western Kansas, but feeders in the eastern part of the state were not as fortunate. During the late 1960s fish kills in the Neosho and Cottonwood rivers led to the closing of several feedlots, including yards that were owned by the Crofoot and Anderson families. Gradually, though, and at the request of government agencies, most yards overcame these difficulties by building large lagoons into which the waste drained. Sometimes the waste was then used for irrigation, thus providing both moisture and fertilizer for crops that were later consumed by the cattle in the lots. The Pratt feedyard became one of the best models in the nation for this type of efficient disposal and reuse of waste from fattening cattle.[14]

While hundreds of Kansas farmers and ranchers participated in the revolution in cattle feeding, the names of several families stand out most prominently. Their operations exemplified the new trends in feeding. E. T. Anderson, one of the earliest large feeders, began buying land and feeding cattle during the early 1900s. He made good money during World War I, then nearly went broke during the 1930s. He continued to deal in cattle, however, and in 1940, with his son Kenneth, purchased a decrepit feedyard near

Modern feedlot near Pratt, Kansas, 1972. The circles of center-pivot irrigation systems are visible between the rows of cattle pens and at the bottom, right. *Courtesy of the Pratt Feedlot, Inc.*

Emporia that eventually became a modern feeding enterprise. They gradually improved and expanded the lot until by the early 1960s it reached a capacity of 20,000 cattle. But Anderson's operation closed down a few years later, when faced with large remodeling expenditures to prevent polluting surface water in the area.[15]

The Crofoot family fed cattle along the Cottonwood River near Strong City and Cedar Point, not far from Anderson's base at Emporia. These men contributed much to the advent of large commercial feeding in the Flint Hills, traditionally the summer home of thousands of grazing cattle. In conjunction with his pasturing operation, J. F. Crofoot began feeding cattle during the depression of the early 1920s. As his sons, Ray, E. C., and Glen, grew older, they first became partners with their father and then in the late thirties developed their own cattle businesses. By the time of World War II the Crofoots had several feeding establishments. Ray Crofoot, operating near Cedar Point, even used a water-powered mill for grinding feed. The old mill continued in operation until the disastrous flood in 1951 destroyed the water wheel and forced conversion to electric power. As the demand for fed cattle rose during the early 1950s, the Crofoots expanded, carving large feedlots from the hills west of Strong City. The hillsides provided shelter for the stock during bad weather, and the pens were easily cleaned because of the natural rock floors. Proper drainage of the lots that lay close to the Cottonwood River, however, eventually proved an insurmountable obstacle. By the early 1960s the Crofoots, now aided by a third generation, had expanded their lots in the Flint Hills to a capacity of over 20,000 head, and were interested in other feeding enterprises outside the state. But stricter pollution standards during the late 1960s drove the feedlots along the Cottonwood River out of business. Girdner, a son of E. C. Crofoot, estimated that to remodel their lots in accordance with government specifications would require an expenditure of over a quarter of a million dollars, a sum that the family chose not to spend. The Crofoots, however, did not give up feeding cattle. E. C. Crofoot and his son Jay moved to the drier climate of west Texas to operate a large feedlot near Lubbock.[16]

While eastern and central Kansas had always had some cattle feeding and had witnessed much expansion after World War II, the western part of the state was more properly the home of the postwar revolution in feeding. It occurred, naturally, in the twenty counties that were mentioned earlier for their large growth in irrigation. As a result, one observer was able to note in 1971 that over half the total cattle feeding in the state was done within a hundred mile radius of Dodge City.[17]

Earl C. Brookover, more than any other individual, led the developments in the western part of the state, beginning his operation in 1951 at a site north of Garden City in the fertile valley of the Arkansas River. Ed Robbins, a rancher from Belvidere, who wanted income from his cattle at times other than during the fall marketing of calves, supplied Brookover with some of his first feeder cattle. The Garden City stockman started with 500 steers, then, using his own and other local capital, gradually increased the capacity so that today the yard has bunk-line space for 42,000 cattle. The turnover rate is about two-and-a-half times a year, allowing over 100,000 cattle to pass through the yards in a single year.

Today, Brookover's feeding enterprise is typical of the many large commercial operations that exist throughout the West. The cattle, most of which come from within a 300-mile radius of Garden City, are either owned by Brookover or fed commercially for others. Brookover's own cattle are usually purchased by order buyers who are stationed throughout the Southeast and Southwest, receiving twenty-five cents per hundredweight for their part in buying cattle. Brookover prefers steers for his operation, purchased at 650 to 700 pounds, fed for 120 days or until most grade choice, and then sold at

Modern feedlot with feed mill in the background. *Courtesy of the Kansas State Board of Agriculture.*

around 1,000 pounds. Heifers, young bulls, and thin cows are also fed at times, but medium-grade steers often make their owner the most profit. Cattle that are owned by others are fed and cared for by the yards' employees at a charge of five cents a head per day, plus the cost of feed, medical care, and branding. Packer buyers come directly to the yards to make their purchases. Trucks bring the light cattle to the feedyards, then haul the finished stock to packers. Upon first arriving in the yards, cattle are routinely vaccinated for red nose, blackleg, and malignant edema, then dipped and wormed to kill external and internal parasites. Each pen of cattle receives its own brand. Cattle are initially fed a diet that contains a high percentage of roughage to gradually "warm them up" for the concentrated ration of grain that follows. Brookover began his feeding enterprise with a random mixture of grain and ensilage that was hand-scooped into bunks from the back of trucks. Today, an ultra-modern, computerized mill that mixes and processes thirty tons of feed an hour, all according to a prescribed formula, provides the diet that is carried to the cattle several times daily. Mechanized feed trucks have replaced scoop shovels. Depending upon which can be purchased at the most advantageous price, alfalfa or some other forage crop and steam-rolled wheat, milo, or corn may make up the basic ration, all mixed according to plan with molasses, minerals, and other necessary feed additives.

Consistent with the vertical integration that has occurred in many agricultural enterprises, some of the four million bushels of grain that Brookover uses each year is produced on his own irrigated farms, making him also a leader in expanding irrigation in southwest Kansas. In 1977, he purchased a ranch just south of Garden City, which had belonged for many years to O. C. Hicks, in order to expand his irrigated farming. Preparations were soon begun for using processed waste from a Garden City packer to supply some of the water for the sprinkler systems that Brookover erected on the Hicks ranch. The completed project was expected to work to the advantage of both the feeder and the packer.

Brookover's feedlot is a clean and efficient operation, with few problems in disposing of waste. Pens are carefully cleaned after cattle are shipped out, and the manure is spread over his land or stored for use after the crops have been removed from the fields. Some manure is also sold to farmers in the area, who use it to fertilize their irrigated crop land.[18]

From the beginning, Brookover has been at the forefront of the changes that have occurred in cattle feeding and irrigation in southwest Kansas. The daily operations of most other commercial yards are similar to those at Brookover's modern factory for making beef; but few yards are operated as efficiently or, most likely, with any more profit. Today, the feedlots operated by Brookover and those run by the many others in western Kansas who have followed his lead are an important stimulus to the local economy, providing markets for the ranchers' calves and an outlet for the abundant grain and forage that is raised in the immediate area. The lots have become the focal points of the communities' agricultural endeavors. In addition, employment is provided for numerous people, who either care for the cattle or shuffle the necessary papers that facilitate the many transactions that must accompany the business. Packers are supplied with quality beef and truckers are provided cattle to haul or meat to carry away to distant urban centers. Millions of dollars are added to the Kansas economy each year as a result of the recent developments in the making of fine beef.

In addition to increasing the number of grain-fattened cattle that came out of Kansas after World War II, the revolution described above affected other segments of the Kansas beef industry as well. Production in the state's best-known area for cattle raising, the Flint Hills, did not escape the changes. During the 1950s and after, the expansion of feeding operations and the increased use of commercial feed supplements significantly changed cattle production in the Flint Hills. In the state's most distinctive beef-producing area, more cow herds began to eat the lush grass that had formerly been reserved for cattle shipped in from the Southwest. Despite the increased number of breeding herds, however, cattle were still shipped in for summer grazing; but even this practice changed as the age of the cattle gradually declined as a result of commercial feeding and changing consumer demands. In 1945, for instance, Wayne Rogler, a pastureman from Chase County, grazed 3,100 three-year-old steers for Dolph Briscoe of Uvalde, Texas. The cattle gained 284 pounds each as a result of their three months on the bluestem. A few years later, E. T. Anderson still pastured over 3,000 three-year-old Matador steers, but the practice soon declined. During the 1950s, two-year-old stock began to dominate. By the late 1960s breeding herds and yearlings accounted for most of the cattle in the Flint Hills. By 1976 Rogler estimated that 30 to 40 percent of the bluestem was used by locally owned cow herds, with the remainder utilized by yearlings.

In addition to the increased consumer demand for grain-fed beef and the commercial feeds that aided winter use of pastures, the general prosperity that cattlemen experienced during and after World War II encouraged residents to buy their own cow herds and to cut down on out-of-state cattle. Stockmen also learned that rising land prices and other production expenses had raised the cost of fattening cattle on grass. Highly mechanized feedyards, using the large grain supplies that became available, fattened cattle almost as cheaply, and did so in less time.[19]

The origin of and the type of cattle that continued to come into the Flint Hills after the war also changed a good deal. High-quality Herefords from the Texas Panhandle and Oklahoma dominated the Flint Hills trade before the 1930s, then cattle from southern Texas became prominent in the movement. Today, yearling steers move into the Flint Hills from several states to the south and east of Kansas, together with those from the traditional sources in the Southwest. Today's cattle are owned mostly by producers in

Kansas and Oklahoma, are of mixed colors rather than straight-bred Herefords, and are generally of poorer quality than most of the earlier stock. Pasturemen refer to them as "#1 and #2 Okies."[20]

The drought of the 1930s and the rising costs of grass fattening encouraged more scientific research in grass utilization during the postwar period. Feeling that research in the use of grassland had fallen behind that in other areas of agriculture, leading stockmen in the Flint Hills helped persuade the state to buy a small tract west of Manhattan for the use of Kansas State College of Agriculture in its research. The benefits from rotating pastures, weed and brush control, and the use of supplemental feeds were demonstrated, as were the harmful effects of overgrazing. The advantages and disadvantages of annual pasture burning also received much study, but as late as 1970 university scientists had not ended completely all of the old arguments. The time of burning, the moisture content of the soil, and the intended use of the pasture were discovered to be critical in the decision on whether to burn. Though some cattlemen have completely dispensed with burning, others still fire their pastures periodically in hopes of gaining better weed and brush control and more forage per acre for their cattle.

Today, cattlemen in the Flint Hills continue to experiment. Some, for instance, are increasing the number of cattle per acre while reducing the length of the grazing period. Normally, a steer is allowed about four acres for the summer grazing season. By cutting the acreage in half and by making sure that all cattle are gone by early July, some cattlemen have found that they can get more gain and profit per acre and that the grass still has time to replenish the food supply to its roots before dormancy in the fall. A July sale to one of the many feedlots and the rising costs of production on grass contributed to this development.[21]

Two decades or so after World War II the Flint Hills exemplified another postwar development in the western beef industry—cattle of different hues had replaced many of the straight-bred Angus and Herefords. This change offended some traditionalists, who argued that the crossbred cattle destroyed the eye appeal of stock and that it mongrelized the traditional breeds. But the multicolored steers and heifers, although sometimes offensive to older stockmen, suggested that the traditional British breeds were being crossbred with each other or mixed with one of the new exotic breeds that had recently been introduced into the United States.

While there had been much crossbreeding during the nineteenth century, when British breeds were being used extensively to upgrade the Longhorn, most large ranchers had settled on straight-bred herds once the cattle had been improved. These straight-bred herds generally dominated the range country until the late 1950s and 1960s. Then, led to a large extent by the work of USDA scientists at the experiment station near Miles City, Montana, and by following scientific advances that had already been made in the development of hybrid seeds, swine, and even chickens, cattlemen also began to seek hybridization. They desired the earlier maturity and greater milking ability from mother cows, the heavier weaning weights from calves, and the better gaining qualities from feeder stock that advocates claimed for crossbred cattle. In the end, cattlemen hoped for larger profits from more beef production with the same quantity of feed. But the breeding of purebreds continued because maximum results from crossbreeding were not attainable without purebreds for use in crossing.

Some ranchers developed sophisticated breeding programs that involved three-way crosses, but this was often a complicated procedure and required more pasture space than many had available. Most simply altered the breed of their bulls, often by running Angus bulls with their Hereford cows or whiteface bulls with their black cows. Cattlemen also used exotic breeds— Charolais, Simmental, Santa Gertrudis, Brahman, Limousin, and others—in their crossbreeding programs. While the Brahman had been in the country for a number of years, most of the exotics came only after World War II or, in the case of the Santa Gertrudis, were developed here through specialized breeding programs.

Few exotics grazed Kansas grass before 1960. Paul Mannell, who farmed southwest of Lincoln, brought some of the first Charolais into the state in 1960, while E. Wallace Johnson, near Towanda, registered the same year the first purebred Santa Gertrudis in the state. Several other exotics were also represented, including M. A. Bell's herd of Highland cattle from Scotland. But most crossbreeding in Kansas followed the trend of mixing Hereford and Angus cattle.

Many of the advantages claimed by advocates of crossbreeding resulted from mixing the traditional British cattle and by introducing exotic blood from continental Europe. Due to their hybrid vigor, calves were larger and better muscled, brood cows matured earlier and gave more milk, and feeder stock gained weight more efficiently. As a result of the many attempts at crossbreeding and because the breed itself had been improved, Angus cattle became more popular in the range country. Shorthorn blood also became more common in the West, although the breed was hampered by a shortage of breeding stock. Conversely, straight-bred commercial Hereford and Angus herds declined in number. Not all crossbreeding, however, had the desired effects, as some herds were downgraded by the use of inferior sires. But cattlemen soon realized that although crossing two animals of poor quality might produce some hybrid vigor, it also resulted in inferior progeny.[22]

While many owners of commercial herds experimented with crossbreeding, producers of purebreds were reluctant at first to endorse crossing, fearing that the purebred business might be injured. But there was little loss of business, as purebred sires and dams were still necessary for the crosses. Herefords, traditionally the most favored cattle, continued to be popular, most crossbreeders using the whitefaces someplace in their programs. Cattlemen who crossbred cattle desired above all the aggressive breeding of the Hereford bull, as well as his superior ability to transmit his desirable characteristics.

Several other developments appeared after World War II in purebred Herefords, some detracting from the breed and others adding to its popularity. During the late 1940s and early 1950s, for example, several prominent stockmen in the West contributed to a change in the Hereford's conformation as they bred and selected shorter, more compact animals. The new Herefords had much eye appeal, style, and heavy muscling; but, after being plied with grain in modern feedlots, they also had too much fat for the modern consumer. As a result, the trend turned back to the long-legged, rangier types of Herefords.

Dwarfism, a problem caused by a recessive gene, became a more serious problem for the breed. Further, most other breeds, especially the Angus, also were affected by dwarfism at about the same time. One government expert estimated in 1952 that 15 percent of the calves born that year were affected by the abnormality. Cattlemen and their breed associations first tended to ignore the problem, while high-grade sires and dams continued to spread the genes throughout the country. Numerous avenues looking toward the detection of the offensive gene, such as insulin injections designed as a possible means of identifying dwarf carriers, were explored by scientists; but the ultimate practical solution involved checking of pedigrees for any known dwarf-carrying ancestry, screening of herd bulls by progeny testing, and the prompt elimination of all animals which proved to be carriers of the defective gene. Thus, by the 1970s, dwarfism as a major industry problem not only had been significantly reduced but for all practical purposes was virtually eliminated.[23]

Artificial insemination and performance-testing were new developments that aided cattlemen. The first allowed a high-quality bull to spread his characteristics to literally thousands of calves, to some even after his death. Performance-testing, which requires the systematic weighing of calves at various stages of development, added scientific evidence to the judgment of cattlemen in selecting the most desirable breeding stock. Superior and inferior sires and dams were more easily identified. Before it had gained popularity, however, some disagreements developed between the people who showed their cattle and the advocates of performance-testing; but by the 1960s the groups worked together to the advantage of both. Most were already convinced by the time the 1976 reserve grand champion Hereford bull at the Denver stock show demonstrated that the same animal could do well in both performance-testing and in the show ring. Clair Parcel, one of the state's early advocates of performance-testing, had raised the bull.[24]

Although the state's breef producers confronted many production and marketing problems during the decades following 1890—some resolved, some not—the cattle industry experienced remarkable growth in its size and in its contribution to the total agricultural economy of the state. Throughout most of the twentieth century, between 35 and 40 percent of the state's total acreage has been used for grazing, which represents more land than that devoted to any other single use. In addition, part of the millions of acres planted to field crops produced forage or feed grains that were used as cattle feed. By 1940 over 64 percent of the cash receipts of Kansas agricultural producers came from the marketing of livestock and its products; over 31 percent of the total receipts derived from cattle and calves alone. By World War II, after the depression and government programs of the 1930s had dealt the hog industry a severe blow, beef cattle were easily the dominant species of livestock in the state. After 1940 there was a temporary decline in the importance of the livestock sector as a whole, relative to that of field crops, but this was not the case with the beef cattle portion of the state's agricultural economy. In 1950 and 1960, for instance, cattle acounted for 34 and 35.7 percent, respectively, of the total cash receipts from the marketing of the state's major farm commodities. This was almost the same as for wheat. Beef gradually increased its share until by 1970 nearly 50 percent of the total cash receipts came from marketing cattle, while that from wheat declined to 22.4 percent. Livestock's contribution as a whole had also risen by this time to almost 64 percent. The land that was used, then, the crops that were fed, and the cash receipts all pointed to the tremendous significance that beef production had attained in the Kansas economy.[25]

Even though beef production increased its contribution to the state's economy during the twentieth century, financial returns to individuals from ranching over an extended period of time were sometimes not large. Considering the capital invested and the amount of work involved, cattle producers often could have made more money in other endeavors. One study of Flint Hills grazing, for example, estimated that landowners received net profits of less than 3 percent on capital invested, capital which in "other forms of investment could readily bring immediate returns of four to six per cent."[26] These figures applied to ranching during the 1960s; but, judging from the many references to no or low profits, they were representative of returns to Kansas beef producers throughout much of the twentieth century, especially the period after the First World War. The profit figures, however, did not include the gains that accrued to property owners as a result of rising land values. In fact, the increased value of the land, especially since the 1930s, may have outstripped the profits from producing cattle. Nor did the study measure the many intangible attractions of raising cattle, such as pride of ownership, continuing a family heritage, enjoying the primitive beauty of the land and the environment as a whole, and the pleasure of improving a product. These advantages, both tangible and intangible, help explain why Kansas and other beef-producing states have never suffered a shortage of cattlemen, and why the nation's consumers have seldom endured a shortage of meat. Through good times and bad, cattlemen can be expected to continue to produce an adequate supply of beef for the nation's consumers.

Notes

CHAPTER 1

1. Kirke Mechem (comp.), *The Annals of Kansas, 1886–1925*, 2 vols. (Topeka: Kansas State Historical Society, 1954, 1956), 1: 176; "Beef Cattle in Kansas," *Report of the Kansas State Board of Agriculture* for the quarter ending September, 1934, p. 153; Richard Goff and Robert H. McCaffree, *Century in the Saddle* (Denver: Colorado Cattlemen's Centennial Commission, 1967), p. 5.

2. Several accounts describe this area. Two of the most analytical are James C. Malin, "An Introduction to the History of the Bluestem-Pasture Region of Kansas: A Study in Adaptation to Geographical Environment," *Kansas Historical Quarterly* 11 (February, 1942): 3–28; and Walter M. Kollmorgen and David S. Simonett, "Grazing Operations in the Flint Hills–Bluestem Pastures of Chase County, Kansas," Association of American Geographers, *Annals* 55 (June, 1965): 260–90.

3. Ibid.; H. R. Hilton, "The Bluestem Limestone Pastures of Kansas," *Twenty-Sixth Report of the Kansas State Board of Agriculture* (1927–1928), pp. 187–89, hereafter cited as *Rept., KSBA;* Malin, "The Bluestem-Pasture Region," 7–11.

4. Kollmorgen, "Grazing in the Bluestem Pastures," 290.

5. *Kansas Stockman,* March 15, 1925, p. 3; February, 1949, p. 8; March, 1956, pp. 14, 66, 68. Hereafter cited as *KS.*

6. *Clark County Clipper,* May 10, 1906; May 9, 1907.

7. Robert W. Richmond, "Cowtowns and Cattle Trails," in *Kansas: The First Century,* ed. John D. Bright (New York: Lewis Historical Publishing Co., 1956), pp. 255–77; Malin, "The Bluestem-Pasture Region," 15–16; John T. Schlebecker, *Cattle Raising on the Plains, 1900–1961* (Lincoln: University of Nebraska Press, 1963), p. 12.

8. Emporia *Gazette,* February 1, 1894. This is a weekly paper; the *Daily Gazette* will be noted as such. Kollmorgen, "Grazing in the Bluestem Pastures," 273–74. In addition, the author noted that, although protein was only a partial

index to the quality of pasture, available evidence indicated that profitable gains in the 1960s were not possible when protein content was less than 8 percent.

9. Malin, "The Bluestem-Pasture Region," 18.

10. Interview, Wayne Rogler, Matfield Green, Kans., August 2, 1977; *The Cattleman,* February, 1967, pp. 46–56.

11. Emporia *Gazette,* October 31, 1895; November 10, 1898.

12. J. J. Moxley, typescript statement on the Flint Hills, March 4, 1970, in Kansas Livestock Association Files, 2044 Fillmore, Topeka. Hereafter cited as KLA Files.

13. Emporia *Gazette,* June 29, 1905.

14. Ibid., August 16, 1894. *Kansas Farmer,* May 16, 1894, p. 2; May 23, 1894, p. 2; August 29, 1894, p. 2. *Fifty-Fourth Rept., KSBA* (1970–1971), pp. 203–204.

15. L. A. Allen, *Our Cattle Industry: Present, Past and Future* (Topeka, 1896), pp. 11–14, pamphlet in Kansas State Historical Society, hereafter KSHS. *The Cattleman,* February, 1934, pp. 28–29. *Kansas Farmer,* March 7, 1894, p. 2; August 15, 1894, p. 9; August 22, 1895, p. 2; September 19, 1894, p. 2; January 9, 1895, p. 18; January 2, 1896, p. 3; October 22, 1896, p. 675; Schlebecker, *Cattle Raising on the Plains,* pp. 13–14.

16. Emporia *Gazette,* July 23, 1896; January 7, 1897; February 11, and 25, 1897; April 8 and 22, 1897; July 1, 1897.

17. *American Hereford Journal* quoted in *KS,* September 15, 1939, p. 17; Jim Orton in *KS,* March, 1951, pp. 12, 14, 102; Martha E. Andrews and Ross H. Bryan, *He Was the Sherman Ranch,* pamphlet in KSHS, n.p., 1970; Cattle Industry Clippings 2: 93–94, in KSHS.

18. *Clark County Chief* (Engelwood), January 1, 1885.

19. Ibid., April 2, 1886; Ashland *Leader,* July 2, 1908.

20. *Clark County Clipper* (Ashland), May 31, 1895; June 26, 1896. Wichita *Beacon* quoted in *Clark County Clipper,* September 24, 1897. J. H. Churchill, "The Cattle Industry of Western Kansas," *Kansas Farmer,* January 21, 1897, p. 35.

21. M. S. Babcock, presidential address in *Report of the Ninth Annual Meeting of the Kansas Improved Stock Breeders' Association* (Topeka: Kansas Farmer Co., 1899), p. 11; *Kansas Farmer,* January 21, 1897, p. 35.

22. Kansas City *Packer* quoted in *Clark County Clipper,* November 26, 1897.

23. *Clark County Clipper,* December 14, 1899; April 5, 1900.

24. Ibid., April 5, 1895; May 13, 1898. For a more extended discussion of fencing, see my "Fencing in Five Kansas Counties between 1875 and 1895" (Master's thesis, University of Kansas, 1968).

25. Charles L. Wood, "C. D. Perry: Clark County Farmer and Rancher, 1884–1908," *Kansas Historical Quarterly* 39 (Winter, 1973): 449–77.

26. Reprinted in *Clark County Clipper,* June 29, 1905.

27. Ibid., November 14, 1907.

CHAPTER 2

1. Some of the material in this chapter appears in my article, "Upbreeding

Western Range Cattle: Notes on Kansas, 1880–1920," *Journal of the West* 16 (January, 1977): 16–28.

2. Edward E. Dale, *The Range Cattle Industry: Ranching on the Great Plains from 1865 to 1925* (1930; reprinted, Norman: University of Oklahoma Press, 1960), pp. 148–56.

3. *Kansas Farmer,* May 30, 1894, p. 3.

4. Ibid., June 6, 1894, p. 4; letter from N. E. Masher and Son, May 30, 1894, p. 5.

5. *KS,* February 1, 1925, p. 4; Donald R. Ornduff, *The Hereford in America: A Compilation of Historic Facts about the Breed's Background and Bloodlines* (Kansas City: Hereford History Press, 1969), pp. 110–19.

6. Enterprise *Chronicle* (Burlingame), in Ford County Clippings 4: 1, in KSHS; C. W. McCampbell, "Seventy Years of Beef Production in Kansas," *KS,* March 1, 1931, p. 53. For Scott's Texas ranch, see Dulcie Sullivan, *The LS Brand: The Story of a Texas Panhandle Ranch* (Austin: University of Texas Press, 1968).

7. Cattle Industry Clippings 3: 89, in KSHS; David I. Day, "Memories of the Crane Ranch," and "More Crane Ranch Memories," *Milking Shorthorn Journal* (May and June, 1941), typed copies in KSHS, n.p.

8. G. W. Glick, "Why I Breed Shorthorns after Half a Century's Experience with Them," *Report of the Ninth Annual Meeting of the Kansas Improved Stock Breeders' Association,* pp. 67–69; Atchison Daily *Globe* Clippings, pp. 98–103, in KSHS; *Kansas Farmer,* November 5, 1896, p. 707; McCampbell, "Seventy Years of Beef Production in Kansas," p. 53.

9. Ibid.; Clyde L. Fitch, "William A. Harris of Kansas: His Economic Interests" (Master's thesis, Kansas State Teachers College, Emporia, 1967), copy in KSHS.

10. *Kansas Farmer Mail and Breeze,* March 10, 1923, p. 3. *KS,* April 15, 1928, p. 22; February 1, 1938, p. 6; March, 1945, p. 43; October, 1964, p. 68. Interview, James G. Tomson, Jr., Wakarusa, Kans., July 23, 1977.

11. *KS,* August, 1942, p. 7; March, 1943, p. 56; August, 1943, p. 7; September, 1953, pp. 22–24. I. D. Graham, "George Grant, First Importer of Aberdeen Angus in the United States," *Thirty-Second Rept., KSBA* (1939–1940), pp. 201–204. McCampbell, "Seventy Years of Beef Production in Kansas," pp. 17, 53.

12. Ibid.; *American Hereford Journal,* January 15, 1941, pp. 30–31. *Kansas Farmer,* March 26, 1896, p. 195. Letters in *Kansas Farmer* from N. E. Masher, May 30, 1894, p. 2; T. F. B. Sotham, April 2, 1896, p. 211. Interview, Clair Parcel, Coldwater, Kans., July 14, 1977.

13. *American Hereford Journal,* June 1, 1924, pp. 4–12, 22–27; Ornduff, *The Hereford in America,* pp. 3–5, 18–20, 30–35.

14. Ibid., pp. 36–37. McCampbell, "Seventy Years of Beef Production in Kansas," p. 53. *KS,* July 15, 1920, p. 9; December 1, 1921, p. 7; April 1, 1940, p. 6. W. A. Morgan in *Thirty-Third Rept., KSBA* (1941–1942), pp. 138–43). *American Hereford Journal,* May 1, 1916, p. 5; December 1, 1940, p. 50.

15. Ibid., June 15, 1918, pp. 28–30; C. W. McCampbell, "W. E. Campbell,

Pioneer Kansas Livestockman," *Kansas Historical Quarterly* 16 (August, 1948): 245–73.

16. Ornduff, *The Hereford in America,* pp. 47, 75.

17. *American Hereford Journal,* July 1, 1916, pp. 6, 15; August 1, 1922, pp. 38–39; July 15, 1924, pp. 6, 10.

18. For additional information on Gudgell & Simpson, two works are especially helpful: Ornduff, *The Hereford in America,* pp. 46, 75–80, 181–204; John M. Hazelton, *A History of Linebred Anxiety 4th Herefords of Straight Gudgell & Simpson Breeding* (Kansas City: Associated Breeders of Anxiety 4th Herefords, 1939), pp. 12–14, 17–23, 83–87, 214. Also helpful is Jay L. Lush, "Line Breeding," *The Cattleman,* March, 1928, pp. 33, 37.

19. Emporia *Gazette,* March 19, 1896; December 27, 1897; January 13, February 10, March 3 and 10, October 20, November 17 and 24, and December 29, 1898.

20. *American Hereford Journal,* June 1, 1935, pp. 88–90.

21. Emporia *Gazette,* November 2 and December 28, 1899. Emporia *Daily Gazette,* February 28 and May 30, 1898.

22. *The Cattleman,* March, 1940, p. 57. Emporia *Gazette,* May 27 and June 24, 1897; December 1, 15, 1898; January 12, March 9, September 28, and December 7, 1899. *KS,* February 15, 1941, p. 38. Dickinson County Clippings 3: 106, 4: 120–22, in KSHS.

23. *Clark County Clipper,* December 21, 1899.

24. Terry H. Harmon, "Soldier Creek Park: The Rockefeller Ranch in Kiowa County, Kansas," *The Trail Guide* 13 (December, 1968): 1–25; Emporia *Gazette,* December 3, 1903.

25. Ibid., April 17, 1902.

26. Ibid., December 29, 1898; December 20, 1900; December 3, 10, and 17, 1903; January 21 and October 20, 1904; December 13 and 20, 1906; January 10, October 24, and November 7, 1907; July 11 and August 13, 1908; February 24 and May 5, 1910; October 26, 1911. *KS,* September 1, 1923, p. 6.

27. Emporia *Daily Gazette,* May 30, 1898; *Kansas Farmer,* February 20, 1895, p. 115.

CHAPTER 3

1. Kansas City Stock Yards Company, *75 Years of Kansas City Livestock Market History,* pamphlet (Kansas City, 1946), pp. 27–29; Edward A. Duddy and David A. Revzan, *The Changing Relative Importance of the Central Livestock Market,* Chicago University School of Business Studies in Business Administration, vol. 8, no. 4 (Chicago: University of Chicago Press, 1938), pp. 5–16; Herrell DeGraff, *Beef Production and Distribution* (Norman: University of Oklahoma Press, 1960), pp. 149–53.

2. *75 Years of Kansas City Livestock Market History,* pp. 4–11; Eva L. Atkin-

son, "Kansas City's Livestock Trade and Packing Industry, 1870–1914: A Study in Regional Growth," (Ph.D. diss., University of Kansas, 1971), pp. 122–30, 156–60, 280, 329, 336–37; Cuthbert Powell, *Twenty Years of Kansas City's Live Stock Trade and Traders* (Kansas City: Pearl Printing Co., 1893), pp. 27–28. *Report of the Federal Trade Commission on the Meat Packing Industry,* part 3 (Washington, 1919), pp. 43–44; hereafter cited as *FTC Rept.*

3. "A Brief History of the St. Joseph Plant," a typescript history, 1938, in miscellaneous records of Swift plant deposited in Spencer Research Library, University of Kansas, pp. 13–14.

4. *The Cattleman,* October, 1933, pp. 15–16; *FTC Rept.,* part 3, pp. 42–43.

5. Alfred D. Chandler, Jr., "The Beginnings of 'Big Business' in American Industry," *Business History Review* 33 (Spring, 1959), reprinted in *Patterns and Perspectives: Interpretations of American History,* vol. 2, 2d ed., Gerald N. Grob and George A. Billias (New York: Free Press, 1972), pp. 96–99; William Z. Ripley, *Railroads: Rates and Regulation* (New York: Longmans, Green and Co., 1912), pp. 139–42.

6. Atkinson, "Kansas City's Livestock Trade and Packing Industry," pp. 214–28; Lewis Corey, *Meat and Man: A Study of Monopoly, Unionism and Food Policy* (New York: Viking Press, 1938), pp. 8–11, 45–47, 158–64; Louis F. Swift, *The Yankee of the Yards: The Biography of Gustavus Franklin Swift* (Chicago: A. W. Shaw Co., 1927), pp. 130–34.

7. G. K. Renner, "The Kansas City Meat Packing Industry before 1900," *Missouri Historical Review* 55 (October, 1960): 18, 20–29.

8. Ibid.; Atkinson, "Kansas City's Livestock Trade and Packing Industry," pp. 214–39; *75 Years of Kansas City Livestock Market History,* pp. 35–37.

9. "The Kansas Livestock Association," n.n., n.d., pp. 1–2; C. W. McCampbell, "The Kansas Livestock Association," n.d., pp. 1–2. Both are typescript accounts of twenty or fewer pages in KLA Files. Also see *First Annual Report of the Kansas State Live Stock Association* (Cottonwood Falls, Kans.: W. C. Austin, 1916), pp. 1–10; "Transcript of Hearings," Board of Railroad Commissioners (1896), case no. 1364, manuscript deposited in KSHS. For additional information on the origin of KLA, see my "Cattlemen and Railroads: The Origin of the Kansas Livestock Association during the 1890s," *Kansas Historical Quarterly* 43 (Summer, 1977).

10. Emporia *Daily Gazette,* March 23, 1896; August 20 and 28, 1897. Emporia *Weekly Gazette,* February 1, 1894; August 12 and 19, and December 21, 1897.

11. Clippings in Kansas Biographical Scrapbook 142: 181–85, 146: 69–70. *KS,* March 15, 1926, p. 5; November 1, 1932, p. 39; March 15, 1926, p. 5; November 1, 1932, p. 39; March 1, 1933, p. 53; April 1, 1937, p. 2. El Dorado *Republican,* July 21, 1909.

12. *KS,* July 1, 1924, p. 3; November 1, 1933, p. 13; February, 1963, pp. 12–13. William E. Connelly, *A Standard History of Kansas and Kansans,* vol. 3 (Chicago: Lewis Publishing Co., 1918), pp. 1361–62.

13. McCampbell, "The Kansas Livestock Association." Mrs. Jesse C. Harper to Glenn Pickett, secretary of KLA, July 28, 1965, in KLA Files. *Clark County*

Clipper, July 4, 1957. *KS*, July 1, 1922, p. 1; March 15, 1926, pp. 5–6; July, 1951, p. 35.

14. Ibid., June 15, 1929, p. 8; May 1, 1931, p. 4; December 15, 1933, p. 5; October, 1956, p. 42; August, 1961, p. 7; April, 1965, p. 8. *American Hereford Journal*, May 1, 1936, p. 36.

15. John Clay, *My Life on the Range* (1924; reprint ed., Norman: University of Oklahoma Press, 1962), pp. 115–18; Charles A. Burmeister, "Six Decades of Rugged Individualism: The American National Cattlemen's Association, 1898–1955," *Agricultural History* 30 (1956): 143–46; Lyle Liggett, *There Is a Time and a Place. . . The History of the American National Cattlemen's Association*, pamphlet (New York: Newcomen Society, 1972), pp. 9–12.

16. Theodore Saloutos and John D. Hicks, *Agricultural Discontent in the Middle West, 1900–1939* (Madison: University of Wisconsin Press), pp. 31–32; Saloutos, "The Agricultural Problem and Nineteenth Century Industrialism," *Agricultural History* 22 (July, 1948): 156–74; W. P. Harrington, "The Populist Party in Kansas," *Kansas Historical Collections* 16 (1923–1925): 403–50.

17. O. Gene Clanton, *Kansas Populism: Ideas and Men* (Lawrence: University Press of Kansas, 1969), pp. 245–51.

18. Samuel P. Hays, *The Response to Industrialism: 1885–1914* (Chicago: University of Chicago Press, 1957), pp. 48–70; Lewis Galambos, *Competition and Cooperation: The Emergence of a National Trade Association* (Baltimore: Johns Hopkins Press, 1966), pp. 199–226, 288–92.

19. C. L. Sonnichsen, *Cowboys and Cattle Kings: Life on the Range Today* (Norman: University of Oklahoma Press, 1950), pp. 236–37.

20. Ripley, *Railroads*, pp. 55, 166–67, 411–12; John F. Stover, *American Railroads* (Chicago: University of Chicago Press, 1961), pp. 117, 171; *Fourteenth Rept., KSBA* (1903–1904), pp. 475–80, 484–97.

21. Lawrence L. Waters, *Steel Trails to Santa Fe* (Lawrence: University of Kansas Press, 1950), p. 172.

22. Ripley, *Railroads*, p. 412; Stover, *American Railroads*, p. 171.

23. Ibid., p. 122; Ripley, *Railroads*, pp. 238–39, 423.

24. *Ninth and Tenth Annual Report of the Board of Railroad Commissioners* (1891), p. v; (1892), p. viii. Hereafter cited as *Rept Bd RR Com.*

25. Gabriel Kolko, *Railroads and Regulation, 1877–1916* (Princeton: Princeton University Press, 1965), p. 51.

26. Edwin O. Stene, *Railroad Commission to Corporation Commission* (Lawrence: University of Kansas Press, 1945), pp. 8–15. *Twelfth Annual Rept Bd RR Com* (1894), pp. 4–5. Emporia *Gazette*, January 14, 1897; January 13, 1898.

27. William F. Zornow, *Kansas: A History of the Jayhawk State* (Norman: University of Oklahoma Press, 1957), p. 218.

28. Emporia *Gazette*, February 11, March 11, and April 15, 1897; December 29, 1898; January 5, 1899. Stene, *Railroad Commission*, pp. 34–40.

29. *Eighth Annual Rept Bd RR Com* (1890), pp. 98–100.

30. Ibid.; *Thirteenth Annual Rept Bd RR Com* (1895), p. 16.

31. Most of the information that follows was taken from three sources: *Kansas*

Farmer, April 16, 1898, p. 248; *Fourteenth Annual Rept Bd RR Com* (1896), pp. 22–31; "Transcript of Hearings" (1896), case no. 1364, in KSHS.

32. *Fourteenth Annual Rept Bd RR Com* (1896), pp. 22–23; "Transcript of Hearings" (1896), pp. 4, 262, 270, 325–26.

33. *Kansas: A History of the Jayhawk State,* p. 147. Zornow failed to give the source for this information. If it came from the printed reports of the various railroads, one might well question its accuracy.

34. "Transcript of Hearings" (1896), pp. 38–40, 131–33.

35. Ibid., pp. 3, 10–13, 176–78, 195–96.

36. Ibid., pp. 12–13, 16–18, 22, 36–37, 54, 251–53.

37. "Transcript of Hearings" (1897), pp. 3–12, 46; *Fifteenth Annual Rept Bd RR Com* (1897), pp. 15–17.

38. Emporia *Gazette,* January 4, 1900.

39. "The Kansas Livestock Association," n.n., n.d., p. 1.

CHAPTER 4

1. Emporia *Gazette,* September 9, 1909.

2. *Fifty-Fourth Rept., KSBA* (1970–1971), pp. 205–206; DeGraff, *Beef Production and Distribution,* pp. 38–50.

3. Ronald E. Johnson, *Prices Received by Farmers for Beef Cattle: United States, by States, Monthly and Annual Average, 1909–1959,* USDA Statistical Bulletin 265 (1960), p. 4; Schlebecker, *Cattle Raising on the Plains,* pp. 17, 19–20, 30, 42, 52, 59–60; Emporia *Gazette,* April 18, 1901. There was a variation of several dollars in the price listings by Schlebecker and those of the USDA Bulletin, probably because Schlebecker's listings included a larger percentage of the stocker and feeder class, which usually sold at a higher price per hundred pounds. One of many examples of the disparity between prices actually received by many cattlemen and those recorded by the USDA was reported in 1915 when a Flint Hills producer sold seventeen carloads of grass-fattened cattle for $9.10 per hundred, or $2.40 above the average price for Kansas cattle, according to USDA statistics. "Cattlemen had made easy money for several years," this stockman said, "and prices held up until September and October of 1919." E. T. Anderson, *A Quarter Inch of Rain* (Wichita: McCormick-Armstrong Co., 1962), p. 131.

4. Gardner P. Walker, "Cattle Industry Cycles," *The Cattleman,* November, 1933, p. 25; *Fifty-Fourth Rept., KSBA* (1970–1971), pp. 205–206.

5. Rudolph A. Clemen, *The American Livestock and Meat Industry* (New York: Ronald Press Co., 1923), p. 291; Schlebecker, *Cattle Raising on the Plains,* pp. 17, 30, 53, 59, 139.

6. Ibid., pp. 60–61; Gene M. Gressley, *Bankers and Cattlemen* (Lincoln: University of Nebraska Press, 1966), p. 277; DeGraff, *Beef Production and Distribution,* p. 131; Wichita *Eagle,* January 27, 1915; M. L. McClure, "Relation of Banking to the Cattle Industry," *Twenty-First Rept.,* KSBA (1917–1918), pp. 68–76.

7. *Forty-Fourth Rept., KSBA* (1960–1961), pp. 185–86; Wichita *Eagle,* January 26 and 28, 1915; Emporia *Gazette,* September 1, 1940.

8. *Kansas Cattleman,* January 5, 1918, p. 7; February 5, 1918, p. 5; May 20, 1918, p. 3. Malin, "The Bluestem-Pasture Region," 21, 27. *KS,* July 5, 1918, p. 6. Emporia *Gazette,* January 21, 1915.

9. Cattle Industry Clippings 4: 61–62, 5: 72–75, 189–95, in KSHS.

10. *Kansas Cattleman,* September 5, 1917, pp. 1, 3; January 5, 1917, p. 3; February 5, 1918, p. 5; February 20, 1918, pp. 3, 6–10; March 18, 1918, pp. 4, 6.

11. Ibid., March 15, 1918, p. 3.

12. Mechem (comp.), *The Annals of Kansas,* vol. 2, pp. 37, 70–71, 146–47, 155, 213, 221, 231–35, 240; *KS,* May 20, 1918, p. 6.

13. *Annals of Kansas,* vol. 2, p. 242; Wichita *Eagle,* January 26, 1915; *Kansas Cattleman,* March 5, 1918, p. 3; Tom G. Hall, "Wilson and the Food Crisis: Agricultural Price Control during World War I," *Agricultural History* 47 (January, 1973): 25.

14. As noted earlier, the value of farm products is probably not the best indicator of livestock's contribution to the Kansas agricultural economy, as the value of all grain fed to stock was apparently tabulated under the heading of crop value when, in fact, grain fed to stock made a contribution to both the crop and livestock sectors. Receipts from farm marketings, which I use for periods after 1925, are a better indication, but these figures were not available for the earlier period. Nor could the contribution of beef cattle be separated from that of the other livestock when value figures were used, but it would probably have been the largest single contributor in most years.

15. Schlebecker, *Cattle Raising on the Plains,* pp. 18–25; Walter M. Kollmorgen, "The Woodman's Assaults on the Domain of the Cattleman," Association of American Geographers, *Annals* 59 (June, 1969): 217–36; *Forty-Fourth Rept., KSBA* (1960–1961), p. 219.

16. *KS,* January 1, 1937, p. 3; Pawnee County Clippings, 2: 47–53, in KSHS.

17. Ibid. Emporia *Gazette,* April 25, 1901; July 25, 1912; August 7, and 21, 1913.

18. *Fifty-Fourth Rept., KSBA* (1970–1971), pp. 207–209. *Kansas Cattleman,* November 1, 1916, p. 15. W. M. Jardine, May 6, 1918; A. J. R. Curtis, May 8, 1918; Forest Kaufman, July 8, 1918; letters to Arthur Capper, in Capper Papers, Box 12:32, KSHS. *Annals of Kansas,* vol. 2, pp. 16, 149.

19. Ibid., pp. 16, 149–54, 187–92, 235.

20. Wichita *Eagle,* January 27, 1915; Emporia *Gazette,* January 21, 1915; Dan D. Casement, "Farm Production of Beef," *Twenty-First Rept., KSBA* (1917–1918), p. 168; *KS,* January 1, 1920, p. 12.

21. Emporia *Gazette,* January 2, 1902. The National Forest land in Kansas was restored to homestead entry in 1915, and 75,000 acres were soon taken by farmers and stockmen during their rush to put land into crop and livestock production during the war.

22. Malin, "The Bluestem-Pasture Region," 8, 21; Dale, *The Range Cattle Industry,* pp. 156–57.

23. Emporia *Gazette,* April 22, July 29, 1915.
24. *KS,* February 1, 1923, p. 16; May 1, 1923, p. 5; March 15, 1925, p. 5; March 1, 1935, p. 11; April 15, 1938, p. 4; January 1, 1942, p. 4; November, 1958, p. 6. Kansas City (Mo.) *Star,* October 5, 1958. *Annals of Kansas,* vol. 1, p. 142. Interview, Evaline Conway, Paola, Kans., August 3, 1977.
25. *Kansas Cattleman,* April 5, 1918, p. 4.
26. *KS,* March 1, 1929, p. 18.
27. Ibid., April 1, 1919, p. 7; Emporia *Gazette,* April 22 and July 29, 1915.
28. Malin, "The Blue-Stem Pasture Region," 23–24.

CHAPTER 5

1. *American Hereford Journal,* July 1, 1920, p. 7; June 1, 1935, p. 9. James C. Malin, *The Grassland of North America* (1947; reprint ed., Gloucester: Peter Smith Reprint, 1967), p. 275.
2. *American Hereford Journal,* October 1, 1932, p. 6.
3. Ibid., November 15, 1921, p. 9; December 1, 1922, p. 58; December 1, 1923, p. 28; December 1, 1924, p. 16B; December 1, 1925, p. 13; December 1, 1928, p. 14; November 1, 1936, p. 14.
4. *Kansas Stockman,* March, 1954, p. 76.
5. Dan D. Casement, "Farm Production of Beef," *Twenty-First Rept., KSBA* (1917–1918), pp. 163–67. *Kansas Cattleman,* November 1, p. 21; December 1, 1916, p. 22. *KS,* March, 1954, p. 76.
6. Ornduff, *The Hereford in America,* pp. 268, 291–92; *KS,* July 1, 1920, p. 16.
7. *American Hereford Journal,* February 1, 1921, pp. 84–85.
8. *KS,* November 1, 1925, pp. 30–33; *Thirty-First Rept., KSBA* (1937–1938), pp. 90–91; F. W. Farley (comp.), *Hazford Place: Modern Herefords,* pamphlet (Kansas City, 1935), p. 3; Ornduff, *The Hereford in America,* pp. 268–69, 293, 295.
9. Ibid., pp. 268, 291–92. *KS,* July 1, 1920, p. 16; July 1, 1922, p. 15. Cattle Industry Clippings 1: 223–26. *Twenty-Eighth Rept., KSBA* (1931–1932), pp. 17–36. *American Hereford Journal,* July 15, 1927, pp. 6–7.
10. *KS,* December 2, 1918, p. 7; Ornduff, *The Hereford in America,* p. 294; *American Hereford Journal,* December 1, 1918, pp. 76–77.
11. Ibid., July 1, 1929, pp. 68–69; July 1, 1945, pp. 216, 240.
12. *KS,* March 15, 1937, p. 2; May 1, 1937, p. 3; July 1, 1937, p. 14; November 1, 1937, p. 13; February 1, 1940, p. 2; December 15, 1940, p. 7. *American Hereford Journal,* January 15, 1937, p. 5; July 15, 1937, pp. 4–8.
13. Ibid., June 15, 1943, pp. 117–19; Edward N. Wentworth, "A Livestock Specialist Looks at Agricultural History," *Agricultural History* 25 (April, 1951): 50; Ornduff, *The Hereford in America,* p. 487.
14. Cattle Industry Clippings 4: 138, 141–42. *American Hereford Journal,* August 1, 1935, p. 4; December 1, 1938, p. 3; June 1, 1940, pp. 20–21.

15. Interview, Clair Parcel, Coldwater, Kans., July 14, 1977.

16. *KS,* September 15, 1920, p. 10; November 1, 1920, p. 10; August 15, 1921, p. 6; May 1, 1926, p. 4; September 15, 1926, p. 7. Cattle Industry Clippings 1: 173–75. *The Cattleman,* August, 1972, pp. 51–52. Interview, Bess Mercer Conley, Delia, Kans., February 9, 1973.

17. *American Hereford Journal,* June 15, 1926, p. 9; November 1, 1926, p. 16.

18. Ibid., June 15, 1921, p. 7; October 15, 1923, p. 15; October 1, 1924, p. 17; July 1, 1937, p. 8. Interview, James O. Greenleaf, Greensburg, Kans., May 15, 1977. Kansas State Livestock Association Clippings 1: 28–29, in KSHS.

19. Kansas City (Mo.) *Star,* March 9, 1952; Kansas City (Mo.) *Times,* June 26, 1962. B. B. Foster to Innis R. Palmer, May 25, 1940, and Foster to Employees, June, 1941, copies in Thomas County Historical Society, Colby, Kans.

20. Interview, E. D. "Dale" Mustoe, Jr., Rexford, Kans., July 13, 1977. Almeda Dible, *Foster Farms, 1912–1954* (1954), pp. 5–15, pamphlet in Thomas County Historical Society.

21. Ibid., pp. 5–20. Interviews, E. D. "Dale" Mustoe, Jr., Rexford, Kans., and Gary Cooper, Colby, Kans., July 13, 1977. *American Hereford Journal,* September 15, 1920, p. 94; December 1, 1921, pp. 22–23; August 1, 1927, p. 6; June 15, 1928, p. 22; July 1, 1931, pp. 54–55; May 15, 1934, p. 6; October 15, 1934, pp. 18–20. Cattle Industry Clippings 4: 94–95.

22. *American Hereford Journal,* October 1, 1944, p. 70.

23. Ibid. Interviews, Claire Parcel, Coldwater, Kans., July 14, 1977, and Walter M. Lewis, Larned, Kans., July 15, 1977.

24. Ibid. *KS,* June, 1953, pp. 35–37. *American Hereford Journal,* March 1, 1921, pp. 58–59; January 1, 1922, pp. 68–69; February 15, 1923, p. 32. Stock Breeders Associations Clippings, pp. 100–101. Cattle Industry Clippings 4: 63.

25. Wichita *Eagle,* July 11, 1968; *American Hereford Journal,* January 1, 1945, p. 163.

26. Ibid., March 1, 1937, p. 3; April 15, 1938, p. 49; August 1, 1939, pp. 6–7; January 1, 1943, p. 66. *KS,* March, 1950, pp. 95–96; November, 1957, p. 32; September, 1971, p. 18. Ornduff, *The Hereford in America,* p. 486.

27. Ibid., pp. 480–81.

28. Interview, Muriel Gregg, Coldwater, Kans., May 15, 1977.

29. Interview, Clair Parcel, Coldwater, Kans., July 14, 1977.

30. Interview, James G. Tomson, Jr., Wakarusa, Kans., July 23, 1977.

31. *KS,* September, 1953, pp. 22–23; Cattle Industry Clippings 4: 53; American Angus Association, *A History of the Angus Breed,* pamphlet, 1973, n.p.; interview, A. G. Pickett, Emporia, Kans., August 2, 1977.

CHAPTER 6

1. *KS,* July 1, 1926, p. 4; April 15, 1928, p. 14; June 15, 1934, p. 4; November 1, 1935, p. 4; May 15, 1937, pp. 1–6. Miscellaneous letters in Livestock Sanitary

Commissioner Files, KSHS. Stubbs Clippings, Vertical File, KSHS. Miscellaneous newspaper clippings in the possession of Bess Mercer Conley, Delia, Kans. Interviews with Mary Atchison, Topeka, Kans., February 24, 1973, and Bess Mercer Conley, February 9, 1973.

2. Ibid. Mercer Clippings, Vertical File, KSHS. Mercer, "How Farmers' Condition May Be Improved," an address given May 21, 1927, copy in KLA Files. *KS,* June 15, 1932, p. 5; December 1, 1923, p. 10; December 15, 1924, pp. 5–14; November 1, 1936, p. 6; May 15, 1937, p. 5.

3. This dispute between cattlemen, railroads, and the Kansas City stockyards centered around the building of a branch rail line to connect unloading facilities with the main part of the stockyards. It will be discussed in more detail in a subsequent chapter.

4. Topeka *Daily Capital,* December 7, 10, and 11, 1913; Topeka *State Journal,* December 10 and 11, 1913. *First Annual Report of the Kansas State Live Stock Association* (1916), pp. 9–15, 42–44; *KS,* March 1, 1932, pp. 8–9. The annual report noted above was apparently the only one ever issued by KLA.

5. James C. Carey, "Dan D. Casement: Viking on a Sea of Grass," *The Trail Guide* 4 (December, 1959): 4–5.

6. *KS,* July 15, 1927, p. 4; March 1, 1929, p. 18. *American Hereford Journal,* March 15, 1945, pp. 12–13. Interview, Raymond E. Adams, Jr., Maple Hill, Kans., July 21, 1977.

7. *Kansas Cattleman,* January 1, 1917, p. 1; April 1, 1917, p. 11. "The Kansas Livestock Association," n.n., n.d., pp. 3–6, in KLA Files.

8. *Kansas Cattleman,* March 5, 1918, p. 4. *KS,* March 1, 1919, p. 4; March 1, 1920, p. 7.

9. Ibid., June 20, 1918, p. 1; December 16, 1918, p. 3.

10. Ibid., May, 1958, pp. 9–10.

11. *Kansas Farmer,* February 21, 1894, p. 4; April 4, 1894, p. 8; March 13, 1895, p. 162; October 23, 1895, p. 675; February 6, 1896, p. 83; February 27, 1896, p. 131. Emporia *Gazette,* March 21 and August 8, 1895; May 19, 1898.

12. *Kansas Farmer,* April 11, 1894, p. 3. Emporia *Gazette,* August 13, 1914. *Kansas Cattleman,* January 1, 1917, p. 8; February 20, 1918, p. 9. F. S. Schoenleber, "Kansas Blackleg Serum," *Twentieth Rept., KSBA* (1915–1916), 259–62. *KS,* March, 1945, p. 107. C. D. Stein, "Blackleg," *Animal Diseases,* USDA Yearbook (1956), pp. 263–65. Kansas State College Clippings 2: 80. Charles R. Kock, "Man Who Licked Blackleg," *K Stater* 15 (October, 1965): 12–14.

13. Ibid.

14. Miscellaneous newspaper clippings in the possession of Bess Mercer Conley, Delia, Kans.

15. *Kansas Cattleman,* February 1, 1917, pp. 8–13. Topeka *Daily Capital,* November 6, 7, 9, and 10, 1914. Schlebecker, *Cattle Raising on the Plains,* 49–50.

16. Ibid. Topeka *Daily Capital,* February 2, 3, 4, 21, 23, and 26, 1914; January 26, 1916. Emporia *Gazette,* February 4, 1915. *First Annual Report of the Kansas State Livestock Association* (1916), pp. 69, 79–84.

17. Topeka *Daily Capital,* November 26 and 28, 1916; December 1 and 2, 1916. *Kansas Cattleman,* January 1, 1917, p. 3.

18. *KS,* May, 1958, pp. 10–11. Mercer to Governor Hodges, September 24, 1914; Hodges to Mercer, September 28, 1914, in Hodges Papers, KSHS.

19. *KS,* October 1, 1924, p. 3; October 15, 1924, p. 5; August 15, 1925, p. 4. *Cattle Raising on the Plains,* pp. 88–89, 108–109.

20. *KS,* April 1, 1919, p. 11.

21. Lewis Nordyke, *Great Round-up: The Story of Texas and Southwestern Cowmen* (New York: William Morrow, 1955), pp. 216–17.

22. *KS,* June 15, 1920, p. 6; August 16, 1920, p. 6; March 1, 1921, p. 7; June 15, 1922, p. 7; February 1, 1923, p. 6; April 15, 1923, pp. 3–5; March 15, 1925, p. 9; July 15, 1925, p. 4; March 1, 1926, pp. 6, 16; April 1, 1926, p. 4; May 15, 1926, pp. 5–6. Interview, Bess Mercer Conley, Delia, Kans., February 9, 1973.

23. *KS,* August 1, 1939, p. 6. Irwin H. Roberts, "Cattle Scabies," *Animal Diseases,* USDA Yearbook (1956), pp. 293–98.

24. *KS,* May 1, 1935, p. 5; *Twenty-Sixth Rept., KSBA* (1927–1928), pp. 138–43; Howard W. Johnson and Albert F. Ranney, "Tuberculosis and Its Eradication," *Animal Diseases,* USDA Yearbook (1956), pp. 213–18.

25. C. A. Manthei et al., "Brucellosis," Ibid., pp. 202–209; Schlebecker, *Cattle Raising on the Plains,* pp. 109, 124–25, 134–35, 164–65, 181, 216.

26. *KS,* February 15, 1931, p. 4; August 1, 1939, pp. 6, 14.

CHAPTER 7

1. Zornow, *Kansas: A History of the Jayhawk State,* pp. 209–24; Robert W. Richmond, *Kansas: A Land of Contrasts* (St. Charles, Mo.: Forum Press, 1974), pp. 189–194. An excellent account of the progressive dimension of Kansas politics during the early twentieth century is the work of Robert S. LaForte, "The Republican Party of Kansas during the Progressive Era, 1900–1916," 2 vols. (Ph.D. diss., University of Kansas, 1965). LaForte describes several of the pressure groups advocating lower freight rates and reform of the state's railroad legislation, but does little with cattlemen as a separate group. He does show, however, that other groups, such as wheat farmers, complained more bitterly about freight rates than did stockmen. The Kansas Federation of Commercial Interests, as LaForte shows, was very active in supporting antirailway legislation, but there was nothing to indicate that the state's cattlemen or KLA took an active role in this organization. For material relating to railways, see especially vol. 1, pp. 169–203, 307–361.

2. Stubbs Clippings, Verticle File; Kansas Biographical Scrapbook 158: 1–10, 19–22, 38, 52, 62, both in KSHS. Emporia *Gazette,* December 2, 1915; Topeka *Daily Capital,* January 26, 1916; *Kansas Cattleman,* January 20, 1918.

3. One of the best sources for information—and colorful language—concerning the relationship of railroads to politics was the Emporia *Gazette;* see especially the

issues for July 2 and 16, 1903; December 3, 1903; March 17 and April 21, 1904; November 30, 1905; March 23, April 19, and August 2 and 16, 1906.

4. Ibid., November 17, 1904; September 27 and November 1, 1906.

5. *Seventeenth Annual Rept Bd RR Com* (1902), pp. 237–46.

6. Stene, *Railroad Commission to Corporation Commission,* pp. 38–39. Emporia *Gazette,* December 8, 1904; March 2, 9, and 23, 1905.

7. Ibid., February 7 and 21, 1907; June 13 and 27, 1907; November 14, 1912.

8. Ibid., June 30, 1908.

9. Letter from C. A. Stannard, ibid., July 28, 1910; letters from D. W. Blaine, Walter W. Underwood, and John S. Dawson, in Stubbs Papers, 1909–1913, KSHS.

10. John F. Stover, *The Life and Decline of the American Railroad* (New York: Oxford University Press, 1970), pp. 116–18.

11. Ibid.; Kolko, *Railroads and Regulation,* p. 218; *Forty-Sixth Annual Report of the Atchison, Topeka and Santa Fe Railway Company* (1940), 27.

12. Stene, *Railroad Commission to Corporation Commission,* pp. 65, 101; "Governor's Statement," in Stubbs Papers.

13. Emporia *Gazette,* February 14, 1901; Topeka *Daily Capital,* August 25 and 26, 1903; *Eighteenth Biennial Rept Bd RR Com* (1903–1904), pp. 92–93.

14. Topeka *Daily Capital,* September 2, 3, and 4, 1903; Emporia *Gazette,* October 25, 1906.

15. *Nineteenth Biennial Rept Bd RR Com* (1905–1906), pp. 82–83, 90–129.

16. Topeka *Daily Capital,* September 2, 3, and 4, 1903; *Fourteenth Rept., KSBA* (1903–1904), p. 518; Emporia *Gazette,* September 10, 1930.

17. *Eighteenth Annual Rept Bd RR Com* (1903–1904), pp. 92–93; *First Annual Report of the Kansas State Live Stock Association* (1916), pp. 9–13.

18. Kolko, *Railroads and Regulation,* pp. 129–51; Nordyke, *The Great Round-up,* pp. 220–25; Ripley, *Railroads: Rates and Regulation,* pp. 499–510; *KS,* June 1, 1924, p. 5; James A. Wilson, "Southwest Cattlemen and Railroad Regulation," *Rocky Mountain Social Science Journal* 7 (April, 1970): 96.

19. Emporia *Gazette,* January 25, 1906; September 22, 1910. Topeka *Daily Capital,* September 23, 1910.

20. Ripley, *Railroads,* pp. 412–28; Stover, *American Railroads,* pp. 182–88; Stover, *The Life and Decline of the American Railroad,* pp. 117–19, 173–76.

21. Ibid.; *Third Biennial Report of the Kansas Public Utilities Commission* (1914–1916), p. 27.

22. Emporia *Gazette,* September 24 and November 26, 1903; Burmeister, "Six Decades of Rugged Individualism," p. 146.

23. Exhibit C-1, Ex Parte No. 123, 1938, pp. 41–45. This is a sixty-page statistical compilation prepared for KLA and the Kansas Corporation Commission by Byron M. Gray for presentation at a rate hearing before the ICC. It gives a statistical history of livestock freight rates in Kansas, along with other data, for the period 1911 to 1938. A copy from ICC is in the possession of the author. Hereafter cited as Exhibit C-1.

24. Stover, *American Railroads,* pp. 182–85; Exhibit C-1, p. 21; *Forty-Sixth*

Annual Report of the Atchison, Topeka and Santa Fe Railway Company (1940), p. 27.

25. *First Annual Report of the Kansas State Live Stock Association* (1916), pp. 25, 82, 132–36; *Kansas Cattleman,* June 5, 1917, p. 3.

26. *First Annual Report of the Kansas State Live Stock Association* (1916), pp. 70, 82, 127–30.

27. Ibid., p. 70; H. O. Caster (comp.), *Kansas Railroads and Public Utilities Commission,* pamphlet (Topeka, 1915), pp. 55–60; Wichita *Eagle,* February 9, 1916; *Kansas Cattleman,* January 1, 1917, p. 9.

28. Ibid., March 1, 1917, p. 6; March 5, 1918, p. 4. Joseph H. Mercer, "How Farmers' Condition May Be Improved," typescript of an address delivered May 21, 1927, in Livestock Sanitary Commissioner Miscellaneous File, KSHS.

29. Kolko, *Railroads and Regulation,* pp. 228–30; Stover, *American Railroads,* pp. 188–93; *Fourth* and *Sixth Biennial Reports of the Public Utilities Commission* (1916–1918), p. 5, (1920–1922), p. 4; *First Annual Report of the Court of Industrial Relations* (1919), p. 12; Exhibit C-1, pp. 41–45. *KS,* June 5, 1918, pp. 3–5; February 1, 1919, p. 33. Walter R. Stubbs, "Public Ownership of Railroads, Waterways and Water Power," *Saturday Evening Post,* June 6, 1914, pp. 3–5, 28–33. Emporia *Gazette,* June 18, 1914. Helpful in understanding the pressure groups that were involved in railroad disputes during the war, as well as the decision of the government to take over the roads, is K. Austin Kerr, *American Railroad Politics, 1914–1920: Rates, Wages, and Efficiency* (Pittsburgh: University of Pittsburgh Press, 1968). Kerr shows that western and southern agricultural shippers were more adamant in opposing rate increases than were any other shippers, and also that they strongly supported government takeover. Shippers of agricultural goods hoped, according to Kerr, to use federal control as a tool for widening their influence over the rate-making process. See especially pp. 101–27.

CHAPTER 8

1. Kansas City Stockyards Company, *75 Years of the Kansas City Livestock Market History,* pp. 11–12; Eva L. Atkinson, "Kansas City's Livestock Trade and Packing Industry," p. 329.

2. *Hereford Swine Journal* (May–June, 1943), p. 13. Emporia *Gazette,* February 4 and 18, March 18, April 8, and August 26, 1897; October 20, 1898.

3. John A. Edwards, *Report of Live Stock Investigation Committee to the Legislature of Kansas,* pamphlet (1907), pp. 1–8, in KSHS; Emporia *Gazette,* February 7, 1907.

4. State of Kansas, *Session Laws* (1907), p. 639; *General Statutes of Kansas Annotated,* vol. 2 (1909), pp. 1, 971; *Revised Statutes of Kansas Annotated* (1923), p. 812; Will K. Reeme to Kansas and Missouri legislators, January 18, 1909, in KSHS.

5. *FTC Rept.,* part 1, pp. 132–33.

6. Ibid., part 3, pp. 51–61, 80–88, 104.

7. Ibid., part 1, pp. 292–93; part 3, pp. 42–43.

8. Ibid., part 1, pp. 284–85, 292–93; part 3, pp. 43–44, 48–49; *75 Years of the Kansas City Livestock Market History*, p. 13.

9. Topeka *Daily Capital*, December 15 and 19, 1913; *Second Biennial Report of the Kansas Public Utilities Commission* (1912–1914), pp. 9–14; *First Annual Report of the Kansas State Live Stock Association* (1916), pp. 26–30, 42, 56–57, 89–92, 94–102, 104; *75 Years of the Kansas City Livestock Market History*, p. 13; *Forty-Ninth Annual Report of the Kansas City Stock Yards* (1919), pp. 6–9.

10. *FTC Rept.*, part 1, p. 46; Clemen, *Livestock and Meat Industry*, pp. 749–52; Harper Leech and John C. Carroll, *Armour and His Times* (New York: D. Appleton-Century Co., 1938), pp. 192–96.

11. *FTC Rept.*, part 1, pp. 46–47, 49.

12. Ibid., pp. 47–53; Clemen, *Livestock and Meat Industry*, pp. 751–55.

13. Topeka *Daily Capital*, January 12, 1904; Emporia *Gazette*, November 26, 1903; September 1, 1904; *Clark County Clipper*, February 16, 1905.

14. James R. Garfield, *Report of the Commissioner of Corporations on the Beef Industry* (1905), pp. xix–xxxv; Clemen, *Livestock and Meat Industry*, pp. 756–60, quoting Francis Walker, "The Beef Trust and the United States Government," *The Economic Journal* (London), December, 1906; Kansas City *Star*, March 5, 1905, in Cattle Industry Clippings 1: 87, 87a, 88, KSHS.

15. *Clark County Clipper*, March 23, 1905; Cattle Industry Clippings 1: 88a–92, KSHS.

16. Saloutos and Hicks, *Agricultural Discontent*, pp. 112–13, 118, 131–32, 145–56, 177, 189, 196, 199–205, 214–25, 238–44.

17. Wichita *Eagle*, February 6, 8, 9, 10, 11, 1916, is the best source for material on the 1916 KLA convention. Also used for this period were the Topeka *Daily Capital*, October 25, 1931; Clemen, *Livestock and Meat Industry*, pp. 769–73. An important sidelight for KLA financial solvency developed from the "war fund" when stockmen agreed to voluntarily tax themselves 5 cents a head on cattle and 2.5 cents on sheep and hogs for the continuance of KLA activities in this area. This tax, according to Mercer, solved the association's financial difficulties for the first time in its history.

18. Ibid. *Kansas Cattleman*, January 1, 1917, p. 4; March 1, 1917, pp. 3, 10; June 20, 1917, p. 3. Tom G. Hall, "Wilson and the Food Crisis: Agricultural Price Control during World War I," *Agricultural History* 47 (January, 1973): 25, 33–36.

19. *FTC Rept.*, part 1, pp. 23–30.

20. For support of the *FTC Report*, see Schlebecker, *Cattle Raising on the Plains*, pp. 76–77; Corey, *Meat and Man*, pp. 75–81. Also see Clemen, *Livestock and Meat Industry*, pp. 16–17, 768–72.

21. *FTC Rept.*, part 1, pp. 24, 33; *KS*, September 5, 1918, pp. 3–4.

22. Ibid.; *FTC Rept.*, part 1, pp. 31, 35–37.

23. Ibid., pp. 38–40; Corey, *Meat and Man*, pp. 78–79.

24. *FTC Rept.*, part 1, pp. 68–72.

25. *Kansas Cattleman,* September 20, 1917, p. 3. *KS,* September 20, 1918, p. 3; August 1, 1921, p. 4.

26. Ibid., August 1, 1919, p. 3: *FTC Rept.,* part 1, 68–70.

27. For examples, see *Kansas Cattleman,* November 5, 1917, p. 6; May 5, 1918, p. 8. *KS,* September 5, 1918, p. 8; August 15, 1919, p. 3.

28. In December, 1917, Joseph P. Cotton, head of the meat division of the Food Administration, had announced that the Big Five were limited to a profit of 2.5 percent on sales of meat, 15 percent on by-products, and a total yearly profit of 9 percent on the average amount of capital used in their businesses.

29. *FTC Rept.,* part 1, pp. 72–73; part 5, pp. 9–11. *Kansas Cattleman,* September 20, 1917, p. 3.

30. *FTC Rept.,* part 5, pp. 12–13.

31. Ibid., part 1, pp. 294–318; part 3, pp. 61–64, 177–78.

32. Ibid., 14–16.

33. *Kansas Cattleman,* April 1, 1917, pp. 6–7; February 5, 1918, p. 4. *KS,* September 5, 1918, pp. 3–4. Corey, *Meat and Man,* p. 76.

34. Ibid., pp. 84–87; *FTC Rept.,* part 1, pp. 76–78; *Kansas Cattleman,* April 1, 1917, pp. 3, 11.

35. *KS,* February 1, 1919, p. 24; *Kansas Cattleman,* February 20, 1918, pp. 6–7.

CHAPTER 9

1. *KS,* January 1, 1920, pp. 9–10; February 1, 1922, p. 6; February 1, 1923, pp. 3, 6.

2. A. B. Genung, *The Agricultural Depression following World War I and Its Political Consequences* (Ithaca: Northeast Farm Foundation, 1954), p. 66; *KS,* March 15, 1937, p. 4; *Thirty-Eighth Rept., KSBA* (1951–1952), p. 407. The KSBA did not begin recording cash receipts figures until 1924, thus the comparison is somewhat misleading, as the lower incomes during the 1920s would have occurred before 1924. The figures are, however, a good indication of the Kansas farm situation during the 1930s when the lowest incomes—$179.2 and $189.9 million—were recorded in 1932 and 1933, respectively. The 1933 figures, and all those subsequent, include government payments.

3. Ibid., p. 409. James C. Malin has made a detailed study of dust storms. For a summary of his findings, see *The Grasslands of North America,* pp. 134–48.

4. *KS,* March 15, 1933, pp. 4, 6; August 15, 1934, p. 11; March 15, 1937, p. 4; March 15, 1938, p. 5. J. W. Lindsey to Arthur Capper, May 31, 1937, Capper Papers, Box 12:32. Government purchases of cattle will be discussed in a subsequent chapter.

5. *KS,* September 1, 1934, p. 4; November 15, 1934, p. 3; March 15, 1935, p. 4; September 1, 1936, p. 3. Interview, Raymond E. Adams, Jr., Maple Hill, Kans., July 21, 1977.

6. Interview, James O. Greenleaf, Greensburg, Kans., May 15, 1977.

7. White, "The Farmer and His Plight," reprinted in *KS,* July 15, 1929, p. 3.

8. Saloutos and Hicks, *Agricultural Discontent,* pp. 103–107. The export market was also affected by tariff policy—to be discussed later—and by this country's inability to adjust the war debt situation. Some American specialty crops continued to find markets abroad, but there was little improvement for the more important crops such as wheat, cotton, and meat. The export of crude foodstuffs amounted to $673 million in 1921, $257 million in 1923, and $421 million in 1927, the high mark of the decade except for 1921. Murray R. Benedict, *Farm Policies of the United States, 1790–1950: A Study of Their Origins and Development* (New York: Twentieth Century Fund, 1953), p. 234.

9. *Kansas Cattleman,* September 5, 1917, p. 6; October 20, 1917, p. 3. *KS,* June 1, 1919, p. 3; December 1, 1921, p. 8; January 1, 1923, p. 11; January 15, 1926, p. 14; March, 1954, pp. 74–76. Cattle Industry Clippings 2: 156–57.

10. Schlebecker, *Cattle Raising on the Plains,* pp. 59, 72, 90, 104, 119, 134, 139, 145, 152.

11. *Fifty-Fourth Rept., KSBA* (1970–1971), p. 206.

12. Clay, *My Life on the Range,* pp. 347–48; Genung, *Agricultural Depression,* pp. 14–15; Saloutos and Hicks, *Agricultural Discontent,* pp. 101–103.

13. Ibid., pp. 93–100; Gardner P. Walker in *The Cattleman,* November, 1933, p. 25; Benedict, *Farm Policies of the United States,* p. 231. Saloutos credits the New Deal innovations in agricultural credit with impeding moves toward stability. These measures were, he said, "of material assistance to the larger farmers and ranchers, but they delayed the elimination of small, inefficient farms which lacked capital, managerial talent, and equipment." See "The New Deal and Farm Policy in the Great Plains," *Agricultural History* 43 (July, 1969): 255. It should also be noted that Saloutos, Hicks, and Benedict occasionally cite indexes that revealed even sharper declines in market prices of agricultural products than were used in this study.

14. Genung, *The Agricultural Depression,* pp. 14–15; Francis W. Schruben, *Kansas in Turmoil, 1930–1936* (Columbia: University of Missouri Press, 1969), pp. 3, 50–51; Benedict, *Farm Policies of the United States,* pp. 247, 260; H. C. M. Case, "Farm Debt Adjustment during the Early 1930s," *Agricultural History* 34 (October, 1960): 173–76; *KS,* March 15, 1934, p. 5; Roy S. Johnson to Arthur Capper, September 20, 1938, in Capper Papers, Box 12:32.

15. Anderson, *A Quarter Inch of Rain,* p. 134; Schlebecker, *Cattle Raising on the Plains,* pp. 74, 89, 104, 119, 135–39; E. W. Sheets et al., *Our Beef Supply,* USDA Yearbook, 1921, p. 304; Ronald E. Johnson, *Prices Received by Farmers for Beef Cattle: United States, by States, Monthly and Annual Average, 1909–1959,* USDA Statistical Bulletin 265 (1960), pp. 4, 25; *Livestock and Meat Statistics, 1957,* USDA Statistical Bulletin 230 (1958), p. 208.

16. *Kansas Farmer Mail and Breeze,* May 7, 1921, p. 3; Sheets, "Our Beef Supply," 275; *KS,* March 15, 1935, p. 5.

17. Benedict, *Farm Policies of the United States,* pp. 277, 314; *KS,* May 15, 1931, p. 6.

18. Ibid., August 1, 1919, p. 9; Wallace County Clippings 1: 7–11, 51–60, 113, 2: 12–14.

19. *KS,* February 1, 1923, p. 16; May 1, 1923, p. 5; November, 1958, p. 6. Interview, Evaline Conway, Paola, Kans., August 3, 1977.

20. *Kansas Cattleman,* January 20, 1918, p. 6; *KS,* September 1, 1925, p. 4; Emporia *Gazette,* December 2, 1915; Stubbs Clippings, in Vertical File, KSHS; interview, O. C. Hicks, Garden City, Kans., July 12, 1977.

21. "The Farmer and His Plight," New York *Times,* reprinted in *KS,* July 15, 1929, p. 15.

22. R. H. Wilcox et al., *Factors in the Cost of Producing Beef in the Flint Hills Section of Kansas,* USDA Bulletin 1454 (1926), p. 25. Kansas production costs compared favorably with those of the two other beef-producing states that were studied. Annual carrying costs for selected areas in Texas and Colorado averaged less for cows—at $24 per head—yet the expenses for a weaned calf amounted to over $39. Of prime importance in determining profits for this type of operation was the fact that the ranches in Texas and Colorado were reported to average about a 60 percent calf crop, while those in the Flint Hills had 83 percent.

23. Malin, "The Bluestem-Pasture Region," 21. *KS,* February 15, 1919, p. 3; April 15, 1930, p. 4; May 1, 1931, p. 2; April 1, 1933, p. 4; April 1, 1934, p. 4; May 15, 1935, p. 5; March 15, 1938, p. 5; April 15, 1939, p. 9.

24. USDA Bulletin 1454, p. 16. Joseph H. Mercer, "Tariff on Livestock and Meats," typescript of testimony before House Ways and Means Committee, May 16, 1928, p. 4, in Livestock Sanitary Commissioner Miscellaneous File, KSHS.

25. Ibid., p. 1. *KS,* April 15, 1927, p. 4; June 1, 1929, p. 4; April 15, 1931, p. 13; June 15, 1931, p. 2; July 1, 1933, p. 6; July 1, 1939, p. 13. *The Cattleman,* February, 1920, p. 5; January, 1938, pp. 17–18.

26. Saloutos and Hicks, *Agricultural Discontent,* pp. 106–107, 376. Schruben, *Kansas in Turmoil,* pp. 4, 51, 64–65, 105–106, 155–60. Niles A. Olsen et al., *Farm Credit, Farm Insurance and Farm Taxation,* USDA Yearbook (1924), pp. 357–62. Mechem (comp.), *The Annals of Kansas,* vol. 2, pp. 248, 407. *Kansas Statistical Base Book* (Lawrence, 1954), p. 17. *KS,* January 15, 1924, p. 11; April 1, 1927, p. 8; April 15, 1932, pp. 5–7; June 1, 1932, pp. 6–7; April 1, 1933, p. 7; March 15, 1935, p. 5; March 15, 1937, p. 3.

27. Ibid., March 15, 1930, p. 10; *Kansas Cattleman,* March 20, 1918, p. 3; *The Cattleman,* March, 1930, pp. 10–13.

28. *KS,* March 1, 1919, pp. 8–10; June 1, 1937, pp. 6–7; July, 1944, p. 5; December, 1952, p. 3. C. W. McCampbell to Will J. Miller, November 8, 1938, in KLA Rate File. C. M. Correll, "K-State Nears Century Mark," *Forty-Fourth Rept., KSBA,* Centennial Edition (1960–1961), p. 137.

29. Cattle Industry Clippings 2: 115, 5: 7–9. *KS,* February 15, 1933, p. 4; March 1, 1933, p. 17; October 1, 1940, p. 35; March, 1944, pp. 30–31; October, 1960, pp. 10–12. Interview, Raymond E. Adams, Jr., Maple Hill, Kans., July 21, 1977.

30. *KS,* February 15, 1922, p. 7.

31. Ibid., May 1, 1923, p. 4; November 1, 1931, p. 46. James Tod, "Wintering the Young Steer," *Twenty-Second Rept., KSBA* (1919–1920), pp. 72–75.

32. Maurice Frink, *Cow Country Cavalcade* (Denver: Old West Publishing Co., 1954), pp. 155–56; Goff and McCaffree, *Century in the Saddle,* pp. 255–70; Bob Lee and Dick Williams, *Last Grass Frontier* (Sturgis: Black Hills Publishers, 1964), pp. 225, 266–70; Nellie Snyder Yost, *The Call of the Range* (Denver: Sage Books, 1966), pp. 238–46. *The Cattleman,* April, 1921, p. 74; September, 1926, p. 11; April, 1927, p. 19; April, 1930, p. 18. *KS,* May 15, 1933, p. 4; October 15, 1933, p. 4; November 1, 1933, p. 19; March 1, 1934, p. 6; June 1, 1934, p. 6; January 15, 1937, p. 5.

33. Ibid., January, 1920, p. 9; March 1, 1920, p. 7; March 1, 1921, p. 14; November 1, 1921, p. 7; September 15, 1929, p. 5; October 15, 1933, p. 13. *The Cattleman,* April, 1921, p. 74; April, 1927, p. 19; April, 1930, p. 18. In 1930, while KLA claimed 12,000 members, the Texas association reported 3,422, after dropping to a low of 2,605 in 1927.

34. *KS,* February 15, 1939, p. 10. The May 15, 1937, issue of the *Stockman,* the journal Mercer had done so much to nurture, announced the inevitable. "This edition of the *Kansas Stockman,*" it said, "is dedicated to the memory of Joseph H. Mercer, whose invaluable service to Kansas and the Southwest is now a matter of History." Mercer had died on May 5, from complications after surgery. This issue of the *Stockman* was filled with short letters from stock raisers all across the state and much of the Southwest commending Mercer's work, and the wide area from which the letters came was an indication of his influence.

35. Ibid., March 1, 1930, p. 6; August 1, 1935, p. 5; June 1, 1937, pp. 3–4; May 1, 1938, p. 5; June 1, 1938, p. 4; April, 1959, p. 4. Emporia *Gazette,* September 22, 1910. Agriculture in Kansas Clippings, pp. 165–66, in KSHS; Kansas Biographical Scrapbook 110: 212–221.

36. Rustling cattle is also encouraged by unusually high market prices for stock, which, apparently, makes the risk worthwhile. This particular stimulus, however, did not operate during the interwar period.

37. *KS,* August 2, 1920, p. 7; August 16, 1920, p. 8; February 1, 1923, p. 6; June 15, 1926, p. 4; October 1, 1930, p. 4; March 1, 1936, p. 53; May 1, 1936, p. 4; June 1, 1936, p. 4; January 15, 1938, p. 4; February 15, 1938, p. 6; March 15, 1938, p. 6; April 1, 1938, p. 15; December 15, 1938, p. 5; March 15, 1939, pp. 3–4; July 15, 1940, p. 5; August, 1947, p. 12. Cattle Industry Clippings 2: 37, 262, 279, 3: 183–85.

38. *KS,* March 1, 1920, p. 13; March 15, 1933, p. 3.

39. Ibid., March 1, 1919, p. 40; April 15, 1919, pp. 8–9, 12; May 1, 1919, pp. 3, 6, 14; June 1, 1919, p. 7; July 15, 1919, p. 3; January 1, 1920, p. 18; February 1, 1920, p. 7; June 1, 1922, p. 4; March 15, 1928, p. 7; July 1, 1931, p. 4; March 15, 1936, p. 7; October, 1955, p. 8; September, 1972, pp. 33–40. *The Cattleman,* April, 1921, p. 5; June, 1927, pp. 17–19. Interview, A. G. Pickett, Emporia, Kans., August 2, 1977.

40. Interview, Evan Koger, Belvidere, Kans., July 15, 1977. *KS,* May 15, 1935, p. 5; June 1, 1939, p. 8. Cattle Industry Clippings, 3: 19. Koger was a

superior source of information. His excellent memory and superb sense of the family's history were invaluable. While he may not admit it, his fine liberal education at Yale no doubt contributed greatly to his awareness of ranching history.

41. The Board of Agriculture began publishing cash receipt figures in 1925. While the cash receipt figures tend to show a pattern different from the farm value figures that were used earlier, cash receipt figures are used here because they are a better indication of the relative importance of the various sectors of Kansas agriculture.

42. *Fiftieth and Fifty-Fifth Repts., KSBA* (1966–1967), p. 87F; (1971–1972), p. 85F.

43. *KS,* March 1, 1920, p. 19; May 1, 1926, p. 3. *Fifty-Fourth Rept., KSBA* (1970–1971), pp. 207, 210.

44. Ibid., p. 206. *Thirty-Eighth Rept., KSBA* (1951–1952), p. 408. *KS,* December 15, 1927, p. 3; March 15, 1930, p. 16.

45. Ibid., May 1, 1937, p. 4; July, 1954, p. 50. Schlebecker, *Cattle Raising on the Plains,* pp. 82–84.

CHAPTER 10

1. Genung, *Agricultural Depression,* p. 5; James H. Shideler, *Farm Crisis, 1919–1923* (Berkeley: University of California Press, 1957), pp. vii, 2–3, 19. Some of the postwar demands were reminiscent of those that had been made earlier during the Populist era.

2. John A. Edwards, *In the Western Tongue* (Wichita: McCormick-Armstrong, 1920), pp. 10–53. *KS,* October 15, 1919, pp. 6–7; November 1, 1919, pp. 7–8; November 15, 1919, pp. 5–7.

3. The Consent Decree and the Stockyards Act will be discussed in the next chapter.

4. Benedict, *Farm Policies of the United States,* pp. 202–205, 233–37; Genung, *Agricultural Depression,* p. 6; Saloutos and Hicks, *Agricultural Discontent,* pp. 372–74; Lynn R. Edminister, *The Cattle Industry and the Tariff* (New York: Macmillan Co., 1926), pp. 1, 76–79, 88. *KS,* March 1, 1921, p. 12; June 1, 1923, p. 9; March 15, 1929, p. 7. *The Cattleman,* January, 1921, p. 21.

5. Edminster, *The Cattle Industry and the Tariff,* pp. 138–40, 186, 240. *KS,* August 15, 1921, p. 5; February 1, 1925, p. 6; March 1, 1926, p. 7; June 1, 1926, p. 14; September 15, 1926, p. 3. Mercer, "Tariff on Livestock and Meats," pp. 1–3.

6. Ibid., pp. 1–5. Benedict, *Farm Policies of the United States,* pp. 250–52, 269, 327–32. *KS,* October 1, 1927, p. 4; November 1, 1927, p. 6; March 15, 1929, p. 7; July 1, 1930, p. 4; August 1, 1930, p. 15; March 15, 1931, p. 15.

7. Benedict, *Farm Policies of the United States,* pp. 329–32, 342, 400; DeGraff, *Beef Production and Distribution,* pp. 96–97.

8. Ibid.; Benedict, *Farm Policies of the United States,* p. 399; Saloutos and Hicks, *Agricultural Discontent,* pp. 527–31. *KS,* July 1, 1935, p. 4; March 15,

1937, pp. 4–5; May 1, 1937, pp. 4–5; March 15, 1938, p. 6; December 15, 1938, p. 5; August 15, 1939, p. 5; February 15, 1940, p. 9.

9. Saloutos and Hicks, *Agricultural Discontent,* pp. 373, 375–78, 380–400; Genung, *Agricultural Depression,* pp. 19–22, 24–35, 51–57; Donald R. McCoy, *Calvin Coolidge: The Quiet President* (New York: Macmillan Co., 1967), pp. 235, 308, 325–28.

10. Schlebecker, *Cattle Raising on the Plains,* p. 117; Homer E. Socolofsky, *Arthur Capper: Publisher, Politician, and Philanthropist* (Lawrence: University of Kansas Press, 1962), pp. 152–58. *KS,* February 1, 1922, p. 6; February 15, 1922, p. 6; April 15, 1924, p. 16; May 15, 1924, p. 3; June 1, 1924, p. 4; June 15, 1924, p. 16; March 15, 1927, p. 7.

11. Joseph H. Mercer to President Coolidge, November 15, 1924, copy in Livestock Sanitary Commissioner Miscellaneous File, KSHS. *KS,* December 1, 1923, pp. 7, 10; December 15, 1924, pp. 5–15; January 1, 1925, pp. 6–8; January 15, 1925, p. 8; March 1, 1926, p. 16; May 15, 1926, pp. 3, 7.

12. *The Cattleman,* December, 1926, p. 11.

13. Marion Clawson, *The Western Range Livestock Industry* (New York: McGraw-Hill Book Co., 1950), pp. 281–83; Clay, *My Life on the Range,* pp. 350–52; Schruben, *Kansas in Turmoil,* pp. 74–76; 90–106. *The Cattleman,* April, 1921, pp. 33–35; July, 1921, pp. 25–27; October, 1921, pp. 7–9, 44; March, 1940, p. 57. *Kansas Farmer Mail and Breeze,* October 8, 1921, p. 4; October 22, 1921, p. 4; October 29, 1921, pp. 3, 11; November 5, 1921, p. 5; November 19, 1921, p. 7; December 17, 1921, p. 19. *KS,* January 1, 1921, p. 8; February 15, 1921, p. 7; August 1, 1921, p. 8; September 15, 1921, p. 5; October 1, 1921, p. 6; October 15, 1921, p. 14; February 1, 1922, p. 7; April 15, 1927, p. 7.

14. Ibid., December 15, 1931, p. 4; Mercer's poll of Kansas bankers in Governor Clyde M. Reed Papers, KSHS; Schruben, *Kansas in Turmoil,* pp. 7–8, 65, 121, 169–70, 216.

15. Ibid., p. 57. Clawson, *Western Range Livestock Industry,* p. 286. *KS,* October 1, 1932, p. 4; November 15, 1932, p. 4; January 15, 1933, p. 4; April 15, 1933, pp. 3, 14.

16. Benedict, *Farm Policies of the United States,* pp. 282–83; Schruben, *Kansas in Turmoil,* pp. 116–17; Clawson, *Western Range Livestock Industry,* pp. 284–87.

17. Ibid., pp. 287–89. *KS,* April 1, 1934, pp. 6–7; February 1, 1937, p. 5; March 15, 1937, p. 7. The contribution of this federal system to Kansas agriculture was indicated by the following: 36,000 Kansas farmers and ranchers were receiving FCA benefits in 1940, and many more had already received them; as of January 1, 1936, 25,837 Federal Land Bank loans for $94.9 million and 21,010 Land Bank Commissioner loans for $44.3 million were outstanding in the state; between 1934 and 1939 the Production Credit Corporation extended $27.5 million to forty-two local Kansas associations; and the Bank for Cooperatives loaned over $4 million to sixty-four cooperative associations in the state between 1934 and 1940. As conditions improved, commercial banks accounted for more of the agricultural paper in the state, reaching 52 percent in 1935. Livestock loans made up about a quarter of the total commercial loans at this time. See reports in *KS,*

February 1, 1936, p. 4; March 15, 1936, p. 7; April 1, 1936, p. 4; June 1, 1936, pp. 3, 14. *Thirty-Second Rept., KSBA* (1939–1940), pp. 32–35.

18. Clawson, *Western Range Livestock Industry,* p. 289.

19. Saloutos and Hicks, *Agricultural Discontent,* pp. 406–410, 419–20, 432–33; Genung, *Agricultural Depression,* pp. 60–64; *KS,* November 15, 1927, p. 3.

20. Ibid., March 15, 1930, pp. 5–6; April 30, 1930, p. 5; June 1, 1930, p. 5; July 1, 1930, pp. 3–5; November 1, 1930, p. 5.

21. Ibid., June 1, 1933, p. 6.

22. Ibid., January 15, 1932, pp. 3–5, 14; March 1, 1932, p. 18; March 15, 1932, p. 5.

23. Dennis A. FitzGerald, *Livestock under the AAA* (Washington: Brookings Institution, 1935), pp. 54–61; Schruben, *Kansas in Turmoil,* pp. 107–113. *KS,* July 15, 1933, p. 4; August 1, 1933, p. 4; August 15, 1933, p. 3; October 1, 1933, pp. 5–6; October 1, 1934, pp. 3–7; October 15, 1934, p. 3; November 1, 1935, pp. 4, 21–25.

24. C. Roger Lambert, "Texas Cattlemen and the AAA, 1933–1935," *Arizona and the West* 14 (Summer, 1972): 137–54; and "Want and Plenty: The Federal Surplus Relief Corporation and the AAA," *Agricultural History* 46 (July, 1972): 390–400.

25. The membership of this committee illustrated the American National's tendency to represent the western range producer more than the midwestern feeder. Charles E. Collins of Colorado was appointed chairman, assisted by Dolph Briscoe of Texas, C. J. Abbott of western Nebraska, J. Elmer Brock of Wyoming, and Hubbard Russell of California.

26. *The Cattleman,* October, 1933, p. 5; January, 1934, pp. 5–6; February, 1934, pp. 6–7; March, 1934, pp. 6–7; April, 1934, p. 10. *KS,* January 1, 1934, pp. 4–5; February 15, 1934, p. 2; April 15, 1934, p. 4; May 15, 1934, p. 4; June 1, 1934, p. 4; June 15, 1934, pp. 4–5; March 15, 1935, p. 6. FitzGerald, *Livestock under the AAA,* pp. 174–83.

27. Donald R. McCoy, *Landon of Kansas* (Lincoln: University of Nebraska Press, 1966), p. 176; Schruben, *Kansas in Turmoil,* pp. 120–21, 158. Kansans had almost 2.9 million beef cattle in 1934, and almost 1.0 million dairy cattle. This represented more beef cattle than the state had had since the early 1900s, and the most milk cows the state has ever had.

28. FitzGerald, *Livestock under the AAA,* pp. 195–200; *KS,* September 1, 1934, pp. 3, 5.

29. Fred Hinkle, *The Saddle and the Statute* (Wichita: McCormick-Armstrong, 1961), pp. 29–30.

30. Schruben, *Kansas in Turmoil,* pp. 129–30; Kansas Emergency Relief Committee Report, "Drought Cattle Operations, the State of Kansas," p. 3, KSHS. This is a typescript account of the Kansas program, and includes maps, charts, and photographs. It, as well as several other volumes related to KERC's work, are neatly bound in leather that was probably made from the hide of a drought-stricken cow.

31. Ibid., pp. 8–10, 13, 17, and map following p. 18; FitzGerald, *Livestock*

under the AAA, pp. 376–77. Osborne County held the distinction of heaviest participation—with 17,733 cattle being sold to the government—followed by Lincoln, 16,487; Russell, 14,559; Mitchell, 13,886; and Smith, 13,445. These are all contiguous counties in the north-central portion of the state. The fewest number of cattle were purchased in Doniphan, 122; Johnson, 192; Wyandotte, 377; Harvey, 424; and Anderson, 465. All of these counties, except Harvey, are located in eastern Kansas.

32. KERC Report, "Drought Cattle Operations, the State of Kansas," pp. 1, 11–12, 27–28, 32–35, 40–47, 53, 64. Slaughtering plants received 25 cents per hundred pounds of dressed weight for butchering and 35 cents for cutting and packaging, plus the hides and all offal. Later, KERC retained the hides. The first canning plant opened in Parsons, August 1, 1934. Others followed in Kansas City, Wichita, Topeka, Leavenworth, Hutchinson, Coffeyville, and Independence. Plants operated twenty-four hours a day, six days a week, and paid their employees 40 to 45 cents an hour.

33. Lewis Nordyke, a historian of the Texas beef industry, noted that "out on the range the tears streamed down the faces of many old cowmen when they saw the government roundup—not because of the drought or the condition of the starving cattle, but because they didn't want the government 'running our business.' Man after man refused to sell to the government, though he had no other market." *Great Round-up*, p. 256. While the quotation would be popular with many of today's cattlemen, it has an unmistakably mythical ring when applied to the real situation during the 1930s, especially in view of the strenuous efforts of many Texans to get the government into the business, the 1,330,218 cattle that were sold to the government, and the $24.5 million that was paid to the weeping "old cowmen."

34. KERC Report, "Drought Cattle Operations, the State of Kansas," pp. 14–15; FitzGerald, *Livestock under the AAA, pp.* 189–91, 205-216, 268–73; C. Roger Lambert, "The Drought Cattle Purchases, 1934–35: Problems and Complaints," *Agricultural History* 45 (April, 1971): 85–91; *The Cattleman,* October, 1934, pp. 9–11.

35. Schruben, *Kansas in Turmoil,* pp. 164–66.

36. Benedict, *Farm Policies of the United States,* pp. 316–20, 350–52, 395–96; Schlebecker, *Cattle Raising on the Plains,* pp. 159–64; 176; State Soil Conservation Committee, "Keeping Kansas Soils Productive through Soil and Water Conservation" (Manhattan, 1952). Kansas received $16.0 million in rental and benefit payments in 1936. Oklahoma was second high with $4.5 million. Schruben, *Kansas in Turmoil,* pp. 168–69.

37. *Thirty-Second Rept., KSBA* (1939–1940), pp. 205–208; Kling L. Anderson, "Range and Pasture," *Quarterly Rept., KSBA,* vol. 65, no. 271 (February, 1946): pp. 92–116. *KS,* April 15, 1934, p. 13. A. E. Aldous, "The Kansas Pasture Situation," *KS,* June 15, 1935, pp. 3, 14, and "Pasture Improvement Plan For Kansas," *KS,* September 1, 1936, p. 3; January 15, 1938, p. 7; November 15, 1938, p. 4.

38. No one, apparently, knows how many ponds had been built in the state prior to 1930, but farmers and ranchers had constructed a few.

39. McCoy, *Landon of Kansas,* pp. 174–76; Schruben, *Kansas in Turmoil,* p. 120.

40. The Water Resources Board of the KSBA has been unable to determine the extent of pond building during this period. The most significant pond-building era for Kansas, however, appeared to be in the 1940s. One estimate claimed that the state had over 72,000 ponds by 1951. See ibid., p. 118; Marcene Grimes, *Government and Natural Resources in Kansas—Water,* pp. 45–46, 59–60, and Marvin Meade, *Government and Natural Resources in Kansas—Soil,* pamphlets (Lawrence, 1957, 1959), pp. 26, 40. Grimes also noted, "The total number of farm ponds in Kansas in 1954 constructed under the various federal and state programs was about 88,000, of which some 16,000 were constructed after 1951." These figures, however, probably omitted privately constructed ponds. Grimes claimed that 8,200 wells were also constructed and 800 springs refurbished between 1936 and 1953.

41. C. M. Schumacher and M. D. Atkins, "Reestablishment and Use of Grass in the Morton County, Kansas, Land Utilization Project," USDA, *Soil Conservation Service TP-146* (March, 1965), pp. 1–13. "Rules of Management for Land Controlled by the Morton County Grazing Association," pp. 1–6, and "By-Laws: Morton County Cooperative Grazing Association," pp. 1–9, copies in possession of author. Meade, *Government and Natural Resources in Kansas—Soil,* pp. 64–68. Cattle Industry Clippings 3: 54–56.

42. In addition to conservation, the state government also assisted cattlemen in other ways. For example, the Drought Relief Committee created in 1930 by Governor Clyde M. Reed no doubt included some cattlemen on its list of aid recipients. Three stockmen, Cal W. Floyd, Arnold Berns, and Will J. Miller, represented livestock interests on the twelve-member committee. The Kansas debt moratorium laws also helped the state's cattlemen. Other debt-adjustment committees, along with the persistent efforts of Governor Landon to reduce freight rates and feed costs, were also of some help to the state's beef producers. Other federal programs aided cattlemen as well, but probably not to the degree of those discussed. The Rural Electrification Act, for example, eventually proved useful; but little was gained from this government effort during the thirties, even though less than 10 percent of rural Kansas was electrified in 1936. McCoy, *Landon of Kansas,* pp. 176–79; Schruben, *Kansas in Turmoil,* pp. 107, 136, 159, 161; Governor Reed to George Juno, January 5, 1931, in Reed Papers, KSHS.

43. Sonnichsen, *Cowboys and Cattle Kings,* pp. xiii–xiv. Also see Casement, "Who Is the 'Real Farmer' Today?", *Breeder's Gazette,* May 6, 1926, reprinted— with a note that the *Stockman* disagreed with many of the views that were expressed—in *KS,* July 1, 1926, p. 6; November 1, 1933, pp. 6, 26. James C. Carey, "Dan D. Casement: Viking on a Sea of Grass," *The Trail Guide* 4 (December, 1959): 1–12; Donald R. Ornduff, *Casement of Juniata: As a Man and as a Stockman . . . One of a Kind* (Kansas City: Lowell Press, 1975), pp. 1–6, 18, 94–97.

44. Dan D. Casement, "Corn-Fed Philosophy," *The Kansas Magazine* (1938), pp. 25–27.

45. James C. Carey, "The Farmers Independent Council of America, 1935– 1938," *Agricultural History* 35 (April, 1961): 70–77. Throughout much of the

New Deal period Casement also had a running debate with William Allen White concerning government aid to the economy. Casement's views never changed, but the correspondence revealed White's gradual acceptance of a larger government role in economic revival. See Carey, "William Allen White and Dan D. Casement on Government Regulation," *Agricultural History* 33 (January, 1959): 16–21.

46. Casement, *The Abbreviated Autobiography of a Joyous Pagan* (Manhattan: Privately Printed, 1944), 3–71. *American Hereford Journal,* April 15, 1945, pp. 20–24, 92–94; May 15, 1945, pp. 12–13; June 15, 1945, pp. 20–21, 40.

47. *KS,* October 1, 1935, p. 14; October 15, 1935, p. 22; December 15, 1935, p. 2; April 15, 1938, p. 3. Senator Arthur Capper, the "Republican New Dealer" from Kansas, discovered much the same situation in two "free-for-all" meetings he held in 1938 and 1939. Much criticism of the existing government programs was expressed, but relatively few Kansas farmers and ranchers expressed any sentiment for discontinuing government aids. Ibid., January 1, 1939, p. 14; January 1, 1940, p. 11. Socolofsky, *Arthur Capper,* pp. 171–74, 182–83; Capper Papers, Box 12:32.

48. *KS,* June 15, 1932, p. 5; February 1, 1933, p. 13. Mercer's political aspirations were cut short by an August primary defeat by C. C. Isely. Both men ran exclusively on the farm parity issue and, according to the *Stockman,* split the rural vote. Mercer's late start also helped defeat him. Along with others, Mercer was promoted by William Allen White, who wrote, "He and I have agreed more nearly on political issues in Kansas than any other two men," and by his campaign manager, Jesse C. Harper, who divided his time between a Clark County ranch and the athletic directorship of the University of Notre Dame. Isely, in turn, was defeated by the incumbent Democrat, George McGill. Ibid., July 1, 1932, p. 4; July 15, 1932, p. 15; August 1, 1932, pp. 4, 15.

49. Ibid., April, 1950, p. 4. Casement, appropriately, was the principal author of the Freedom Resolution.

50. Ibid., September, 1960, p. 6.

CHAPTER 11

1. Shideler, *Farm Crisis,* pp. 28–30. Exhibit C-1, pp. 41–45. *KS,* March 1, 1919, p. 4; March 15, pp. 6–7, September 1, 1921, pp. 1, 7. In addition to increased tariffs, railroads filed $677 million in undermaintenance claims against the government, many of them fraudulent, and were actually paid $222 million. Stover, *The Life and Decline of the American Railroad,* p. 174.

2. Exhibit C-1, pp. 41–45; Kolko, *Railroads and Regulation,* p. 230; *KS,* September 15, 1921, p. 6; April 15, 1922, p. 16; February 1, 1923, pp. 5–6.

3. Ibid., August 1, 1925, p. 5; August 15, 1925, pp. 3, 5; October 15, 1925, p. 3; March 1, 1926, p. 6; August 1, 1926, p. 3; March 15, 1934, p. 7; June 15, 1934, p. 4.

4. Mercer, "How Farmers' Condition May Be Improved," pp. 2–12. *KS,*

August 15, 1923, p. 16; February 1, 1924, pp. 5–7; March 15, 1928, p. 5; March 15, 1932, p. 15; September 15, 1936, pp. 2, 4. The sale-in-transit provision permitted stock sold at small, country sale points to be shipped from the point of origin to their final destination at the single, long-haul rate, which was less expensive than two separate rates. Stockyards and railroads rightly felt that this discriminated against the large central markets. The feed-in-transit privilege allowed stockers and feeders to be carried to feeding areas at 85 percent of the fat stock rate, then the full rate was paid from the place of feeding to the central market. Towards the end of the 1930s, the rail lines petitioned to adjust this practice, apparently because they believed shippers were transporting fat stock to points near central markets at the reduced rates, then completing the haul by truck. See clipping from *The National Wool Grower,* April, 1939, p. 13; J. A. Farmer, Western Rail Carriers representative, to W. P. Bartel, secretary of ICC, December 19, 1940; "Joe," traffic manager of Kansas City Stockyards Company, to Will J. Miller, December 26, 1940; C. E. Childe, transportation manager of Omaha Stockyards, to Miller, December 30, 1940, all in KLA Rate File.

5. Stene, *Railroad Commission to Corporation Commission,* pp. 49, 101–106; State of Kansas, *Session Laws* (1920), pp. 36–47; *Thirteenth Biennial Report of Kansas Corporation Commission* (1934–1936), pp. 12–16; *KS,* September 1, 1938, p. 4.

6. Ibid., January 1, 1938, pp. 4–5; March 15, 1938, pp. 4, 7; May 15, 1938, pp. 2, 7–8; August 1, 1939, p. 4. *Fourteenth Biennial Report of Kansas Corporation Commission* (1936–1938), pp. 75–78. Exhibit C-1, pp. 41–45; J. F. Stevick, Santa Fe Rate Expert, to Will J. Miller, May 8, 1941, in KLA Rate File.

7. *KS,* February 1, 1919, p. 27; March 1, 1919, p. 46; April 1, 1926, p. 5; *Kansas Farmer Mail and Breeze,* January 3, 1920, p. 18; Schruben, *Kansas in Turmoil,* pp. 2–3.

8. Exhibit C-1, pp. 53–60. *KS,* March 15, 1936, p. 8; May 15, 1939, p. 15.

9. Ibid., March 15, 1929, p. 8; March 15, 1931, p. 15; October 1, 1931, p. 4; November 1, 1931, p. 4; May 15, 1932, p. 4; November 1, 1932, p. 18. "Kansas Corporation Commission Report on Docket 18203," 1938, copy in KLA Rate File.

10. Interviews, Evan Koger, Belvidere, Kans., July 15, 1977; A. G. Pickett, Emporia, Kans., August 2, 1977; and Wayne Rogler, Matfield Green, Kans., August 2, 1977.

11. Exhibit C-1, pp. 53–58; Clawson, *The Western Range Livestock Industry,* p. 173; E. W. Sheets et al., *Our Beef Supply,* USDA Yearbook (1921), pp. 281–84.

12. Corey, *Meat and Man,* pp. 189–96. Leech and Carroll, *Armour and His Times,* pp. 354–57. *The Cattleman,* May, 1937, p. 5. *KS,* March 1, 1923, pp. 8–9; May 1, 1923, p. 3; July 15, 1923, p. 16; September 1, 1924, p. 4; March 15, 1935, p. 4; May 15, 1935, p. 7; May 1, 1936, pp. 7–8, 10.

13. Shideler, *Farm Crisis,* p. 27; Clemen, *Livestock and Meat Industry,* pp. 782–85. *KS,* July 15, 1929, p. 4.

14. Benedict, *Farm Policies of the United States,* pp. 181–82, 199. *KS,* August

1, 1919, p. 10, August 15, 1919, pp. 7, 10, 13; September 1, 1919, pp. 10–11; October 1, 1919, pp. 1, 9; March 1, 1920, pp. 36–42.

15. Ibid., February 1, 1920, p. 6; March 1, 1920, pp. 15, 29; April 15, 1920, p. 8; May 15, 1920, p. 3; June 1, 1920, p. 1. *The Cattleman,* February, 1920, pp. 17–18; State of Kansas, *Session Laws* (1920), pp. 68–72.

16. Benedict, *Farm Policies of the United States,* pp. 183, 352; Clemen, *Livestock and Meat Industry,* pp. 788–89. *KS,* February 1, 1921, p. 10; July 1, 1921, pp. 4–5; September 1, 1921, p. 4; June 1, 1922, p. 15; T. H. Ingwerser, of Swift and Company, testimony, in Transcript of Marketing Conference, Kansas City, 1927, p. 21, in KLA Rate File.

17. Ibid. *KS,* July 15, 1929, p. 4; September 15, 1929, pp. 5–6; January 15, 1931, p. 4; June 1, 1932, p. 4.

18. Ibid., March 1, 1920, pp. 8, 30–31; July 1, 1931, p. 13; August 1, 1931, p. 4; June 1, 1932, p. 4; June 15, 1933, p. 4; March 1, 1938, p. 42.

19. Ibid., March 1, 1919, pp. 14–15; March 1, 1920, p. 8; June 1, 1921, p. 7; August 1, 1921, pp. 6–7; September 15, 1922, p. 16.

20. Ibid., January 1, 1920, pp. 7, 10, 14–16; November 1, 1922, pp. 4–5; February 1, 1924, p. 8; December 15, 1924, pp. 8–11; March 15, 1925, p. 14; January 15, 1930, pp. 5–7; June 1, 1930, p. 5. *Kansas Farmer Mail and Breeze,* May 7, 1921, p. 3; Senator Capper to Mercer, January 5, 1932, in Capper Papers, Box 12:32; E. W. Baker, *Livestock Estimates Anticipation Receipts Aid Orderly Marketing,* USDA Yearbook (1927), pp. 429–31.

21. E. G. Nourse and J. G. Knapp, *The Co-Operative Marketing of Livestock* (Washington: Brookings Institution, 1931), pp. 9–13, 40–54, 103–108, 157–59; Saloutos and Hicks, *Agricultural Discontent,* pp. 56–57; Theodore Macklin, *Cooperation Applied to Marketing by Kansas Farmers,* Bulletin 224 (Kansas Agricultural Experiment Station, 1920), pp. 7–10; Ralph Snyder, *We Kansas Farmers: Development of Farm Organizations and Cooperative Association in Kansas as Gleaned from a Lifetime of Experience and Contact with them* (Topeka: F. M. Steves & Sons, 1953), pp. 21–26, 77. *KS,* November 15, 1921, p. 16; March 1, 1923, pp. 6–7; February 1, 1924, p. 8; May 1, 1924, p. 4. Emporia *Gazette,* April 11, 1907.

22. Nourse and Knapp, *The Co-Operative Marketing of Livestock,* pp. 38, 113, 148–50, 236–37; R. H. Elsworth, *Statistics of Farmers' Cooperative Business Organization, 1920–1935,* Bulletin 6 (Farm Credit Administration, 1936), pp. 65–66, 118, 126; M. C. Puhr, *Farmer Co-ops in Kansas,* pamphlet (Wichita Bank for Cooperatives, 1938), KSHS.

23. *KS,* October 1, 1920, p. 8; September 15, 1921, p. 6; DeGraff, *Beef Production and Distribution,* pp. 150–52. During and after World War II the number of community auctions multiplied at a much slower pace, according to DeGraff, but an increase in volume of several hundred percent during the 1940s was probably more striking than the increase in numbers had been during the 1930s.

24. *KS,* March 15, 1937, p. 5; June 1, 1937, p. 3; June 15, 1937, p. 3; August 1, 1937, p. 4; March 15, 1938, p. 7; March 15, 1939, p. 3; October 1, 1939, p. 36. One of the earlier community sale barns in Kansas, built at Alma during World War I, came to serve the local community in a variety of ways in addition to the

exchange of livestock. The theater-like arrangement of the seats in the sale barn was particularly suitable for band concerts, spelling bees, and various other functions of the local schools. Some of the activities of the annual county fair were also held in the barn. Interview, Dorothy Schmanke, Topeka, Kans., June 11, 1973.

25. *KS,* April 15, 1928, pp. 7–8; March 15, 1929, p. 8. Nourse and Knapp, *The Co-Operative Marketing of Livestock,* pp. 176–77.

26. Ibid., pp. 180–81. *KS,* March 15, 1922, pp. 4, 16; April 1, 1922, p. 4; September 15, 1922, p. 10; April 1, 1934, pp. 3, 8. Edward A. Duddy and David A. Revzan, *The Changing Relative Importance of the Central Livestock Market,* Chicago University School of Business—Studies in Business Administration, vol. 8, no. 4 (Chicago: University of Chicago Press, 1938), pp. 48–53.

27. DeGraff, *Beef Production and Distribution,* pp. 152–53; *The Cattleman,* February, 1939, p. 13; James R. Gray, *Ranch Economics* (Ames: Iowa State University Press, 1968), p. 450.

28. *KS,* February 1, 1922, p. 8; October 1, 1939, p. 36. *The Cattleman,* November, 1930, pp. 34–39; Duddy and Revzan, *Central Livestock Market,* pp. 44–47, 73–86; DeGraff, *Beef Production and Distribution,* pp. 150–53.

29. *KS,* March 1, 1928, p. 80; April 15, 1928, pp. 7–10; March 15, 1929, p. 7; May 1, 1931, pp. 4–6; April 15, 1932, p. 3; April 1, 1936, p. 4. Transcripts of Marketing Conferences held in Kansas City, July, 1927, and Chicago, October, 1927, both in KLA Rate File. Typescript of an address by Senator Capper over WIBW Radio, pp. 1–7; S. S. Spencer, October 1, 1934, and D. M. Hildebrand, May 22, 1936, to Capper; Senator Robert D. Carey to Senator Hugo L. Black, April 24, 1936, all in Capper Papers, Box 12:32. *The Cattleman,* October, 1927, p. 9; April, 1928, p. 15; April, 1934, p. 17.

30. Duddy and Revzan, *Central Livestock Market,* p. 53.

31. Fred N. Howell, "Some Phases of the Industrial History of Pittsburg, Kansas," *Kansas Historical Quarterly* 1 (May, 1932): 286; "Meat Packing of Prime Importance to Kansas," *Kansas Business Magazine* 3 (February, 1935): 8–9. The Hill plant was reported to have begun packing horse meat for human consumption in 1907. The supply of horses came mostly from Montana and Wyoming sheepmen who captured and sold wild horses. No "useful" horses were slaughtered, the plant officials claimed, as these were sent to the South as workhorses. Most of the meat was salted and packed for sale in Europe, especially France and the Scandinavian countries. By-products and horses too old to provide palatable meat were processed into dog and fox food. Ibid., 4 (September, 1936): 10–15.

32. Corey, *Meat and Man,* pp. 189–95.

33. "Threat to Kansas Packing Industry," *Kansas Business Magazine* 3 (December, 1935): 5, 26; Duddy and Revzan, *Central Livestock Market,* pp. 59–61; C. P. Wilson and H. M. Riley, *Recent Trends in the Livestock and Meat Industry in Kansas,* Bulletin 355 (Manhattan: Kansas Agricultural Experiment Station), pp. 7–13; Schruben, *Kansas in Turmoil,* pp. 9, 69, 123–24, 172–73.

34. *KS,* May 15, 1923, pp. 3–4; February 1, 1924, pp. 10–11. *The Cattleman,* November, 1934, pp. 11–13. DeGraff, *Beef Production and Distribution,* pp. 162–63.

CHAPTER 12

1. *KS,* August, 1942, pp. 5–6; February, 1943, p. 3; March, 1943, p. 8; September, 1946, p. 14; April, 1950, pp. 18–19. *Fifty-Eighth Rept., KSBA* (1974–1975), p. 220. Schlebecker, *Cattle Raising on the Plains,* pp. 172, 186–87.

2. Ibid., pp. 193–94. *KS,* December, 1948, p. 7; January, 1949, p. 7. Cattle Industry Clippings 3: 154, 160.

3. Ibid., 154; *Thirty-Fifth Rept., KSBA* (1945–1946), pp. 37–50.

4. Schlebecker, *Cattle Raising on the Plains,* p. 203.

5. Ibid., pp. 205–206; Topeka *Daily Capital,* August 10, 1952; Cattle Industry Clippings, 4: 76.

6. Schlebecker, *Cattle Raising on the Plains,* pp. 207–208, 223–25; *Fortieth and Fifty-Eighth Repts., KSBA* (1956–1957), pp. 6–12; (1974–1975), p. 220.

7. *KS,* July, 1949, p. 7. *Thirty-Fifth* and *Forty-First Repts., KSBA* (1945–1946), pp. 7–10; (1957–1958), 7–13. Schlebecker, *Cattle Raising on the Plains,* pp. 181, 197–98, 216–18, 229–30.

8. "Beef Cattle in Kansas," *Quarterly Report of the Kansas State Board of Agriculture* (September, 1934), pp. 134–51. *American Hereford Journal,* February 1, 1920, pp. 66, 148–49; December 1, 1922, pp. 26–27.

9. *Forty-Third, Fifty-Fourth, Fifty-Eighth* and *Fifty-Ninth Repts., KSBA* (1959–1960), pp. 6–12, 21–24; (1970–1971), p. 75F; (1974–1975), p. 71F; (1975–1976); p. 71F. *KS,* June, 1949, p. 39; November, 1959, p. 19. Cattle Industry Clippings 5: 32, 121–25, 198–99.

10. *Thirty-Ninth, Forty-Ninth,* and *Fifty-First Repts., KSBA* (1953–1956), pp. 73–75; (1965–1966), p. 106; (1967–1968), pp. 52–55. Cattle Industry Clippings 4: 175; 5: 20, 29–32, 35–36. Interview, Evan Koger, Belvidere, Kans., July 15, 1977.

11. *Thirty-Ninth, Forty-Second, Forty-Fourth, Fiftieth, Fifty-Second,* and *Fifty-Fifth Repts., KSBA* (1953–1956), pp. 6–11; (1958–1959), pp. 6–11; (1960–1961), pp. 13–20; (1966–1967), pp. 94–95; (1968–1969), pp. 6–12; (1971–1972), pp. 8–14. Cattle Industry Clippings 5: 121–25. Interviews, O. C. Hicks, Garden City, Kans., July 12, 1977; and Dale Mustoe, Rexford, Kans., July 13, 1977.

12. *Fifty-Third* and *Fifty-Ninth Repts., KSBA* (1969–1970), p. 78F; (1975–1976), p. 175.

13. *Fifty-First* and *Fifty-Ninth Repts., KSBA* (1967–1968), p. 16F; (1975–1976), pp. 8, 14F.

14. Cattle Industry Clippings 5: 23, 110–11, 117; *Fifty-First Rept., KSBA* (1967–1968), pp. 52–55.

15. Anderson, *A Quarter Inch of Rain,* pp. 80–90, 103, 131, 169, 187; Cattle Industry Clippings 5: 110–11, 117.

16. *KS,* January 1, 1940, p. 15; March, 1953, p. 18; April, 1958, p. 5; January, 1962, p. 54; October, 1963, pp. 12–16. *Forty-First Rept., KSBA* (1957–1958), pp. 44–46. Cattle Industry Clippings 2: 201; 5: 23, 110–11, 117.

17. Ibid., 5: 121–25.

18. *KS,* January, 1952, pp. 6–7; November, 1957, p. 25. *Forty-Sixth Rept., KSBA* (1962–1963), pp. 58–59. Interviews, E. C. Brookover, Jr., and Sanky Ruth,

Garden City, Kans., July 12, 1977; and O. C. Hicks, Garden City, Kans., July 12, 1977.

19. *KS,* May, 1945, p. 5. Cattle Industry Clippings 3: 174–75; 4: 175; 5: 12–13. *The Cattleman,* February, 1967, pp. 52–56; August, 1972, p. 51. Interview, Wayne Rogler, Matfield Green, Kans., August 2, 1977.

20. Ibid.

21. Ibid.; *KS,* April, 1970, pp. 44–45; *The Cattleman,* August, 1972, pp. 53, 112.

22. *KS,* September, 1944, p. 9. Cattle Industry Clippings 4: 170, 177, 194; 5: 1, 63. Interviews, Clair Parcel, Coldwater, Kans., July 14, 1977; A. G. Pickett, Emporia, Kans., July 23, 1977.

23. *Thirty-Ninth Rept., KSBA* (1953–1956), pp. 45–47; *American Hereford Journal,* September 15, 1942, p. 17; June 15, 1943, p. 264; January 1, 1944, p. 93. Schlebecker, *Cattle Raising on the Plains,* pp. 219–20, 233. Interview, Clair Parcel, Coldwater, Kans., July 14, 1977.

24. Ibid. *Thirty-Ninth Rept., KSBA* (1953–1956), pp. 45–47.

25. *Fifty-Fourth and Fifty-Ninth Repts., KSBA* (1970–1971), p. 85F; (1975–1976), p. 88F.

26. Kollmorgen, "Grazing in the Bluestem Pastures," 260–90.

Bibliography

MANUSCRIPTS AND MANUSCRIPT COLLECTIONS

Board of Railroad Commissioners. Transcripts of Hearings. Topeka, 1896, 1897. Kansas State Historical Society (KSHS).

Capper, Arthur. Gubernatorial and Senatorial Papers. 1915–1919, 1919–1949. KSHS.

Hodges, George H. Gubernatorial Papers. 1913–1915. KSHS.

Kansas Corporation Commission. Exhibit C-1 of hearing before ICC on Ex Parte No. 123. 1938.

Kansas Emergency Relief Committee Report. "Drought Cattle Operations, the State of Kansas." 1935. KSHS.

Kansas Soil Conservation Service. Typescript Reports to Regional Headquarters. 1945, 1952–1953, 1956. KSHS.

Livestock Sanitary Commissioner, State of Kansas. Miscellaneous File. KSHS.

McCampbell, C. W. "The Kansas Livestock Association." N.d. In Kansas Livestock Association Files, 2044 Fillmore, Topeka, Kansas.

Moxley, J. J. Typescript Statement on the Flint Hills. March 4, 1970. KLA Files.

Reed, Clyde M. Gubernatorial Papers. 1929–1931. KSHS.

Reeme, Will K. Open letter to Missouri and Kansas Legislatures. January 18, 1909. KSHS.

Stubbs, Walter R. Gubernatorial Papers. 1909–1913. KSHS.

Swift and Company. Miscellaneous Records for St. Joseph Plant. Spencer Research Library, University of Kansas.

"The Kansas Livestock Association." N.n., n.d. KLA Files.

Transcript of Marketing Conference. Kansas City, July 15, 16, 1927. KLA Files.

Transcript of Marketing Conference. Chicago, October 20, 1927. KLA Files.

NEWSPAPERS, CLIPPING FILES, AND TRADE JOURNALS

Agriculture in Kansas Clippings. 1881–1928. KSHS.

Anderson County Clippings. Vol. 3. KSHS.

Ashland *Leader*. 1907–1908.

Atchison *Daily Globe* Clippings. KSHS.

Cattle Industry Clippings. Vols. 1 (1890–1935), 2 (1936–1940), 3 (1940–1950), 4 (1951–1963), 5 (1951–Present). KSHS.

Cattleman, The (Ft. Worth). 1920–1970.

Clark County Chief (Englewood). 1885–1887.

Clark County Clipper (Ashland). 1892–1893, 1895–1908.

Clark County Clippings. Vols. 1 (1886–1940), 2 (1940–1944), 3 (1944–Present). KSHS.

Daily Drovers Telegram (Kansas City, Mo.). Selected issues.

Dickinson County Clippings. Vols. 3, 4. KSHS.

Earth, The (Chicago). 1904, 1913, 1924–1925, 1933–1934.

Emporia *Daily Gazette*. 1894–1897.

Emporia *Weekly Gazette*. 1894–1916.

Ford County Clippings. Vol. 4. KSHS

Ford County Globe (Dodge City). April, 1883.

Kansas Business Magazine (Topeka). 1930–1940.

Kansas Cattleman (Manhattan and Topeka). 1916–1918.

Kansas City (Mo.) *Star*. Selected issues.

Kansas Farmer (Topeka). 1894–1920.

Kansas Farmer Mail and Breeze (Topeka). 1920–1924.

Kansas Biographical Scrapbooks. KSHS.

Kansas State Agricultural College Clippings. Vol. 2. KSHS.

Kansas State Livestock Association Clippings. KSHS.

Kansas Stockman (Topeka). 1918–1975.

Livestock-Stockyards Clippings. KSHS.

Lyon County Clippings. Vol. 4. KSHS.

Lyon County Democrat (Emporia). 1894.

Meat Clippings. Vol. 1 (1937–1936). KSHS.

Mercer, Joseph H., Clippings. Vertical File. KSHS.

Montgomery County Clippings. Vol. 6. KSHS.

News for Farmer Cooperatives (Washington, D. C.). 1934–1936.

Pawnee County Clippings. Vol. 2. KSHS.

Stockbreeders' Associations Clippings. KSHS.

Stubbs, Walter R., Clippings. Vertical File. KSHS.

Topeka *Daily Capital*. Selected issues.

Wallace County Clippings. Vols. 2, 3. KSHS.

Bibliography

GOVERNMENT PUBLICATIONS

Allen, T. Warren, et al. *Highways and Highway Transportation.* U. S. Department of Agriculture Yearbook. 1924.

Anderson, Kling L. "Range and Pasture." *Quarterly Report of the Kansas State Board of Agriculture,* vol. 65, no. 271 (February, 1946).

Baker, E. W. *Livestock Estimates Anticipation Receipts Aid Orderly Marketing.* USDA Yearbook. 1927.

"Beef Cattle in Kansas." *Quarterly Report of the Kansas State Board of Agriculture* for the quarter ending September, 1934.

Board of Railroad Commissioners, State of Kansas. *Annual and Biennial Reports.* 1890–1910.

Carver, Thomas N. *The Organization of Rural Interests.* USDA Yearbook. 1913.

Court of Industrial Relations, State of Kansas. *First Annual Report.* 1918–1920.

Elsworth, R. H. *Cooperatives Growing in Membership and Scope of Operation.* USDA Yearbook. 1927.

———. *Statistics of Farmers' Cooperative Business Organizations, 1920–1935.* Bulletin 6. Farm Credit Administration, Cooperative Division. 1936.

Garfield, James R. *Report of the Commissioner of Corporations on the Beef Industry.* 1905.

Hoover, Leo M. *Kansas Agriculture after 100 Years.* Bulletin 392. Kansas Agricultural Experiment Station, Manhattan. 1957.

Jardine, W. M. *Secretary's Report to the President.* USDA Yearbook. 1926.

Johnson, Howard W., and Albert F. Ranney. "Tuberculosis and Its Eradication." *Animal Diseases.* USDA Yearbook. 1956.

Johnson, Ronald E. *Prices Received by Farmers for Beef Cattle: United States, and by States, Monthly and Annual Average, 1909–1959.* USDA Statistical Bulletin 265. 1960.

Kansas Emergency Relief Committee. "Public Welfare Service in Kansas, 1934, 1935." 1936.

———. "Social Welfare Service in Kansas, 1936." 1937.

Kansas Public Service Commission. *Biennial Reports.* 1924–1932.

Kansas Public Utilities Commission. *Biennial Reports.* 1911–1924.

Kansas State Board of Agriculture. *Annual* and *Biennial Reports.* 1889–1976.

Livestock and Meat Statistics, 1957. USDA Statistical Bulletin 230. 1958.

Macklin, Theodore. *Cooperation Applied to Marketing by Kansas Farmers.* Bulletin 224. Kansas Agricultural Experiment Station, Manhattan. 1920.

McCampbell, C. W. *George W. Glick, Outstanding Kansas Citizen and Stockman.* Circular 283. Kansas Agricultural Experiment Station, Manhattan. 1952.

———. *Col. W. A. Harris.* Circular 308. Kansas Agricultural Experiment Station, Manhattan. 1954.

Manthei, C. A., et al. "Brucellosis." *Animal Diseases.* USDA Yearbook. 1956.

Olsen, Nils A., et al. *Farm Credit, Farm Insurance and Farm Taxation.* USDA Yearbook. 1924.

Bibliography

Parr, V. V. *Beef Raising from Grass Alone: A Sound Practice in Ranching.* USDA Yearbook. 1927.

Report of the Federal Trade Commission on the Meat-Packing Industry. 1918–1920.

Part 1: Summary.

Part 2: Evidence of Combination among Packers.

Part 3: Methods of the Five Packers in Controlling the Meat-Packing Industry.

Part 4: The Five Larger Packers in Produce and Grocery Foods.

Part 5: Profits of the Packers.

Part 6: Cost of Growing Beef Animals. Cost of Fattening Cattle. Cost of Marketing Live Stock.

Roberts, Irwin H., and N. G. Cobbett. "Cattle Scabies." *Animal Diseases.* USDA Yearbook. 1956.

Schumacher, C. M., and M. D. Atkins. "Reestablishment and Use of Grass in the Morton County, Kansas, Land Utilization Project." USDA, *Soil Conservation Service TP-146.* March, 1965.

Sheets, E. W., et al. *Our Beef Supply.* USDA Yearbook. 1921.

State Conservation Commission. "Conservation in Kansas." Report to Governor Robert B. Docking. 1972.

State Corporation Commission of Kansas. *Biennial Reports.* 1932–1940.

State Soil Conservation Committee. "Keeping Kansas Soils Productive through Soil and Water Conservation." A Progress Report on Soil Conservation Districts. Manhattan. 1952.

———. "Soil Conservation in Kansas." *Reports.* 1967, 1968.

State of Kansas. *General Statutes of Kansas Annotated,* vol. 2. 1909.

———. *Revised Statutes of Kansas Annotated.* 1923.

———. *Session Laws.* 1907, 1909, 1911, 1913, 1919, 1920, 1921.

Stein, C. D. "Blackleg." *Animal Diseases.* USDA Yearbook. 1956.

Stokdyk, E. A. *Cooperative Marketing by Farmers.* USDA Yearbook. 1940.

U. S. Bureau of the Census. *Census of Agriculture, 1964, Statistics for the State and Counties, Kansas.* 1967.

U. S. Crop Reporting Board. *Prices Received by Farmers, United States, 1908–1955; Crops, Livestock, Livestock Products, Monthly and Annual or Seasonal Average Prices.* USDA Statistical Bulletin 180. 1956.

Wilcox, R. H., et al. *Factors in the Cost of Producing Beef in the Flint Hills Section of Kansas.* USDA Bulletin 1454. 1956.

Wilson, C. P., and H. M. Riley. *Recent Trends in the Livestock and Meat Industry in Kansas.* Bulletin 355. Kansas Agricultural Experiment Station, Manhattan. 1952.

INTERVIEWS AND LETTERS

Adams, Raymond E., Jr. Tape-recorded interview with author. Maple Hill, Kans.

July 21, 1977. Deposited in Southwest Collection (SWC), Texas Tech University.

Atchison, Mary. Unrecorded interview with author. Topeka, Kans. February 24, 1973.

Brookover, E. C., Jr., and Sanky Ruth. Unrecorded interview with author. Garden City, Kans. July 12, 1977.

Conley, Bess Mercer. Unrecorded interview with author. Delia, Kans. February 9, 1973.

Conway, Evaline. Tape-recorded interview with author. Paola, Kans. August 3, 1977. In SWC.

Cooper, Gary. Tape-recorded interview with author. Colby, Kans. July 13, 1977. In SWC.

Greenleaf, James O. Tape-recorded interview with author. Greensburg, Kans. May 15, 1977. In SWC.

Gregg, Muriel. Tape-recorded interview with author. Coldwater, Kans. May 15, 1977. In SWC.

Hicks, O. C. Tape-recorded interview with author. Garden City, Kansas. July 12, 1977. In SWC.

Jackson, Charles R. Tape-recorded interview with author. Coldwater, Kans. May 14, 1977. In SWC.

Koger, Evan. Tape-recorded interview with author. Belvidere, Kansas. July 15, 1977. In SWC.

Lemon, George C. Tape-recorded interview with author. Pratt, Kans. July 15, 1977. In SWC.

Lewis, Walter M. Tape-recorded interview with author. Larned, Kans. July 15, 1977. In SWC.

Mustoe, E. D. (Dale). Tape-recorded interview with author. Rexford, Kans. July 13, 1977. In SWC.

Parcel, Clair. Tape-recorded interview with author. Coldwater, Kans. July 14, 1977. In SWC.

Pickett, A. G. Tape-recorded interview with author. Emporia, Kans. August 2, 1977. In SWC.

Rogler, Wayne. Tape-recorded interview with author. Matfield Green, Kans. August 2, 1977. In SWC.

Schmanke, Dorothy. Unrecorded interview with author. Topeka, Kans. June 11, 1973.

Weaver, Marietta. Tape-recorded interview with author. Mullinsville, Kans. July 14, 1977. In SWC.

Letter from Benjamin B. Foster to Innis R. Palmer. May 25, 1940. Copy in Thomas County Historical Society Library, Colby, Kans.

Letter from Benjamin B. Foster to Employees. June, 1941. Copy in Thomas County Historical Society Library, Colby, Kans.

Bibliography

UNPUBLISHED THESES AND DISSERTATIONS

Atkinson, Eva L. "Kansas City's Livestock Trade and Packing Industry, 1870–1914: A Study in Regional Growth." Ph.D. dissertation, University of Kansas, 1971.

Fitch, Clyde L. "William A. Harris of Kansas: His Economic Interests." Master's thesis, Kansas State Teachers College, 1967.

LaForte, Robert S. "The Republican Party of Kansas during the Progressive Era, 1900–1916." Ph.D. dissertation, University of Kansas, 1965.

Olson, Ross A. "A Study of Structural Changes in the Livestock Economy of Kansas." Master's thesis, Kansas State University, 1967.

Skeen, Lydia A. "The History of the Cattle Industry of the Flint Hills of Kansas." Master's thesis, Kansas State University, 1938.

Wood, Charles L. "Fencing in Five Kansas Counties between 1875 and 1895." Master's thesis, University of Kansas, 1968.

PAMPHLETS AND MISCELLANEOUS REPORTS

Allen, L. A. *Our Cattle Industry, Present, Past and Future.* Address before Kansas State Board of Agriculture. 1896. KSHS.

American Angus Association. *A History of the Angus Breed.* 1973. KSHS.

Andrews, Martha E., and Ross H. Bryan. *He Was the Sherman Ranch.* 1970. KSHS.

Atchison, Topeka & Santa Fe Railway Company. *Forty-Sixth Annual Report.* 1940.

Bulletin of Yale University. Obituary Record. No. 104. New Haven, Conn. 1946.

Caster, H. O. (comp.). *Kansas Railroads and Public Utilities Law as It Concerns the Public Utilities Commission.* Topeka: State Printer, 1915.

Catalogue of the Shannon Hill Herd of Short Horn Cattle, Atchison, Kans. 1895. KSHS.

Dible, Almeda. *Foster Farms, 1912–1954.* 1954. Thomas County Historical Society Library.

Duddy, Edward A., and David A. Revzan. *The Changing Relative Importance of the Central Livestock Market.* Chicago University School of Business—Studies in Business Administration, vol. 8, no. 4. Chicago: University of Chicago Press, 1938.

Edwards, John A. *Report of Live-Stock Investigation Committee to the Legislature of Kansas.* Topeka: n. p., 1907.

Farley, F. W. (comp.). *Hazford Place: Modern Herefords.* Kansas City: Hereford Journal Co., 1935.

Grimes, Marcene. *Government and Natural Resources in Kansas—Water.* Lawrence: University of Kansas Government Research Center, 1957.

Kansas City Stock Yards Company. *Annual Live Stock Reports.* 1884–1941.

———. *75 Years of Kansas City Livestock Market History.* Kansas City: n.p., 1946.

Kansas Improved Stock Breeders' Association. *Report of the Ninth Annual Meeting.* Topeka: Kansas *Farmer* Co., 1899.

Kansas State Live Stock Association. *First Annual Report.* Cottonwood Falls, Kans.: W. C. Austin, 1916.

Liggett, Lyle. *There Is a Time and a Place . . . The History of the American National Cattlemen's Association.* New York: Newcomen Society, 1972.

McCarty, Harold H., and C. W. Thompson. *Meat Packing in Iowa.* Iowa Studies in Business, no. 12. Iowa City: State University Press, 1933.

Meade, Marvin. *Government and Natural Resources in Kansas—Soil.* Lawrence: University of Kansas Government Research Center, 1959.

Morton County Cooperative Grazing Association. By-laws.

Puhr, M. C. *Farmer Co-ops in Kansas.* Wichita: Bank for Cooperatives [1938]. KSHS.

Rules of Management for Land Controlled by the Morton County Grazing Association.

· ARTICLES AND PERIODICALS

Burmeister, Charles A. "Six Decades of Rugged Individualism: The American National Cattleman's Association, 1898–1955." *Agricultural History* 30 (1956): 143–50.

Carey, James C. "The Farmers Independent Council of America, 1935–1938." *Agricultural History* 35 (April, 1961): 7–77.

———. "William Allen White and Dan D. Casement on Government Regulations." *Agricultural History* 33 (January, 1959): 16–21.

———. "Dan D. Casement: Viking on a Sea of Grass," *The Trail Guide* 4 (December, 1959): 1–12.

Case, H. C. M. "Farm Debt Adjustment during the Early 1930s." *Agricultural History* 34 (October, 1960): 173–81.

Casement, Dan D. "Corn-Fed Philosophy." *The Kansas Magazine* (1938), pp. 25–27.

Chandler, Alfred D., Jr. "The Beginnings of 'Big Business' in American Industry." *Business History Review* 33 (Spring, 1959). Reprinted in *Patterns and Perspectives: Interpretations of American History,* vol. 2, 2d ed., edited by Gerald N. Grob and George A. Billias. New York: Free Press, 1972.

Cheever, Lawrence O. "John Morrell and Company." *The Palimpsest* 47 (April, 1966): 145–92.

Dale, Edward E. "The Cow Country in Transition." *Mississippi Valley Historical Review* 24 (June, 1937): 3–20.

———. "The Ranchman's Last Frontier." *Mississippi Valley Historical Review* 10 (June, 1923): 34–46.

Day, David I. "Memories of the Crane Ranch," and "More Crane Ranch Memories." *Milking Shorthorn Journal* (May and June, 1941).

Dusenberry, William. "Constitutions of Early and Modern American Stock Growers' Associations." *Southwestern Historical Quarterly* 52 (1950): 255–75.

Fay, C. R. "The Success of Cooperation among Livestock Producers in the United States of America." *Southwestern Political and Social Science Quarterly* 9 (1928–1929): 452–63.

Feder, Earnest. "Farm Debt Adjustments during the Depression: The Other Side of the Coin." *Agricultural History* 35 (April, 1961): 78–81.

Galambos, Lewis. "The Agrarian Image of the Large Corporation, 1879–1920: A Study in Social Accommodation." *The Journal of Economic History* 28 (September, 1968): 341–62.

Greenman, Judd. "A Great Stock and Packing Business." *Annual Review of Greater Kansas City* (1908), p. 54.

Hall, Tom G. "Wilson and the Food Crisis: Agricultural Price Control during World War I." *Agricultural History* 47 (January, 1973): 25–46.

Harmon, Terry H. "Soldier Creek Park: The Rockefeller Ranch in Kiowa County, Kansas." *The Trail Guide* 13 (December, 1968): 1-30.

Harrington, W. P. "The Populist Party in Kansas." *Kansas Historical Collections* 16 (1923–1925): 403–450.

"History of Kansas City Stock Yards." *Hereford Swine Journal* 3 (May/June, 1943): 12–17.

Howell, Fred N. "Some Phases of the Industrial History of Pittsburg, Kansas." *Kansas Historical Quarterly* 1 (May, 1932): 273-94.

Koch, Charles R. "Man Who Licked Blackleg." *K-Stater* 15 (October, 1965): 12–14.

Kollmorgen, Walter M., and David S. Simonett. "Grazing Operations in the Flint Hills-Bluestem Pastures of Chase County, Kansas." Association of American Geographers, *Annals* 55 (June, 1965): 260-90.

———. "The Woodsman's Assault on the Domain of the Cattleman." Association of American Geographers, *Annals* 59 (June, 1969): 215-39.

Lambert, C. Roger. "The Drought Cattle Purchase, 1934–1935: Problems and Complaints." *Agricultural History* 45 (April, 1971): 85–93.

———. "Texas Cattlemen and the AAA, 1933–1935." *Arizona and the West* 14 (Summer, 1972): 137–54.

———. "Want and Plenty: The Federal Surplus Relief Corporation and the AAA." *Agricultural History* 46 (July, 1972): 390–400.

Link, Arthur S. "The Federal Reserve Policy and Agricultural Depression of 1920–21." *Agricultural History* 20 (July, 1946): 166–75.

Malin, James C. "An Introduction to the History of the Bluestem-Pasture Region of Kansas: A Study in Adaptation to Geographical Environment." *Kansas Historical Quarterly* 11 (February, 1942): 3–28.

Matson, C. H. "A Giant Kansas Farm." *The World's Work* 4 (July, 1902): 2327-2329.

May, Irvin M. "Cotton and Cattle: The FSRC and Emergency Work Relief." *Agricultural History* 46 (July, 1972): 401–413.

McCampbell, C. W. "W. E. Campbell, Pioneer Kansas Livestockman." *Kansas Historical Quarterly* 16 (1948): 245–73.

Renner, G. K. "The Kansas City Meat Packing Industry before 1900." *Missouri Historical Review* 55 (October, 1960): 18–29.

Saloutos, Theodore. "The Agricultural Problem and Nineteenth Century Industrialism." *Agricultural History* 22 (July, 1948): 156–74.

――――. "The New Deal and Farm Policy in the Great Plains." *Agricultural History* 43 (July, 1969): 245–55.

Stubbs, Walter R. "Public Ownership of Railroads, Waterways and Water Power." *Saturday Evening Post,* June 6, 1914, pp. 3–5, 28–33.

"Unparalleled Sale at Hazford Place." *American Hereford Journal* 28 (July 1, 1937): 7–14.

Walker, Don D. "From Self-Reliance to Cooperation: The Early Development of the Cattlemen's Association in Utah." *Utah Historical Quarterly* 35 (1967): 187–201.

Wentworth, Edward N. "A Livestock Specialist Looks at Agricultural History." *Agricultural History* 25 (April, 1951): 49–53.

Wilson, James A. "Southwest Cattlemen and Railroad Regulation." *Rocky Mountain Social Science Journal* 7 (April, 1970): 89–97.

Wood, Charles L. "The Development of an Enclosure System for Five Kansas Counties, 1875–1895." *The Trail Guide* 14 (March, 1969): 1–20.

――――. "C. D. Perry: Clark County Farmer and Rancher, 1884–1908." *Kansas Historical Quarterly* 39 (Winter, 1973): 449–77.

――――. "Cattlemen and Railroads: The Origin of the Kansas Livestock Association during the 1890s." *Kansas Historical Quarterly* 43 (Summer, 1977): 121-39.

――――. "Upbreeding Western Range Cattle: Notes on Kansas, 1880–1920." *Journal of the West* 16 (January, 1977): 16–28.

BOOKS

Anderson, E. T. *A Quarter Inch of Rain.* Wichita: McCormick-Armstrong Co., 1962.

Atherton, Lewis. *The Cattle Kings.* Bloomington: Indiana University Press, 1961.

Benedict, Murray R. *Farm Policies of the United States, 1790–1950: A Study of Their Origin and Development.* New York: Twentieth Century Fund, 1953.

Bright, John D. (ed.). *Kansas: The First Century.* New York: Lewis Historical Publishing Co., 1956.

Casement, Dan D. *The Abbreviated Autobiography of a Joyous Pagan.* Manhattan: Privately printed, 1944.

Cheever, Lawrence O. *The House of Morrell.* Cedar Rapids: Torch Press, 1948.

Clanton, O. Gene. *Kansas Populism: Ideas and Men.* Lawrence: University Press of Kansas, 1969.

Clawson, Marion. *The Western Range Livestock Industry.* New York: McGraw-Hill Book Co., 1950.

Clay, John. *My Life on the Range.* 1924. Reprint. Norman: University of Oklahoma Press, 1962.

Clemen, Rudolph A. *The American Livestock and Meat Industry.* New York: Ronald Press Co., 1923.

Connelley, William E. *A Standard History of Kansas and Kansans.* Vol. 3. Chicago: Lewis Publishing Co., 1918.

Corey, Lewis. *Meat and Man: A Study of Monopoly, Unionism and Food Policy.* New York: Viking Press, 1950.

Dale, Edward Everett. *The Range Cattle Industry: Ranching on the Great Plains from 1865 to 1925.* 1930. Reprint. Norman: University of Oklahoma Press, 1960.

DeGraff, Herrell. *Beef Production and Distribution.* Norman: University of Oklahoma Press, 1960.

Dykstra, Robert R. *The Cattle Towns.* New York: Alfred A. Knopf, 1968.

Edminster, Lynn R. *The Cattle Industry and the Tariff.* New York: Macmillan Co., 1926.

Edwards, John A. *In the Western Tongue: A Collection of Speeches and Letters.* Wichita: McCormick-Armstrong Co., 1920.

FitzGerald, Dennis A. *Livestock under the AAA.* Washington: Brookings Institution, 1935.

Fletcher, Robert A. *Free Grass to Fences: The Montana Cattle Range Story.* New York: University Publishers Inc., 1960.

Frink, Maurice. *Cow Country Cavalcade: Eighty Years of the Wyoming Stock Growers Association.* Denver: Old West Publishing Co., 1954.

————, W. Turrentine Jackson, and Agnes Wright Spring. *When Grass Was King.* Boulder: University of Colorado Press, 1956.

Galambos, Louis. *Competition and Cooperation: The Emergence of a National Trade Association.* Baltimore: Johns Hopkins Press, 1966.

Gates, Paul W. *History of Public Land Law Development.* Washington: Government Printing Office, 1968.

Genung, A. B. *The Agricultural Depression following World War I and Its Political Consequences.* Ithaca: Northeast Farm Foundation, 1954.

Goff, Richard, and Robert H. McCaffree. *Century in the Saddle.* Denver: Colorado Cattlemen's Centennial Commission, 1967.

Gray, James R. *Ranch Economics.* Ames: Iowa State University Press, 1968.

Gressley, Gene M. *Bankers and Cattlemen.* Lincoln: University of Nebraska Press, 1966.

Hays, Samuel P. *The Response to Industrialism: 1885–1914.* Chicago: University of Chicago Press, 1957.

Hayter, Earl W. *The Troubled Farmer, 1850–1900: Rural Adjustment to Industrialism.* DeKalb: Northern Illinois University Press, 1968.

Hazelton, John M. *A History of Linebred Anxiety 4th Herefords of Straight*

Gudgell and Simpson Breeding. Kansas City: Associated Breeders of Anxiety 4th Herefords, 1939.

Hinkle, Fred. *The Saddle and the Statute.* Wichita: McCormick-Armstrong Co., 1961.

Kansas Statistical Base Book. Lawrence: University of Kansas Bureau of Business Research, School of Business, 1954.

Kerr, K. Austin. *American Railroad Politics, 1914–1920: Rates, Wages, and Efficiency.* Pittsburgh: University of Pittsburgh Press, 1968.

Kolko, Gabriel. *Railroads and Regulations, 1877–1916.* Princeton: Princeton University Press, 1965.

Kraenzel, Carl F. *The Great Plains in Transition.* Norman: University of Oklahoma Press, 1955.

Laude, G. A. *Kansas Shorthorns: A History of the Breed in the State from 1857 to 1920.* Iola: Laude Printing Co., 1920.

Lee, Bob, and Dick Williams. *Last Grass Frontier: The South Dakota Stock Grower Heritage.* Sturgis: Black Hills Publishers, 1964.

Leech, Harper, and John C. Carroll. *Armour and His Times.* New York: D. Appleton-Century Co., 1938.

Malin, James C. *The Grasslands of North America: Prolegomena to Its History with Addenda and Postscript.* 1947. Reprint. Gloucester: Peter Smith, 1967.

Markley, Walt. *Builders of Topeka.* Topeka: Capper Printing Co., 1934.

McCoy, Donald R. *Calvin Coolidge: The Quiet President.* New York: Macmillan Co., 1967.

———. *Landon of Kansas.* Lincoln: University of Nebraska Press, 1966.

McCoy, Joseph G. *Historic Sketches of the Cattle Trade of the West and Southwest.* Kansas City: Ramsey, Millett and Hudson, 1874.

Mechem, Kirke (comp.). *The Annals of Kansas, 1886–1925.* Vols. 1 and 2. Kansas State Historical Society, 1954, 1956.

Nordyke, Lewis. *Great Round-up: The Story of Texas and Southwestern Cowmen.* New York: William Morrow, 1955.

Nourse, E. G., and J. G. Knapp. *The Co-Operative Marketing of Livestock.* Washington: Brookings Institution, 1931.

Ornduff, Donald R. *The Hereford in America: A Compilation of Historic Facts about the Breed's Background and Bloodlines.* 1957 Reprint. Kansas City: Hereford History Press, 1969.

———. *Casement of Juniata: As a Man and as a Stockman . . . One of a Kind.* Kansas City: Lowell Press, 1975.

Powell, Cuthbert. *Twenty Years of Kansas City's Live Stock Trade and Traders.* Kansas City: Pearl Printing Co., 1893.

Richmond, Robert W. *Kansas: A Land of Contrasts.* St. Charles, Mo.: Forum Press, 1974.

Ripley, William Z. *Railroads: Rates and Regulation.* New York: Longmans, Green and Co., 1912.

Saloutos, Theodore, and John D. Hicks. *Agricultural Discontent in the Middle West, 1900–1939.* Madison: University of Wisconsin Press, 1951.

Sanders, Alvin H. *Short-Horn Cattle: A Series of Historical Sketches, Memoirs and Records of the Breed and Its Development in the United States and Canada.* 2d ed. Chicago: Sanders Publishing Co., 1901.

———. *The Story of the Herefords.* Chicago: Breeder's Gazette Print, 1914.

———. *A History of Aberdeen-Angus Cattle.* Chicago: New Breeder's Gazette, 1928.

Schlebecker, John T. *Cattle Raising on the Plains, 1900–1961.* Lincoln: University of Nebraska Press, 1963.

Schruben, Francis W. *Kansas in Turmoil, 1930–1936.* Columbia: University of Missouri Press, 1969.

Shideler, James H. *Farm Crisis, 1919–1923.* Berkeley: University of California Press, 1957.

Snyder, Ralph. *We Kansas Farmers: Development of Farm Organizations and Cooperative Associations in Kansas as Gleaned from a Lifetime of Experience and Contact with Them.* Topeka: F. M. Steves and Sons, 1953.

Socolofsky, Homer E. *Arthur Capper: Publisher, Politician, and Philanthropist.* Lawrence: University of Kansas Press, 1962.

Sonnichsen, C. L. *Cowboys and Cattle Kings: Life on the Range Today.* Norman: University of Oklahoma Press, 1950.

Steen, Herman. *Cooperative Marketing.* New York: Doubleday, Page & Co,, 1923.

Stene, Edwin O. *Railroad Commission to Corporation Commission.* Government Research Series, no. 2. Lawrence: University of Kansas Press, 1945.

Stover, John F. *American Railroads.* Chicago: University of Chicago Press, 1961.

———. *The Life and Decline of the American Railroad.* New York: Oxford University Press, 1970.

Sullivan, Dulcie. *The LS Brand: The Story of a Texas Panhandle Ranch.* Austin: University of Texas Press, 1968.

Swaffar, Paul. *Look What I Stepped In.* Kansas City: Lowell Press, 1972.

Swift, Lewis F. *The Yankee of the Yards: The Biography of Gustavus Franklin Swift.* Chicago: A. W. Shaw Co., 1927.

U. S. Bureau of the Census. *Historical Statistics of the United States, Colonial Times to 1957.* Washington: Government Printing Office, 1960.

Waters, Lawrence L. *Steel Trails to Santa Fe.* Lawrence: University of Kansas Press, 1950.

Webb, Walter P. *The Great Plains.* New York: Grosset and Dunlap, 1931.

Yost, Nellie Snyder. *The Call of the Range: The Story of the Nebraska Stock Growers Association.* Denver: Sage Books, 1966.

Zornow, William F. *Kansas: A History of the Jayhawk State.* Norman: University of Oklahoma Press, 1957.

Index

Index